Electing the House

The Adoption and Performance of the US Single-Member District Electoral System

Jay K. Dow

University Press of Kansas

Published by the University

Press of Kansas (Lawrence,

Kansas 66045), which was

organized by the Kansas

Board of Regents and is

operated and funded by

Emporia State University,

Fort Hays State University,

Kansas State University,

Pittsburg State University,

the University of Kansas,

and Wichita State University

Published by the University Press of Kansas (Lawrence,
Kansas 66045), which was organized by the Kansas
Board of Regents and is operated and funded by Emporia
State University, Fort Hays State University, Kansas State
University, Pittsburg State University, the University of
Kansas, and Wichita State University

Library of Congress Cataloging-in-Publication Data

Names: Dow, Jay K. (Jay Kent), 1962– author.
Title: Electing the House : the adoption and performance
of the US single-member district electoral system / Jay Kent
Dow.
Description: Laurence, Kansas : University Press of Kansas,
[2017] | Includes bibliographical references and index.
Identifiers: LCCN 2016047597
ISBN 9780700624096 (cloth : acid free paper)
ISBN 9780700624102 (pbk. : acid free paper)
ISBN 9780700624119 (ebook)
Subjects: LCSH: United States. Congress. House—Election
districts—History.
Classification: LCC JK1341 .D69 2017 | DDC 328.73/07345—
dc23
LC record available at https://lccn.loc.gov/2016047597.

British Library Cataloguing-in-Publication Data is available.

Printed in the United States of America

10 9 8 7 6 5 4 3 2 1

The paper used in this publication is recycled and contains
30 percent postconsumer waste. It is acid free and meets the
minimum requirements of the American National Standard
for Permanence of Paper for Printed Library Materials
z39.48–1992.

CONTENTS

ILLUSTRATIONS

Image and Figures

Tables

PREFACE AND ACKNOWLEDGMENTS

The idea for this book took shape when I was privileged to attend two Jack Miller Center Summer Institutes on teaching America's founding principles and history. I was surprised by my inclusion in the programs because, although I taught a class in founding-era political thought at the University of Missouri, I had made my academic career on statistical studies of electoral systems in contemporary elections. These institute conversations with some of the leading graduate students and faculty in American political thought and development made me realize that I couldn't provide a satisfactory answer to the simple question of how and why we came to elect the House of Representatives as we do. I've always believed one of the primary benefits of the academic profession is that one can pursue one's intellectual interests wherever they lead, and my interests were shifting from the contemporary performance and political implications of election systems to understanding their origins and development. I had been recently promoted to full professor and was in a good position to read and learn as much as I could about the political thought on elections in the early republic, American political development, and the long history of congressional elections. This book is the beginning of that process.

On its face my academic pedigree suggests that I'm best suited for my original vocation of statistical analyses of electoral systems. I completed my dissertation under the guidance of Mel Hinich at the University of Texas at Austin, and Mel was one of the most accomplished scholars of his generation in this field of inquiry. However, I was also greatly influenced by Walter Dean Burnham, and his presence is felt throughout the manuscript. Dean Burnham taught me many things, including that one needs to understand history to place empirical findings in context and that one can gain great insights from very basic electoral data and simple analysis. This book owes much to Dean Burnham's influence a full quarter-century after I last took a seminar from him.

More immediately, I am deeply indebted to the University of Missouri Kinder Institute on Constitutional Democracy for providing financial assistance that allowed me to conduct research at Chicago's Newberry Library and, more importantly, for creating a campus-wide network of scholars interested in basic questions of US constitutional governance. The Kinder Institute provides a forum for the collaboration and discussion of ideas among scholars from different academic backgrounds and perspectives, all of whom share a deep commitment to constitutional democracy and the American polity. In this, I owe particular acknowledgments to my colleagues Justin Dyer and historian of the early republic Jeff Pasley. Professors Dyer and Pasley codirect the Kinder Institute and were instrumental in establishing the intellectual environment where I could discuss the ideas in this book. I am also indebted to Pev Squire, who shared his considerable expertise on the development of American legislatures as I pursued my inquiry on their election. These conversations in conferences, colloquia, seminars, and department hallways moved this project forward in a way that would not have been possible otherwise. I also benefited from the assistance of the University of Missouri Research Council, which granted me a research leave to write. The Research Council also funded my work at the National Archives Center for Legislative Archives, where I obtained material that provided richer context for several chapters. In acknowledging Research Council support, I am simultaneously recognizing the assistance of my former department chair, John Petrocik. This gentleman had to support me and the project for it to secure institutional backing, and I very much appreciate his effort on my behalf.

Finally, the most significant acknowledgments and deepest expressions of gratitude go to my family, including daughters Rachelle and Laurel and, especially, my wife, Debbie. Debbie did not marry a scholar. She married a guy barely out of high school who over the course of our thirty-five-year marriage slowly became one. Her patience and support in this process is incalculable and extends well beyond anything specific to this project. For that and everything else I am profoundly grateful.

Electing the House

1 House of Representatives Elections and American Political Development

> We are all Republicans, we are all Federalists.
> *Thomas Jefferson, first inaugural address*

The United States elects its House of Representatives from single-member districts using the plurality rule. This method selects the candidate with the most votes, even if less than a majority, from a geographically contiguous district. This electoral system is an anomaly. For most of the world, an electoral system—the rules by which citizens' votes are translated into legislative seats—means proportional representation. Of the world's approximately thirty or so established and unquestioned democracies, only four—the United Kingdom, India, Canada, and the United States—rely exclusively on single-member district (SMD) plurality rule to elect their national legislature. For the United States perhaps the more striking fact is that nowhere is this mandated. The Constitution grants the states the authority to elect representatives in the manner of their choosing, subject to restrictions that Congress may choose to impose.

In the nation's early years the states exercised this privilege and elected their representatives using a variety of methods. For example, New Jersey elected its representatives at-large for the first five congresses, then changed to SMD, then reinstituted at-large elections, and finally opted for dual-member-district elections (DMD) from 1812 to 1814, after which it used at-large elections. Vermont's representatives were elected from single-member districts until the Thirteenth Congress, when the state switched to at-large elections, until the Seventeenth Congress when it used single-member districts for one cycle before reinstating at-large elections. New York relied on SMD during much of this period, but created some multimember constituencies in the early nineteenth century. In contrast, Virginia relied exclusively on SMD elections to elect its representatives in the early republic.

The Virginia exception aside, fluidity in House election methods was the rule, not the exception, in the nation's early years. Congress eventually asserted its prerogative in the mid-nineteenth century and required states to elect their representatives from single-member districts. This practice, now as much by tradition as by law, is well established.

This book asks how this came to be and whether it is a good thing. How did the United States evolve from a decentralized process for electing the House of Representatives to a SMD system that is so ingrained that even those well versed in American government often think it has always been that way? Understanding the development of US electoral processes is central to understanding the evolution of American political processes more generally. Much has been written about when the presidency and the judiciary changed and solidified into the institutions we know today, but as Ira Katznelson and John S. Lapinski argue, Congress remains "on the outside edge" of the study of American political development.[1] If the development of Congress is an undertilled field, then the development of House election processes is nearly virgin forest. This is a key missing component of our general knowledge of the development of American political institutions. Such knowledge also allows us to better understand the place of elections in US democratic governance. Different election methods privilege different values and standards, and in the periods when these were most fervently debated the advocates of different means of election made explicit the distinct understandings of the objectives fulfilled by elections. The struggle over how to elect the House of Representatives clarifies the potential benefits, liabilities, and trade-offs that are necessarily a part of selecting one way to elect the chamber rather than another.

In recent years an increasing number of voices, including academics, advocates, politicians, and others, have argued that the United States SMD "first-past-the-post" electoral system is outdated and should be replaced by other electoral arrangements that are presumably more capable of reflecting and capturing the distribution of national political preferences. Our "winner-take-all" system, so the argument goes, produces representational disenfranchisement, uncompetitive elections, civic disengagement, polarized and contentious politics, political gridlock, and a host of other perceived ills that will be remedied by changing to some other system to elect our representatives.

I think that these arguments are terribly misguided and that the United States is well served by winner-takes-all legislative elections. The SMD plurality system is uniquely well suited to American republican ideals of good governance, the institutions created to support these ideals, and the contemporary social and political environment in which national legislative elections are contested. However, entering this discussion is challenging, in part because the current debate is rarely framed in systemic terms. That is, the discussion pays relatively little attention to the place of the SMD system within the broader context of a system of government predicated on the dispersal of political power and its operation in a heterogeneous society that still embraces classically liberal values. Nor is the discussion greatly informed by American political thought and history. All of this is unfortunate because the way we elect our representatives is part of a corpus of political institutions and processes that were selected and implemented to advance a particular understanding of good and proper government. Yet the discussion is largely bereft of serious engagement with these ideas and their relationship to elections. Critics seldom devote attention to understanding why and how the SMD plurality system was universally adopted and institutionalized, whether the system performs well according to the objectives it was intended to fulfill, and whether these objectives are themselves still desirable.

I seek to answer these questions in the following chapters. To be clear, the book is less a response to the critics of the method used to elect the House of Representatives than it is a study of why the SMD plurality system was adopted and institutionalized, and an affirmative argument about its merits in selecting the US House of Representatives. In making this argument, however, I address many of the objections raised by critics of the system and in the process hope to assuage the concerns of skeptics and remind others of the many virtues of our current electoral processes. The simple argument of this book is that when the American SMD, first-past-the-post method of electing representatives is understood within the context of American political thought, when we recall the history of its establishment and institutionalization, and when we consider its contemporary application, its merits will be more clearly understood and appreciated.

So why does the way we elect members of the House of Representatives merit a book-length study? There are several reasons. Foremost, the House of Representatives is our most important government body, and the manner in which it is elected, more than any other single feature of our political institutions and processes, influences the character of national politics. The Framers certainly believed the House to be the central organ of government, as do scholars of contemporary American politics. The powers of government are largely the powers of Congress, which helps explain why the Constitution's first article is as long as the rest of the document combined. With this in mind, scholars agree that the method used to elect the lower chamber of any national legislature is the most important determinant of the nature of citizen representation, characteristics of its political parties and party politics, the ability for citizens to hold government accountable for its performance in office, and a host of related considerations that are central to democratic governance. The United States is no exception. It is the SMD plurality electoral system that most directly shapes national politics, and it is this system—replicated at the statehouse level—that is the focus of those who wish to change the manner in which we elect our representatives. Both critics and advocates of the United States SMD system understand that if one changes the method used to elect the House of Representatives one changes many other things as a consequence.

Equally important, understanding the adoption and institutionalization of the US SMD system greatly increases our general knowledge about the origins and development of electoral institutions and processes. Political scientists generally treat electoral systems as fixed and exogenous because our interests often lie in using these structures to explain other things, such as the characteristics of political parties and party systems. But of course, electoral systems are not fixed and exogenous. They are selected, imposed, modified, and often, as in the United States, eventually become so ingrained in the fabric of government that one hardly ever seriously considers their provenance. Yet as Lipset and Rokkan remind us, choosing and imposing an electoral system is the core element in the grand strategy of politics. "The party strategists will generally have decisive influence on electoral legislation and opt for the systems of aggregation most likely to consolidate their position, whether through increases in their representation, through strengthening of the preferred alliances, or through safeguards against splinter movements."[2] If one wins the battle over the electoral system, one eventually wins many other battles as well.

Stein Rokkan also provides the key insight that helps explain the politics surrounding the adoption and institutionalization of electoral systems: in Western democracies it has generally been the case that particular electoral systems are advocated, implemented, and consolidated in response to franchise expansion and mass mobilization.[3] Most of our understanding of the origins of electoral systems comes from European polities and the emergence of left-socialist parties and the enfranchisement of working-class citizens in the late nineteenth and early twentieth centuries. In this regard, the European experience is quite different from that of the United States. On this side of the Atlantic the major episode of franchise expansion and mobilization occurred prior to industrialization and the establishment of large, urban workforces.[4] Specifically, in the United States mass franchise and mobilization dates to the Jacksonian era, and it was in this period that the major legislative efforts to mandate SMD plurality-rule elections for House of Representatives elections came into force. The leaders of the nascent parties believed that the SMD winner-take-all system was the best way to manage the rapidly changing political environment in the decades preceding the Civil War. This system became increasingly entrenched during successive periods of franchise expansion in the twentieth century. Indeed, one hears echoes of the political battles over the SMD plurality system when women obtained complete enfranchisement in the early twentieth century and when African Americans obtained full franchise in the civil rights era. The SMD plurality-rule system was the Federalists' solution to tyranny of the majority under the expectation of universal franchise, and the Jacksonian-Whig era parties' response to the electoral volatility and uncertainty that accompanied franchise expansion and mass mobilization. The US single-member district system's establishment and consolidation cannot be understood without reference to the history of electoral participation.

For some, the fact that partisan politics advanced the institutionalization of the US SMD electoral system compromises its normative standing. Since the system emanated as much from crass politics as high-minded republican ideals, the SMD system enjoys no more standing than any of its potential alternatives. It is undeniable that politicians learned very early in American history that geographically defined, single-member districts present several avenues for partisan advantage. The most obvious of these is gerrymandering district boundaries to benefit candidates of a particular party or to benefit incumbent office holders regardless of partisan affiliation. Subsequent chapters argue that the practical significance of using the SMD system for partisan purposes both is overstated and certainly is not a feature that distinguishes the SMD system from other electoral arrangements. All electoral systems present opportunities for nefarious behavior. Still, taking the party politics critique at face value, it is entirely unclear why we would consider the partisan origins of the SMD winner-take-all system to be a bad thing. People who argue in this vein seem to take it as an article of faith that strong political parties and partisan politics is bad, and in doing so consciously or unconsciously reflect the ideas of the Progressives and the Progressive Era that was devoted to limiting the power of political parties and affiliated politicians. These ideas, which resonate as strongly today as at any point in American history, are reflected in the direct primary, campaign finance regulations, and a host of other restrictions on the ability of political parties to organize and contest elections.

For all the bad press they receive, political parties are among the most fundamental and basic of all democratic institutions. As E. E. Schattschneider reminds us, "The political parties created democracy . . . and modern democracy is unthinkable save in terms of parties."[5] For democratic governance, strong political parties and partisanship are a virtue, not a vice. Strong parties provide governing alternatives, structure the vote, and increase the ability of ordinary citizens to hold representatives accountable for their actions in office. Indeed, when political observers assess the quality of democratic governance around the world, invariably the first questions they ask about any nation center on the strength of political parties, especially parties outside of government. The existence of a viable alternative to the incumbent government is the first requirement of any nation worthy of being called a democracy. An overlooked consequence of the crass partisanship that advanced the institutionalization of the SMD plurality system as the selection process for the national legislature is that the SMD system itself further consolidated American political parties as mass political institutions. The American SMD system contoured the salient features and characteristics of our political parties, which are distinct in their emergence, organization, and function from those in much of the democratic world, and are especially well suited to the American political landscape.

That said, partisan politics only goes so far in explaining the adoption and institutionalization of the SMD plurality system. Political institutions and processes exist in an intellectual environment, and to take root and grow these must advance the ideals and values that are privileged in that setting. The US SMD system did not become institutionalized simply because politicians wanted it that way; it became institutionalized and is maintained precisely because it fits so comfortably within the corpus of political thought that informs our collective understanding of good governance. The liberal democratic values that permeate the American experience place particular premium on the dispersion of political power and the ability of citizens to hold government officials responsible for their performance in office and motivates a system of representation that balances representatives' ability to know and effectively represent their constituents with enhancement of their ability to pursue great national objectives. These values are not anachronistic: they are as relevant to the United States today as they were at the founding.

Arguing the importance of ideas in explaining the adoption and institutionalization of the US single-member district electoral system injects one into the middle of a debate in American political development.[6] Its antecedents are familiar to many in the form of the Charles Beard thesis that the economic position of the Framers dictated the Constitution's structure and that the economic interests of elites determine political institutions and processes. If the Beardian thesis is correct, then normative ideas and values have little purchase in explaining political development. Economics and historical direction drive development, as reflected, for example, in the adoption and institutionalization of the SMD system. To understand how SMD elections came to be the method we use to elect the House of Representatives all one must do is determine why this electoral system is more advantageous to economic elites than some other system. Voilà, it is explained. Nobody believes the strong form of this argument; however, there remains an active discussion about the extent to which ideas matter in explaining US political development.[7]

The debate's outline is captured in a recent exchange between George Thomas on one hand and Karen Orren and Stephen Skowronek on the other.[8] Its crux is whether political thought or institutional and historical analysis should drive the study of American political development.[9] Advocates of the former view, including Thomas, James Ceaser, and Rogers Smith, privilege the place of ideas, culture, and normative values in the study of American political development. Scholarship in this tradition emphasizes understanding and interpretation, rather than description and explanation, in making sense of the development of American political institutions and processes. It is political and social ideas that help us comprehend and assess the development of American political institutions and the role they play in American politics and government. The primary purpose of American political development as an academic endeavor is to elucidate those ideals that enable us to better understand our polity and make prescriptive statements that contribute to its health and maintenance.[10] Thomas contrasts this with "value-free" institutionally and historically focused scholarship, his exemplar of which is Orren and Skowronek's *The Search for American*

Political Development. Their approach to development encourages scholars to focus on tangible institutions and relate our knowledge of these to broader questions in "mainstream" political science.[11] This is not an unreasonable characterization since Orren and Skowronek argue that the central purpose of American political development is to acquire "cumulative," "falsifiable" knowledge about the development of the American polity that has "significant implications for studying both the past and present."[12] They also caution against American political development scholarship drifting in a direction that makes it a "preserve of normative reflection."[13]

In this I purse a path most clearly articulated by Robert C. Lieberman that recommends "relaxing the common focus on order" by emphasizing the complex interplay between ideas, institutions, conflict, and opportunity that allows us to better understand the development of political processes and traditions.[14] All scholars of American political development agree that ideas matter; they matter because political institutions are themselves manifestations of values, and ideas shape and perpetuate these institutions. Institutions derive from ideas, but they also derive from accident and force, the strategic machinations of politicians, tradition, and things as pedestrian as pragmatic compromise. Ideas do not cause institutions so much as they favor and privilege certain types of institutions. The discussion over how to elect Congress, both historically and today, admits several viable selection methods, but because of the ideas that have shaped the American experience these are a small subset of the available methods for electing a legislature. Orren and Skowronek are certainly correct that institutions themselves enjoy a certain autonomy in that they tend to perpetuate and entrench themselves even when intellectual currents shift. They also correctly emphasize that ideas must have "empirical referents"—they must tangibly manifest themselves someplace in our political system to merit our attention—and that a political development field that does not contribute to the broader discipline of political science by the standards of the discipline will be deservedly marginalized.

I argue that the ideas encapsulated in the Federalist and Anti-Federalist debates transcend American history and continually shape our understanding of the purpose of the House of Representatives, proper representation, and electoral processes. Ideas, especially important ones, tend to be stable and enjoy a certain longevity. If so, then why did the national government enact a SMD mandate in 1842 but ignore state petitions for a constitutional mandate in the early nineteenth century? Why did the SMD system become solidified in the latter nineteenth century and further reinforced in the civil rights era? The ideas underlying the SMD system are relatively constant but gain more purchase at some points in our political history than at other points. Simply, we want to understand "what makes an idea's time come?"[15]

This leaves the question of what constitutes political development or, more simply, how do we know development when we see it? Orren and Skowronek's characterization of political development as "a durable shifting in governing authority," where "governing authority" means the legal entity authorized to exercise power and make relevant decisions, is particularly well suited for studying how we came to elect the House. The adoption and institutionalization of the SMD system is principally a story of changing governing authority. Prior to the mid-nineteenth century, states determined how to elect their representatives. By the early twentieth century governing authority unquestionably resided in the national government, which told states how they would elect their representatives. To understand how we went from a decentralized authority that produced several methods of House election to universal application of the SMD system requires that we trace this evolution in governing authority. This shift in authority, however, can be understood, explained, and normatively assessed only with reference to the ideas that shape how we as a society think about electoral democracy.

This opens a second discussion in American political development; specifically, which ideas matter? In this, I build on James Ceaser's notion of "foundational ideas," which he defines as the "first cause or ultimate justification" in political development in that these ideas set in motion and shape the development of political institutions and processes.[16] Ceaser describes foundational ideas through analogy to a pyramid, the base of which consists of foundational ideas on which other ideas are placed. These ideas provide the "context in which statesmen must act."[17] Scholars of American political thought are quite adept at tracing the subtleties and nuances of the many ideas that have shaped the American experience, and these contours and nuances are important. However, one must see the forest for the trees, and in American electoral politics the foundational concepts of liberalism and republicanism are central. This book argues that the basic parameters of the Federalist and Anti-Federalist debate surrounding the ratification of the Constitution shaped how we came to think about electing Congress. Consequently, developing these foundational concepts as they pertain to elections is necessary. That is not to say other ideas haven't shaped this dialogue. The Progressive Era sociology certainly influenced how we think of elections, and this will be given its full due. In the task at hand, understanding why we came to elect members of the House in the manner we do and assessing the performance of this system, it is the ideas that trace to the early republic that allow one to make sense of these questions in a manner that is simply not possible otherwise. The tension and interplay between liberal and republican values as reflected in the Federalist and Anti-Federalist understandings of representation and elections set in motion the adoption and institutionalization of the SMD system, the foundation for its evaluation, and the challenges to it.

The Federalist and Anti-Federalist debates encapsulate two visions of the House of Representatives and its election, raising questions of what the principal authors of these writings really believed about representative government. Although of scholarly interest, the private thoughts of the Framers are not relevant to the project.[18] This is because the writings that surrounded the constitutional ratification struggle were political documents. They sought to influence the state ratification conventions and have to be understood in that context. These writings distilled, sharpened, and sometimes oversold to the point of hyperbole two distinct visions of American government. Some of these authors, including Madison himself, advocated positions with which we know they personally disagreed. The Federalist and Anti-Federalist writings were public documents written to advance political arguments crafted to win a political battle. They encapsulate internally consistent, distinct ideas about the House of Representatives and its election that resonated at the time and have continued to resonate throughout US history. These understandings of representative government took on a life of their own and reside in the American consciousness regardless of what Madison, Hamilton, Cato, or the Federal Farmer held in their hearts and minds. In this analysis, I am not interested in Madison's or Cato's innermost thoughts. Rather, I'm interested in what they wrote, and I take these texts, indeed all texts used in this book, at face value because that's how they were intended to be read. Public debates rest on public ideas.

American political thought provides both an empirical foundation for understanding the adoption and longevity of the SMD system; more importantly, it provides the normative benchmarks by which its performance may be assessed. The performance of any electoral system can be assessed only by normative foundations privileged by these ideas.[19] However, grounding an argument in favor of the SMD plurality system in the context of political thought is unusual. With only a few notable exceptions, the best known of which is Harvard Law professor Lani Guinier's *The Tyranny of the Majority*, contemporary discussions of US elections largely ignore political thought.[20] Instead, commentators and critics overwhelmingly focus on the political objectives that they would like to see realized, such as increased support for minor parties, greater numbers of racial minorities or women in the legislature, or some other objective, where these are understood to be hindered by the SMD plurality system and more likely to be achieved by some other electoral arrangement. What often emerges, then, are thin arguments about the utility of particular electoral processes for achieving particular objectives, with scant attention paid to political thought, contemporary theory or empirics, or the political context beyond current politics. While debates about the relationship between electoral arrangements and particular political objectives certainly have value, serious discussion of electoral reform has to be informed by a more complete understanding of the relationship between elections and American democratic thought and the performance of the US SMD system by the standards valued by contemporary scholars of electoral institutions and practices.

Finally, it's important to establish at the outset that one of the traditional explanations for the US single-member district system, namely that we inherited it from the British, is largely incorrect. Historian Michael Kammen dismisses this explanation as "simplistic and perhaps misleading" because it points far too strongly to a presumed linage from British colonial institutions to those debated in the founding era.[21] Most of the American colonial assemblies were established between 1619 (Virginia) and 1683 (New York), and these evolved into "efficient law-making and representative institutions" by the early 1700s.[22] However, representation in these assemblies had little to do with the single-member district system as we understand it today. This is because colonial representation was corporate representation. It was towns, villages, counties, and other corporate entities that received representation, not individual citizens.[23]

To represent a town, a collection of houses, means that the town has some identifiable interest that is separate and distinguishable from the interests of the citizens who comprise it. Today it is difficult to imagine what this even means, but not so in the colonial era. Eighteenth-century British representation was corporate representation; it was landed or commercial or other identifiable interests that received representation. It was these corporate interests that were brought into Parliament, and parliamentarians represented these interests, not citizens or even specific classes of citizens. And so it was on this side of the Atlantic, only here the relevant corporate entity was the township. J. R. Pole writes: "The towns were the political constituencies of the provincial assemblies . . . the town was to New England what the corporation was to the British parliamentary system; and the townspeople of New England loved their towns far more than they loved their provinces. The town, both in its social and political life, maintained a strong sense of corporate identity."[24] The town gave citizens "their political existence" and the town was the basic political unit; few questions merited conveyance to a colonial legislature, and when they did it was the town's interest that was to be represented.[25] The town was the legislative constituent.[26] It was only in the late colonial period that the received corporate understanding of representation evolved to "the novel but attractive notion that the state was really composed of all its individual members."[27]

Consequently, the idea of representing a town, as a town rather than as a convenient collection of individuals, resonated. So while freemen had the vote, they voted in the spirit of furthering the corporate interest, and even "the humblest members of the town" who lacked the franchise still "felt that their interests, involved with those of their town, were included in its representation."[28] Representation was thus both corporate and virtual, and this was accepted until the rise of popular sovereignty and idea of individual representation in the late colonial period.[29] If representation is of the corporate type, which is what the British brought to the New World, then districts have no meaning apart from defining the relevant corporate entity. If a district is a county, it's still just a county, not a collection of citizens for individual representation. The United States single-member district system that emerged at the founding, in contrast, is predicated on the representation of individuals in a legislative assembly. This idea of a representational district as a territorial grouping of citizens to provide for their individual representation simply did not exist until the late colonial period, long after the establishment of the states' legislative chambers.

In addition, these corporate entities typically selected more than one representative. Representatives were allocated to towns and villages, and towns and villages often received multiple representatives. Each Massachusetts town, for example, could send up to one representative for every forty qualified voters to the General Court's House of Representatives.[30] Indeed, territorial districting for the Massachusetts General Court's lower chamber didn't even exist until 1857.[31] The Virginia House of Burgesses was initially a unicameral assembly with two burgesses selected from each county.[32]

Later in its colonial history the House of Burgesses evolved into a bicameral assembly, but with representation still based on two members selected from corporate entities such as towns and counties. Likewise, other states' assemblies were predicated on corporate representation, and many of these corporate entities sent multiple representatives to their state assembly.[33] This pattern holds well into the eighteenth century.

Simply, in the colonial era there was nothing that looked like the single-member district system for the representation of individuals. The theoretical understanding of representation that we now accept didn't exist when the colonies established and consolidated their governments and the entities that were to be represented. To call these corporate entities "districts" is misleading, and regardless these were often entitled to multiple representatives. To whatever extent one wishes to convey a sense of continuity with the British experience, the most one can say is that the idea of popular sovereignty and individual representation emerged in conjunction with the late colonial and revolutionary eras, and the idea that constituencies could be geographically determined presented a transition from previous understanding of representation and governance. We didn't "inherit" the single-member district system from the British in any meaningful sense.

Thematic Overview

The book begins with the place of elections in founding-era American political thought. Specifically, what did the Framers expect of elections and electoral institutions? This is not an exercise in Framer worship. Period and early republic writers often differed sharply on the proper objectives of electoral processes, and these ideas still resonate in the American psyche. However, I do view founding writers—Federalist and Anti-Federalist—as advancing coherent, albeit very different, understandings of the purpose of elections in republican government, and these values and understandings transcend our history. The Federalist and Anti-Federalist debate over the House of Representatives and its proper election presents competing visions of republican government and elections that echo throughout American history. The foundations of this debate are often unstated and, indeed, often unrecognized predicates of both historical and contemporary discussions about how to best elect the lower chamber of our Congress. Both visions are firmly grounded in the republican and liberal traditions and recommend the SMD system.

In the United States we accept these principles of republican governance.

If one rejects republican democracy in favor of some other model of democracy—say, direct democracy—then the argument of this book will carry little weight because one rejects the underlying assumption that republican objectives are the benchmark against which the performance of the electoral system is assessed. There is more nuance to this argument than captured in the blunt question, "What does American political thought expect of elections and electoral institutions?" The United States has been influenced by many ideas. However, as Rogers M. Smith, the primary advocate for the "multiple traditions" understanding of American political thought, explains, even this thesis holds "that Americans share a *common* culture but one more complexly and multiply constituted than is usually acknowledged . . . above all, recognition of [these multiple traditions] does not imply any denial that America's liberal and democratic traditions have great normative and political potency."[34] Many voices have spoken on the place of elections in the American tradition, and these voices have not always agreed. However, there is a body of thought, a corpus of principle that may be distilled from the founding writings that point to core values and objectives widely agreed on in the American experience. I use these principles and objectives as the lens through which to interpret and argue the merits of the US winner-take-all electoral system.

The first underlying premise of my argument is that the theory of republican government that shaped the founding and later eras recommends winner-take-all congressional elections and provides the normative and positive standards by which the electoral system's performance should be judged. If one is prepared to concede that the proper standards by which to assess the merits of the US SMD system are those germane to the American variety of republicanism and that its performance should be assessed in the contemporary political and social context in which it operates, then I believe one can make a strong argument that there is no serious alternative to our current electoral system. This assumes that these ideals continue to resonate and inform our understanding of the place of elections in contemporary US government. I believe they do. To be clear, I do not hang all of my argument on American exceptionalism. However, any discussion about democratic institutions and processes that is not informed by the political and social history of the resident nation is surely misguided. Arguments about the merits of the US electoral system must center on the normative standards and social objectives that the system was meant to advance, and why these are more or less appropriate for the political, social, and historical circumstances of the United States than other objectives that one might wish the electoral system to fulfill.

More generally, the SMD plurality-rule electoral system, like any other electoral system, is overlaid on a particular polity, and its performance and influence on aggregate politics are a function of both the rules themselves and the application of those rules to a particular time and place. One cannot assess the relative merits of US electoral processes without considerable reference to the appropriate intellectual, historical, and social context. In particular, understanding the relative merits of United States electoral processes and institutions without firmly grounding the discussion in the American experience is impossible. This helps us better understand what aspects of its performance are intrinsic to the rules themselves and what aspects are a function of application in the United States.

There are reasons why American political thought seldom enters the discussion about the US winner-take-all legislative electoral system. Most important is the fact that the Framers seldom explicitly deliberated the merits of electoral processes. Apart from Madison's famous discussion of representation in *Federalist No. 10*, references to elections by Madison and Hamilton in their respective papers on the national legislature, and arguments advanced by prominent Federalists such as Jonathan Jackson and Anti-Federalist writers such as the Federal Farmer and Brutus, there are relatively few period writings to inform our understanding of the proper electoral institutions in American government.

With respect to this critique, while it is true that relatively little attention was paid to electoral processes in the Constitutional Convention and the Federalist and Anti-Federalist debates, it is also true that there was more discussion of electoral processes during the constitutional and early republic eras than is commonly recognized. It turns out that there is much in the written record that informs us about why our electoral processes evolved from practices to institutions, and the relationship between these institutions and both period and contemporary understandings of good government. This dialogue occurred not just among leading Federalist and Anti-Federalist writers, but in the ratifying conventions, state house debates, and other forums. This discussion intensifies considerably in the first half of the nineteenth century and re-emerges periodically in subsequent periods in American history. The most important of these periods was the Jacksonian era debate over electoral processes. Specifically, under authority granted by the Constitution's first article, section four, the 1842 Apportionment Bill mandated for the first time that states adopt the SMD system for electing their House of Representatives. The ensuing debate over this provision of the apportionment bill demanded that participants revisit our understanding of republican government and craft arguments—some echoing those of the founding generation, others novel—about how best to elect representatives in a national polity that was rapidly becoming politically mature and modern. The national conversation about the SMD system and its alternatives is an episodic, if not continuing, discussion in American political history.

A second premise from which I argue the merits of the US SMD plurality system is the broad features of the contemporary political community. By that, I simply mean what do we as a polity look like? Are we a largely consensual polity, or are we deeply divided along social, economic, religious, or other lines? This is important because perhaps the greatest and most commonly cited advantage of alternative, especially proportional, electoral systems is that these foster representation along multidimensional lines. In a fragmented society parties representing ethnic, religious, regional, and other demographic divisions, or parties that represent policy issues highly salient to a relatively small portion of the electorate, can secure representation in the national assembly. Open-list proportional representation in Belgium, for example, ensures that at least some legislative parties organize around Dutch-speaking and Francophone interests. This is a good thing because history shows that the penalty for systematically excluding clearly defined communities from representation is often bloodshed.

Does this characterization fit the United States? There is no doubt that the United States is more politically polarized than in the recent past. However, it is important to place US political polarization in context. One can point to a host of nations that are polarized to the extent that the underlying lines of political cleavage are pronounced enough to threaten the stability of the political system. We, in contrast, agree on broad principles and squabble at the margins. There is something called the "American Creed," and it is widely accepted. By and large, we agree on a market economy, limited government, civil liberties, and many other things that often distinguish us from other political cultures. Further, by some measures the United States is becoming more consensual, not less, over time. If the so-called culture wars defined the 1990s, social progressives are slowly but irreversibly taking the field. Public attitudes toward issues such as race, gay and lesbian rights, and similar considerations today are nearly unrecognizable from those of the civil rights and Stonewall eras. Not to be left behind, economic conservatives have won many hearts and minds. Regardless of the outcome of the continual debates over budgets and taxes, we will never again see 70 percent marginal tax brackets. One may see increased government regulation and oversight of financial markets, but interest rates on savings accounts are unlikely to be set by government rule as they were through much of the mid-twentieth century, nor for that matter will we see airfares set by a resurrected Civil Aeronautics Board nor a telephone monopoly granted to a new Ma Bell.

The third premise underlying my argument is that serious evaluation of the US SMD plurality-rule system has to be informed by comparative analysis. We are not the only nation that uses this electoral system, and the performance of the US SMD plurality-rule system cannot be easily understood in isolation. Among the several things one learns by comparing the US SMD plurality-rule system with its application in other nations is that its performance on several dimensions is quite different here than elsewhere. For example, if one believes the strong version of Duverger's Law that SMD plurality systems systematically thwart the emergence of strong, nationally competitive third parties, one then has to explain the results of the 2010 British national election in which the Liberal Democrats forced the second governing coalition since the end of World War Two. Indeed, the Liberal Democratic Party's 22 percent vote share in 2010 was about the same as its vote share in several past national elections. Likewise, as of this writing, five parties are represented in the Canadian House of Commons, and the Indian lower chamber, which is also elected under the SMD system, recently hosted several parties competing under four broad electoral alliances.

Comparing the SMD plurality system in the United States with that of other nations also informs much about this electoral system's performance relative to normative goals. Our electoral rules have been in place for generations, providing much leverage for understanding their effects across time. We can also comparatively assess the relative performance of SMD and other electoral rules domestically. Alternatives to the SMD system have long been applied in the United States. Indeed, the use of multimember districts was the norm for state house elections in the United States after the Civil War.[35] As recently as the early 1960s, nearly half of all state legislators were elected from multimember districts.[36] Single transferable vote, cumulative voting, and other allocation rules have all made appearances in US elections. Ironically, given the contemporary debate, the single-member district system was strengthened during the civil rights era in response to the Supreme Court's application of the Fourteenth Amendment's equal protection clause in its "one-man, one-vote" jurisprudence. Alternative electoral processes were often discarded precisely because they were thought to offer a vehicle through which the potential voting power of racial minorities could be weakened.[37]

Chapter Outlines

The next chapter focuses on broad themes in founding-era thought relevant to the selection of the House of Representatives. It highlights the tension between liberalism and republicanism and argues that the framing generation's challenge was to obtain the benefits promised by republicanism while mitigating the threats that republican government presents to liberal values. They did so by advancing a synthetic understanding of constitutional government in which the structure of elections was integrated into the larger constitutional architecture. The chapter focuses on three key areas of difference between the Federalists and Anti-Federalists: civic virtue, the public good, and the prevention of tyranny. Differences over these considerations shaped each group's respective understanding of the purpose of elections and their role in constitutional governance. The chapter concludes with a brief illustration of the argument applied to the Senate.

Chapter 3 details the Federalists' and Anti-Federalists' visions of the House of Representatives and its election. It begins by arguing that one cannot make a persuasive argument about how to best elect a representative assembly unless one has a clear understanding of its purpose. The Federalists believed the House was principally a forum for the articulation and scrutiny of ideas. Elections should select those most virtuous and capable of discovering and advancing a broadly defined public good, a group they defined as the natural aristocracy. The political interests that inform debate should be balanced and made harmless in the constituency at the electoral stage, and elections were secondary to checks and balances in the prevention of tyranny. The Anti-Federalists thought the House should be a forum for the balancing and reconciliation of distinct interests and that elections should serve as a vehicle to bring these interests into the chamber. They also believed that virtue principally resided in the "middling" classes and that elections should be organized to select members of this group to serve as legislators. In addition, for the Anti-Federalists elections were the primary bulwark against tyranny; the constitutional architecture should thus be simple enough for citizens to hold representatives accountable for their actions in office. Each of these visions is complete and irreconcilable, and both still resonate in American political discourse, introducing a tension that cannot be completely resolved.

The fourth chapter is empirical and traces House election methods in the early republic from 1788 to 1824 and the nascent parties' responses to these methods. The states used four methods to elect the first few Congresses exclusive of nomination processes and vote thresholds necessary for election: SMD election; general-ticket election; at-large election in which a state's electors could vote for all House candidates, each of whom had to be affiliated with a district; and combined SMD and multimember district elections. The larger states eventually gravitated toward the SMD system, while smaller states often maintained general-ticket elections. However, this pattern is not as strong as previously suggested; election systems were often determined as much by political advantage as by state size and heterogeneity. Importantly, the protoparties understood the incentives induced by the electoral systems they promulgated. After 1800 parties rarely fielded more than the optimal number of candidates for any given system, the protoparties coordinated supporter votes on particular candidates by means of such methods as handbills and broadsheets, and the vote shares of secondary candidates fell precipitously. By the end of the era the SMD and general ticket were the two electoral systems used to elect the House, with most states opting for the former.

Chapter 5 is in many ways the book's core chapter. It traces the politics of the Jacksonian-Whig era, which ultimately resulted in Congress mandating the SMD system for House elections as part of the Apportionment Act of 1842. It first details efforts to mandate SMD elections through constitutional amendment in the early nineteenth century, then reviews the politically volatile electoral setting of the Jacksonian-Whig era. The chapter argues that the electoral instability and uncertainty of the late 1830s and 1840s motivated the SMD mandate in 1842 and its retention for the balance of the antebellum period. In doing so, it discusses two events that were catalysts for the SMD mandate—the New Jersey and Alabama general-ticket elections that were used to preclude Whigs from those states' respective congressional delegations. The inclusion of the SMD mandate in the 1842 Apportionment Act was made possible by the brief period of Whig political ascendancy in the early 1840s. The chapter reviews the chamber debates surrounding the Apportionment Act, which presented a self-conscious attempt to recreate founding-era arguments about the proper means of electing the House. This chapter also analyzes five key House votes concerning support for and opposition to the SMD mandate. The politically unstable electorate motivated the SMD mandate, but its adoption and resilience is owed to the consistency of American political ideas about representative assemblies and their election.

The following chapter focuses on the single-member district's consolidation and institutionalization in the Progressive Era. It traces the institutionalization of the single-member district system from the post-Reconstruction period until 1930. In doing so, it documents the nearly complete shift from the states to the national government in governing authority for federal elections. Congress refined the system by adding the requirements that districts be compact and contiguous, and contain approximately equal population. These requirements remained in effect until the 1920s, when Congress failed to reapportion following the 1920 census. This census revealed a significant population shift from rural to urban areas, driven by the First World War. Legislators blocked reapportionment for a decade until the passage of the Permanent Apportionment Act of 1929 that shifted the process from Congress to the executive branch. The act required districting but was silent on the "compact, contiguous and equal population" requirement.

The great question of the Progressive Era, and the Populist period before it, is why the SMD system emerged unscathed and indeed strengthened. Virtually every electoral practice was subject to reform, and the Progressives were deeply skeptical of legislative institutions, preferring as few boundaries between citizens and lawmaking as possible. I argue that it was the dearth of Progressive political thought with respect to republican governance that precluded their providing a cogent alternative to SMD elections. Combined with the enfranchisement of women and enactment of other reforms such as the direct primary, this insulated the SMD system from the otherwise large-scale electoral changes of the era.

The seventh chapter covers the years 1930 to the present day, which I refer to as the court years. The chapter details how the federal courts established modern districting practices and argues that these strengthened the single-member district system in the contemporary period. The court's "one person, one vote" jurisprudence in the 1960s and the pursuit of voting rights for African Americans were deeply intertwined. The pursuit of these objectives within the constraints of districts being compact and contiguous and containing equal population forced Congress, the courts, and voting rights activists to explicitly recognize that the achievement of one normative objective necessarily requires the diminution of other normative objectives. SMD elections were seen as the best vehicle for advancing the voting rights and political influence of underrepresented populations. The central feature of the period is the interconnected relationship between the court's equal protection jurisprudence and the maintenance of the Voting Rights Act protections. This is reflected in the congressional debates that surrounded the "one person, one vote" rulings, the Voting Rights Act, and the subsequent congressional (1967) reiteration of the SMD mandate. This forced the court to address a number of complex legal and political questions. The court created a sometimes muddled jurisprudence, but one that clearly established the SMD system as one of the few election methods likely to satisfy the "one person, one vote" requirement and protect the political rights of racial minorities. Whether the court's reasoning on these question is right or wrong, the SMD system was unarguably strengthened in the context of franchise expansion.

Chapter 8 is quite distinct from the preceding chapters. Its purpose is to empirically assess the current performance of the US SMD system. In doing so, the chapter provides evidence that the SMD system functions well in practice. It begins by noting the necessary trade-offs inherent in any electoral system; for the SMD system these center on trade-offs imposed by the requirement that districts be compact and contiguous and most importantly that they contain equal population. The chapter reminds the reader that SMD elections do not automatically produce two-party systems. The United States is the only strong example of Duverger's Law, and there are many contextual and historical factors beyond the electoral system that structure our party systems. The balance of the chapter is organized around the theme of "fair" elections and argues that the US system performs well and is fair. It does so by focusing on three subjects. First, it discusses gerrymandering and argues that there are significant limits to the practical importance of gerrymandering and that less-gerrymandered districts often reduce the likelihood of securing other desirable objectives. Further, reapportionment and redistricting reduces any biases favoring one party or the other. It then evaluates the partisan fairness of the system by estimating seats-vote curves in recent US elections. These show that the SMD system produces few national electoral biases favoring one party and also relatively responsive elections. On balance the SMD system applied to US House elections produces high-quality congressional representation for most citizens. It selects officeholders that represent their constituents well and that span the US ideological spectrum, with many representatives properly classified as moderates while others hold more extreme views in accordance with the distribution of these views in society. Many of the criticisms generally levied against the US SMD system simply do not withstand close scrutiny.

The book concludes by presenting an argument for the US SMD system. In doing so, it harkens back to the original Federalist and Anti-Federalist dispute over the purpose of the House of Representatives, good and proper representation, and corresponding principles of election. I argue that the crux of this founding-era debate continues to capture the essence of contemporary debates over House elections and the single-member district system, and argue that these visions provide a useful foundation for understanding and explaining the adoption, institutionalization, and contemporary merits of the single-member district system. In particular, most critiques of the US single-member district system are grounded in a distinctly Anti-Federalist understanding of republican governance. The chapter synthesizes the merits of the SMD system in House of Representatives elections and argues that any electoral system necessarily advances some normative values at the expense of others. There is no perfect way of electing a representative assembly, and public discourse is best served by considering the trade-offs across systems rather than searching for the "best" system. Still, the SMD system fits most comfortably with American political values and the institutions created to support those values. Many critiques of the SMD system fail to recognize the importance of electoral instructions conforming to the existing constitutional architecture and the trade-offs inherent in any electoral process. The chapter does advocate modest changes to the House SMD system to make it more consistent with the founders' vision of advancing the public good, and also addresses existing concerns about its application. Foremost among these is making congressional districts more heterogeneous by reducing their number. The creation of more-heterogeneous districts by construction makes it more difficult to gerrymander, will encourage representatives to be more sensitive to a wider range of political perspectives, and perhaps most importantly will make the chamber more conducive to the pursuit of a broadly national public good.

Whether one agrees with this conclusion favorable toward the US SMD system or not, sensible discussion of the United States election process must be grounded in political thought germane to the American experience, the broader constitutional architecture within which electoral processes reside, and an informed understanding of the political history surrounding the development of these institutions and their empirical performance in application. If the book contributes to this discussion it will have served its purpose.

2 Founding-Era Thought and the Selection for Office

> If the structure of American government was
> crafted by the Federalists, the spirit of American
> politics has more often been inspired by the Anti-
> Federalists.
>
> Saul Cornell, The Other Founders:
> Anti-Federalism and the Dissenting
> Tradition in America, 1788–1828

Members of the US House of Representatives represent people, not places. US senators represent places, not people. That distinction is made in every American government course, accompanied by the instructor's silent prayer that students won't enquire too closely about why it is that representatives are elected from geographically defined districts or what it means for senators to represent states in their corporate capacity. This distinction is difficult to clarify in part because it is an oversimplification. Elected officials in the United States represent interests where the sense of these interests was to be gathered and articulated directly by citizens, or indirectly through the state legislatures or through presidential electors, depending on the branch and its constitutional role. The distinction is also difficult to clarify because both the founding era and the contemporary era selection processes for each chamber reversed this logic. In the early republic several states elected representatives in a manner designed to maximize state influence in the House of Representatives, while today the direct election of US senators is the selection method most consistent with representing citizens in an assembly.[1] For these reasons, Americans often think of representatives as representing places while senators represent people, albeit rather unequally.

This and the following chapter are primers on early republic thought important for understanding the SMD system in American government. Together they sketch the foundation for explaining its adoption and its institutionalization, and, I argue later, for assessing its performance. In doing so, the chapters clarify the relationship between the selection process and the constitutional objectives that the House of Representatives was expected to fulfill. Throughout I argue that SMD plurality election, even though not universally implemented in the early republic, is the system best suited to giving the Framers' overall goals and priorities effect with respect to the House of Representatives. Electoral institutions are part of the larger constitutional architecture and cannot be understood apart from it.

To fully appreciate the centrality of SMD plurality elections in the US expression of liberal democracy, one has to outline the most salient premises, features, and objectives of the political system and ask if these are best served by this system, or whether other electoral arrangements could be equally satisfactory or superior. The US SMD plurality rule system is best evaluated in terms of whether it facilitates broader objectives such as advancing the collective welfare, protecting political minorities, and providing for the type of citizen representation that most resonates in the American experience. Whether the priorities that recommend the SMD winner-takes-all system in House elections are still relevant or even desirable is open to question. I believe that they are, but save that discussion for later. The chapters' purpose is narrower: it is to persuade the reader that the SMD plurality system is a logical component of the overall constitutional system as envisioned in the framing era. Naturally, the more that one agrees that these objectives are still important and realized by the constitutional framework, the more weight this argument carries in ongoing discussions about proper electoral processes and institutions. Evidence that these goals and priorities still resonated in the mid-nineteenth century and still do even today is provided by their importance in explaining the system's universal adoption and perpetuation.

To understand why we elect representatives as we do requires that one explore in some detail the republican and liberal values that so influenced the framing generation and that continue to structure American politics. The United States was founded by men profoundly influenced by the writings of Harrington, Sidney, Locke, and others who articulated an individualistic view of society and who sought political institutions and processes that recognized and protected basic rights.[2] These writers instilled in the Americans certain principles, including that sovereignty ultimately rests with the people and that the legislature is the principal branch of government.[3] Central to this is the liberal tradition that emphasizes minimizing the danger of tyranny, especially government-promulgated tyranny, and fostering commerce and industrious pursuits. Equally important is republicanism, which centers on cultivation of civic virtue, discovery and pursuit of the public good, and the importance of civic engagement in developing citizenship and society.

Liberalism and republicanism enjoy an uneasy coexistence. They are mutually supportive in that both privilege the individual and celebrate his/her place in the political process, but they are in tension because less than omniscient and less than altruistic humans may govern in a manner that threatens liberal values. The public good "discovered" by representatives may demand the abrogation of citizens' basic rights and liberties. Madison points to this danger, perhaps nowhere more clearly than in *Federalist No. 48* where he reminds us that "an elective despotism is not the government we fought for." Republican government can threaten liberal values, and these values must be protected.[4]

The national discussion, both historical and present, over how to elect the House of Representatives dates to the founding-era debate over ratification of the Constitution. The Federalists and Anti-Federalists embraced different understandings of American society, the proper objectives of government, and the role of the House of Representatives in securing those objectives. These differences over where civic virtue resides, how to develop it and bring it into government, how to discover and advance the public good, and how best to reduce the danger of tyranny had far-reaching implications for how to elect the House of Representatives. This debate brings the assets and liabilities of particular electoral methods into sharper relief. The Federalist understanding of representative democracy recommends using the plurality rule to elect representatives from large, heterogeneous, single-member districts. Anti-Federalist thought recommends electing representatives by majority vote from small, homogeneous districts or using majority-runoff elections or what we now call instant-runoff voting. Each group's conception of society, the good, and the problem of tyranny were logically linked to their preferred electoral methods. One cannot get from the Federalists' understanding of civic virtue, the public good, and the problem of tyranny to instant-runoff voting. Likewise, Anti-Federalist thought precludes electing representatives from large districts or with less than an electoral majority. The values, assumptions, and reasoning of this debate underlie the adoption of the SMD system and discussions of US elections in subsequent eras, and

they deeply inform our understanding of the relationship between democratic values and electing a representative assembly.

The Founders—both the Federalists and the Anti-Federalists—embraced
a synthetic understanding of government as meaning a constitutional architecture in which all component parts, including the selection of its members,
must fit together in a specific way to achieve desired objectives. The method
used to select each branch is inseparable from its constitutional role. The
Federalists advocated a relatively complex constitutional design in which the
dispersion of political power and mutual checks among the branches served
as the primary bulwark against tyranny. To secure the public good in such
a constitution requires a particular kind of representative and a particular
kind of electoral system to obtain such representatives.[5] The Anti-Federalists,
in contrast, advocated a simpler constitutional design in which electoral
accountability was the primary protection against government-promulgated
tyranny. Their vision requires a different type of representative selected
through a different electoral process. One cannot separate the respective Federalist and Anti-Federalist political objectives from the constitution needed
to achieve these objectives, from the model of representation recommended
by these visions or from the electoral institutions needed to give these goals
effect. These components must be unpacked and made clear to fully understand the place of the SMD system in US government.

My treatment of founding-era political thought may seem selective to
those well acquainted with the subject. For those most familiar with the lit-
erature on electoral systems, especially those critical of the US SMD system,
it may seem less familiar and unnecessary, yet nothing is more central to
understanding the process under which electoral institutions and processes
are established, institutionalized, and evaluated. The difficulty is that while
constitutional-period writers were quite explicit about these foundations,
their discussions of elections were fewer. To be sure, there are more founding-era writings that speak to elections than is often recognized, and these
have sometimes gone unnoticed because they are lost in the great debates
about republican government, the powers of the national government and
its component branches, and other subjects that captured the imagination of
the founding generation. Still, these writings are of immense value because
in addition to informing us about how the Framers thought about electing
the House, they present the genesis of an intellectual tradition that spans
our history. The references to legislative elections by the delegates to the
Constitutional Convention in *The Federalist Papers*, in Anti-Federalist letters

and pamphlets, and in other period writings demonstrate that the founders thought seriously about elections and how these enhanced or detracted from the overall objectives of the political system. Subsequent generations seeking to reform American elections have appealed to these ideas to justify their respective arguments about how best to elect representatives.

One of the most fundamental questions about American government is how and why the SMD plurality system came to be the method we use to elect the House of Representatives. While strategic politicians chose to adopt it in response to specific social and political circumstances, the system could not be imposed and become part of the national political fabric without a normative and intellectual foundation that recommended its adoption and permanency. While the SMD plurality system did not become a permanent feature of US elections until the mid-nineteenth century, these foundations date to the early republic. The echoes of Federalist and Anti-Federalist debates are heard in every discussion of electoral reform since the founding era. This grounding is also central for assessing the performance of the SMD system and proposals for reform because the more that one accepts these premises and objectives, and believes these are still relevant today, the more difficult it is to argue that the SMD plurality system is deficient in any serious way.

Ultimately, any argument advocating SMD plurality elections, or any other electoral system for that matter, must center on what government is supposed to do. What is the purpose of our political system? Within this broad context, what are the purposes of the branches of government and how do they contribute to this overall purpose? Do the means used to select the members of government advance or inhibit these objectives? These are the foundational premises for any conversation about the efficacy of our electoral institutions because they set the ground rules, so to speak, for discussion. If one cannot agree on the standards and objectives served by a political system, then it is pointless to argue about the efficacy of electoral processes because there is no consensus on how one might assess their contribution toward achieving these goals; we are simply talking past one another.

The Framers' Objective: Republican Government in a Liberal Society

The Framers sought to establish a government capable of protecting individuals from the arbitrary and capricious actions of both their government and their neighbors while simultaneously advancing what Madison calls the "permanent and aggregate interests of the community."[6] These objectives reflect the two major ideological currents that shaped the United States and its political institutions and processes. The first is liberalism, with its emphasis on protecting individual rights and economic opportunity. In the American tradition one principal, if not the principal, responsibility of government is to protect these rights and liberties. Echoing Locke, Jefferson famously asserts in the Declaration of Independence that "governments are instituted among men" precisely to secure and protect fundamental rights. The prohibitions listed in the Constitution's first article, ninth section, and in the Bill of Rights guard against the most egregious violations of rights by the government and are the clearest expressions of our indebtedness to the English tradition of "liberty from" the abuses of a tyrannical state. The *Federalist* and other period writings repeatedly argue the importance of promoting "justice," meaning the protection of rights, especially the rights of the minor party.[7] This is not possible, Madison argues, under direct democracy, in which "measures are too often decided, not according to the rules of justice, and the rights of the minor party, but by the superior force of an interested and overbearing majority."[8] The Framers celebrated those qualities that define us as individuals and thought them worthy of protection.

The second current is republicanism. Republican thought views society as an organic whole rather than a collection of separate and distinct interests, and as possessing a public or collective good that is discovered and pursued through deliberation, especially deliberation in legislative assemblies. The prerequisite for republican government is civic virtue, defined as "a disinterested attachment to the public good, exclusive and independent of all private and selfish interest."[9] Republican thought enjoys a much older pedigree than liberalism, and the lineage that most influenced the American tradition traces, albeit somewhat indirectly, to the ancients as reflected in Aristotle's famous dictum that man seeks "not merely life alone, but the good life" and that "political society exists for the sake of noble actions, and not of mere companionship."[10] David F. Epstein puts it nicely when he observes that the Framers believed that "men are free when they engage in political life—not when they are merely benignly neglected."[11] Reflecting this tradition, when speaking of "liberty" the Framers most often mean "political liberty" or the "liberty to" participate in public affairs and enjoy the personal and societal benefits that accompany civic engagement. A central tenet of republicanism is this belief that civic engagement is the foundation for both personal development and the creation of a society worth living in.

In this spirit, the Framers recognized and sought to promote the personal and collective fulfillment and development that come from being part of and participating in a self-governing political community.

The framing generation's challenge was to obtain the benefits promised by republicanism while mitigating the threats that republican government presents to liberal values. The received solution advocated by Montesquieu, and most clearly advanced on this side of the Atlantic by John Adams in his *Thoughts on Government*, was to rely on a "mixed" system of government to protect basic rights and privileges. In England where Lockean liberalism and its attendant focus on the protection of the individual gained fullest expression, rights were primarily expected to be protected by a government in which the Commons, the Lords, and the Monarch each had their own separate "views and interests" and their own governmental functions, and mutually checked each other.[12] The Framers were deeply impressed by Montesquieu's insight that a system of government in which each branch has its own functions, its own interests, and its own perspective is best capable of protecting liberty. Still, the United States has no hereditary aristocracy to balance the many, and regardless, the Framers would settle for nothing less than a "strictly republican" government, meaning a government in which the branches are either directly elected as in the case of the House of Representatives, or indirectly selected by the people as was the case for the remaining branches.[13] The entire constitutional structure ultimately had to rest on elective consent. The Americans had to find the "republican remedy" for the "republican disease," that is, craft a popular government capable of discovering and advancing the public good while minimizing the danger of tyranny."[14]

We generally understand that the Federalists were more influenced by the liberal tradition, while the Anti-Federalists emphasized republican themes. As a general statement, this is generally wrong, although the mistake is easy enough to understand. Hamilton begins *The Federalist* by pointing to the proposed constitution's implications for "particular interests" and "local institutions."[15] These are not the words of a man who sees the United States as an organic, undifferentiated whole. Likewise, Hamilton is not very charitable toward the ancient republics. While he concedes that the "petty republics of Greece and Rome" dazzled us with "a transient and fleeting brilliancy," in the main one recoils with "horror and disgust at the distractions with which they were continually agitated."[16] In contrast, the Anti-Federalists steep their writings in classical republican imagery. They recoil against the "aristocratic" elements of the Constitution, argue the importance of equality centered on the "middling" class, and extol the importance of civic virtue. To drive home the point, the pseudonyms of prominent Anti-Federalists include A Plebian, Brutus, Cato, Centinel, and Cincinnatus, leaving little doubt about where they turned for inspiration.

In truth it was the Federalists who borrowed most extensively from republican foundations, while the Anti-Federalists placed greatest emphasis on liberal values. The Federalists repeatedly invoke the importance of republican themes such as civic virtue and an expansive notion of the public good. After all, Hamilton, Madison, and John Jay wrote the *Federalist Papers* under the pseudonym Publius, paying homage to the Publius Varerius Publicola, a much-revered Roman statesman and general.[17] Most Anti-Federalist writings reflect greater liberal influence than republican, as reflected in their arguments for the importance of representatives speaking for local interests and the protection of liberty. Still, this distinction between the Federalists and Anti-Federalists is easily overdrawn. In reality, the Federalists and Anti-Federalists were deeply influenced by both lines of thought. What is more important is that the Federalists and Anti-Federalists differed in their understanding of how to balance republican and liberal values. These differences motivate distinct constitutional designs and methods to select its component branches. The Federalists embraced an expansive conception of the good, sought to minimize the reliance on virtue to advance the public good, and advocated a complex constitutional architecture that relied primarily on internal checks and the dispersion of power to thwart tyranny. The Anti-Federalists embraced a limited conception of the good; placed greater emphasis on civic virtue to protect liberty; and advocated a simpler, more transparent government in which elections, coupled with greater powers reserved for the states, were the primary protections against tyranny. How to properly balance republican and liberal objectives underlies all founding debates about how we elect federal office holders. If we do not understand these foundations, all subsequent arguments are built on sand.

Three Key Considerations

To understand the place of the SMD system in American government, it is beneficial to explore the Federalists' and Anti-Federalists' understandings of civic virtue, the public good, and the prevention of tyranny in some detail. These, more than any other considerations, illustrate differences in Federalist and Anti-Federalist thought over advancing and balancing republican and liberal values in the constitutional architecture, as reflected in the purpose of the House of Representatives, what constitutes good and proper representation, and the electoral institutions necessary to give these visions effect. These are the primitives that underlie the more familiar discussion of Federalist and Anti-Federalist representation; developing these considerations in some depth helps to clarify the underlying assumptions and values embedded in any electoral system, and also permits one to trace how changes in our understanding of these considerations have influenced how we believe our representative assembly should be elected.

I have already suggested the outlines of this discussion. The Federalists thought civic virtue resided primarily in the natural aristocracy, while the Anti-Federalists generally believed that virtue resided in the middling classes. The Federalists advanced a more ambitious notion of the public good than did the Anti-Federalists, and finally, the Federalists emphasized checks and balances and the dispersion of political power to thwart tyranny, while Anti-Federalists advocated for a simpler, more transparent government in which electoral accountability protects our rights and liberties. This sketch misses the nuances and contours of these generalizations, and how these considerations underlie two complete but very different understandings of the purpose of the House of Representatives and its election.

Civic Virtue

The Founders agreed that the success of republican self-governance depended on what Jefferson called "the spirit of our people."[18] No popular government, they believed, could long survive without "disinterested attachment to the public good, exclusive and independent of all private and selfish interest" in both the governors and the governed.[19] To them, the alternative to being guided by civic virtue in our collective capacity was rule by terror.[20] The immediate postrevolutionary period did not foster great confidence that the Americans possessed sufficient virtue for successful self-governance. Writers from the Carolinas to Massachusetts denounced the increasingly vain and licentious behavior of the Americans, as reflected in a growing taste for luxury, speculation, decreased religious faithfulness, and a variety of other behaviors.[21] On the eve of the Constitutional Convention, Federalist John Jay lamented that "too much has been expected from the virtue and good sense of the people," while New Jersey governor and Convention participant William Livingston bluntly concluded that "the American people do not exhibit the virtue necessary to support a republican government."[22]

Patrick Henry described the American polity as "dangerously sick."[23] All agreed that republican government could not be predicated solely on the civic benevolence of the rulers and the ruled, but neither could virtue be discarded as a key, indeed necessary, foundation for self-governance.[24] Their challenge was to locate, cultivate, and bring into the public sphere as much civic virtue as possible, recognizing the limitations of virtue as a foundation for self-governance. Federalists and Anti-Federalists alike wrestled with the question of how much civic virtue was necessary for self-governance; how to locate, nurture, and develop it; and how to make best use of it in government. The consequence for failing to do so was not lost on the Framers, all of whom were quite familiar with the decline and collapse of the ancient republics from their want of virtue.

The Founders' thought on civic virtue is inseparable from their understandings of the society for which they sought to craft a government. The Federalist and Anti-Federalist models of republican government derived from the geographic extent of United States and its social heterogeneity. The Federalists celebrated the size of the United States and its diversity of the talents, livelihoods, and even the values of its people. In such a society one could sensibly ask where virtue is more or less likely to reside. What orders of men are likely to be more virtuous and what orders are likely to be less virtuous? For the Federalists, civic virtue principally resided in the natural aristocracy. In contrast, the Anti-Federalists idealized small, relatively homogeneous republics, and viewed the geographic extent of the United States and the diversity in the habits and manners of its inhabitants as obstacles to cultivating virtue and bringing it into government. For this reason, they argued that republican government was best suited to smaller polities, which by their nature are apt to be homogeneous. In such polities virtue is likely to be distributed more uniformly across citizens. For the Anti-Federalists virtue principally resided in the great middling class of yeoman farmers, artisans, and tradesmen. As Melancton Smith argues in the New York ratifying convention, such men are "more temperate," possess "better morals," and are less ambitious. The yeomanry should be brought into government precisely because members of this class can better sympathize with, and understand, the bulk of the citizenry, and are thus better capable of determining and pursing the national good.

The Federalists were deeply skeptical that civic virtue provides an adequate foundation for US government. They rejected as "unrealistic the traditional republican reliance on patriotism . . . [and] . . . the restraints of conscience" to advance the public good and protect against tyranny.[25] Madison's admonition that "if men were angels, no government would be necessary" reflects a pragmatic understanding of mankind and an unwillingness to rely on selfless behavior and good deeds to structure American government.[26] In this spirit they drafted a constitution that minimized reliance on benevolence to achieve the desired outcomes. Instead, "ambition" would be made to "counteract ambition" so that the mutually antagonistic actions of presumably less than altruistic individuals protects liberties and advances the general good. This does not mean that the Federalists thought civic virtue was unimportant; they considered it very important, indeed necessary, for republican governance. The "aim of every political constitution," Madison argues, "is ... to obtain for rulers men who possess most wisdom to discern, and most virtue to pursue, the common good of the society; and ... to take the most effectual precautions for keeping them virtuous whilst they continue to hold their public trust."[27] Virtue must be brought into the political process; however, it is a supplement, what Madison calls "an auxiliary precaution," to more effective means of protecting liberty and advancing the good.

For the Federalists virtue was a characteristic of the few. It existed in the natural aristocracy, that elite class of men composed of "the most eminent professional men ... and men of large property."[28] Members of this class had "a high sense of honor, possess abilities, ambition, and general knowledge" and came primarily "from the landed estates."[29] Anti-Federalist writer Federal Farmer counted no more than "about four or five thousand" such men in a nation of three million souls. George Washington agreed, surmising that "the few ... who act upon principles of disinterestedness are, comparatively speaking, no more than a drop in the ocean."[30] The Federalists believed that members of this natural aristocracy of talent, accomplishment, and "proven merit" possessed the wisdom to "best discern the true interest of their country" and were imbued with such "patriotism and love of justice" that they would be unlikely to sacrifice the public good to "temporary or partial considerations."[31] Their view stems from a tradition that held that economic independence was necessary for one to selflessly engage in public service from a disinterested perspective.[32] The Federalists believed that virtue also resided in the citizenry, albeit to a lesser extent than in the natural aristocracy. Madison points to the importance of citizen virtue in the Virginia ratifying convention by reminding delegates that "we ought not to rely on the virtue of rulers; depend rather on the 'great republican principle, that the people will have [enough] virtue and intelligence to select men of virtue and wisdom.'"[33] Citizens must at least possess sufficient virtue to select the most virtuous to represent them. The Federalists also made the untraditional argument that a strong central government and the encouragement of commercial pursuits were compatible with civic virtue and even strengthened it. Energy and stability in government, they believed, "is essential to national character" and to the "repose and confidence in the minds of the people," and an "irregular and mutable legislation" is both "odious to the people" and "an evil in itself."[34] A capable government promotes virtue by being stable, effective, and, above all else, fair. If government is arbitrary and capricious, or simply incompetent, then there are few incentives to contribute to one's political community or even to play by the rules.

The Anti-Federalists viewed civic virtue as more than an "auxiliary precaution," it was the central element of successful self-government. For them, virtue principally resided in the natural democracy. This natural democracy, from whom many representatives would be drawn, consisted of "the general yeomanry, the subordinate officers, civil and military, the fishermen, mechanics and traders, many of the merchants and professional men."[35] These citizens earned their livelihood from "middling and small estates, industrious pursuits, and hard labor." They were also less accustomed to "combining great objects," and possessed "less ambition and a larger share of honesty."[36] For the Anti-Federalists, republican governance "depends on . . . devotion to fellow citizens and to country so deeply instilled as to be almost as automatic and powerful as the natural devotion to self-interest."[37] To them, this was a characteristic of the industrious middle, not elites. The Anti-Federalist concern for virtue is reflected, for example, in their general preference for a religious test for holding office that they believed would ensure that public officials possessed at least a minimum level of virtue.[38] The Anti-Federalists were especially concerned with what they saw as deficiencies in the Constitution's ability to foster virtue and bring it into government. The Constitution would fail to develop a virtuous citizenry, would bring the least rather than the most virtuous into office, and would undermine the existing national stock of civic virtue. It would do so by distancing citizens from their government so that few would learn proper civic skills, and would lessen the ability of citizens to identify the most virtuous to represent them. The strong Federalist Constitution would enable the crafting of laws so ill-suited for Americans that it would change their dispositions and values in a manner incompatible with self-governance. By undermining virtue, the Constitution contained the seeds of its own destruction.

The Anti-Federalists were deeply influenced by the Montesquian thesis that republics rest foremost on the good behavior of both the ruled and rulers and that virtue is best developed in small, participatory republics characterized by relative equality of circumstance. In such a nation civic virtue is distributed more uniformly among its citizens and is nurtured by close communities, labor in the trades, artisanal activities, and, especially, in connection with the land.[39] Jefferson's belief that "those who labor in the earth are the chosen people of God, if ever he had a chosen people, whose breast he had made his particular deposit for substantial and genuine virtue" captures much Anti-Federalist sentiment.[40] The Anti-Federalists were especially uneasy with the Federalist vision of a large, commercial republic that they believed would promote avarice and exacerbate inequality and, as a consequence, undermine civic virtue.[41] Anti-Federalist Cato warned that "the progress of a commercial society begets luxury, the parent of inequality, the foe to virtue, and the enemy to restraint." In the eyes of many Anti-Federalists, wealth made one less virtuous and more susceptible to the temptation of usurping the government for private gain.[42] The excesses and inequities of urban commercialism fostered self-serving behavior and presented a threat to the viability of republican self-governance. The Anti-Federalists did not oppose commerce, but believed it should rest on an agrarian and artisan foundation, and rejected the notion that self-serving men who engage in private practices for private gain, especially those with commercial spirit, would bring the necessary virtue to the government.[43] In remarks latter echoed by Jefferson in his first annual address, the Pennsylvanian Centinel thought that while "commerce is the handmaiden of liberty" "the merchant, immersed in schemes of wealth, seldom extends his views beyond the immediate object of his gain; he blindly pursues his seeming interest, and sees not the latent mischief."[44] It is the excesses of commercialism and the accumulation of great wealth that undermines virtue and threatens the republic.[45] In contrast, communities characterized by face-to-face interactions among citizens of similar circumstances nourish civic virtue.

All Americans, regardless of their support of or opposition to the Constitution, believed that popular sovereignty depended on civic virtue and that participatory democracy increased the national stock of civic virtue. The relationship between virtue, interests, and social strata is one of the foundations of Federalist and Anti-Federalist conceptions of good and proper representation and, hence, elections. Each group's writings on virtue are theoretical in the sense that their respective ideas are predicated on different foundations. Federalist republicanism depends on application to a large, diverse nation. In such a nation, if virtue is primarily the province of the natural aristocracy, then these men should form the corpus of the legislature, and one must adopt electoral institutions that allow citizens to identify these men and bring them into the government. Anti-Federalist republicanism requires obtaining the benefits of a small, rather homogeneous polity. If virtue principally resides in the "great middling class," then this recommends a different type of representative and electoral processes that allow citizens to choose the most virtuous from among this largely undifferentiated mass. One of the most lasting Anti-Federalist contributions to American political discourse was to "democratize" civic virtue.[46] Virtue resided principally in the middle stratum of industrious, hardworking citizens. This idea of democratized virtue gained considerable traction in the early nineteenth century and played an important role in the changing electoral practices of the era.

The Public Good

In republican thought the purposes of civic engagement and self-rule are the enlightenment of men, the development of a community, and the discovery and pursuit of the collective good. In contemporary discussions we tend to overlook the extraordinary emphasis that late-colonial and early-republic thinkers placed on government's role in advancing the collective or public good. Gordon Wood reminds us that no term other than "liberty" was invoked more by the revolutionary and framing generation than the "public good."[47] Madison's Tenth Federalist paper alone makes no fewer than seven distinct references to the "public good," the "collective good," and the "good of the whole." The liberal tradition, especially as reflected in the writings of John Locke, is not dismissive of a greater public good, but views it as something coincidental or a by-product of individuals pursuing their private good. While the Founders were sympathetic to this perspective, they went well beyond it by recognizing that the "common interest [is] . . . an entity to itself, prior to and distinct from the various private interests of groups and individuals."[48] Whether one recalls the reference in the Constitution's preamble to the "General Welfare" or the ratification debate's numerous invocations of the "public" or "collective good," the Framers clearly believed that a public good exists and that it is more than the summation of individual good or, for that matter, the good of any particular generation. The public good is, as Madison says, "permanent," "aggregate," and defined in terms of the collective welfare of the community, including its future members.[49]

The Framers were sparse in their descriptions of the public good. The Constitution's preamble, inter alia, speaks of establishing justice, meaning protecting the rights of the minor party, and promoting the general welfare. The Federalists, Hamilton in particular, justify government powers—especially congressional powers such as the power to tax and spend, regulate commerce, and advance the sciences and useful arts—on the grounds that these contribute to the public good. Anti-Federalist writers likewise appeal to the public good in justifying their visions of desirable government. However, the Federalists and Anti-Federalists had very different visions of what constitutes the public good and how best to secure it. Their respective understandings motivate the founding debate over the size and scope of the national government and the powers entrusted to it. These differences reveal much about the relationship between the greater social and political objectives expressed through the Constitution and the place of electoral institutions in achieving these objectives. In particular, since the republican tradition emphasizes the role of debate and discussion in discovering the public good, and since the government's powers to pursue the good are largely legislative powers, the Federalist and Anti-Federalist understandings of the public good tells us much about the selection of its members.

The Federalists place the most weight on the public good in defining and justifying political institutions, and they advocate a correspondingly strong national government with powers commensurate with the demands inherent in advancing the good in a large and growing nation. To the Federalists, the public good was discovered through the debate of "enlightened and virtuous" legislators whose views are informed by the interests of their constituents, but transcend and surpass these to "discern the true interest of their country."[50] Accepting the idea of a relatively broad national interest, these writers embraced the positive benefits of government action. The Federalist Papers begin with an impassioned call for a strong government capable of meeting the needs of its citizens. Publius then continues nearly uninterrupted from the twenty-third to the forty-sixth paper to advocate expansive and strong national government powers. In doing so, he articulates the foundational Federalist position that "a constitution, at least equally energetic with the one proposed" is required to preserve the union and meet the needs of its citizens.[51] Such a government, Hamilton intoned, "ought to contain in itself every power requisite to the full accomplishment of the objects committed to its care, and the complete execution of the trusts for which it is responsible; free from every other control but a regard to the public good and to the sense of the people."[52] The government had to be strong enough to establish and enforce property rights; promote commerce, science, and the useful arts; protect basic rights; and defend itself. To be sure, the Federalists believed in national government of limited scope, but they sought significant powers within that scope. The purpose of these powers was to enable legislators to pursue and secure the greater public good.

The Anti-Federalists dismissed the notion of an expansive national good. They instead advanced a narrow, very different understanding of the public good and the role of the House of Representatives in securing it. As Herbert Storing writes, they were "defenders of the status quo" who "saw in the Framers' easy thrusting aside of old forms and principles threats to four cherished values: to law, political stability, the principles of the Declaration of Independence, and to federalism."[53] The Anti-Federalists were conservatives in the truest sense of the word. To be sure, there were divergent voices among Anti-Federalists, but the common thread linking these writers was a strong preference for a government that placed primary emphasis on the protection of liberty, which, to the Anti-Federalist mind, was nearly synonymous with advancing the good. Anti-Federalist Brutus writes, "The preservation of internal peace and good order, and the due administration of law and justice, ought to be the first care of any government."[54] This does not mean that the Anti-Federalists failed to acknowledge the positive benefits of government action; they did acknowledge it, but the scope of these actions was limited to considerations such as national defense. Even these responsibilities were viewed with some caution. Brutus speaks for many Anti-Federalists when he warns that "standing armies in time[s] of peace are dangerous to liberty" and calls attention to "that dangerous engine of despotism a standing army."[55] Even such basic entities as the regulation of commerce were seen as dangerous precisely because doing so could impinge on individual liberties. For the Anti-Federalists, the public good is nearly synonymous with the protection of private rights.[56]

Consistent with this constrained view of the public good, the Anti-Federalists advocated for a central government with few responsibilities extending beyond such basic entities as mutual defense. They considered more extensive responsibilities dangerous and were deeply apprehensive regarding the proposed powers of the national government. Brutus begins his series of essays by pointing to the dangers of the national government's possession of what he considered unfathomable powers: "This government is to possess absolute and uncontroulable power, legislative, executive and judicial, with respect to every object to which it extends. . . . The powers of the general legislature extend to every case that is of the least importance—there is nothing valuable to human nature, nothing dear to freemen, but what is within its power. It has the authority to make laws which affect the lives, liberty and property of every man."[57] The Anti-Federalist preference for more bounded government powers is not unexpected, given that the good itself is more limited. These writers were especially critical of the "necessary and proper" clause, which they viewed as providing the national government with an open grant of authority. When combined with the national government power to tax and the Article VI "national supremacy" clause, this clause threatened the very existence of the states as viable political entities. The Anti-Federalist preference for maintaining political power at the state level was driven in large part by their understanding of the public good, which beyond being more circumscribed was also more parochial.[58] Whatever the public good is, it is more likely to be defined and realized at the state and local levels of government.

This brief recitation reminds us that it was the Federalists who possessed the stronger notion of a national public good and favored arming the House of Representatives with sufficient, competent powers to obtain it. The Federalists are also clear about what the public good is not. Foremost, the public good is not simply the aggregate of the individual good. Writing of the good, Wood concludes: "The common interest was not . . . simply the sum or consensus of the particular interests that made up the community. It was rather an entity in itself, prior to, and distinct from the various private interests of groups and individuals . . . politics was conceived to be not the reconciling but the transcending of the different interests of the society in the search for the single common good."[59] This classically republican understanding deeply impressed the Federalists and is clearly reflected in their writings. Epstein similarly argues that while the good of individual citizens is a key component of the public good, it does not define the good: the interests of the community are an "aggregate" because the community is a nonhierarchical whole; none of the parts has a higher dignity than the others. But the whole is more than the sum of its parts because the whole has a permanence that the parts (individual men) lack. The present parts have no higher dignity than the future parts.[60] Simply, the Federalists were neither utilitarians nor pluralists. The public good is defined only in terms of the collective well-being of the whole nation, including its future inhabitants. The public good is something that transcends specific interests; it is discovered through debate that is informed by interests but surpasses them. In contrast, the Anti-Federalists largely disputed the Federalist insistence that the public good is permanent and transcends the individual good. For example, Thomas Paine writes that the "public good is not a term opposed to the good of individuals; on the contrary it is the good of every individual collected."[61] To Paine and other prominent Anti-Federalists, the common good is closer to the aggregated individual good and is obtained through brokered compromises among competing interests.

These differences motivate different types of representation. There is no reason to believe that the representative able to transcend specific interests to advocate for a broader, less temporal national good is the same representative who will successfully negotiate with chamber peers over legislation affecting constituent interests. Different electoral processes are needed to select each of type of representative.

The Prevention of Tyranny

The liberal objective of the Constitution was the prevention of tyranny. As with bringing civic virtue into government and advancing the public good, the means to reduce the likelihood of tyranny has consequences for the constitutional architecture and the selection of its membership. Not surprisingly, the Federalists and Anti-Federalists also disagreed over how best to reduce the likelihood of tyranny, with attendant consequences for the election of the House of Representatives. Specifically, the Federalists relied most heavily on checks and balances to reduce the likelihood of government-promulgated tyranny, while the Anti-Federalists believed electoral accountability to be the surest safeguard against tyranny. The problem faced by the framing generation was that these two prescriptions for minimizing the danger of tyranny are mutually antagonistic; enhancing one necessarily reduces the efficacy of the other. The simpler and more transparent a constitution, the easier it is to both legislate and assign responsibility to officials for government actions and hold them electorally accountable, while the more complexity introduced into the government through checks and balances, the less likely it is that the government can promulgate tyrannical legislation in the first place, but the more difficult it is for citizens to assign responsibility to officials and hold them electorally accountable for government actions. The Framers understood that they must necessarily emphasize one solution at the expense of the other. Since each approach to minimizing the danger of tyranny has significant consequences for electing the House, it is useful to develop these two understandings more deeply.

The major constraint the Framers faced in designing a republican government capable of protecting rights and liberties was that they did not create three coequal branches of government. The legislature is necessarily more powerful than the executive and judiciary.[62] Only the Congress can initiate potentially tyrannical legislation, including taxation, and only the House of Representatives enjoyed full democratic legitimacy because it was the only directly elected branch of government. To the Founders, this combination of extraordinary powers and what Madison calls the House of Representatives' "supposed influence over the people" owing to its direct election meant that "it is against the enterprising ambition of this department that the people ought to indulge all their jealousy and exhaust all their precautions."[63] In the framing era, when one speaks of reducing the likelihood of government tyranny one is often speaking of legislative tyranny, in particular tyranny promulgated by the House of Representatives.[64]

Constitutional checks and balances were intended to reduce the likelihood of tyranny. Specifically, the framers designed a complex government where in period usage "complex" meant a system of government predicated on the separation of powers and functions and the dispersion of political power. Complex or "mixed" government introduces different interests—traditionally the interests of the one, the few, and the many—into the government through separate branches of government that exercise distinct powers. These branches and corresponding interests check and balance one another, and in doing so prevent tyranny because no one interest gains ascendancy over the others.[65] In contrast, "simple" government includes direct democracy, a government with unchecked legislative supremacy, or a government with very clearly defined boundaries for its component branches.

While both the Federalists and the Anti-Federalists advocated separation of functions and powers, they differed deeply over what constitutes a properly designed government and over the proper selection and composition of the House of Representatives. Madison's famous dictum that "ambition must be made to counteract ambition" is the key underpinning of a distinctly Federalist understanding of balanced government, in which the "opposite and rival interests" of those occupying the branches of government safeguard against tyranny. If the House and the Senate have different legislative priorities owing to differences in the way their memberships are selected, the differences in their terms of office, or differences due to their relative sizes, these chambers are as likely to be antagonistic as cooperative. Such antagonism slows or stops the legislative process, and in doing so makes it difficult for the House to enact potentially tyrannical laws. The presidential veto is an additional check against tyranny should the chambers cooperate, as is the judiciary's power of review. Gridlock, to use the modern term, was the Founders' principal safeguard against tyranny.

The Anti-Federalists also believed in separation of powers and functions, but, to borrow Madison's words, they thought these were at best an auxiliary precaution against tyranny.[66] To the Anti-Federalists the best guarantee of liberty was the electoral check granted to the enfranchised. For electoral accountability to work properly one has to be able to assign responsibility to one's legislator, and to each branch of government, for governmental actions. Consequently, the Anti-Federalists advocated clearly delineated powers between the branches and fewer checks. This simpler government allows citizens to clearly identify the sources of tyranny, whether the source be a branch of government or particular officials within a branch. In this respect, part of the conflict between the Federalists and Anti-Federalists centered on the extraordinary complexity necessary to give constitutional checks and balances effect. To work properly, the Constitution's checks and balances require the select blending of powers across branches, especially for the purpose of strengthening the weaker branches against the House of Representatives.[67] The Anti-Federalists believed that one's ability to assign responsibility for government actions was obscured by the extensive checks and balances needed to give this precaution effect.

Rather than creating a complex government, the Anti-Federalists sought to introduce complexity *within* the House of Representatives. From the Anti-Federalist perspective, the House of Representatives was to be comprised of different "orders" of men distinguished by place, wealth, abilities, and other attributes. In Herbert J. Storing's words, the House represents "'orders' in the community—not hereditary orders but the . . . balance of different parts of the community, their different interests, their different claims to rule."[68] To the extent to which this internal complexity exists, they expected House-promulgated tyranny to be averted by preventing any one order from becoming ascendant over the others. Internal complexity ensures that when one order of men becomes overly powerful, the others have an institutional platform from which to check their ascendance.

The Federalists and the Anti-Federalists were keenly aware of the need for proper electoral institutions to give effect to their respective solutions to the problem of tyranny. The Federalists understood that a system of government designed to reduce the likelihood of tyranny through properly constructed checks and balances does so at the expense of electoral accountability. Consequently, one has to place a high premium on obtaining representatives of the highest virtue and wisdom in the first place. Likewise, the Anti-Federalists understood that since their solution to tyranny was electoral accountability and the internal complexity of the House of Representatives, then the organizational structure of the government must be such that voters could clearly assign credit or blame to elected officials for their actions, while simultaneously generating the necessary legislative complexity so that all interests or orders of men are represented and none dominates the political process. The electoral institutions that give these two visions effect are quite different; indeed, they are incommensurable. One necessarily chooses between these two approaches to minimizing the danger of tyranny, and from this choice follows the appropriate electoral institutions.

Systemic Government and Selection for Office

Creating a system of popular government that combined and enhanced liberal and republican virtues while minimizing their respective liabilities required that the Framers adopt a systemic view of government, where "systemic" means that all of the parts of the government—all parts of the Constitution—had to fit and work together to achieve the desired objectives. The desired objective was a republican government in a liberal society, that is, a government that cultivated and made use of civic virtue and was capable of identifying and advancing the collective good while at the same time minimizing the danger of tyranny. To achieve this goal, the legislative, the executive, the judiciary, federalism, and other key aspects of constitutional design were not crafted separately and in isolation, but were instead created jointly in anticipation of how they would function in unison. In doing so, the Framers paid due attention not only to the respective powers and checks granted to the branches, but equally to their terms of office, membership qualifications, and, most importantly, the means of selection for each office necessary to furthering these goals. Without due care in the selection processes, balance would be forfeited and the constitutional structure would be incapable of achieving its twin objectives.

This understanding is most clearly articulated in the Federalist 47–51 sequence in which Madison explains the relationships among the branches of government. In doing so, inter alia, he makes two very important points. The first is that the key organizational principle of American government is separation of functions and the dispersion of political power. His *Federalist No. 47* prologue raised no eyebrows among his Federalist and Anti-Federalist contemporaries: "The accumulation of all powers, legislative, executive, and judiciary, in the same hands, whether of the one, the few, or many, and whether hereditary, self-appointed, or elective, may be justly pronounced the very definition of tyranny."[69] His second point is that the primary constitutional design challenge is to maintain separation of functions and powers. To do so from the Federalist perspective requires a complex constitutional design that selectively blends powers across branches to strengthen each branch against encroachments by the others. "In the next place, to show that unless these departments be so far connected and blended as to give to each a constitutional control over the others, the degree of separation which the maxim requires, as essential to a free government, can never in practice be duly maintained."[70]

The fundamental point for elections is that this blending of powers is necessary because one cannot rely on constitutional delineations of authority, what Madison calls "parchment barriers," to maintain this dispersion of power. Separation of powers and checks and balances work only if each department has "a will of its own" and officeholders have the "personal motives" to maintain their independence and authority. A "will of its own" means that the members of each branch should see the political world somewhat differently and behave accordingly in pursuing their own objectives. The House of Representatives was directly elected, the Senate selected by state legislatures, the executive selected by the Electoral College, and federal judges appointed precisely so that the selectors of each office differed, with different goals and priorities, and as a consequence each officeholder was responsible to, and reflected the values of, a different composition of the American polity. Likewise the terms of office: two, four, and six years for representatives, the president, and senators, respectively, and during good behavior for federal judges, fostered different outlooks and objectives among holders of these offices.

Representatives are more concerned with immediate circumstances than the president, while senators have an even longer-term perspective. Federal judges who hold lifetime appointments presumably adjudicate for the ages.

The anticipated effect of different means of selection and terms for the offices was that the inhabitants of each branch would see the political world differently. Representatives would view the world in a manner not unlike their constituents, senators from the perspective of state legislators, and presidents from the perspective of electors chosen in a manner determined by their state legislature, while federal judges would keep their own counsel informed by the tenets of legal scholarship.

While the Federalists and Anti-Federalists agreed that separation of powers was, as John Adams wrote, the sine qua non of good government, they disagreed over the extent of complexity needed to guard against tyranny and whether the self-interest of office holders or their civic virtue should be the primary device that maintains separation of powers. The Federalists emphasized the importance of self-interest and power seeking in maintaining separation of powers and functions. Madison writes: "This policy of supplying, by opposite and rival interests, the defect of better motives, might be traced through the whole system of human affairs, private as well as public . . . [the] . . . aim is, to divide and arrange the several offices in such a manner as that each may be a check on the other; that the private interest of every individual may be a centinel over the public rights."[71]

While it is mutual checks that maintain the separation of functions and powers, it is electoral institutions that provide the behavioral foundations necessary to give these effect. To the Federalists, electoral institutions shaped the preferences, incentives, and rewards required for separation of powers to fulfill its anticipated constitutional role. Simply, the constitutional framework of separation of functions and powers does not work in the absence of properly designed elections. Most important, the electoral institutions were directly embedded in the Constitution—state legislative selection of the Senate, the Electoral College selection of the president—or were assumed to be widely implemented in the case of the SMD plurality system for the House of Representatives, and were those selection processes considered best suited to further the overall objectives fulfilled by the Constitution.

In contrast, the Anti-Federalists advocated greater reliance on civic virtue to maintain both the distribution of power and protection against tyranny. In his first letter Anti-Federalist Centinel challenges Madison by questioning: "Suppose a government could be formed and supported on such principles, would it answer the great purposes of civil society; if the administrators of every government are actuated by views of private interest and ambition, how is the welfare and happiness of the community to be the result of such jarring adverse interests?" For Centinel and other Anti-Federalists the only way that electoral accountability can function properly is if citizens know to whom responsibility for government actions should be assigned, and this is possible only if citizens can determine such responsibility. This is made possible by a simpler constitutional design. Centinel continues: "The highest responsibility is to be attained, in a simple structure of government, for the great body of the people never steadily attend to the operations of government, and for want of due information are liable to be imposed on."[72] Only when responsibility can be assigned is it possible for a people to check the tyrannical actions of the government. The prerequisite for this is a simple constitutional structure.

A Brief Illustration: The Senate

Our interest is not the role of checks and balances in preventing tyranny and helping representatives discover and advance the public good, but rather how the electoral system facilitates these objectives in the overall constitutional architecture. It is here that there is much that accounts for the establishment and institutionalization of the SMD plurality system and provides a normative recommendation for its use. However, it is easiest to motivate this argument through a brief digression on the upper chamber of Congress. Under the original Constitution, US senators were selected by the state legislatures, a practice that continued until the Progressive Era and the passage of the Seventeenth Amendment in 1913. The question is, why did the Framers choose state legislative appointment? To answer that question one has to first understand what it means to represent states in a legislature, and second, the purpose of the Senate as understood by the Framers.

To represent a state, a geographic entity, means to represent it in its corporate capacity. As discussed in the first chapter, by "corporate capacity" one means that a state as a state has some identifiable and defined interest that is separate and distinguishable from the interests of the citizens who comprise it. In the founding era the basic unit of legislative representation was the township or county, with little regard for their respective populations. It was the corporate entity, the town or county, that formally received legislative representation, not its residents.[73] At the Constitutional Convention and in the ratification debates, the normative justification for equal state representation in the Senate and the manner in which senators would be appointed hinged critically on one's acceptance or rejection of corporate representation. While supporters and skeptics of state corporate capacity spoke in several contexts, the most focused forums for these arguments were the debates over how to extend federalism protections to the states. To "protect" states means that one must be protecting *something*, in particular something that would otherwise not be protected by legislators in the House of Representatives or by a similarly comprised and selected second legislative chamber. That something is the rights and privileges of states as states.

Among the most forceful advocates of the corporate capacity argument was delegate Luther Martin, who left the Convention over objections to several decisions, including population-based state representation in the House of Representatives.[74] Immediately following the Convention, he justified state corporate capacity in a speech to the Maryland House of Delegates by appealing to natural law, arguing: "that each state when formed was in a state of nature as to the others, and the same rights as individuals in a State of Nature."[75] According to this view, states are entities that have rights and privileges in and of themselves, these rights and privileges obtain equally to all states, they are distinct from the rights and privileges of the citizens who comprise the states, and, just like those for individuals, these rights and privileges merit constitutional protection.[76]

Of course, many disagreed with the state corporate capacity argument. James Madison is the best-known dissenter, but skepticism regarding this line of reasoning was articulated during the Convention by several delegates, perhaps none more clearly than Roger Wilson: "Can we forget for whom we are forming a government? Is it for *men*, or for the imaginary beings called *states*? Will our honest constituents be satisfied with metaphysical distinctions?"[77] So far as Wilson and like thinkers were concerned, states have no rights or interests beyond those of their respective citizens, and it is citizens who should be represented in both the House and in the Senate.

It is not for us to judge whether states do or do not have corporate interests. That question was settled by the Connecticut Compromise and the Constitution's ratification.[78] Rather, stipulating that states have corporate interests and that these are given meaning through a federal form of government, two implications for state representation and the selection of senators follow. The most familiar is that states have to be equally represented in the legislature. If states are represented in the legislature and their interests are separate and distinct from the interests of the citizens who compose them, then state population is irrelevant to representation. If one agrees with Luther Martin that all states are created equal, then they are entitled to equal representation. In the absence of a belief that states possess corporate capacity, there is no normative justification for equal state representation in the Senate.

More central to our purposes, the corporate capacity premise has significant implications for how one selects members of the Senate. In particular, there is no obvious argument for direct citizen participation in the choice of senators. If one seeks to protect state interests as distinguished from citizen interests, then one presumably wants to use the selection mechanism most capable of discovering, articulating, and protecting the former. Constitutional Convention delegate John Dickinson of Delaware proposed the method thought best for doing so that eventually became Article I, Section 3, of the original Constitution, mandating that state legislatures select US senators. The justification for legislative rather than citizen selection was precisely that state legislators were in the best position to judge the interests of their states and to select senators who would further these interests. As Dickinson argued, "The sense of the states would be better collected through their governments; than immediately from the people at large."[79] Senators appointed by state legislatures were assumed to be in the best position to comprehend and advocate the interests of their respective states. They were also expected to protect the states against excessive encroachment by the national government, in particular by the House of Representatives, because those who failed to do so would be replaced at the earliest possible moment by others who would fulfill this responsibility more diligently. In the Convention Dickinson argued the received founding-era wisdom that citizen selection of senators was antithetical to the institution's purpose. Citizen election would fail to capture "the sense of the states"; worse, directly elected senators would be willing accomplices to the House in extending the reach of the national government relative to the states. In this view, state legislature selection of senators is a key federalism protection for the states under the original US Constitution.

State legislative selection is also recommended by the purposes served by the Senate in the overall constitutional framework. The Senate serves two additional purposes under the original Constitution. The first is to defend against rash and unreflective decisions made by the more numerous House of Representatives. Madison captures this sense in the early Convention debates on the Senate. In his view, the role of the Senate is "first to protect the people against their rulers: secondly to protect the people against the transient impressions into which they themselves be led . . . a numerous body of representatives, were liable to err also, from fickleness and passion."[80] In the Framers' view, the House of Representatives was likely to pursue objectives of a momentary and transient nature often adverse to the long-run well-being of the nation. The House pursues such policies because of its greater numbers, because it is directly elected, and because representatives have brief terms. All of these attributes make the chamber susceptible to passionate, unreflective behavior rather than dispassionate reason. This deficiency is remedied by the Senate. Under the original constitution, the Senate is the responsible chamber.[81] Its selection by the state legislatures was intended to ensure that only the most "distinguished characters" served in the chamber. Combined with its smaller size and six-year terms, this was intended to produce more enlightened, thoughtful, and dispassionate governance. The chamber was expected to provide stability and enable citizens to hold their government accountable for its long-term performance.[82]

Equally important, the Senate is the key institutional connection between the states and the national government. The Senate not only exists to protect state interests in the federal structure, but properly selected it ensures harmony between the two levels of government when the national government is proactive. When Dickinson formally proposed "that the second branch of the national legislature be chosen by the legislatures of the individual states," he justified statehouse selection on the grounds that this mode of selection "will more intimately connect the state governments with the national legislature."[83] This ensures that the national government and states are more likely to be in agreement and cooperate when the national government acts. George Mason summarized this argument immediately before the question was put to a vote:

> The state legislatures also ought to have some means of defending themselves against the encroachments of the National Government. In every other department we have studiously endeavored to provide for self-defense. Shall we leave the states alone unprovided with the means for this purpose? And what better means can we provide than giving them some share in, or rather to make them a constituent part of, the national establishment . . . the second branch of the national legislature should flow from the legislature of each state, to prevent encroachments on each other and to harmonize the whole.[84]

It is precisely because the upper chamber represents states rather than citizens that the states "secure their authority" in the national government and are "harmonized" with it. This provides the link between the national and state governments

One can reasonably agree with Dickinson that the direct election of US senators, as is now required under the Seventeenth Amendment, compromised the ability of the chamber to protect the long-term interests of states because senators are now more responsive to the immediate interests of citizens. Whether such strong federalism protections are or are not desirable depends on one's political preferences, but it is unarguable that the original constitutional selection process was purposefully selected to facilitate the Senate's intended purpose in the overall constitutional structure. The state corporate interest premise combined with federalism in which states have a central independent place in governance, and the desire to elevate the most distinguished citizens to the chamber, provides the justification both for equal state representation in the Senate and for insulation of senatorial selection from direct citizen input. The Framers instituted state legislative selection of US senators rather than direct election precisely because legislative selection advanced the intended purpose of the Senate, while citizen election would inhibit it. This selection mechanism was intended to fulfill a particular purpose, and when the selection process was changed so was the chamber's ability to fulfill that purpose.

Conclusion

In the American balance of liberal and republican ideals, the Federalists embraced a public good that was expansive, truly national in character, and discovered by enlightened and virtuous representatives drawn from the natural aristocracy. Their principal solution to government-promulgated tyranny was mixed government predicated on a rather complex system of checks and balances. The behavioral foundations needed to give the constitution effect were embedded in the selection method for each office. The Anti-Federalists believed in a more circumscribed and parochial good, with interests represented by virtuous legislators drawn from all social classes. They further believed that electoral accountability was the best bulwark against tyranny. These foundations—a broad notion of the public good combined with complex government constructed primarily to check the House, or a more narrowly defined good combined with a preference for electoral accountability made possible by a simpler, more transparent constitution—present very different conceptions of a US government. To the Framers, the parts of each constitutional model are linked. A government with extensive responsibilities and powers is best checked internally; a government with fewer responsibilities and powers, and a correspondingly simpler architecture, is properly checked by the electorate. Recognizing this helps explain the respective Federalist and Anti-Federalist preferences for electoral institutions, and also provides a basis for interpreting subsequent debates over US elections.

These are the broadest strands of founding-era political thought relevant to understanding electoral institution processes. The key considerations center on the idea that the Framers sought to create a republican government in a liberal society, and this necessarily introduces a tension that is not easily solved in a strictly republican form of government. Liberal values are placed under stress in a system of government predicated on popular sovereignty. The primary insights for understanding how the Framers sought to solve this problem come from the Federalist and Anti-Federalist debate over separation of functions and powers and their respective views toward primary reliance on checks and balances or electoral accountability to minimize the danger of tyranny. These solutions may not be brokered; they are mutually antagonistic. One must choose among them. More broadly, the Framers designed a systemic government in which all the component parts, including the selection methods and their induced behavioral motivations, must fit together for the overall constitutional structure to achieve its overall objective of enabling a strictly republican government to exist in a liberal nation.

The following chapter discusses how these predicates and values are reflected in the Federalist and Anti-Federalist understandings of the purpose of the House of Representatives within the broader constitutional architecture, good and proper representation, and the electoral processes necessary to implement and secure these ideals. What emerges are two distinct understandings of House elections, both of which continue to resonate in American political discourse. Contemporary discussions of the House of Representatives and its election reflect both the Federalist and Anti-Federalist visions of legislative elections without recognition that these visions are founded on different assumptions, ideals, and political objectives and that in their purest form they are in conflict rather than harmony. Chapter 3 disentangles and clarifies these two understandings of the House and its election.

3 The Founding-Era House of Representatives and the SMD System

The aim of every political constitution is, or ought to be, first, to obtain for rulers men who possess most wisdom to discern, and most virtue to pursue, the common good of society.

James Madison, Federalist No. 57

It is deceiving a people to tell them they are electors, and can choose their legislators, if they cannot, in the nature of things, choose men from among themselves, and genuinely like themselves.

The Federal Farmer, Essay No. 7

In George Mason's memorable words, the House of Representatives is "to be the grand depository of the democratic principles of the government."[1] The House is the democratic chamber: it is where the people are represented. Compared to the Senate, where states are represented and selection was driven by the desire to obtain the most distinguished members and to foster harmony between the national government and the states, the proper selection method for the House is both simpler and significantly more complex. It is simpler in the sense that the people are represented in the House and are entitled to choose their own representatives. It is more complex because the constitutional objectives fulfilled by the House are more extensive than those for the Senate, and this must be reflected in its selection method. This chapter outlines the purpose of the House of Representatives, the corresponding model of representation recommended by this understanding, and how this is incorporated into the selection method for the chamber. In doing so, it presents competing Federalist and Anti-Federalist visions of the House and its election that still resonate today. Contemporary discussions about electoral processes and representation are often poorly distilled versions of the founding-era debates, and would benefit immensely from being reminded of their antecedents and the terrain that has already been covered.

It is fitting to begin this chapter with George Mason's words because in many ways Mason straddled the boundaries that separated the Founders. He contributed greatly to the Constitutional Convention only to decline to sign the document, instead devoting his energies to opposing its ratification in his native Virginia. Mason opposed ratification because he believed that the proposed government would eventually devolve into a "tyrannical aristocracy."[2] Federalist representation, which he described as the "shadow only of representation," ranked high on his list of constitutional defects that would eventually promulgate tyranny because the laws would be "made by men little concerned in, and unacquainted with, their effects and consequences."[3] Mason's critique still resonates today. Like all of the Founders, Mason struggled with the complexities and nuances of democratic assemblies, representation, and elections. His enthusiasm for popular sovereignty was tempered by a recognition that "much had been said against democratic elections" and that "much might be said."[4]

Those interested in congressional government are generally acquainted with the Federalist and Anti-Federalist differences over the House of Representatives. The Federalists sought representatives drawn from the "natural aristocracy" of virtuous and wise citizens who would govern for the greater good. Madison famously advocated a system of representation to "refine and enlarge" the public's views by passing them through these "enlightened" representatives.[5] To obtain such representatives, the Federalists sought to elect members of the House from relatively large, heterogeneous districts, using the plurality rule, and to have them serve for what was then considered the fairly lengthy term of two years. Further, representatives should have the discretion to pursue the public good unencumbered by excessive restraints imposed by their constituents. The Federalists believed the candidates most likely to emerge and win such elections would be those "men who possess the most attractive merit, and the most diffusive and established characters." These were precisely the men in whom constituents could place their trust to secure great national objects.[6] Such representatives would serve the country well because they were not like their constituents; they would be citizens of superior ability, wisdom, and virtue.

The Anti-Federalists also sought virtuous representatives to govern for the greater good, but believed that citizens would find such representatives from among themselves and those with whom they were most closely acquainted. The Anti-Federalists thought the House of Representatives should mirror society and that representatives should "think, feel, reason and act" like those on whose behalf they legislated.[7] In his third letter, Brutus provides one of many Anti-Federalist statements to this effect: "The very term, representative, implies, that the person or body chosen for this purpose, would resemble those who appoint them—a representation of the people of America, if it be a true one, must be like the people." The Anti-Federalists placed an especially high premium on holding representatives accountable for their performance in office and fidelity to constituents. To fulfill these objectives the Anti-Federalists believed representatives should be elected by majorities from small, homogeneous districts. Legislative accountability was enhanced by this correspondence and annual election, and because citizens were deeply familiar with their representatives and their actions in office. Representatives would serve their constituents well precisely because they were indistinguishable from them.

Like any simplification, this summary is a caricature. Federalist and Anti-Federalist thought and the ensuing debate was much deeper and centered on the purpose of the House of Representatives, and from this follows proper representation, how to select representatives with desirable qualities, and how much autonomy representatives should enjoy. The two positions were irreconcilable. The Federalists could not imagine a more poorly constructed government than one that established a large legislative chamber comprised of members who "think, feel, reason and act" like the citizens on whose behalf they legislate. For many Anti-Federalists, the thought of being governed by "the most diffusive and established characters" smacked of returning to the subjugation they endured as subjects of the British Empire.[8] The Federalists won the constitutional battle, but the Anti-Federalists arguably won the hearts and minds of the Americans. Popular rhetoric says that we want representatives to be typical citizens and responsive to our preferences. Still, we lament their difficulty in pursuing great national objects.

The SMD plurality system is a necessary and integral, although unwritten, part of the Constitution. I make this argument by first discussing the purpose of the House of Representatives. It is impossible to construct a compelling argument about how best to elect a representative assembly unless one has a clear understanding of the purpose of that assembly. From this follows the proper model of representation, by which I mean the qualities that define good representation and how these contribute positively to governance. Next I consider more deeply what it means to "choose" one's representative or, more accurately, what it means to be represented by a representative of one's choice. Since contemporary critics argue that SMD plurality elections inhibit citizens from being represented by those of their own choosing, it is instructive to remind ourselves of how the Framers thought about this question. For the Framers whether one was represented by a legislator of one's choice encompassed three key elements. The first is popular sovereignty reflected in the right to vote for a representative. Here it is important to understand the conflict between virtual and actual representation that was at the heart of the revolutionary generation's basis for separation from Great Britain. This section highlights those aspects of virtual representation that positively influenced the Framers' thinking about proper government. This section also discusses the relationship between enfranchisement and electoral institutions. Second, I review the distinctions between plurality and majority electoral systems. Plurality is essential to the Federalist vision, while it is antithetical to that of the Anti-Federalists, who required that elections generate majorities. The third element explores period understandings of whether representatives should enjoy extensive autonomy from their constituents, or whether representatives should be responsive to constituents' demands. In many ways, accountability is the core of the constituent and representative relationship. These three elements—popular sovereignty, electoral thresholds, and the extent of legislative autonomy—form the period foundation for whether one was represented by a legislator of one's choice.

These competing visions of the House of Representatives produce a corpus of ideas that argue that the Federalist conception is primarily realized by SMD plurality elections. The Anti-Federalist model can be realized by an SMD system creating either natural or manufactured majorities. The preferred Federalist and Anti-Federalists electoral processes are predicated on different assumptions and democratic values. It is these democratic values, reflected in a particular constitution and applied to a given society, that drive electoral methods. The Framers' arguments provide the intellectual foundation for the adoption and institutionalization of the SMD plurality system in the United States and the basis for assessing its performance and continued use. I believe that if critics of the House of Representatives and its elections better understood these foundations, they would question their own assessments and preferred remedies for perceived deficiencies in US elections and representation. Eventually one has to decide whether the SMD plurality system is beneficial or harmful to US representative government. I leave that discussion for later in the book; for now it will suffice to better understand the Framers' arguments as they understood these arguments.

The Purpose of the House of Representatives

Today the purpose of the House of Representatives seems clear: its purpose is to legislate. The public distain for Congress as reflected in low levels of approval for both the institution and its members provides ample evidence that Congress's inability to legislate efficiently as exemplified by "gridlock" and claims that "Washington is broken" demonstrates that we think legislative inaction is a defect in our government. The Framers would be appalled. To them, legislative inaction is as much an indication of the chamber functioning properly as is legislative action. This is because the Congress, like the entire constitutional structure, was intended to balance the objectives of republicanism and liberalism. Congress is charged with securing "the public good *and* private rights."[9] Both objectives privilege inaction over action. The discovery of an unambiguous public good is a rare thing indeed, and the protection of citizens from a potentially tyrannical government more often than not involves slowing, rather than expediting, the legislative process.[10]

To the Founders, the House of Representatives was the institution primarily responsible for fulfilling the republican objective of discovering and advancing the public good. Founding-era writings distinguish the House from the other branches of government in this respect. No framer of significance discusses the presidency, the judiciary, or even the Senate as the chief institutional platform for the discovery and advancement of the collective good. These branches certainly contribute to the collective welfare by bringing different perspectives of the good into the governing process and by exercising their respective responsibilities, but their principal contribution is to slow the House so that time and the reflection that delay affords enables the public and their representatives to more clearly see the good uncorrupted by momentary passion and transient impulse.[11]

The Federalists and Anti-Federalists differed immensely in their understandings of how republican government advances the good. As a consequence, the House of Representatives serves a different purpose for each group. For the Federalists the primary purpose of the House is to provide a forum for deliberation and discovery of the good. The House of Representatives is first and foremost a venue for the articulation and scrutiny of ideas.

It is the peoples' representatives who discover and pursue the good, not the people themselves. The Anti-Federalists also thought the chamber advances the good, but it does so by bringing well-defined notions of the good into the House, which serves as a location for finding compromise among the distinct interests brought forward by representatives of the various constituencies.[12] Deliberation to discover the good, Anti-Federalists believed, should primarily take place in the constituency among citizens, not in the chamber. The received good is then conveyed to representatives, whose responsibility it is to enact the will of the people through the legislative process.[13] They do so by reconciling these distinct interests into something that approximates the general good.

The Federalists and Anti-Federalists also thought that a properly designed and elected House could contribute to protecting against tyranny. Both groups agreed the key was balancing interests so that no single interest dominates the political processes. However, they differed over whether such balance is best achieved in the constituency or within the chamber—that is, should the narrow interests of citizens be primarily balanced and rendered harmless in constituencies constructed for that purpose, or should they be balanced within the legislative chamber itself? The Federalists sought to keep interests out of government and consequently emphasized balancing and reconciling these within constituencies. District heterogeneity was intended to ensure that no single interest dominated the constituency and to make sure that representatives were sensitive to many perspectives. The Anti-Federalists thought that constituent interests should be brought into government and balanced in the chamber. This works only if representatives are informed about and responsible to well-defined interests and advocate these against other such interests in the chamber.

These distinct understandings motivated different assemblies and different election processes to populate these assemblies. A House of Representatives intended to discover the good through deliberation is properly staffed by members who have been exposed to a variety of interests and views in their constituency and have latitude to use this knowledge to pursue the good. A House of Representatives that serves as a venue for reconciling competing interests is properly staffed by representatives who have clear understandings of their constituents' interests and are held to account in advocating them against the interests brought into the chamber by other representatives. These respective purposes impose prerequisites that constituencies and representatives must fulfill. Each perspective presents a complete vision of the House of Representatives and how to best elect it. Exploring these visions more deeply allows us to more clearly see the relationship between competing democratic values and how distinct electoral arrangements furthered these values.

The Federalists

The Federalists justify republican government on the grounds that only a representative assembly chosen by the people can "discern the true interest of their country" and act for the public good as "proper guardians of the public weal."[14] In this view, the purpose of the House of Representatives is to discover and legislate toward a broadly national and permanent good. Their belief that "the public voice, pronounced by the representatives of the people, will be more consonant to the public good than if pronounced by the people themselves" summarizes an important aspect of their political thought, and also says much about period understandings about the usefulness of direct democracy for advancing the public good.[15] This implies nothing about the Framers' view of citizen competency. It is irrelevant whether the people are enlightened. Had "every Athenian citizen been a Socrates," Madison says about ancient Greece, "every Athenian assembly would still have been a mob."[16] The problem was to find electoral processes that encouraged directly elected legislators tied to local constituencies to pursue a national good.

The Federalist solution begins with Madison's observation that while representatives must be "acquainted with all their local circumstances," they must also "comprehend and pursue great and national objectives."[17] To do so, representatives must be capable of transcending parochial and temporal interests. Election from large, heterogeneous districts helps representatives comprehend great national objectives in two ways. The first is that such districts are conducive to the election of the most virtuous men, and these are precisely the representatives most capable of valuing, understanding, and pursuing a broadly defined national good. The Federalists believed that the greater public good was not the primary concern of most citizens, who neither understand it nor privilege it over local or immediate interests. Rather, as Epstein argues, in the founding era the public good was thought to be "the concern of a kind of elite; wise representatives" who shared "this concern with . . . the most considerate and virtuous citizens."[18] To "pursue great and national objectives," representatives must be those "whose wisdom may best discern the true interest of their country, and whose patriotism and love of justice will be least likely to sacrifice it to temporary or partial considerations."[19] Only the natural aristocracy fits this description.

There is no guarantee, however, that citizens will elect such "fit characters." The Federalists were keenly aware that men of "local prejudices" and "sinister designs" are regularly elected to office. The second Federalist argument for large, heterogeneous districts is that these facilitate the election of representatives with desirable qualities, in part because such districts provide greater numbers of "fit characters" who might seek office, and "consequently, a greater probability of a fit choice."[20] Large districts also reduce the ability of unworthy candidates to "practice with success the vicious arts, by which elections are too often carried."[21] In particular, such districts reduce the efficacy of appeals by demagogues and make it harder for the unworthy to bribe or scheme their way into office.

To understand how locally elected representatives could pursue the national good, first recall that for the Federalists the major impediment to securing the public good is the "spirit of party" and interested factions.[22] Madison laments that differences among citizens have "divided mankind into parties, inflamed them with mutual animosity, and rendered them much more disposed to vex and oppress each other, than to co-operate for their common good."[23] These differences, which the Framers believed resulted from immutable characteristics, are "sown into the nature of man." As long as we are free to differ in our political and social preferences, such differences will exist. For the Federalists, the only remedy is to elect the most distinguished men possible and then place them in a constitutional framework that makes best use of their virtue and directs their interested ambition into socially beneficial directions. Such virtuous and civic-minded men were expected to be the most capable of overcoming and minimizing the spirit of party and faction in the legislature. Virtue, however, is a thin thread on which to hang obtainment of the public good.[24] The Framers recognized that even the best, most enlightened representatives will fall well short of the classical republican ideals. Madison maintains that "enlightened statesmen will not always be at the helm" and further that "it is in vain to say that enlightened statesmen . . . will be able to render [clashing interests] . . . subservient to the public good."[25] Legislators will not be brilliant altruists, nor would it help if they were. The problem is how to elect the best possible representatives—those with the most virtue and wisdom—recognizing that these traits will still be found wanting relative to our aspirations and that while these traits will make recognition and pursuit of the greater good more likely they will not guarantee it.

Large districts, even if they elect virtuous representatives, are insufficient for securing the public good; districts must also encompass multiple and distinct interests. For the founders, district heterogeneity largely followed from size: the larger the district, the greater number of interests contained within it. For the Federalists, constituencies could not be "communities of interest."[26] It is only when districts encompass multiple communities of interest that virtuous representatives can potentially comprehend the public good. Drawing electoral districts to encompass multiple interests ensures that legislators are exposed to a variety of perspectives. In contrast, the Federalists thought legislators drawn from small districts, which by their very nature are homogeneous, would be "unduly attached" to "local circumstances and lesser interests" and "too little fit to comprehend and pursue great and national objects."[27]

Large, heterogeneous districts also prepare representatives to contribute to legislative discussion because their arguments are informed and challenged by a greater number of perspectives. Importantly, this preparation occurs in the constituency at the electoral stage. To gain election in the first place, legislators must be exposed to and address and win the confidence of many different interests. When representatives enter the chamber they will not be the proverbial villagers who have never crossed the hill to visit the village on the other side. Similarly, such districts contribute to republican ideals of good citizenship by encouraging residents who are presumptively divided by interests and values to discuss and debate these among themselves. In such districts one has the opportunity to participate in political discourse with neighbors and fellow residents of different political mind, with corresponding benefits for civic education and engagement.[28]

Finally, large, heterogeneous districts also advance the liberal objectives of the House of Representatives by making it more difficult for majority factions to form and enter the House of Representatives. Echoing Hanna Pitkin, Andrew Rehfeld argues that the Federalists embraced "a vision of political representation that kept interests out of the legislature in service to the public good."[29] While both the Federalists and the Anti-Federalists advocated balancing interests in the legislature to prevent tyranny, the Federalists believed that balancing interests in the constituency, not in the legislature, was the more effective way to prevent tyranny and to keep any one or few groups from becoming too powerful. In large districts, narrowly defined interests primarily check and balance themselves in the constituency, not in the House of Representatives.

Electoral districts, of course, can be too large, with detrimental effects on legislator knowledge and understanding of constituent needs and interests. Madison expresses the concern that in overly large districts representatives would be "too little acquainted with all their local circumstances and lesser interests" and that a proper balance between these extremes must be found.[30] In obtaining this mean, the Federalist preference is clearly for larger districts. Still, even properly sized districts may admit specific interests to reach the Congress, but these will be fewer and farther between, and more easily balanced and "rendered harmless" in the chamber, and if not, externally checked. In contrast, small districts increase the likelihood that a single interest will dominate the constituency and enter the chamber. From the Federalists' perspective, tyranny of the majority becomes more probable. "The smaller the society, the fewer probably will be the distinct parties and interests composing it; the fewer the distinct parties and interests, the more frequently will a majority be found of the same party; and the smaller the number of individuals composing a majority, and the smaller the compass within which they are placed, the more easily will they concert and execute their plans of oppression."[31] In homogeneous districts minority voices are lost; even if there is no absolute majority interest it is easier for a small number of powerful interests to coordinate to the detriment of others in the political community. For the Federalists, small political societies, whether small republics or small legislative districts within great republics, are tyrannical political societies.

The Anti-Federalists

The Anti-Federalists thought the purpose of a House of Representatives was to enact the will of the people. It exists to legislate the good as expressed by the people, albeit a good that is more limited and local than the Federalists' good. Melancton Smith, speaking before the New York ratifying convention, makes this the center of his speech: "It [is] the fundamental principle of a free government, that the people should make the laws by which they were to be governed. He who is controlled by another is a slave; and that government which is directed by the will of . . . any number less than the *will of the community*, is a government for slaves."[32] The Anti-Federalists define the will of the people as synonymous with the good, while the Federalists thought that the will of the people, assuming it could somehow be determined, was typically an impediment to securing the public good. More importantly, the Anti-Federalists primarily thought of representative government as a practical alternative to direct democracy in discovering and advancing the public will. Smith continues, "Experience has taught mankind that legislation by representatives is the most eligible and the *only practicable* mode in which the people of any country can exercise this right."[33] This distinguishes the Anti-Federalists from the Federalists in a very important respect. The Federalists wrote of the theoretical benefits of representative democracy relative to direct democracy, and certainly did not think of representative government as a pragmatic necessity for governing on a national scale. By thinking of the national good as the will of the community, and representative government as a practical way to execute this will, the Anti-Federalists embraced a different understanding of the House of Representatives and its proper election.

For Melancton Smith and other Anti-Federalists the community possesses a will; the question is, how is it expressed?[34] The answer is that legislators have to press local and particular interests that are then brokered and reconciled into something approaching the community will.[35] The likelihood of reconciling interests is, as one might expect, inversely related to the disparity of these interests. In a small, relatively homogeneous nation, where the government has few responsibilities, the brokering and compromise necessary to reach mutually acceptable accommodation and something approximating the popular will presents few obstacles. In a large, heterogeneous nation, where government has extensive responsibilities, it likely no such reconciliation is possible. The Anti-Federalists idealized the former society and government, and in such it is only possible to achieve the good if representatives advocate the interests of their constituents in the legislature. The Federal Farmer, perhaps the most extensive Anti-Federalist commentator on the legislature and its election, makes this point when he informs us that he is "fully convinced that we must organize the national government [to] . . . secure . . . more effectually the different interests in the community." Interests must be collected, brought into the chamber, and advocated.

The Anti-Federalists believed interests were closely tied to the "orders of men" in the community. For these writers, the "what" to be represented are "orders of men" defined by interests and their standing among the many or the few. Federal Farmer speaks to this when he emphasizes the importance of achieving balance in the legislature. "I advanced the idea of balancing the several orders of men in a community, in forming a general representation. . . . Each order must have a share in the business of legislation actually and efficiently."[36] Here the term "orders" does not mean the traditional hereditary distinction of the commons, the aristocracy, and the monarchy familiar from the old world, but rather "balance of the different parts of the community, their different interests, and their different claims to rule," whether these parts "be the many and the few or any other fundamental differentiation."[37] The Anti-Federalists believed that the natural aristocracy should be represented, but in proportion to their numbers just like any other well-defined order or community of interest.[38] Federal Farmer continues: "I contend for uniting and balancing their interests, feelings, opinions, and views in the legislature; we may not only so unite and balance these as to prevent a change in the government by the gradual exaltation of one part to the depression of others, but we may derive many other advantages from the combination and full representation."[39] The House of Representatives provides a forum in which the interests affiliated with these orders are balanced and reconciled.

For the Anti-Federalists, the House of Representatives functions properly only when local interests are introduced and advanced in the chamber. This is possible only if representatives represent well-defined local interests. As Allen and Lloyd put it, "the heart of their method was to arrange representation in such a manner as to safeguard interests."[40] The Anti-Federalists believed that a good government is not one in which interests simply inform debate over the public good, but rather their amalgamation and reconciliation is the public good. This recommends majority election from small, homogeneous constituencies. Federal Farmer's advocacy of balancing the distinct interests of different orders of men expresses the view that men's respective interests are often, perhaps more often than not, different and antagonistic. The assembly is where these distinct interests are articulated and advanced, and the legislative process is to find mutual accommodation among them through negotiation and reconciliation. One cannot escape the view that these writers largely viewed politics as an arena in which there are winners and losers, and the best that can be achieved is mutually acceptable compromise.[41]

Representation

It is difficult to provide an exact analogue to the contemporary use of the phrase "to be represented by a representative of one's choice" in the founding era. In the Framer's minds there were at least three components to representation, and these could be disentangled so that people whom we would reasonably consider democrats in modern usage, could disagree about the extent of applicability of these to the Americans. The first and by far the most important component is popular sovereignty, meaning citizens have the right to vote for their representatives. This discussion centered first and foremost on the relationship between virtual and actual representation, but also on the implications of broad electoral franchise. Second is the distinction between plurality and majority electoral systems. While this may seem to be splitting fine hairs, the subject's underpinnings are applicable and inform the implications of a variety of voting procedures and processes. The final component is the extent of legislative autonomy enjoyed by representatives. Should representatives be trustees afforded extensive latitude to do as they see fit, or should they be delegates from constituencies and subject to their control while in office? At some level, the extent of "choice" one has in representation depends on whether that "choice" exists only at the moment of election or implies a certain amount of fidelity after the ballots are counted. The Federalist and Anti-Federalist differences over these considerations explain much about their preferred method for electing the House of Representatives, and also inform us about the underpinnings of a variety of electoral processes.

Virtual Representation and Actual Representation

Every school child knows that while the American Revolution had many sources, its genesis is most firmly grounded in the dispute with Great Britain over representation. The rallying cry "No taxation without representation" was more than a slogan; it pointed to a deep division between an older understanding of the relationship between parliamentarians and citizens and a competing understanding emerging in political thought.[42] In the older tradition one's lack of franchise or parliamentary representation was not necessarily a disservice because parliamentarians governed for the common good of all. Under "virtual" representation "those elected by a few are presumed to represent all."[43] This is normatively defensible so long as "there is a communion of interest and sympathy in feelings and desires between" the representatives and "the people in whose name they act."[44] However, virtual representation in the English tradition is representation of a very particular kind; it is the representation of interests, not of people. It is trading or agricultural or other interests that are represented and given voice in parliament, and so long as some representative speaks for a particular interest it is of little concern whether a *particular* constituency defined by that interest is represented; rather, what matters is that *some* constituency defined by that interest is represented.[45] The representative drawn from the latter speaks for all similarly situated constituencies. Despite having no representatives of their own in parliament, the Americans, so English proponents of virtual representation argued, had suffered no injury and had no just cause for rebellion because others spoke on their behalf. Of course, the American position, momentarily setting aside the viability of virtual representation in the New World, was that no parliamentarian shared a "communion of interest and sympathy in feelings and desires" with the colonists, and thus virtual representation failed the Americans on its own terms.[46]

The founders rejected virtual representation as we do now. Nothing less than popular sovereignty through actual representation was a normatively defensible basis for government legitimacy.[47] Citizens must vote for their representatives. This is correct, but it is also incomplete. It is correct in that the Framers entertained nothing other than popular sovereignty as reflected in the right of the people to vote for their own representatives. However, several important aspects of the normative foundations of virtual representation migrated quite successfully to this side of the Atlantic.[48] The Federalists were deeply influenced by the premium that virtual representation placed on identifying and advancing the collective good. The purpose of the legislature for both English defenders of virtual representation and the Federalists was to discover and legislate to the common good. Both groups rejected the idea that legislators represented and pressed local interests; rather, to the extent to which representatives conveyed local sentiments and desires, these were useful primarily for informing broader discussions of the national good. Madison's invocation of the "permanent and aggregate good" borrows heavily from this line of thinking, and does not distinguish him and many other proponents of American poplar sovereignty from those English parliamentarians who still thought virtual representation a viable means to republican objectives.[49]

The problem faced by the founders, especially the Federalists, was how to elect the best people to Congress—those most inclined to understand, discover, and value the greater public good—stipulating popular sovereignty. Herein lies one of the most important facts about the United States for understanding the adoption of the single-member district plurality system: franchise in the late colonial and early republic eras was quite broad. The revolutionary experience undermined arguments for limited franchise and, according to estimates by Alexander Keysar, at the founding upward of 60 to 70 percent of adult white men could vote.[50] To place this figure in context, in Great Britain well under 25 percent of men could vote.[51] The eventual right to vote, at least for white males, was largely a foregone conclusion.[52] Consequently, the founders anticipated that elections would be contested under something approaching universal white male suffrage. The problem was how to elect the natural aristocracy to the House, given that the electorate would not be limited to this class.[53]

The Federalists' solution was election from large, heterogeneous electoral districts under plurality rule. In their view, this system increased the likelihood of filling the chamber with the natural aristocracy when elections were contested under broad franchise. As Jean Yarbrough argues, "Hamilton and Madison defend the large electoral district . . . because it makes the principle of popular election safe. The expanded district solves the problem of how to select the best men without restricting the right to vote."[54] Large districts promote large numbers of candidates, and these candidates are unlikely to have the ability to sway voters based on any sort of personal connection—say, economic dependence on the candidate—with members of the electorate. Candidates likely to win such elections are those who display superior personal qualities and are able to bridge the disparate interests in the constituency. The important and often overlooked point is that the SMD plurality system was in part motivated by the desire to obtain the most virtuous and enlightened representatives under a nearly universal right to vote. Under a restrictive franchise, as was the case in Europe well into the late nineteenth and twentieth centuries, there is no reason to believe SMD plurality elections were necessary for electing the most worthy to office. If only those on the top rung of the class ladder can vote, then any electoral system will work satisfactorily in this regard.

Pluralities and Majorities

Given that the people will elect their own representatives, the question turns to what vote threshold is appropriate for the election of a representative. Should a representative enjoy the majority support of his or her constituency, or is plurality support sufficient? A central critique of SMD plurality elections is that those who do not vote for the winner are "disenfranchised" or that their vote "does not count" in some sense. Commonsensically, we think there is a considerable difference in the normative legitimacy enjoyed by a legislator elected with the overwhelming support of his or her constituency relative to a legislator elected with a modest plurality of the vote. That said, we also lament the uncompetitiveness of House of Representatives elections, and seem to think that significant electoral majorities say less about the correspondence between representatives and their constituents than about the possibility that elections are less pristine than portrayed by Norman Rockwell. The Framers thought carefully about the differences between plurality and majority election, and each of the two founding-era visions of republican government requires a distinct electoral threshold as a component of its design. To achieve its objectives, the Federalist model demands that representatives be elected under the plurality rule, while the Anti-Federalist vision compels natural or constructed majorities.

The Federalists require that representatives be knowledgeable about the various interests that comprise the constituency and that no single interest dominate the views held by the representative. For the Federalists, plurality in conjunction with constituency heterogeneity provides incentives for legislators to appeal to coalitions of minorities, and district heterogeneity makes it more likely that these coalitions will be fluid. Legislators cannot easily establish a base of support built on one or two interests and expect to remain in office. This system also furthers the Federalist goal of selecting the natural aristocracy because this class of men most clearly possesses the ability to span and engage disparate groups and interests. Equally important, while plurality election guarantees that candidates can win with less than a majority of the vote, it also guarantees that incumbents can be defeated with less than an electoral majority. Plurality rule better enables coalitions of minorities to unseat incumbent representatives, providing additional incentives for representatives to be sensitive to the views of the various groups composing their constituencies.

This line of reasoning also helps explain why districts cannot be "communities of interest" and, if using district elections, why they must elect a single representative. If a district is sufficiently large to encompass distinct interests, it would defeat the Federalist purpose if it elected multiple representatives because each representative would likely be responsive to one or a few of the interests that define the district.[55] To the extent to which this is true, one would not expect representatives to see beyond their "local prejudices" and pursue a greater and transcendent good. In the Federalist view, representatives must hear and be responsive to many voices.

In contrast, the Anti-Federalist vision imposed majority rule. The Federal Farmer describes the choice between majority and plurality elections as "the most important question in the business of elections."[56] He objects to plurality rule on several grounds, the first of which is his agreement with Madison that this method will select for office "men of influence," his less than charitable moniker for the natural aristocracy. Melancton Smith, speaking at the New York ratifying convention, echoes this objection, arguing that "if the elections be by plurality . . . none but the great will be chosen—for they easily unite their interest—The common people will divide, and their divisions will be promoted by the others. There will be scarcely a chance of their uniting, in any other but some great man. A substantial yeoman of sense and discernment, will hardly ever be chosen. It appears that the government will fall into the hands of the few and the great. This will be a government of oppression."[57] The Federalists and Anti-Federalists agree that plurality elections tip the electoral scales in favor of the natural aristocracy at the expense of the natural democracy, but to good or ill effect depending on one's perspective. In contrast, majority elections make it much more likely that elections will be "tolerably equal" and foster the election of members of the yeomanry. If a candidate requires the support of a majority, he must have the confidence of the broad body of citizens, and these citizens will be in a better position to judge the virtue and character of candidates. Since in the Anti-Federalist mind civic virtue principally resides in the great middle, members of this class will secure election, and virtue will be brought into government.

The Anti-Federalists also advocated majority rule on the grounds that since the good is discovered in the constituency, representatives must have a very clear idea of what the constituents want. It is nonsensical to speak to the interests and priorities of a heterogeneous constituency characterized by fluidity and the election of representatives by plurality. Such a constituency has no clearly defined idea of the good. This is not the case when majority rule is applied to homogeneous constituencies. Majorities are easier to obtain in homogeneous constituencies, and such majorities send a clearer signal about the good as understood by constituents. If no natural majority is obtained, then majorities should be constructed by runoff or similar election. As the Federal Farmer writes, "if no man have a majority . . . the voters may examine the characters of those brought forward, accommodate, and proceed to repeat their votes till some one shall have that majority."[58] Constructed majorities ensure that representatives have a clear, unambiguous understanding about the views within the constituency and the agreements and compromises reached by constituents in settling on a representative. Such constructed majorities, obtained either by runoff elections or by "instant runoff voting" are fully within the Anti-Federalist vision for House elections. Whether these majorities are natural or manufactured, officeholders must have the support of most of their constituents.

The Federalist and Anti-Federalist difference over whether representatives should be elected by plurality or majority follows from their respective understandings of the purpose of the House of Representatives. If one wants to balance and reconcile interests in the constituency rather than in the chamber, and elect representatives most capable of understanding different ideas of the good, then plurality election applied to single-member districts is appropriate. If one seeks to reconcile and broker interests in the chamber, and elect members who "think, feel, reason and act" like those they represent, then majority rule is preferable. The important point is that the rule used to aggregate votes and determine winners follows from the purpose of the chamber. Since the Federalists and Anti-Federalists had very different views of its purpose, they advocated different electoral thresholds.

Trustees and Delegates

In the founding era the final component of what it means to elect a representative of one's choice centered on the nature of the legislator and constituent relationship. To elect a representative implies things about the postelection relationship between the representative and those he represents, in particular legislative responsibility and accountability to their constituents. Specifically, to what extent should legislators exhibit fidelity to the wishes of those who elect them, and how does one best encourage such fidelity? The founders disagreed sharply on both of these questions, with significant implications for proper electoral processes. For the Federalists, giving effect to the legislature's ability to seek and advance the public good requires that representatives have the discretion to pursue the truth wherever it leads. Representatives should enjoy considerable discretion to set aside immediate constituent interests for the greater good. The Federalists certainly believed that this warrant has limits, and that there must be means to ensure that the constituents enjoy a "proper degree of influence" in the conduct of legislative business. That said, the Anti-Federalists placed considerably more weight on legislative fidelity to constituents. In doing so, they required that representatives faithfully advocate and advance the specific interests of their constituents in the chamber, leaving little room for legislative discretion and demanding greater attention to questions of how best to guide, control, and, if necessary, punish representatives. These differences are reflected in each group's preferences over the length of representatives' terms, the proper restraints and sanctions that can be imposed on representatives, and the electoral processes that facilitate the preferred model of legislative accountability and responsibility.

Madison most clearly discusses the legislator and constituent relationship in *Federalist Paper No. 56*, which emphasizes that each representative "must be acquainted with the interests and circumstances of *his* constituents."[59] Being "acquainted" with the "interests and circumstances" of one's constituents is rather tepid language if one expects representatives to press their interests and circumstances in a Congress populated by legislators advocating the interests and circumstances of their constituents. Madison's language is purposeful because the Federalists believed that pressing specific and local interests is antithetical to obtainment of the national good.[60] Legislators must faithfully bring forward their constituents' interests in the chamber for the purpose of informing debate over the national good, but not to advance these for local advantage. Madison then details why one would expect such familiarity and the sources of legislative fidelity to constituents. Familiarity follows from district election, which necessarily requires representatives to know a well-defined geographic location in some detail. If one "divides the largest state into ten or twelve districts," Madison says it "will be found that there will be no particular local interest . . . which will not be within the knowledge of the representative of the district."[61] Legislative fidelity owes primarily to electoral "dependence on the people," but also to representatives' sense of "duty," "honour," "gratitude," and "ambition itself."[62] Legislators will not ignore their constituents if they wish to be reelected. In addition, the natural aristocracy is especially sensitive to considerations of duty and honor.

For the Federalists, giving effect to the legislature's ability to seek and advance the public good requires that representatives have the discretion to follow their consciences and best judgments. The only way that representatives can find the collective good is by enjoying the freedom to do so without undue interference from constituents. Representatives must be of the "trustee" rather than "delegate" type. While Edmund Burke was chastising his own electors in Bristol for seeking to instruct his actions in the House of Commons, he also deeply influenced the Federalists when he wrote:

> Parliament is not a congress of ambassadors from different and
> hostile interests; which interests each must maintain, as an agent

and advocate, against other agents and advocates; but parliament is a deliberative assembly of one nation, with one interest, that of the whole; where not local purposes, not local prejudices, ought to guide, but the general good, resulting from the general reason of the whole. You choose a member indeed; but when you have chosen him, he is not a member of Bristol, but he is a member of parliament.[63]

A year before the Constitutional Convention, George Washington, in a letter to his nephew and future Supreme Court justice Bushrod Washington, captured a more nuanced view of the constituent-representative relationship that is close to the received Federalist spirit on the question. "In national matters . . . the sense, but not the law of the district may be given, leaving the delegates to judge from the nature of the case and the evidence before them."[64] To make such discretion work in practice requires virtuous representatives in the first place, electoral accountability, and, as Hamilton points out in one of the Federalists' canonical passages on legislative accountability, the fact that legislators will be governed by the same laws they promulgate.

Is it not natural that a man who is candidate for the favour of the people, and who is dependent on the suffrages of his fellow citizens for the continuance of his public honours, should take care to inform himself of their disposition and inclinations, and should be willing to allow them their proper degree of influence upon his conduct? This dependence, and the necessity of being bound himself . . . by the laws to which he gives his assent . . . are the strong cords of sympathy between the representative and the constituent.[65]

For the Federalists, such independence for representatives is necessary to discover and pursue the public good. Representatives cannot be agents of their constituents because citizens of even large and heterogeneous constituencies neither know nor advocate the national interest. This is even truer for small constituencies. Two-year terms, rather than the customary one-year term for state representatives, while still brief, also give legislators more latitude to pursue the good while insulated from momentary passions and pressure.

Giving representatives the latitude to discover and implement the public good sets a high bar for the types of citizens who should serve as representatives. In particular, representatives should be knowledgeable, enlightened, and above all else virtuous. If one elects a trustee, which in Federalist thought is necessary if one's theory of politics places the search for the general good above all else, representatives have to be the most virtuous and enlightened citizens available. As Madison's quote that introduces this chapter argues, "The aim of every political constitution is, or ought to be, first, to obtain for rulers men who possess most wisdom to discern, and most virtue to pursue, the common good of society."[66] This is not rhetoric; Federalist representation fails unless representatives are of this sort.

The Anti-Federalists place a significantly greater premium on legislative fidelity to constituents because representation, in their view, facilitates "the direct expression of the will of the people" in furtherance of the public good.[67] Representatives must therefore be agents or delegates for their constituents. The key underpinning of this idea of representation was put rather frankly by Cato in his seventh letter, in which he quotes Demosthenes: "There is one common bulwark with which men of prudence are naturally provided, the guard and security of all people, particularly of free states, against the assaults of tyrants . . . distrust," in particular not trusting that the interest of the represented will be the same as the interest of those who represent, and fearing that representatives will be tempted to follow their own interests.[68] The Anti-Federalists were also especially sensitive to what in the present era we call Lord Acton's Maxim: even good men can be tempted by power to pursue ends harmful to their electors. These considerations motivate the necessity of keeping representatives on a short leash.

Fostering this oversight and control requires that representatives be drawn first and foremost from small homogeneous districts because such districts guarantee that representatives are like their constituents, with a corresponding commonality of interest. This does not mean that representatives can be anybody from the community; even the Anti-Federalists thought that representatives should be among the best and brightest, but the best and brightest or, as Federal Farmer puts it, their "best informed" from among otherwise typical citizens.[69] According to the Federal Farmer, "the substantial part of the [natural] democracy . . . are a numerous and valuable set of men, who discern and judge well, but from being generally silent in public assemblies are often overlooked; they are the most substantial and best informed men in the several towns."[70] In addition to commonality of interest, fidelity is fostered foremost by short terms of office, recall, and a latent sympathy for the right of constituents to instruct their representatives. In his fifth essay Cato argues that "if annual elections were to exist in this government . . . you will never want men to execute whatever you design."[71] With respect to instruction and recall, an Anti-Federalist writing under the pen name Amicus summarizes that "there are, I fear, a few persons among us, so wise in their own eyes, that they would if they could, pursue their own will and inclinations, in opposition to the instructions of their constituents. In doing so, they may perhaps, once in a hundred times, act for the interest of those they represent."[72] Still, instruction and recall had largely fallen out of favor by the 1780s, and for the Anti-Federalists their purpose could largely be accomplished by the proper selection of representatives in the first place.

Two Visions of American Democracy and Electing the House

The preceding two chapters present two different understandings of United States government and election of the House of Representatives. Their purpose was to detail the normative and positive foundations that underlie the Federalist and Anti-Federalist preferences for electing the House. As Richard Katz argues, electoral systems are manifestations of values and are designed to capture and further those values.[73] The Federalists and Anti-Federalists embraced different values, preferences, and understandings of the country for which they sought to form a government, and in doing so they advocated different electoral institutions and processes to further their respective goals. These distinct visions transcend our history and introduce a tension in American politics that is not easily reconciled. The Federalists carried the day, and we are governed under their Constitution. The Anti-Federalists, as will become clearer in subsequent chapters, captured our imagination. Our visions of the legislature and its election are more consonant with Anti-Federalist values, although one has to reconcile this with the place of such values in the extant Constitution.

To understand how this dialogue transcends our history and how it informs election processes, it is useful to summarize these respective visions. Both the Federalists and the Anti-Federalists were deeply influenced by the republican and liberal traditions, and both embraced a systemic understanding of the Constitution, including the electoral processes that give it effect. On balance, it was the Federalists who were more deeply influenced by the republican values that informed the founding era, as reflected in their expansive notion of the public good and understanding that the purpose of the legislative chamber was to provide a forum for deliberation and discovery of a truly national good. The Anti-Federalists were more deeply influenced by the liberal tradition, as reflected in their relatively circumscribed notion of the national good, their embracing of introducing interests into the chamber, and their insistence on majority rule. For the Federalists the primary purpose of elections was to select the best legislators and educate them so they could effectively pursue the greater good. For the Anti-Federalists the primary purpose of elections was to prevent legislative tyranny and enforce legislative accountability and responsibility. Federalists' and Anti-Federalists' preferences for electoral processes each require a particular constitution. The organizing principle of the Federalist constitution—our extant Constitution—is the dispersion of political power. Where power is dispersed and government action requires the concerted efforts of all three branches, there is a premium placed on deliberation to discover the public good because these ideas have to influence many political actors. The legislative deliberation that informs debate in the chamber also informs the other branches and the public. To govern under such a constitution requires enlightened representatives and a deliberative assembly. The Anti-Federalist constitution, which existed only in the minds of these writers, forms a simpler government in which the legislature provides a forum for the reconciliation and brokering of political interests and is externally checked by a vigilant electorate. Such a political process requires representatives who are focused on the immediate interests of their constituents, and once the will of the people is expressed through the legislative chamber, this process recommends legislative supremacy with little interference from the executive or the judiciary branches.

These distinct underlying principles give rise to the two understandings of House elections presented in the early part of this chapter. These are the Federalist advocacy of electing the natural aristocracy from large, heterogeneous districts using plurality rule and the Anti-Federalist preference for electing representatives from the great middling class using majority rule from small, homogeneous constituencies. What is central is recognition that these Federalist and Anti-Federalist differences are predicated on distinct normative values and understandings of the polity for which the government is formed. For the Framers, if one advocates one or the other one has accepted the complete, systemic vision of the United States, the purpose of its government, and the values that motivate each vision of republican government in a liberal society. The Federalists and Anti-Federalists advanced different visions of the American polity, the proper balance in securing republican and liberal values, the purpose of the House of Representatives, and a host of other considerations. Each vison is a complete whole. As stated

THE FOUNDING-ERA HOUSE OF REPRESENTATIVES

in the opening of this chapter, one cannot get from Federalist values and understandings of the American polity to instant runoff voting, nor can one get from the Anti-Federalist understanding of these considerations to SMD plurality applied to large, heterogeneous congressional districts. Choose we must.

The importance of making these foundations clear is threefold. First, these provide a conceptual way of understanding the principles underlying any discussion of electoral systems. If one advocates this system or that system, one has to engage in the same discussion as occupied these first two chapters. Electoral systems operate in a larger constitutional architecture and embody a host of normative values and assumptions about the polity to which they are applied. In contemporary discussions these primitives are seldom made clear. In the specific case of the United States, this discussion has to explicitly recognize that the Framers did have such a discussion and were fully aware of these underpinnings. This does not mean the Framers were necessarily right; after all, the purpose of this chapter was to make clear these arguments as they understood them. By the same token, these cannot be ignored. If the Framers' assumption that instant runoff voting was incommensurable with advancing a greater public good in the republican sense was wrong, then it is incumbent on advocates of such electoral processes to explain why the Framers were wrong. More generally, discussions of electoral systems, especially those centered on the merits and liability of given systems, must make these foundations clear because nothing is more central than assessing the efficacy and utility of electoral processes.

Second, this discussion provides us with normative benchmarks by which to assess the efficacy of electoral processes. Do our election methods contribute to or detract from the objectives we seek to fulfill? How do we judge whether our electoral institutions function well or poorly? In either case, one has to articulate those values by which the performance of our electoral system is to be judged. If one believes the argument that the Federalist and Anti-Federalist constitutional preferences formed complete understandings of the government and how to best elect its component branches, then such assessment will invariably be grounded in one of these visions. If one prefers the Federalist conception, then the SMD plurality system is an integral part of it. One might reasonably prefer the Federalist vision and still find the SMD plurality system wanting, but in such cases one then knows to diagnose the poor performance by assessing where in the constitutional system the current manifestation of SMD elections differs from that envisioned at the founding. Similarly, if one prefers the Anti-Federalist vision of American society and politics, then one can sensibly assess what constitutional changes are necessary for this system to effectively contribute to this different vision of American government. At the end of the day, these are practical questions. Do our political aspirations focus on engaging the diversity of the nation, or are we more inclined to focus on "communities of interest"? Do we want representatives to be drawn from the modern equivalent of the natural aristocracy, or do we prefer representatives to be more like typical citizens and the legislature to more closely approximate the cultural demographics of the United States? Do we believe there are great, national objectives to be obtained, or is the national good best advanced by something more akin to interest group liberalism? Are we prepared to prevent government-promulgated tyranny by hobbling the efficiency of government, or would we rather our government be more efficient and rely on elections to safeguard our liberties? Lastly, if the answers to these questions presuppose a particular constitutional architecture, are we prepared to make changes to that architecture to facilitate preferred electoral processes?

Finally, this discussion prepares the ground for interpreting the modern debate about electing the House that emerged in the first third of the nineteenth century. Attempts to mandate the SMD system began very early after the founding, but gained considerable momentum with the rise of modern party politics in the 1820s and 1830s. The Federalist and Anti-Federalist arguments and assumptions were adapted for the rise of modern party politics, but the underlying founding-era arguments provide continuity that transcends our political history. As is well known, the Federalists ceased to be a major electoral force in the early years of the nineteenth century, but the Whigs and Jacksonians returned to these arguments, albeit in a manner consistent with the emergence of modern political parties and electoral campaigning, ultimately appealing directly to the founding arguments and underlying assumptions and values when Congress finally mandated SMD elections in 1842. I explore in depth the politics of the SMD mandate in the fifth chapter, but in the next chapter it is useful to turn to a descriptive survey of the election processes of the early years of the republic.

In the first few years of the republic the states were faced with the task of simply figuring out how to elect representatives for a new government, and the relationship between practices that were useful for populating statehouses and colonial assemblies and those useful for filling a national representative assembly with powers that were yet to be clearly defined. In doing so, they balanced many things: popular preference for districts or at-large elections, the desire to increase state influence in the new national congress, practical politics centered on the protoparty Federalist and Anti-Federalist split, and simple historical inertia. The following chapter provides an overview of this electoral landscape. The most striking feature of the early republic was how much discretion states exercised in adopting and changing electoral processes. In hindsight, this is not too surprising for a new nation, but even those well versed in American political history may not have appreciated the fluidity in electoral processes in the early republic.

4 House of Representatives Elections in the Early Republic, 1788–1824

> A law has also passed in [Pennsylvania] providing for the election of members of the House of Representatives. . . . The act proposes that every citizen throughout the state shall vote for the whole number of members allotted to the state. This mode of elections will confine the choice of characters of general notoriety, and so far be favorable to merit. It is however liable to some popular objections urged against the tendency of the new system. In Virginia I am inclined to think the state will be divided into as many districts as there are to be members. In others . . . a middle course be taken. It is perhaps to be desired that various modes should be tried, as by that means only the best model can be ascertained.
>
> *James Madison letter to Thomas Jefferson,*
> *October 8, 1788*

One of the most significant events in US government, now all but lost to history, occurred on September 13, 1788. On that day the Confederation Congress, which had governed the United States under the Articles of Confederation since 1781, passed a brief resolution that read in part: "Whereas the convention assembled in Philadelphia . . . did, on the 17th of September [1787] report to the United States Congress assembled, a constitution for the people of the United States . . . and whereas the constitution so reported . . . has been ratified . . . RESOLVED . . . that the first Wednesday in March next, be the time, and the present seat of congress the place for commencing proceedings under the said constitution."[1] The Confederation

Congress directed the states to elect their representatives and in doing so ordered its own demise. One species of government passed peacefully to another. The Election Ordinance of 1788, as the above resolution is known, initiated the most intense and focused period of discussion and planning of elections witnessed before or since in any democratic nation. Each of the thirteen states had full autonomy to elect their share of the first class of sixty-five representatives as they saw fit and, while not working completely with a tabula rasa, had the discretion to adopt nearly any means to select their delegations. They had six months to do so.

The methods proposed to elect representatives can largely be consolidated into three basic questions: Should representatives be elected in districts or at large? Should citizens be allowed to vote for all of a state's representatives or just one? Should candidate election require a plurality or majority of the vote? These considerations presented many ways to elect representatives. For example, New Hampshire opted to use the general ticket to elect its three-member delegation and adopted a process intended to ensure that only candidates who enjoyed majority support were elected. States that districted were obligated to draw boundaries, and this raised the question of whether districts should contain an equal population, as much as practicable, and also introduced the possibility that legislators would draw districts for political advantage. Massachusetts's election law mandated that its eight districts contain roughly equal population, but the Federalist-dominated legislature led them to underrepresent citizens in the western part of the state, which was sympathetic to Anti-Federalists.[2] In what is perhaps the best-known early example of gerrymandering, the Anti-Federalist–controlled Virginia legislature led by Patrick Henry drew James Madison's district specifically to thwart his election to the government he had done so much to craft. Madison won anyway.[3]

This chapter reviews the ways the House of Representatives was elected from the founding to the early Jacksonian era. It presents the menu of election methods adopted by the Americans. In doing so, it details the state-level adoptions of means to elect their congressional delegations and overviews the nation's electoral landscape as it moved into the period when the SMD system was eventually mandated. If we seek to understand the benefits and liabilities of the SMD system, then it is useful to survey the various systems that have seen application and the arguments for and against their use in a particular political context. The abstract Federalist and Anti-Federalists debates over representation and elections suddenly and forcefully became the backdrop to tangible disputes over how to elect representatives. State legislators were forced to wrestle with balancing their principles, obtaining political advantage, and managing the practical administration of elections. Decisions had to be made quickly and in the face of considerable uncertainty over how these methods would work in practice.

It is useful to briefly clarify here the ways that representatives were elected in the early republic. The most common method was the standard single-member district plurality system (SMD) in which electors received a single vote that was cast for a district-affiliated candidate. This was used by, for example, New York and is the same method used today. The general ticket (GT) used by several states, including Connecticut, New Jersey, and New Hampshire, selected candidates in a statewide election. Electors possessed as many votes as there were seats to be filled. These votes could not be cast cumulatively; for example, electors could not allocate two votes to an individual candidate.[4] A third method required candidates to stand for election in a district, but electors could vote for a candidate in each of the state's districts. Georgia and Maryland used this system in the first two federal elections; this method appears similar to SMD plurality election but was actually an at-large method. Like the general ticket, it permitted electors to cast ballots for all of a party or faction's candidates. The defining characteristic that makes an at-large election at-large is how votes are allocated and cast, not whether candidate names are attached to districts. To distinguish this method from the SMD system, I refer to it as at-large single-member district (AL-SMD). A fourth method that saw application was the combined single-member and multimember district system (SMD-MMD). Some states, most notably Pennsylvania, used both single-member and multimember constituencies. In the multimember constituencies citizens typically voted in a manner identical to the general ticket system.[5] One purpose of electing from multiple-member districts was to enable states to preserve corporate entities such as counties rather than breaking them up to create additional single-member districts. Another less laudable purpose was to secure political advantage by swamping a viable political minority in a district sufficiently large to guarantee the majority faction or party all of the district's seats. States that adopted this system usually did so following a reapportionment when their legislative representation increased. Finally, states that possessed only a single House seat elected their representative at large (AL).

The methods of casting ballots in the early republic bore little resemblance to the way we vote today. Votes could be cast viva voce, or by reporting one's vote or votes directly to an election judge. Typically, however, electors wrote the names of as many candidates as there were positions to be filled on a slip of paper and handed this to an election judge. Pennsylvania's guideline for selecting its eight representatives was fairly standard: "Every person coming to elect representatives shall deliver in writing on one ticket or piece of paper the names of eight persons to be voted for as representatives."[6] Requiring a written ballot posed few hurdles to the enfranchised. The founding-era literacy rate among white men in New England exceeded 90 percent.[7] Those who could not write but were otherwise eligible to vote could generally report votes to an election judge or deposit a ballot filled out by a trusted person. These were not secret ballots in the sense we know today, although there was sometimes an effort to maintain confidentiality in the process. Maryland, for example, required that the ballot be folded. The judge could not unfold them until all ballots were cast.[8] Still, the government-printed secret ballot we know today did not exist, and would remain unavailable for a century. Voting was a public act.[9]

These ways of selecting representatives also admit different thresholds for election. The Anti-Federalists were especially alarmed at the prospect of electing representatives with very small pluralities, which was quite possible in a preparty era when widely dispersed voters could not easily coordinate their ballots for a few viable candidates. In particular, the general ticket presented an acute problem of narrowing the field so that winning candidates received more than a trivial vote share. In an era before organized political parties, there was often little commonality in the lists submitted by electors residing in different parts of a state, even if they had the same political leanings. Connecticut and New Jersey sought to ameliorate this problem by using nomination processes. Connecticut allowed electors to nominate as many persons as there were seats to be filled. The state's five representatives were then selected from a final pool consisting of the twelve leading nominees. New Jersey used a similar method, but for the purpose of establishing a list of eligible candidates. This list was published about two weeks before the election so electors would have sufficient time to distinguish viable from less viable candidates. New Hampshire pursued a different tack by requiring candidates to secure a majority of the vote to win election. If insufficient candidates met this requirement, the state held a runoff election to fill any remaining seats.[10] States that used SMD elections also faced the small plurality problem, albeit to a lesser extent. Most were content to elect the candidate with the greatest vote share regardless how small. Massachusetts was not, and required winning candidates to secure a majority of the vote. If no candidate in a district obtained a majority, the district held a runoff election between the two leading candidates.[11]

This discussion is not intended to catalog the various methods used to elect the early Congresses, but rather to show the variety of potential and actual ways to elect representatives that were in play in the early years of the republic. Single-member and multimember constituencies, at-large elections, and a variety of nomination and electoral thresholds all saw application in the nation's early years. Four systems were used to elect the first House, even without considering differences in nomination or threshold requirements. The universe of potential ways to elect representatives available to the states was even greater. Madison's conjecture that the states would implement "various modes" of election was indeed perceptive.

The next section of this chapter focuses on the election to the First Congress that met from March 1789 to March 1791. Most states passed their election laws between October and December of 1788. This brief period witnessed a flood of documents, legislative debates, and personal correspondence advocating for and against means to select the entire corpus of national offices, including presidential electors, senators, and representatives. These are sometimes repetitive, loosely reasoned, and overtly partisan, but within these texts are principles that capture why states adopted particular ways to elect their representatives. These build on Federalist and Anti-Federalist ideals, but also on the anticipated effects of election methods applied to a particular time and place.

Following this, I trace the ascendance of the SMD plurality system through the balance of the first party era. The ways that states elected their representatives in the early Congresses introduced inertia into these processes that carried through to the Jacksonian period. However, these methods were not entirely static. There was some fluidity in election methods, and as new states were admitted to the union they had to revisit these arguments anew. There are two key considerations that help us better understand why Congress eventually mandated the SMD system. The first is the rapid ascendancy of SMD elections after the first few federal elections. By the second apportionment about half the states used either SMD or SMD-MMD elections, with about 70 percent of all representatives elected from single-member districts under the plurality rule. This figure remained more or less constant until the middle years of the Jacksonian period. The second is why some states maintained the general ticket throughout the period and why some newly admitted states, such as Missouri, adopted the general ticket rather than SMD election. By the first years of the nineteenth century the single-member district system had become the way most of the House membership was elected, although several states continued to elect their representatives at large.

Electing the House in the First Party Era

The First Congress

In the First Congress the House of Representatives was elected in roughly equal measure from single-member districts and at large. Most of the southern states used single-member districts, as did New York and Massachusetts in the north. Pennsylvania, New Jersey, Connecticut, and New Hampshire opted for the general ticket. Georgia and Maryland required representatives stand for election in a district, but allowed electors to vote for candidates in all districts. This method, for reasons explained previously, was an at-large system that more closely resembles the general ticket than standard SMD plurality election. Finally, Delaware and Rhode Island used at-large elections because each elected a single representative. Of the First Congress's sixty-five representatives, 40 percent—twenty-six, to be exact—were elected from single-member districts by plurality rule.

Table 4.1 presents the ways the states elected their House delegations for the first two Congresses. These Congresses were elected under the original constitutional apportionment of representatives and met between 1789 and 1793. The Constitution was ratified without the benefit of a national census to determine the apportionment of representatives among the states. The Framers worked with their best estimates of state population, which had to suffice until the first national census in 1790. The chamber changed size between the First and Second Congresses because of the admission of Vermont and Kentucky to the Union in 1791 and 1792 respectively.

The primary choice the states had to make in the first federal election was whether they would elect their representatives from districts or statewide. This debate was generally framed in terms of whether electors had the right to vote for a state's entire delegation or for a single representative. It was understood that granting electors a single vote meant they had the right to vote for a candidate in a district. Multiple votes meant that electors had the right to vote for the state's entire congressional delegation statewide by general ticket. However, this debate carries more significance than just the

Table 4.1. Election Methods for the Constitutional Apportionment

State	First Congress (1789–1791)	Second Congress (1791–1793)
Connecticut	GT (5)	GT (5)
Delaware	AL (1)	AL (1)
Georgia	AL-SMD (3)	AL-SMD (3)
Kentucky	—	SMD (2)
Maryland	AL-SMD (6)	AL-SMD (6)
Massachusetts	SMD (8)	SMD (8)
New Hampshire	GT (3)	GT (3)
New Jersey	GT (4)	GT (4)
New York	SMD (6)	SMD (6)
North Carolina	SMD (5)	SMD (5)
Pennsylvania	GT (8)	SMD (8)
Rhode Island	AL (1)	AL (1)
South Carolina	SMD (5)	SMD (5)
Vermont	—	SMD (2)
Virginia	SMD (10)	SMD (10)
House Membership	65	69

The number in parentheses is the number of representatives apportioned to each state under the constitutional apportionment preceding the first census.
Source: Kenneth C. Martis, *The Historical Atlas of United States Congressional Districts: 1789–1983.*

choice between single-member district and at-large election. The question was presented in terms of whether the constitution confers a federal right to vote for multiple candidates. Under the Constitution, one could vote in federal elections if one was qualified to vote for the lower chamber of one's state legislature. The states determined if one was so qualified.[12] However, if one was qualified to vote in federal elections, it was unclear whether the states could limit electors to a single vote. Such concerns were not unreasonable. After all, the Constitution does not permit states to require that representatives reside in a particular district, so how could a state impose the seemingly comparable restriction that a voter must reside in a district?[13] More generally, the distinction between single and multiple votes is central to any discussion of electoral systems because the ability to cast multiple votes opens up a host of potential ways to elect representatives while the single-vote restriction reduces the number of viable methods.

This debate quickly took on Federalist and Anti-Federalist tones. Federalists often favored at-large election and granting electors as many votes as representatives to be elected.[14] The Federalist *Pennsylvania Mercury*, for example, argued that a person's right to vote for all of a state's representatives is "a *federal right* given to them by the Federal Constitution, and which the state cannot take from them."[15] New York assemblyman Brockholst Livingston, Princeton classmate of James Madison and brother-in-law of John Jay, reasoned that "the constitution gave every man a right to vote for six men [New York's apportionment], and it would be an arbitrary stride of power to restrain him to vote for only one."[16] Those of Anti-Federalist persuasion generally avoided the question of whether the Constitution conferred such a right, instead advocating the advantages of casting a single vote in a district on grounds familiar from the ratification debates. Livingston's assembly colleague Samuel Jones responded that "if six men were to be voted for throughout the state, the people would be obliged to vote for men they could not know."[17] In Massachusetts the Real Farmer reiterated the most classical Anti-Federalist argument that "the perfection of the portrait consists in its likeness . . . [and for] an equal and real representation . . . the . . . districts in which representatives shall be chosen, should be as small as the nature of the case, and the Constitution, will admit of."[18] To obtain a real representation one has to elect "several persons . . . of different ranks and interests."[19] This is not possible under the general ticket that would advantage elites, but is instead achieved by electors casting a single vote in a compact district.

The question of how much importance to place on unified state representation in the House of Representatives also influenced the choice of election method. Those who favored advancing state interests in the chamber advocated for the general ticket. Writing in the *Baltimore Journal*, Civis maintained that "we may therefore with propriety conclude, that as no particular corner of a state, can have any separate interest to advocate in the general government, the most eligible method would be . . . [election by] the people at large."[20] Pennsylvanian Numa pointed to the advantages of the method eventually adopted by Maryland and Georgia because "when members are chosen by the whole state they will consider themselves servants of the whole state, and not suffer themselves to be misled by local prejudices or interests of a few men who often govern counties or districts."[21] Those skeptical of state representation, mostly Anti-Federalists, emphasized the importance of representing smaller political communities. Speaking in New Jersey, Publius Secundus Americanus argued that "electing one representative for each [district], the freeman's vote is of some consequence" and is recommended because "the people should be acquainted with the men they choose."[22] Americanus foresaw that general ticket elections would exacerbate partisan conflict while district elections would help prevent "the states from falling into parties."[23]

Of deeper interest is why any state adopted at-large elections. Both the Federalists and Anti-Federalists advocated district elections, making it unclear why the general ticket method was entertained at all. In Virginia, Confederation Congress member Edward Carrington reported to James Madison that "the district plan in the fullest extent is adopted by a union of Federalists and Anti-Federalists, so that no proposition could be offered against it."[24] One would expect similar correspondence in all states. It is true that Federalists were sympathetic to at-large election, which they believed advantaged the election of "characters of general notoriety." Still, the United States adopted the Federalist Constitution and with it the ability to create large, heterogeneous congressional districts. If political principle mattered above all else, no Anti-Federalist should have supported the general ticket and neither would any Federalist, absent a strong argument that it would elect better representatives than districts containing about 30,000 residents. Few such arguments were made. Indeed, appeals such as those of Civis and Numa placed the Federalists in the awkward position of defending the state corporate interest argument they so resolutely denied at the drafting stage. As a matter of practical politics if not principle, it was the Federalists who most strenuously argued for granting citizens multiple ballots and the Anti-Federalists who argued for a single vote.

Political advantage played a large if not the largest part in driving states' selection of the method to elect the First Congress. The Federalist-controlled New Jersey and Connecticut legislatures adopted the general ticket with well-placed confidence that Federalists would control the congressional delegations. Likewise, solidly Federalist Maryland allowed voters to cast ballots for candidates in each district because it would ensure a Federalist sweep in the first House elections. The Pennsylvania Federalists did the same thing without the additional administrative burden of creating districts. Pennsylvanian Benjamin Rush, Federalist signer of the Declaration of Independence, was frank about his state's decision to use the general ticket: "By obliging the whole state to vote in one ticket, it is expected that the Federalists will prevail by a majority of two to one in the choice of representative for the lower house of congress."[25] However, at-large election is risky if one is unsure about the political leanings of the enfranchised. South Carolina's political divisions were geographic, with the low country dominated by the Federalists and the Midlands and Appalachian backcountry by Anti-Federalists. A joint committee of the low-country-controlled South Carolina legislature recommended the general ticket to the full assembly, but this was wisely defeated by Federalists in favor of district elections. This owed less to political ideals than the recognition that the weight of the electorate resided outside the low country and would determine the state's congressional delegation.[26] This fear was well founded as Anti-Federalists won three seats in the state's first class of five representatives. Politically divided New Hampshire implemented the general ticket and returned a mixed delegation of proadministration and antiadministration legislators, showing that political coalitions and coordination between leaders of the two factions and their respective voters were not yet well established.

The received explanation for states' choice to use SMD or at-large election is size; larger states typically used SMD election while the smaller states gravitated toward the general ticket.[27] This is correct, but the pattern took a few years to become clear. In the first federal election only eleven states had any decision to make at all, and the relationship between size and election method is weak. Pennsylvania, which adopted the general ticket, was not just geographically large; its population was second only to Virginia. Connecticut was geographically compact, but its population exceeded that of both Carolinas, each of which districted. Indeed, Pennsylvania and Connecticut alone accounted for thirteen of the First Congress's twenty representatives elected by general ticket. If Maryland and Georgia are properly classified as states that used at-large elections, then there is little relationship between state size and election process in the First Congress. Of the five largest states (Virginia, Massachusetts, Pennsylvania, New York, and Maryland), three adopted SMD elections and two elected representatives at large. Of the five smallest states (North Carolina, South Carolina, New Jersey, New Hampshire, and Georgia), three used at-large elections and two used the SMD method. Connecticut, the state with the median population, elected at large. One has to squint hard to see a pattern in these data. In the end, political principle, practical politics, and the simple need to elect a delegation drove electoral selection for the First Congress.

Electing the House in the Balance of the First Party Era
Following the first House election, state political leaders took stock of their methods for electing representatives. Most stood pat, but Pennsylvania switched from the general ticket to SMD elections for the second federal election, while Maryland and Georgia both adopted the SMD method for the

Table 4.2. State Election Methods for the House of Representatives in the Third through Seventh Congresses

State	Third Congress (1793–1795)	Fourth Congress (1795–1797)	Second Apportionment Fifth Congress (1797–1799)	Sixth Congress (1799–1801)	Seventh Congress (1801–1803)
Connecticut	GT (7)	GT (7)	GT (7)	GT (7)	GT (7)
Delaware	Al (1)	AL (1)	AL (1)	AL (1)	AL (1)
Georgia	GT (2)	GT (2)	GT (2)	GT (2)	GT (2)
Kentucky	SMD (2)	SMD (2)	SMD (2)	SMD (2)	SMD (2)
Maryland	SMD (8)	SMD (8)	SMD (8)	SMD (8)	SMD (8)
Massachusetts	MMD (14)[a]	SMD (14)	SMD (14)	SMD (14)	SMD (14)
New Hampshire	GT (4)	GT (4)	GT (4)	GT (4)	GT (4)
New Jersey	GT (5)	GT (5)	GT (5)	GT (5)	GT (5)
New York	SMD (10)	SMD (10)	SMD (10)	SMD (10)	SMD (10)
North Carolina	SMD (10)	SMD (10)	SMD (10)	SMD (10)	SMD (10)
Ohio	—	—	—	—	AL (1)
Pennsylvania	GT (13)	SMD-MMD (13)[b]	SMD-MMD (13)[b]	SMD-MMD (13)[b]	SMD-MMD (13)[b]
Rhode Island	GT (2)	GT (2)	GT (2)	GT (2)	GT (2)
South Carolina	SMD (6)	SMD (6)	SMD (6)	SMD (6)	SMD (6)
Tennessee	—	AL (1)	AL (1)	AL (1)	AL (1)
Vermont	SMD (2)	SMD (2)	SMD (2)	SMD (2)	SMD (2)
Virginia	SMD (19)	SMD (19)	SMD (19)	SMD (19)	SMD (19)
House Membership	105	106	106	106	107

a. One representative was elected at large.
b. PA 4th elected two representatives by block vote.

Source: Kenneth C. Martis, *The Historical Atlas of United States Congressional Districts: 1789–1983*.

third federal election. The admission of Kentucky and Vermont increased the number of states using SMD elections by two, so that by the late 1790s this method of electing representatives was clearly ascendant. Of the Fourth Congress's 106 representatives, over 80 percent were elected from single-member districts.

There was relatively little change in electoral systems after the first few federal elections. Pennsylvania returned to the general ticket for the Third Congress and then reinstituted districts for the Fourth Congress. Georgia used the general ticket to elect its representatives to the Third Congress and maintained this system until the 1842 mandate. Still, for the balance of the first party era, states rarely changed their method of election from that in place in 1800.

That said, by the Fourth Congress the large state–small state pattern was well established. As table 4.2 shows, the states that used the general ticket—Connecticut, Georgia, New Hampshire, New Jersey, and Rhode Island—had little in common besides being small in population and, for the most part, in geography.[28] Three reasons are generally cited to explain large states' preference for districting and small states' preference for the general ticket. These follow from the premise that the larger states were more socially and politically heterogeneous than the smaller states. The first is that SMD election helped the large states better secure representation for disparate populations in the various regions of a state. The homogeneity of the small states precluded the need to district for this purpose.[29] Second, the small states had better defined and agreed-on state interests that were more easily advanced by selecting representatives at large. If an entire state delegation is unified by a common election in a statewide vote, it is more likely to represent and press state interest in the chamber. Partisan advantage also helps explain small-state preference for the general ticket. Since these states were more politically homogeneous, the majority party or faction can more easily use at-large elections to control the state's entire House delegation. Finally, at-large election also helped the small states protect themselves against the large states by electing unified delegations to Congress, since the large-state delegations were presumably divided by district elections.[30]

Keeping in mind that we are extrapolating from a very few cases, these explanations raise a number of questions. It stretches the imagination to believe that leaders of large state majority factions districted for the noble purpose of securing the representation of concentrated political minorities.

They may have been forced to do so in politically contentious state houses. but the framing generation was not as politically magnanimous as our primary school teachings would lead us to believe. It is also unclear why corporate representation would be more important to the small states than the large states. A large state such as Federalist-leaning Massachusetts could probably have increased its influence in the chamber by electing a unified or nearly unified House delegation. Finally, the most important political division between the states postfounding was not large state versus small state, but north versus south or, more accurately, slaveholding versus non-slaveholding. If state commonality and interest drove election method, any pattern in election method should correspond to geography; it does not. Also, the first two newly admitted states, Vermont and Kentucky, were small yet adopted SMD election.

A more complete understanding of the large state–small state pattern is realized by recognizing that the components of the size explanation are not mutually exclusive and are very difficult to disentangle. Election methods were driven by state heterogeneity—whether it is political, economic, or cultural, all of which blend together; the desire to secure corporate representation; and the desire to secure partisan advantage. These considerations came together more easily in the smaller states than in the larger ones, and this is reflected in their respective choices in electoral system. State political leaders quickly learned that the general ticket was especially advantageous if one could be certain of obtaining an electoral majority. For this reason, the small states used the general ticket to elect unified or nearly unified congressional delegations.

The more interesting pattern is that adoption of the general ticket usually benefited the Federalists, and this happened almost exclusively in states without a western frontier. Single-member districts were almost universally adopted by newly admitted states. In the Fifth Congress, for example, Connecticut, New Hampshire, New Jersey, and Rhode Island were represented entirely by Federalists while Georgia was the sole general ticket state to elect Anti-Federalist representatives. The Federalists were politically strongest in the small, established states while the Anti-Federalists and later Republicans were strongest in the larger states, especially in the western regions of those states. In the fifth congressional election Pennsylvania Republicans carried the state's five westernmost districts, while the eight districts won by the Federalists were all in the eastern half of the state.[31] The same pattern appears in Virginia, where the Tidewater was solidly Federalist and all

Table 4.3: State Election Methods for the House of Representatives in the Eighth through Twelfth Congresses

	Third Apportionment				
State	Eighth Congress (1803–1805)	Ninth Congress (1805–1807)	Tenth Congress (1807–1809)	Eleventh Congress (1809–1811)	Twelfth Congress (1811–1813)
Connecticut	GT (7)	GT (7)	GT (7)	GT (7)	GT (7)
Delaware	AL (1)	AL (1)	AL (1)	AL (1)	AL (1)
Georgia	GT (4)	GT (4)	GT (4)	GT (4)	GT (4)
Kentucky	SMD (6)	SMD (6)	SMD (6)	SMD (6)	SMD (6)
Louisiana	—	—	—	—	AL (1)
Maryland	SMD-MMD (9)[a]	SMD-MMD (9)[a]	SMD-MMD (9)[a]	SMD-MMD (9)[a]	SMD-MMD (9)[a]
Massachusetts	SMD (17)	SMD (17)	SMD (17)	SMD (17)	SMD (17)
New Hampshire	GT (5)	GT (5)	GT (5)	GT (5)	GT (5)
New Jersey	GT (6)	GT (6)	GT (6)	GT (6)	GT (6)
New York	SMD (17)	SMD-MMD (17)[c]	SMD-MMD (17)[c]	SMD-MMD (17)[d]	SMD-MMD (17)[d]
North Carolina	SMD (12)	SMD (12)	SMD (12)	SMD (12)	SMD (12)
Ohio	AL (1)	AL (1)	AL (1)	AL (1)	AL (1)
Pennsylvania	SMD-MMD (18)[b]	SMD-MMD (18)[b]	SMD-MMD (18)[b]	SMD-MMD (18)[b]	SMD-MMD (18)[b]
Rhode Island	GT (2)	GT (2)	GT (2)	GT (2)	GT (2)
South Carolina	SMD (8)	SMD (8)	SMD (8)	SMD (8)	SMD (8)
Tennessee	GT (3)	GT (3)	GT (3)	GT (3)	GT (3)
Vermont	SMD (4)	SMD (4)	SMD (4)	SMD (4)	SMD (4)
Virginia	SMD (22)	SMD (22)	SMD (22)	SMD (22)	SMD (22)
House Membership	142	142	142	142	143

a. Two candidates were elected in district 5.
b. Eleven candidates were elected by MMD from districts 1, 2, 3, and 4: 3 from 1st, 3 from 2nd, 3 from 3rd, 2 from 4th.
c. Two candidates were selected by the joint district 2 and 3.
d. Four candidates were elected by MMD: 2 from 2nd and 2 from 6th.

Source: Kenneth C. Martis, *The Historical Atlas of United States Congressional Districts: 1789–1983*.

Table 4.4. State Election Methods for the House of Representatives in the Thirteenth through Seventeenth Congresses

| State | Thirteenth Congress (1813–1815) | Fourteenth Congress (1815–1817) | Fourth Apportionment | | |
			Fifteenth Congress (1817–1819)	Sixteenth Congress (1819–1821)	Seventeenth Congress (1821–1823)
Alabama	—	—	—	AL (1)	AL (1)
Connecticut	GT (7)	GT (7)	GT (7)	GT (7)	GT (7)
Delaware	GT (2)	GT (2)	GT (2)	GT (2)	GT (2)
Georgia	GT (6)	GT (6)	GT (6)	GT (6)	GT (6)
Illinois	—	—	AL (1)	AL (1)	AL (1)
Indiana	—	AL (1)	AL (1)	AL (1)	AL (1)
Kentucky	SMD (10)	SMD (10)	SMD (10)	SMD (10)	SMD (10)
Louisiana	AL (1)	AL (1)	AL (1)	AL (1)	AL (1)
Maine	—	—	—	—	SMD (7)
Maryland	SMD-MMD (9)[a]	SMD-MMD (9)[a]	SMD-MMD (9)[a]	SMD-MMD (9)[a]	SMD-MMD (9)[a]
Massachusetts	SMD (20)	SMD (20)	SMD (20)	SMD (20)	SMD (13)
Mississippi	—	—	AL (1)	AL (1)	AL (1)
Missouri	—	—	—	—	AL (1)
New Hampshire	GT (6)	GT (6)	GT (6)	GT (6)	GT (6)
New Jersey	DMD (6)	GT (6)	GT (6)	GT (6)	GT (6)
New York	SMD-MMD (27)[b]	SMD-MMD (27)[b]	SMD-MMD (27)[b]	SMD-MMD (27)[b]	SMD-MMD (27)[b]
North Carolina	SMD (13)	SMD (13)	SMD (13)	SMD (13)	SMD (13)
Ohio	SMD (6)	SMD (6)	SMD (6)	SMD (6)	SMD (6)
Pennsylvania	SMD-MMD (23)[c]	SMD-MMD (23)[c]	SMD-MMD (23)[c]	SMD-MMD (23)[c]	SMD-MMD (23)[c]
Rhode Island	GT (2)	GT (2)	GT (2)	GT (2)	GT (2)
South Carolina	SMD (9)	SMD (9)	SMD (9)	SMD (9)	SMD (9)
Tennessee	SMD (6)	SMD (6)	SMD (6)	SMD (6)	SMD (6)

House Membership	182	183	185	186	187
Vermont	GT(6)	GT (6)	GT (6)	GT (6)	SMD (6)
Virginia	SMD (23)	SMD (23)	SMD (23)	SMD (23)	SMD (23)

a. Two candidates were elected in district 5.

b. Twelve candidates were elected by MMD: 2 from 1st, 2 from 2nd, 2 from 12th, 2 from 15th, 2 from 20th, 2 from 21st.

c. Fourteen candidates were elected by MMD: 4 from 1st, 2 from 2nd, 2 from 3rd, 2 from 5th, 2 from 6th, 2 from 10th.

Source: Kenneth C. Martis, The Historical Atlas of United States Congressional Districts: 1789–1983.

areas west of the Blue Ridge were Republican.[32] Further, in the early nineteenth century all newly admitted states adopted SMD plurality elections, if not initially then after their apportionment reached about three or four representatives.[33] Of the eight states admitted to the Union after the founding until the 1820s that elected more than one representative, only one—Tennessee—used the general ticket, and then only for one apportionment cycle, after which it switched to SMD elections. Put simply, every state admitted after the founding in the first party era instituted SMD elections. A good predictor of state electoral system in the first party era is simply distance from the Atlantic Ocean.

Learning the Electoral System Ropes in the First Party Era

One of the most striking features of early republic elections is how quickly voters and the protoparties adjusted to the incentives provided by the various methods used to elect the House. Different election systems privilege different numbers of viable competitors and hence the optimal number of candidates that should stand for election. The SMD plurality-rule system encourages like-minded citizens to band behind a single candidate. This helps avoid splitting the vote and electing a candidate from another party. Consequently, elections in such districts should eventually gravitate toward two-candidate contests, with each candidate affiliated with a different faction or party. The empirical regularity in which the SMD plurality system tends to organize elections around two parties is known as Duverger's Law, and results from voters seeking to avoid "wasting" votes by casting them for candidates unlikely to win and also to the tendency of this system to "magnify" the seats won by the major party relative to its vote share. Ballots for a third- or lower-ranking candidate are wasted in the sense that only the two leading candidates are competitive for election. The difference between the first- and second-place finish determines party control of the seat; the difference between second and third does not. If voters want to influence the election outcome they have an incentive to vote for their most preferred candidate among the two leading candidates.[34] The SMD plurality system also tends to reward the leading party with extra legislative seats relative to its vote share. This "mechanical" effect obtains because minor parties that receive votes are unlikely to win any seats. Since these parties have detracted from the vote shares of the major parties but not their seat shares, the majority party receives legislative seats out of proportion to its vote share.[35] Multimember constituencies provide similar incentives, with the number of viable candidates increased in proportion to the number of representatives selected in each district.[36] In chapter 8 I argue that Duverger's law is less of a "law" and more of a tendency in explaining party systems, but in the early republic one clearly observes the emergence of coordination between political elites in the latter's endorsement of specific candidates and in the number of candidates standing for election.

The general ticket, especially if it is used to elect a large number of representatives, presents a more difficult problem for like-minded citizens to coordinate on an optimal number of candidates. If voters return a complete ballot and vote only for candidates representing their preferred party, then parties should offer no more candidates than there are seats to be elected. In this case, the leading candidates will have equal vote shares and all will be elected to the House. In effect, a general ticket ballot is a ballot for a political party, with the winning party taking all of the seats. The difficulty is that party leaders and like-minded voters may not agree on candidates or voters may simply not return a complete ballot. Under such circumstances the vote shares of candidates representing the same party or faction will differ, with the consequence that more than one party elects representatives to Congress. The likelihood of this scenario depends on how easily party leaders and voters can coordinate on a set of candidates. The ease of doing so depends on whether there are various factions within a party, how many representatives the state elects, the ease of communication with electors, and similar considerations.[37] General ticket elections, especially in the absence of organized political parties, are more likely to be a free-for-all.

Image 4.1 is an electoral broadsheet that illustrates how the early parties coordinated on candidates in the face of these difficulties. The Democratic-Republican broadsheet was published in Delaware in 1807 endorsing the election of Constitutional Convention participant John Dickenson as Delaware's House representative. It is signed by several Democratic-Republican notables, including Declaration of Independence signatory George Read, former Delaware governor David Hall, and Reuben Gilder, who served in the Revolutionary War as a surgeon and later became a well-established Baltimore physician. For Democratic-Republican voters the broadsheet went some ways toward solving the candidate coordination problem as it advocated a single candidate for Delaware's single seat in the House. For Dickenson the endorsement was still insufficient for election, as Federalist Nicholas Van Dyke won the seat. Nonetheless, the broadsheet shows that

Meeting

OF THE

DEMOCRATIC REPUBLICAN

CONFEREES,

Of the State of Delaware.

At a meeting of the Democratic Republican conferees of the State of Delaware, convened in the town of Dover, on the 4th. of August 1807, in pursuance of previous appointment, for the purpose of selecting suitable characters, to be voted for and supported by the Democratic Republicans of the State of Delaware, at the ensuing general election, for the office of Governor and Representative to Congress; David Hall was called to the chair, and John Hamm appointed secretary.

Upon consideration,

It was resolved unanimously, That Joseph Haslett be and he hereby is selected by this meeting as a suitable character to be voted for and supported by the Democratic Republicans of the State of Delaware, for the office of Governor, at the ensuing general election.

Resolved unanimously, That John Dickinson be and he is hereby selected by this meeting as a suitable character to be voted for and supported by the Democratic Republicans of the State of Delawre, at the ensuing general election, as a candidate to represent this State in the Congress of the United States.

Resolved further, That this meeting do recommend the above named candidates to the citizens of the State of Delaware, as worthy of their suffrages and support, at the ensuing general election, and as possessing in an eminent degree, that patriotism, and those abilities, which are the sure pledges of a faithful discharge of public duty.

Resolved, That the foregoing proceedings be signed by the conferees from the several counties in this State, and be published in handbills, for the information of our fellow-citizens.

Signed,

DAVID HALL,	GEORGE READ,
JOHN FISHER,	WILLIAM BELL,
JOHN WAY,	JOHN ADAMS,
JOHN MERRITT,	ROBERT JAMISON,
PETER WILLIAMS,	THOMAS LOWBER,
WILLIAM D. WAPLES,	JOHN FARISS,
FERDINAND CASSON,	WALTER DOUGLASS,
REUBEN GILDER,	JOHN CAREY,
JOHN COLLINS,	MITCHELL KERSHAW.
JOHN HAMM.	

Dover, August 4, 1807.

Image 4.1. Maryland Federalist Election Broadsheet, 1807. Used by permission of the Library Company, Philadelphia, PA.

even in the nation's earliest years the emerging parties adopted strategies to compete effectively under the electoral rules in force.[38]

The difficulty in systematically evaluating how well citizens and political leaders responded to the incentives provided by selection methods is due to the dearth of election data from the early republic. Fortunately, this deficiency has been greatly ameliorated by the A New Nation Votes project conducted under the auspices of Tufts University and the American Antiquarian Society.[39] This project has collected House election returns for many early republic elections from available ballots, period newspaper and broadsheet reports, county histories, and other sources. These data provide considerable information on many early House of Representatives elections. The collection is not complete; for any state that elected by district, we may not have returns for all districts in any election year. For example, for Virginia in 1789 we have complete returns for six districts; for the remaining districts we know only the name of the winner and perhaps one competitor. Still, the information on these six First Congress elections is considerable, and the collection will become more complete over time. For any election—single-member district, multimember district, or general ticket—for which we have data, these data are complete. These contests cover the corpus of election laws that saw application in the nation's first years before reliable returns became more readily available in the Jacksonian period. These data show that, remarkably early, our voters and political leaders were increasingly able to coordinate on fewer, more viable candidates. These data document the nation's rapid transition to organized, competitive elections.

Table 4.5 presents an example of general ticket returns. Displayed are

Table 4.5. New Hampshire 1806 General Ticket Election Returns

Within Party Finish Order	Republican	Votes	Federalist	Votes
1	Jedediah K. Smith	5,773	Samuel Tenney	3,685
2	Clement Storer	5,695	Caleb Ellis	3,625
3	Peter Carlton	5,695	David Hough	3,596
4	Francis Gardner	5,680	Thomas W. Thompson	2,838
5	Daniel M. Durrell	5,123	Silas Betton	2,825
6	John Wheeler	934	Samuel Quarles	132
7	Timothy Farrer	798	Nathanial Shannon	105
	9 Others	<100	13 Others	<100

Source: *A New Nation Votes: American Election Returns, 1787–1825.*

the results of the 1806 election, in which New Hampshire elected five Republicans to the Tenth Congress. The names of the elected are in italics along with their vote receipts. Among the Republicans, Jedediah Smith had the highest number of votes and Daniel Durrell ranked last. The general ticket presents a question of how to calculate vote shares. In New Hampshire an elector could vote for five candidates, so if 10,000 people returned complete ballots there are 50,000 votes distributed across some number of candidates. However, no candidate could receive more than 10,000 votes. Consequently, I calculated a candidate's vote share as the percentage of the maximum possible number of votes that he could receive. In the 1806 New Hampshire election 46,504 distinct votes were cast for the five available seats, so no candidate could receive more than 9,301 votes.[40] Based on these figures, Jedediah Smith received a majority of 62 percent. The last elected representative, Daniel Durrell, received a majority of 55 percent. To facilitate comparison with SMD and MMD elections, I define the winning plurality under the general ticket as the minimum vote share needed to gain election. In 1806 this was 55 percent. Similarly, the first or maximum losing vote share was Samuel Tenney's 39.6 plurality.

A particularly notable aspect of the New Hampshire election is how quickly the vote trails off after each party's fifth-ranked candidate. For both the Republicans and Federalists, the fifth-ranked candidate received a vote share comparable to the first-ranked candidate; however, the sixth-ranked candidate received only a fraction of the vote of the fifth-ranked candidate. In general ticket elections the vote difference between the first-place finisher and the last elected finisher is often very small because electors typically vote a straight ticket. This means that the difference in the pluralities of candidates from the same party or faction will often be negligible, and the leading party, as in the above example, will sweep the election and win all seats. Based on the complete returns, in 1806 New Hampshire had about 9,400 total electors, of whom about 5,700 voted for Republicans and 3,700 for Federalists. For each party there were five leading candidates and no more. Electors clearly distinguished these candidates from the others.

To better understand early House elections, I graphed the number of candidates and vote shares for elections in Delaware, New Jersey, Massachusetts, and Virginia from the first federal election until 1820. I selected these states because they implemented a broad range of electoral laws and also include states from New England, the mid-Atlantic, and the South. These graphs provide visual insight on when and how well candidates, parties, and voters adjusted to the incentives provided by these electoral systems. In essence, they capture the steepness of the election learning curve. It turns out it was very steep, meaning that regardless of the system, parties, candidates, and voters quickly adjusted to the method used to elect representatives.

It is important to understand that these graphs do not present a story about Duverger's Law. At best, the Federalists and Republicans might be described as protoparties, and there was little in the structure and organization that would allow one to make sensible statements about how the parties and their affiliated voters responded to electoral processes. Further, the period after 1800 is one of single-party dominance. Beginning with the Seventh Congress in 1801 through the balance of the era, the Republicans maintained overwhelming control of the House of Representatives, with their majority often exceeding 70 percent of the seats. Simply, after 1800 relatively few Federalists were elected to the House. Consequently, graphs detailing the number of candidates competing for seats and their associated vote shares do not mean that two parties are competing for these seats; quite often two Republicans were competing. That said, there were certainly states and districts with a strong Federalist presence, and also districts that were competitive and contested by both groups.

Figure 4.1 graphs Delaware's elections from the first House election until 1820. Delaware's experience nicely illustrates how quickly citizens and political leaders responded to the incentives provided by election methods. Delaware elected a single representative from the First (1789) to the Twelfth Congresses (1811), and then a second representative through the Seventeenth (1821) Congress. The at-large election of one representative effectively made the state a single-member district. Delaware then used the simplest application of the general ticket to elect two representatives until 1822, when it reverted back to a single representative. The figure presents the number of House of Representatives candidates per seat and the winning pluralities though these Congresses.

In the state's first federal election five candidates received respectable vote shares. Federalist John Vining won with a 44 percent plurality, and Anti-Federalist Rhodes Shankland finished second with almost 24 percent of the vote. By the fourth election in 1794 two candidates, Federalist Henry Latimer and Republican John Patton, combined to win over 95 percent of the vote; Patton was elected with a 51 percent majority. From that point forward Delaware's House elections were almost always contested by two primary candidates per seat, with this pattern only briefly altered in 1806 when three

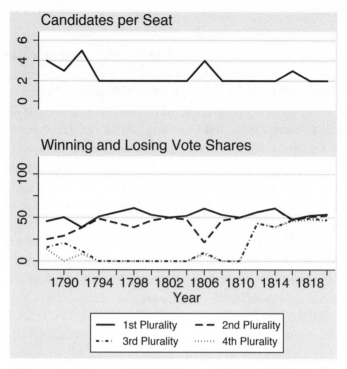

Figure 4.1. Delaware: 1789–1820. Source: A New Nation Votes.

Republicans entered the field, securing pluralities of approximately 21, 10, and 8 percent respectively. Federalist James M. Broom won the election handily with over 60 percent of the vote.

In 1812 the election system changed to electing two candidates by general ticket, and the vote difference between the first- and second-place candidates, and the third- and fourth-place candidates, immediately collapsed. In this election Federalists Thomas Cooper and Henry M. Ridgely were elected with nearly identical vote shares of 56 percent. Republicans Richard C. Dale and David Hall finished third and fourth respectively, with pluralities of approximately 43 percent. In effect, the election became a majority contest between two party slates.

By 1816 Delaware's political environment became more competitive, demonstrating one of the very few instances in which a representative from each party was elected under the general ticket. In this case Federalists failed to coordinate well, and two minor Federalist candidates won a combined vote share of just over 10 percent. This was sufficient to allow Republican Willard Hall to secure the second seat by a fraction of a percent over the second Federalist candidate, Caleb Rodney. In the absence of the two additional candidates, the Federalists would have won both seats handily. Nonetheless, the overall pattern in elections is clear. By 1798 most elections were contested by two primary candidates per seat. When the state elected a single representative, winning candidates generally secured a majority of the vote. The second-place candidate was always competitive, and third- and lower-place candidates received negligible vote shares. The vote share of the second loser increased dramatically in 1812 when a second seat came into play, but as expected the number of candidates remained about two per seat, and the minimum winning plurality remained approximately 50 percent of the vote.[41] In Delaware at least, the protoparties understood the rules and competed accordingly.

New Jersey presents an interesting example of election irregularities, malfeasance, and corruption. As Figure 4.2 suggests, this was also true in the early republic. New Jersey's political environment was significantly more complex than Delaware's. It elected five or six representatives, depending on the apportionment, in a politically contentious state in which electoral rules and practices were sometimes changed quickly for political advantage. After 1800 the Republicans dominated the state so overwhelmingly that in 1803, 1804, 1810, 1816, and 1818 the Federalists mounted no organized attempt to contest these elections. Throughout most of the early republic New Jersey used the general ticket to elect representatives. It switched to SMD plurality elections for the 1798 election and to dual-member districts in 1813. Both changes advantaged the Republicans during brief periods of increased Federalist strength. In 1796 Federalists swept the House election on the general ticket. Recognizing that their support was geographically concentrated in the north, the Republican-controlled assembly districted for the 1798 election, leading to the election of three of their own to the Sixth Congress.[42] Republicans again changed the rules in 1812 when they postponed the general ticket election scheduled for that autumn until spring 1813, when the state's six representatives would be elected from dual-member districts. This strategy worked well as two Republicans were elected from the northern First District. The smaller pluralities in 1814 owe to the Federalists contesting, although in vain, this election in response to the 1812–1813 shenanigans. This election notwithstanding, the Republicans enjoyed an overwhelming advantage, as reflected in very high winning pluralities. In 1802–1804, 1810, and 1816–1829 Republican candidates swept the general ticket with close to 100 percent or more of the possible vote. That

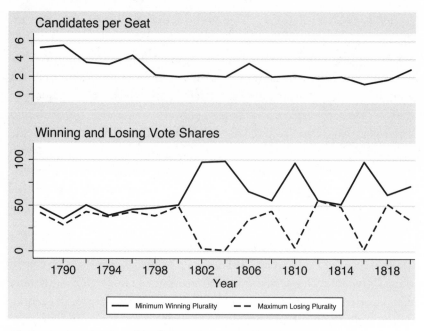

Figure 4.2. New Jersey: 1789–1820. Source: A New Nation Votes.

said, the number of candidates per seat approached two or fewer as the state moved into the nineteenth century. Combined with the 1798 and 1812–1813 rule changes, this clearly illustrates that political leaders understood that electoral systems shape results and that these could be changed to one's advantage.

Figure 4.3 graphs the average number of candidates per district and the first- through fourth-place pluralities in Massachusetts. Massachusetts relied almost exclusively on single-member districts during this period, but election was by majority rather than plurality rule. If no candidate secured a majority, subsequent elections were held until a candidate emerged with a majority of the vote. The majority requirement generally invited candidate entry into the election because one might attempt to advance to a runoff field more advantageous to one's eventual election. However, the Massachusetts system was not a true runoff because any candidate who competed in the first round could also stand in subsequent elections. In practice, weaker candidates often stood aside or received few votes, but elections that failed to generate a majority sometimes witnessed several rounds of voting before a candidate was elected. For example, the November 1796 election in the Eastern First District saw three candidates split the vote with pluralities

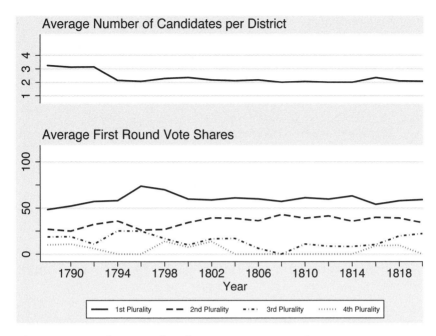

Figure 4.3. Massachusetts: 1789–1820. Source: A New Nation Votes.

between 28 and 40 percent. The second round in February 1797 was contested by the same three candidates, who finished in the same order with none receiving a majority. Finally, the two leading candidates stood for a third election in May with Federalist Isaac Parker obtaining 53 percent of the vote. In the first two federal elections most districts required multiple ballots to elect a representative. Thereafter elections were typically decided in the first round, with this becoming more common over time. Following the second apportionment about two-thirds of all district elections were decided on the first ballot. After 1802 multiround elections were uncommon, and electoral majorities were almost always secured on the first ballot.

Consistent with this, the average number of candidates competing per district declined significantly between 1794 and 1796, and stabilized around two per district for the balance of the first party era. Likewise, the average first-round vote share increased during roughly the same period, settling between 50 and 60 percent for the remainder of the era. This is not surprising since the pattern of political competition stabilized in Massachusetts in the early 1800s, with Republicans dominant in the eastern and far western parts of the state, while Federalist strength was concentrated in central Massachusetts. The central Massachusetts fifth and sixth districts,

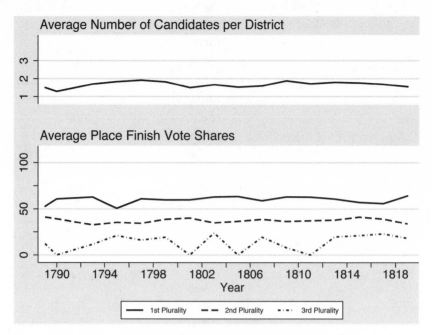

Figure 4.4. Virginia: 1789–1820. Source: A New Nation Votes.

for example, consistently elected Federalists to Congress while the eastern districts, excluding Boston, were reliably Republican. The districting system in Massachusetts, along with the experience of competing under the majority requirement, routinized political competition. The fortunes of Republicans and Federalists waxed and waned with the political tides, but both parties were always competitive for a share of the Massachusetts congressional delegation.

Figures 4.4 displays similar information for Virginia, which elected its representatives from single-member districts using the plurality rule. The Old Dominion enjoyed long experience with district elections defined by corporate entities. In colonial times it elected its House of Burgesses from dual-member districts that corresponded to county boundaries.[43] The number of candidates seeking election in these districts averaged about four, decreasing to about three or so immediately before the revolution.[44] When the state adopted SMD plurality elections for federal elections it was unsurprising that the number of vote recipients per district rarely exceeded two. Election-return data for Virginia are spotty for the first few elections. For example, for the 1797 House election we have compete returns for only twelve of Virginia's nineteen districts. Of these twelve districts, only eight were competitive in that two or more candidates received substantial vote shares. Still, having complete returns for twelve of nineteen House elections in 1797 is remarkable, and the proportion of complete returns increases in time. Figure 4.4 graphs the average number of candidates per district per year and the average vote-share pluralities for the competitive elections. The average number of candidates per election-year graph includes those districts where only one candidate received votes, while the vote shares are calculated only for those districts where two or more candidates received votes.

The most obvious characteristic of these elections is that the average number of candidates per district over the period never exceeds two. This is primarily because a significant number of elections were uncontested. For example, in 1801 we have complete information on twelve district elections, and only six of these featured two or more candidates. Throughout the first-party era in Virginia roughly 40 percent of House contests were uncontested. A typical example of competition in these districts is provided by Republican John Randolph's experience. Randolph was elected in 1799 from the Virginia Piedmont Seventh District, defeating Federalist Powhatan Bolling with approximately 60 percent of the vote. In 1801 he was elected from the same district unopposed. Following the 1801 reapportionment, Virginia's House delegation increased to twenty-two; Randolph's district was redrawn with modest boundary changes, and Randolph was again elected to the House unopposed, as he was in 1805 and 1807. Some districts were more compet-itive. For example, Virginia's Fifth District, located in the western part of the state following the 1802 reapportionment, featured contested elections in the five cycles between 1803 and 1811, with Republicans winning four of these elections and the Federalists capturing the seat once. Likewise, the Tidewater Virginia Twelfth District returned exactly the same record during this period. In addition, many districts, especially toward the latter part of the period, were contested by two Republicans with no Federalist opposition. For example, no Federalist won in the Virginia Third District after 1797, and no Federalist contested an election after 1813. Many of these two-candidate contests after 1810 were among Republican candidates.

The vote shares tell a similar story. These are again only calculated for the competitive races, but in these the average winning share in a cycle tended to be a comfortable majority of about 60 percent. The average second-place finish was in the 37 percent range, and when a third candidate competed, their vote shares over the period were just over 10 percent. The first- and second-place pluralities are quite smooth because these are averaged over several contests in each cycle, whereas third-place pluralities exist only in a handful of elections. Overall, the figure presents a picture of electoral stability. Candidate entry into these elections was selective, with a large percentage of races are uncontested. Competitive districts tended to lean either Federalist or, more commonly, Republican. In the more competitive districts winners still generally obtained office with a comfortable vote margin. The Virginia political world was largely stable and predictable, and political elites and citizens responded accordingly, as reflected in the decision to stand or not stand for election or to vote for tertiary candidates.

It is not important to explore the weeds here, but one can get a sense of district competition and how it developed by looking at examples of elections in individual districts across time. The difficulty in studying districts across time is that they are not static; districts are rearranged and changed with each new apportionment. The reapportionment after the first census increased Virginia's House representation from ten to nineteen, so district numbers from the first two Congresses bear little relationship to those in the third. Under the first apportionment Virginia's Fifth District was in the center of the state. Following reapportionment that number was assigned to a district in the southwest. It is worth noting here that the general practice of assigning numbers to districts itself dates to the nineteenth century. In the early republic districts were more often identified by geographic entities, such as the name of the largest county in the district. In addition, following reapportionment the geographic extent of districts was greatly reduced. As a general rule, at best one can study within-district political competition in an apportionment period.

Fortunately this is not true for Maryland. Maryland apportionment did not change between 1803 and 1822, and because of that the state experienced only minor redistricting. Indeed, the boundaries for some districts remained largely unchanged for these two decades.[45] Figure 4.5 shows the vote shares for Federalist and Republican candidates in the Maryland Second and Seventh Districts during this period. These districts are directly across the Chesapeake from each other on the western and eastern shores respectively. In at least one respect, these districts are atypical in that both were relatively competitive during the period. Federalists tended to do better in the western Second District but also ran competitively in the eastern shore, winning in 1816 and nearly so in 1820.

The important feature of this figure is not that these districts witnessed

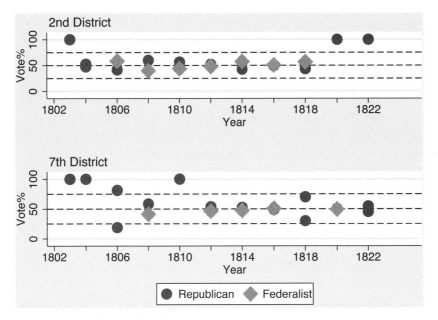

Figure 4.5. Maryland: 1803–1822. Source: A New Nation Votes.

two-party competition in the sense we understand today; they did not. These were organized factions and protoparties, not modern political parties. What is important is that when these districts were contested it was by two candidates. Also, in these years Republicans dominated Maryland politics—Republicans won about three-quarters of the House elections during this period. This dominance often enticed multiple Republican candidates to enter races, as was the case in 1804 in the Second District, and in 1806 and 1818 in the Seventh District. In this respect, the Maryland experience was typical in that single-member districts tended to attract two candidates even when it was clear that there was little party competition. In some sense, the 1804 election in the Second District and the 1806 and 1818 elections in the Seventh District were more closely related to contemporary primary elections. Regardless, candidates, political leaders, and electors were learning, and one manifestation of that was learning to not crowd the field.

Conclusion

At the founding the states chose how to elect their representatives. As Madison's letter to Jefferson at the beginning of this chapter reveals, these choices were conscious and considered, not simply a continuation of existing colonial practices. Even states such as Virginia and Massachusetts that had extensive experience with representative democracy had to reassess election practices because of the differences between representing corporate entities such as towns and counties and representing citizens under the new Constitution. The voluminous documentary evidence from the first federal election shows that these decisions were not lightly considered. The states chose election processes and often experimented with them before settling on an approach that would carry them through the next half century. These choices were influenced by the state's history, their cultural and political characteristics, and the desire to achieve particular political objectives or to increase state influence in the national legislature. Most of this experimenting occurred in the nation's first decade, with a subsequent pattern of electoral system quiescence extending through the first third of the nineteenth century.

Throughout this period different principles and patterns emerged that shaped the subsequent national discussions about electing the House of Representatives. Foremost among these was the understanding that the way a House delegation is elected is the prerogative of the state. It is true that constitutional amendments were introduced to mandate SMD elections for the House early in the nation's history, as discussed in the next chapter. However, the idea that it was the proper place of the national government to mandate how the states would elect representatives was never seriously entertained at the beginning of the nation's history. A bedrock principle of founding-era governance was that elections are a state-level activity and control of these processes resides in the states. So far as House elections were concerned, this bedrock began to crumble in the middle years of the nineteenth century.

The second important pattern that emerges is the ascendancy of the SMD system in House elections. By 1800 the vast majority of representatives were elected from single-member districts, and most of these by plurality rather than majority rule. This raises the question of why the states gravitated toward the SMD plurality system despite being free to adopt any system they saw fit. The large-state and small-state dichotomy clearly has purchase here; the large states used SMD elections, and the states that used the general ticket were all small. That said, the normative foundations for SMD plurality elections also helps explain the gradual voluntary agreement by most states that this method was the best way to elect a representative assembly. These values became increasingly entrenched in the early years of the nineteenth century, and reflect the decline of corporate representation as a normative concept. The political dominance of the Republicans in the Era of Good Feelings also removed the necessity of at-large elections to secure unified congressional delegations since the Federalists were not competitive in many jurisdictions.

The third major pattern that emerges in this era is that political leaders and citizens quickly learned how to compete effectively under the electoral rules in force in their states. The volatility of the first few elections settled quickly, and thereafter excess candidates under any electoral rule disappeared and voters coalesced around the few viable candidates in any given election. The ability of like-minded political leaders, factions, and parties to do so depended critically on their ability to recognize the incentives provided by each election method and respond accordingly. It is not surprising that political leaders could do so very early in our history. They had lengthy experience with elections under the colonial system, and the learning curve was steep. The primary question for political leaders was how to select optimal rules for a given state and time, given that suffrage was broad and increasing.

This state of the electoral world raises a number of questions. The most significant is why party leaders in the late Republican era and Whig-Jacksonian era would seek to disrupt this political world by imposing electoral methods on the residual states that used either the general ticket or multimember constituencies, and how they could do this so effectively that they overcame the ingrained opposition to even desirable changes, given that election authority was vested with the states. There is no simple answer to this question, but an important component of any answer is understanding the electoral implications of moving from a period of relative political quiescence in the Era of Good Feelings to the tumultuous politics of the Jacksonian and Whig Era. This is the subject of the next chapter.

5 The Jacksonian-Whig Era and the 1842 SMD Mandate

Establish the precedent that party malice is to be gratified, and party vengeance satiated by this vexatious and tyrannical process, and you may as well at once organize a corps of bandits, to enforce your savage and despotic orders.

North Carolina Whig representative
Kenneth Rayner, speaking in Congress
on the contested New Jersey general ticket
election, December 18, 1838

The Majority should govern, but the minority be heard.

Tennessee Whig representative Thomas
Dickens Arnold, speaking in favor of the
SMD requirement, April 26, 1842

The requirement that states elect representatives from single-member districts was mandated by the Apportionment Act of 1842. With this statute Congress acted under its understood powers under the Constitution's first article, fourth section, which states that "Congress may at any time by law make or alter such regulations" in regard to how states elect representatives. This prerogative is largely unquestioned today, but it was deeply disputed in the antebellum period. While it took a couple of election cycles for all states to implement the law, it quickly became the governing authority for House elections and has been renewed on several occasions without significant controversy.[1]

The Apportionment Act of 1842 is arguably one of the most important pieces of legislation in US history. In addition to codifying the principle that Congress can determine how the states elect their representatives, it reduced the size of the House of Representatives for the first and only time and ultimately required the chamber to deliberate under the Article 1, Section 5, provision that "each House shall be the Judge of the Elections, Returns and Qualifications of its own Members" when four states subsequently ignored the law.[2] It also motivated the first presidential signing statement of consequence when President Tyler questioned the constitutionality of the requirement. Understanding why Congress mandated SMD elections and, in particular, why it did so in 1842 is central to understanding the adoption of electoral systems and for understanding the evolving relationship between the national government and the states in the conduct of federal elections. The single-member district requirement did not suddenly emerge out of nowhere. The issue was repeatedly debated in the early nineteenth century, and proposed constitutional amendments requiring such election secured Senate support on multiple occasions before dying in the House. These antecedents form the political lineage that ultimately produced the 1842 act.

This chapter first discusses attempts to mandate SMD election in the early nineteenth century. I then overview the politically volatile electoral environment of the Jacksonian-Whig era and explain why it created incentives for the Whigs to seek the requirement that representatives be elected from single-member districts. It is difficult to exaggerate the differences between the electoral politics of the Jacksonian-Whig era and that of today. The differences are so significant and consequential that it is impossible to understand the SMD requirement without this background. The exceptionally dynamic, partisan, and volatile political context of the Jacksonian-Whig period motivated party leaders, especially Whig leaders, to standardize national elections under the SMD system. Two catalytic events eventually prompted Congress to act. The first was the contested 1838 New Jersey general ticket election in which the Democratic-weighted House of Representatives awarded New Jersey's seats to the Democratic ticket. The second was Alabama's 1841 switch from SMD election to the general ticket for the purpose of denying the Whigs any seats in that state's five-member congressional delegation. The penultimate section of the chapter focuses on the congressional politics surrounding the bill's drafting and passage. The SMD mandate was a Whig party reform, but the chamber debates and subsequent support for the bill reveal a more nuanced understanding of support for the requirement.

The politically unstructured environment of the mid-1820s gave rise to the Democratic-Whig era. Specifically, the Era of Good Feelings between about 1817 and 1825 gave birth to the Jacksonian Democrats and later the Whigs.[3] The Democrats valued egalitarianism and a limited role for government, opposed economic elites, especially banking and financial elites, and had a general fear of market economies. They were influenced by the Anti-Federalist tradition as reflected in their belief that the House should reflect the American population and have a preference for protecting state prerogatives, and placed a premium on *stare antiquas via*, meaning deference to practices established by tradition.[4] The Whigs were the political heirs of the national wing of the Jeffersonian Democratic-Republicans. This branch of the Jeffersonian Republicans counted James Madison in its membership and advocated a strong national government, the encouragement of trade and commerce, and a deliberative assembly led by enlightened leaders in pursuance of a greater national good.[5] To be sure, the Whigs attracted a number of former Federalists but rejected many of the old values, foremost among them the Federalists' overt emphasis on elitism. To speak of the Whig Party as opposition to Andrew Jackson or the Jacksonian Democrats is, as Michael F. Holt points out, a "literary convenience."[6] The Whigs began as a congressional caucus that opposed Jackson; however, they did not develop as a true political party until the late 1830s. Only then did the Whigs hold nominating conventions, systematically contest elections at both the national and state levels; and, most importantly, capture and organize a significant portion of the electorate. This is important because the imposition of a national mandate for single-member district House elections can only be understood in the context of systematic two-party competition for control of Congress, and this did not fully emerge until the late 1830s.

While the intensely partisan and uncertain electoral setting of the late 1830s and early 1840s motivated the SMD requirement, it would not have been possible without an intellectual and normative foundation that recommended such election. Even the most cynical politician had to justify his actions in terms of political values and ideals; members of Congress did so. One of the most important aspects of the debates over the Apportionment Act is that its participants appealed to the founders and their respective understandings of elections in the wider constitutional architecture to justify their positions. The bill was debated at a time when no legislator possessed living memory of the founding, so all based their arguments on founding texts, including Madison's *Notes of Debates in the Federal Convention of 1787*, *The Federalist Papers*, and the various records of debates in the state ratifying conventions. The Apportionment Act of 1842 presents one of the earliest and most significant instances of legislators supporting or opposing government action principally on framing-era intent.

Antecedents to the 1842 Apportionment Act Mandate

Attempts to require that members of the House of Representatives be elected from single-member district elections long predate the 1842 Apportionment Act. The preferred vehicle for doing so was constitutional amendment, and these almost always included provisions for changing the Electoral College as well. These proposed amendments obliged states to elect representatives from single-member districts and select presidential electors from these same districts. Each state's legislature would then select its two remaining presidential electors in the same manner as senators. The selection process for president would dovetail exactly with the selection of the House and Senate. Importantly, these amendments also often precluded redistricting between apportionments and required that districts consist of contiguous territory and contain as near as possible equal population.

Representative John Nicholas of Virginia introduced the first of these proposals in 1800. The Nicholas resolution was referred to committee, which returned an adverse recommendation, and it went no further in the chamber. Importantly, the proposal was rejected partially on the grounds that "the objects directly contemplated therein are already within the limits of the legislative authority of the government of the United States. . . . To convert to a constitutional provision . . . seems to be both superfluous and inconvenient."[7] Congress, so the committee argued, already enjoyed the right to regulate House elections, and thus a constitutional amendment was unnecessary. In 1800 at least, Congress appeared to believe that it could determine how representatives were elected.

More sustained efforts to constitutionally require SMD election emerged in the 1810s and 1820s. These proposals often came at the behest of the states. No fewer than six states petitioned Congress to propose an amendment requiring the SMD system. These states included New Jersey and Connecticut, both of which used the general ticket.[8] Records illuminating why states would petition Congress to eliminate their own prerogatives are few, but a letter from Thomas Jefferson to James Monroe on the Electoral College probably captured the essence of these motivations. Jefferson recognized that "all agree that an election [of presidential electors] by districts would be best, if it could be general . . . [but so long as] . . . ten states choose by their legislators or by a general ticket, it is folly and worse than folly for the other six not to do it."⁹ States that chose presidential electors by general ticket or through their state legislatures produced a unified block of votes for a single candidate. This increased their influence relative to states that chose by districts because the latter's votes were typically split among candidates. If all agreed that district election is best, then the only way out of this conundrum was to require that all states elect by district. States that used the general ticket would support such a mandate if they could be assured that all other states were equally bound.¹⁰ The same principle applied to the selection of representatives. States that used the general ticket to elect representatives increased their influence relative to states that used districts and would be reluctant to give this up unless assured that all other states would do so as well.

The most serious attempts to enact a constitutional amendment came between 1816 and 1822, and these obtained the necessary two-thirds Senate approval in 1819, 1820, and 1821 before dying in the House of Representatives.¹¹ The first of these proposals was introduced by North Carolina representative Israel Pickens on instruction from his state legislature. Subsequent proposals were introduced by New Jersey senator Mahlon Dickerson, also on instruction. As Dickerson remarked, the timing was "auspicious for undertaking the proposed amendment, as there is less of party animosity now than there has been at any period since the establishment of our government."¹² The Era of Good Feelings reduced the partisan obstacles to a constitutional amendment, and many senators were given license from their statehouses to support one.

Dickerson's arguments in favor of an SMD mandate centered on the familiar ground of the place of elections in a constitution that balances republican and liberal values. The House, he stated, is "emphatically called the popular branch, to distinguish them from the Senate, which may still be considered as a representation of the states."¹³ The "popular branch is . . . the main stay and strong hold of the republican principles of our government" and as such "ought to be a representation of the people."¹⁴ It "should be a fair representation . . . of the citizens—the people at large."¹⁵ Like Mason, Dickerson considered the House "the grand depository of the democratic principle." Then, channeling his inner Madison, he castigated the general ticket on the grounds that it suppressed "the voice of the minorities," with this tyranny "practiced under the specious garb of Republicanism."¹⁶ He also addressed the state safety issue noted by Jefferson, arguing that such an amendment "does not abridge the rights of any states, but adds to the security of all."[17] Despite failing to produce an SMD mandate, Dickerson's contribution is notable because his remarks would not have been out of place in any founding-era debate on elections.

In contrast to 1800, in the 1820s there was less certainty that such a mandate was within the legislative authority of Congress. Members of Congress divided over whether its Article I, Section 4, authority to regulate the "time, place and manner" of House elections included determining the methods states use to elect their representatives. Dickerson did not believe that Congress possessed legislative authority, and believed that only a constitutional amendment could bind states in this manner. According to Dickerson, the purpose of Article I, Section 4, was to "guard against a possible case, of a combination of particular states, to stop the process of Government, by refusing to send Representatives to Congress."[18] The provision protects the national government from the states, especially the larger states, by precluding the latter from grinding the former to a standstill by simply refusing to elect representatives. In this view, Congress does not have the authority to dictate to the states *how* they elect their representatives, only that they *must* elect representatives. If this is correct, then the only foundation for an SMD mandate is constitutional amendment.

Virginia senator Barbour, who personally favored district election, led the opposition to so amending the constitution. Barbour's objection stemmed both from a reverence for the document, which he wished to protect from "adventures after theoretical perfection" and from his belief that Congress possessed the necessary legislative authority, although an authority that was best unused.[19] Importantly, Barbour raised the issue of states' rights for the first time, asking, "What delinquency have the states committed to produce a forfeiture of their rights? What reason presents itself to justify this curtailment of their privileges?"[20] The limits of constitutional authority to legislate and the federal-state balance of powers became among the most salient considerations in Congress's decision to impose the SMD mandate two decades later.

The attempts to amend the Constitution to require that representatives be elected from single-member districts had largely run their course by 1826.[21] Attention turned to presidential elections, with the election of Andrew Jackson following the public indignation over the "corrupt bargain" that led to the selection of John Quincy Adams by the House of Representatives in 1824.[22] The tumultuous politics following these elections ultimately brought the question of a uniform national system for the election of representatives back to the forefront of debate. By perhaps extraordinary coincidence, Adams would be one of the principal players in 1842 since he was the only former US president to subsequently sit in the House of Representatives. However, before turning to the apportionment bill it is useful to understand the political environment in which Congress found itself during this period.

Elections in the Jacksonian-Whig Era: 1824–1850

Modern electoral politics emerged in the Jacksonian-Whig era. This period witnessed the emergence of political parties, the mass enfranchisement and mobilization of the white male electorate, and election campaigns.[23] Walter Dean Burnham describes the years between the 1820s and 1830s as witnessing a "democratic revolution" in American politics resulting from the "development of a permanently embedded, closely competitive party system."[24] Historian Alexander Keyssar concurs, explaining that broadening franchise and increased voter turnout were driven by party competition for office: "By the 1830s, competition between Whigs and Democrats dominated political life, reflecting the creation of a strong and vibrant national party system; not only were elections systematically contested, but both party loyalty and party identification [became] prominent elements of public life. In this competitive political culture, the issue of suffrage reform inescapably attached itself to partisan rivalries."[25] Between about 1810 and 1830 the states eliminated virtually all franchise restrictions except race and gender. Property and tax-paying requirements, residency requirements, even citizenship requirements were dropped in rapid succession as conditions to vote.[26] The parties enfranchised and mobilized white males to create and maintain political advantage in this extraordinarily competitive political environment.

Three graphs that present voter turnout, the number of cast ballots, and the stability of party vote shares respectively capture the most salient aspects of elections in this period. For context it is useful to keep in mind that the US population nearly doubled between 1820 and 1840. Less than 10 million were counted in the 1820 census, whereas the 1840 census records approximately 17 million Americans.

Figure 5.1 plots the potential electorate and the House election voter turnout rate between 1820 and 1850. The potential electorate consists of those eligible to vote; the turnout rate is the percentage of those eligible to vote who cast ballots.[27] All else equal, one would expect a doubling of the potential electorate because of population increase. In fact, this is exactly what we observe: the pool of potential voters increased from about 1.6 million to just

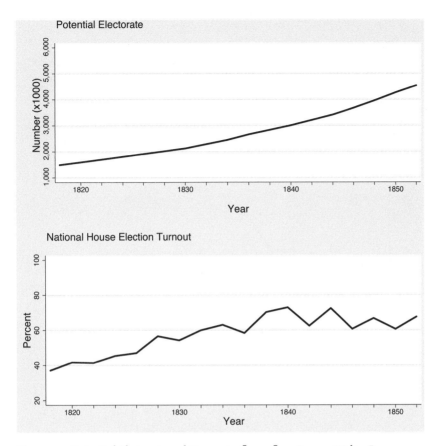

Figure 5.1. *Potential Electorate and Turnout: 1820–1850. Source: Walter Dean* Burnham, Voting in American Elections, *and US Census.*

over 3 million in two decades. However, the rate at which these men cast ballots also increased. In two decades election turnout roughly doubled, from about 30 percent of the potential electorate to about 70 percent. The major inflection point in turnout is between the 1824 and 1828 presidential elections, when the rate roughly doubled.[28]

The cumulative effect of these two trends was a near *quadrupling* of the active electorate between 1820 and 1840, and it went up from there. Figure 5.2 presents the total number of cast ballots in House of Representatives elections between 1820 and 1850. The combined effect of expanded franchise, population growth, and party mobilization of voters was an enormous increase in votes. The Sixteenth Congress convening in 1819 was elected by 300,000 ballots. Approximately 2 million ballots elected the Twenty-Seventh

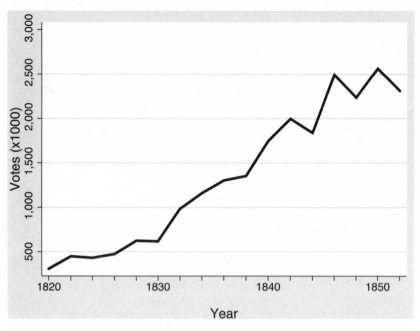

Figure 5.2. Total Ballots Cast: House Elections, 1820–1850. Source: Walter Dean Burnham, Jerome M. Clubb, and William Flanigan, State-Level Congressional, Gubernatorial and Senatorial Election Data for the United States, 1824–1972.

Congress, which passed the Apportionment Act of 1842. Michael F. Holt, the foremost scholar of Whig-era politics, reports that the median percentage increase across states in cast ballots between just 1832 and 1836 was between 25 and 30 percent.[29] A few state-level examples further illustrate this immense increase in voter participation. Just over 47,000 ballots were cast in Massachusetts in the 1832 presidential election, while in the 1840 election Massachusetts recorded nearly 125,000 ballots, an increase of over 160 percent. Massachusetts's population increased in these eight years, but not by 160 percent. In the same period Missouri saw approximately 27,000 ballots increase to 51,000, while Indiana recorded an increase from 61,000 votes to 85,000 votes.[30] To appreciate the magnitude of this increase in the active electorate, consider that approximately 104 million ballots were cast in the 1992 presidential election and 122 million votes were cast in the 2012 presidential election. That represents an increase of about 17 percent. The percentage increase in ballots cast in House elections between 1820 and 1842 exceeded 500 percent. In sum, in the 1820s and 1830s white men received the vote, and they used it.

The problem faced by parties was that mass enfranchisement and mobilization was risky because it created an uncertain political environment. One could not easily predict how the newly enfranchised would vote, and mobility meant that new voters with dubious political loyalties migrated to established jurisdictions. Partisanship was emerging, which, by its nature, has a stabilizing effect on elections because partisans, not surprisingly, tend to vote for the party with which they identify. This provides political parties with a semipredictable level of electoral support. However, in the era's early years these ties were not sufficiently rooted to well-structured voting and elections.[31] From the perspective of party leaders, the American political universe in the 1830s must have looked like an immense rising tide with little indication of when it would ebb or even the direction it would take at any given moment. These leaders had to try to manage this political world, one largely of their own making but also one beyond their ability to control or even fully anticipate.

This notion of uncertainty can be made more precise by calculating electoral volatility for the Jacksonian-Whig and, for comparison purposes, contemporary periods. Electoral volatility is simply the absolute difference in a party's vote share in two proximate elections summed over all parties.[32] It measures how well vote shares in a given election correspond to vote shares in the next election. Volatility is low if parties get about the same vote share across elections. If there are significant vote swings, then volatility is high. Electoral volatility measures uncertainty in the sense that it captures how well one can predict future performance based on past results. If electoral volatility is low, then one can make such inferences with greater confidence. If volatility is high, then one cannot. The question is how "high" is high? One way to answer this is by comparing Jacksonian-Whig period electoral volatility with the present era's.

The Figure 5.3 graph of electoral volatility captures two interesting features. The first is the extraordinary level of volatility before about 1836. Organized protoparty competition collapsed in 1820, with the effectively unopposed election of President James Monroe initiating the "Era of Good Feelings." Subsequent elections organized around individuals, including Andrew Jackson, William Crawford, Henry Clay, and John Quincy Adams. The high volatility in the mid-1820s reflects this unstructured political environment and, especially, the vitriolic 1824 and 1828 elections that produced

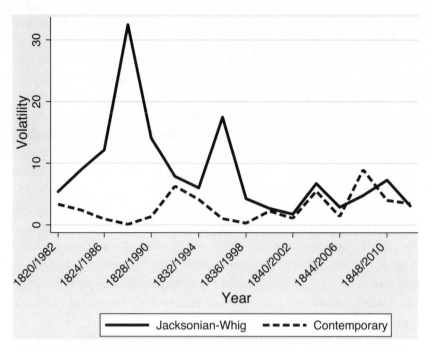

Figure 5.3. Electoral Volatility: Jacksonian and Modern Eras. Source: Gerald G. Rusk, A Statistical History of the American Electorate.

charges of a "corrupt bargain" and the subsequent outright presidential election of Andrew Jackson in 1828. The 1830s spike corresponds to the high-water mark for the Anti-Mason party, which received double-digit vote shares in these congressional cycles.[33] Still, by about 1830 the emergence of the Democrats under Jackson and his successors and a few years later the Whigs under Clay was underway and electoral volatility declining. By the late 1830s the Jacksonian-Whig era clearly entered a new period. Michael F. Holt describes these years as witnessing a "realignment" characterized by heightened voter interest, increased issue differences between the parties, and ideological polarization.[34] Importantly, though, Holt correctly argues that the reduced electoral volatility of the late 1830s did not capture "stability in voting patterns. Instead [it masked] movements of the voters into and out of the participating electorate."[35] Partisanship was emerging and movements from "standing" vote choices were fewer and smaller, but it had not yet solidified into the structuring force it is today.

To understand why the Whigs sought to mandate the single-member district system. one has to appreciate the nature of politics in the 1830s.[36]

Foremost, it was about economics, specifically the "roller-coaster" economy. Economics was "the predominant influence shaping American political development in these years," and it was economics that structured electoral politics.[37] The volatile economy forced the parties to "formulate clear and contrasting economic policies" and molded "officeholders in the respective parties into disciplined phalanxes who supported their rival programs in state and national legislative bodies in order to establish contrasting records to take to the electorate."[38] The parties were organized around different "economic constituencies, if not . . . different classes."[39] The Whigs did better in hard economic times; in 1841, with control of both the presidency and Congress, they should have been in a position to enact their policies to the satisfaction of their electorate. However, Whig president William Henry Harrison died only thirty days after taking office, leading to the inauguration of Vice President John Tyler, a man with very tenuous Whig affiliation who spent more time thinking about the Constitution than the economy.[40] Tyler subsequently vetoed much of his own party's economic legislation, to the disillusionment of Whig voters, who, while not prepared to vote Democratic, were prepared to abstain in upcoming elections.[41] As a result, Whig electoral fortunes were bleak in 1842, and most anticipated a shift in party control in the Twenty-Eighth Congress.

In the 1840s the electorate was active, polarized, and fluid, and the Whigs were increasingly disadvantaged. It is easy to assume that with increasing partisanship party leaders sensed their world was solidifying and could plan accordingly, but this would be misleading. Mapping a river while still in the river is difficult, and in 1842 party leaders were in the political river. Their frame of reference was the near past, and the political and sectional tensions that would ultimately destroy the Whigs were certainly sensed, if not clearly visible. In addition to being relatively unstable, period politics was often nasty. In this respect, two events drove home the point that the fate of parties and control of Congress depended heavily on election rules. The first was the contested New Jersey House election of 1838; the second was a decision by the Alabama legislature to switch from SMD election to the general ticket for the 1841 election.

The New Jersey House election clarified the stakes inherent in using the general ticket in deeply divided and competitive states. The 1838 election produced a dead-heat finish between the Democratic and Whig House tickets, with a spread of only 171 votes out of over 28,000 cast determining the election of one or the other ticket.[42] New Jersey Whig governor William Pennington challenged ballots recorded in two towns that, if struck, would elect the Whigs. However, Democratic secretary of state James Westcott recognized these votes, producing both Democratic and Whig claims to the state's five House seats. The responsibility to adjudicate contested House elections rests with the chamber. The Twenty-Sixth Congress, however, wanted party control; indeed, control of the House depended on how these five seats were awarded.[43] The Democrats possessed the largest plurality, but were shy of a majority due to the Anti-Masons' possession of a handful of seats. Further, conservative Democrats sided with the Whigs in some organizational votes, including the election of Whig Robert Hunter as Speaker of the House. It was unclear how these legislators would vote on the New Jersey seats. As the House discovered, resolving a disputed general ticket election is more complex and the stakes much higher than in an SMD election. As Tennessee Democrat Aaron Brown noted, if the chamber sought to uncover improper New Jersey ballots then the "whole state would have to be ransacked."[44] Eventually a Democratic-controlled special committee recommended the Democratic-weighted chamber seat to the Democratic ticket, prompting committee Whigs to issue a rare minority report alleging that partisan gain had determined the outcome.[45] The Democratic slate was ultimately seated by a chamber vote held under a bare quorum.[46] The disputed election placed the chamber in a position to determine an entire congressional delegation, in this case a delegation that would determine control of the chamber. The implications of this experience were not lost on its participants.

More controversy followed when Alabama's Democratic-controlled legislature changed the state's electoral system from single-member district to the general ticket for the 1841 congressional election. The proposal's architect was Governor Arthur P. Bagby, who saw the general ticket as a device to check a perceived increase in Whig Party support and protect state interests, especially slaveholding interests, against northern abolitionists.[47] Bagby's immediate objective was to keep Whig candidates from winning the state's western and southernmost Third and Fifth Districts, centered on Tuscaloosa and Mobile respectively. He also viewed the general ticket as most conducive to the "perpetuity of the sovereignty of the states" because it would elect a united delegation.[48] The Democrats were strongest in northern Alabama and probably constituted a majority of the state's electors.[49] However, districting enabled the Whigs to count on winning two and possibly three districts.[50] The politics of changing the election system boiled down to a bare-knuckle partisan fight with only superficial and tepid appeals to normative justifications. Journalist and future secessionist leader William Lowndes Yancey argued for the general ticket because "in three districts out of five, the Whigs have the power of electing a majority of congressional representatives, while actually a minority of 6000 votes."[51] Yancey's math was probably correct, but the only issue was whether the Democrats would control Alabama's congressional delegation. The matter was momentarily settled by the legislature, which allowed Alabama to schedule a May general-ticket election to select a delegation in time for a special session Congress had set to convene later that month. When Congress met, Alabama was represented by five Democrats. Even though the election outcome reflected the majority sentiments of the state's voters, the strategic machinations did not sit well with Alabamans; in an August referendum they voted to return to the district system, a decision that was subsequently ratified by the state legislature as its first order of business in 1841.[52] This reversal notwithstanding, Alabama presented a clear example of changing an election process solely for political advantage, in this case eliminating an entire party from congressional representation.

The political context of the 1830s to 1840s set the stage for the legislative mandate of single-member district elections. What was needed was an instrument for doing so. Constitutional amendment was no longer viable, given the difficulty such a proposal would have in obtaining a two-thirds majority in either chamber. However, any legislative approach would have to have a suitable foundation. Such a vehicle presented itself in the form of the 1840 decennial census. The census required congressional reapportionment, and with that came the opportunity to legislate House selection itself.

The Apportionment Act of 1842 and the SMD Mandate

The Apportionment Act of 1842 was introduced in the second session of the Twenty-Seventh Congress. Vermont Whig Horace Everett brought it to the House on January 22, although it was not considered by the chamber until April 20. Between April and June it motivated the deepest and most comprehensive examination of elections since the founding. The second session of the Twenty-Seventh Congress counted 241 representatives, of whom 142 were Whigs. Seven states selected their representatives by general ticket, with seventeen Whigs and fourteen Democrats so chosen. The Senate seated forty-eight, of whom twenty-six were Whigs. The Whigs held modest majorities in both chambers, but these were very thin for the purposes of this bill. This was especially true in the Senate, where if the fourteen senators representing states that selected by general ticket chose to uphold their states' prerogative, there was little chance that the SMD mandate could pass. The states that elected by general ticket were generally small, but beyond this characteristic there was no pattern that linked them. They encompassed all regions, including the South, New England, and the Midwest.[53]

The introduced bill addressed only the apportionment question. About a week later New Jersey Whig representative William Halstead proposed the districting provision in an amendment added as the bill's second section. The act's two subjects—the size of the chamber and the districting requirement—were inextricably linked. First was the population-to-seats ratio or, simply, how many citizens each legislator represents. A smaller ratio means a larger chamber and vice versa. Advocates of a smaller ratio placed a premium on the chamber more closely resembling the national polity. Those advocating a larger ratio primarily thought of the chamber as a deliberative body that served as a forum for discovery of the national good. The districting requirement spoke to state and federal balance in the constitutional system and, in particular, the meaning of Congress's authority to regulate the "times, places and manner" of House elections. Debate over the bill followed the partisan and regional divisions of the second party system, but each party emphasized different considerations. Democrats, most of whom favored a larger chamber, focused their remarks on the constitutional propriety of requiring the states to elect representatives from single-member districts. Most Democrats preferred single-member district elections, but not at the expense of usurping traditional state authority. The Whigs divided over the ratio question. Most wanted a smaller chamber but some, most notably John Quincy Adams, advocated a larger House. However, they were united in support of the districting mandate. House Whigs devoted their energy primarily to arguing the constitutionality of the SMD mandate, while their Senate colleagues focused on the purpose of the House and the types of representatives selected by each system.

Both sides agreed that the debate should be guided by founding-era intent and not political gain.[54] In this spirit there were few references to the New Jersey and Alabama elections, although early-twentieth-century historian James Woodburn argues that these helped motivate the bill and formed the backdrop against which it was debated.[55] The debate certainly addressed partisan and state advantage under the various election systems, but these pragmatic considerations were relegated to tertiary status in the proceedings. The most admissible arguments were predicated on political values, and these were based on appeal to founding texts including the *Federalist Papers*, the records of debates in the state ratifying conventions, and Madison's recently published *Notes of Debates in the Federal Convention of 1787*.

However, how each side read these documents and used them to support or oppose the apportionment act was quite different. Historian Martin H. Quitt captured these differences, writing that the "Whigs gave greater weight to the intentions of the framers, Democrats to the expectations of the ratifiers."[56] This pattern is unmistakable. In several instances opponents of the districting requirement quite literally inventoried state ratification debates that supported their interpretation of the "time, place and manner" clause. The Whigs, in contrast, advocated what Johanna Nicol Shields aptly calls "progress through retrogression," a return to the Federalist vision of an assembly populated by enlightened representatives who were their constituents' trustees and who could pursue the good "independently, rationally and deliberatively."[57] In crafting such arguments Whigs naturally relied heavily on the drafting convention and *The Federalist*.

These two provisions produced a corpus of proposals and speeches that was voluminous even by the standards of an era when a seeming qualification for serving in Congress was the ability to sustain a marathon-length speech.[58] In doing so, the debate went well beyond partisan divisions to encompass comprehensive exploration of the nature of federal and state relations, the purpose of the House of Representatives, and proper representation. These debates present one of the "most significant moments in the evolution of electoral systems in the United States" and constitute nothing short of a self-conscious attempt to reexamine the collective understanding of elections and representation.[59]

Even without the districting mandate, the apportionment component of the bill was significant enough. The first congressional apportionment provided one representative for every 30,000 citizens. In the ensuing years this number had been only modestly increased with the chamber growing to compensate for increased population. Following the 1830 apportionment each House member represented 47,000 citizens, with the chamber totaling 244 seats. However, by 1842 population growth meant that the initially adopted ratio of 50,179 would produce a House with 305 members. Such a startling increase in membership forced Congress to reconsider how it conducted business.

Democrat Richard Davis of New York opened the proceedings by observing that he "had never seen more disorder and less decorum and efficiency in any legislative body."[60] Davis was not being hyperbolic; the press referred to the House as "the bear garden" because it was such an unruly and vitriolic place.[61] Drawing inspiration from the Anti-Federalists, Davis contended for a larger chamber elected in such a manner to "get more of the people into the House and fewer Gentlemen."[62] He dismissed concerns that a larger House would exacerbate chamber order and efficiency problems because a more numerous representation would facilitate the election of "voting men, not talking men."[63] Kentuckian John B. Thompson, in contrast, articulated the Federalist-inspired and more widely accepted Whig perspective near the end of debate: "Large assemblies are always tumultuary; and the spirit of a mob seems to pervade the numbers of a mob . . . destroy by numbers, the calmness, and quietude, and facility of intercommunication requisite for deliberation,—and your House of hundreds will be inert and emasculated as to all unity and concentration of purpose: like any other mob . . . led by passion and leaders, and not from reason and deliberation."[64] There is no daylight between Thompson's sentiments and the Federalist's over fifty years earlier. Others expanded along these lines.[65] Democrat Francis Pickens of South Carolina recommended a smaller chamber on the grounds that this would "increase the power of the House" relative to the Senate, an advantage that would be lost if they added "to its numbers [and] make it a mob." Pickens also pointed warily to the increasing power of the new party leaders, warning that in large assemblies power is concentrated "in the hands of a few, who then would become dictators of the republic." [66]

Others favored a House of Representatives significantly larger than its current membership. A few days after Wise's speech, Democratic representative Charles Atherton of New Hampshire presented the canonical Anti-Federalist argument:

> The reason for establishing a representative government was because the whole people could not assemble and determine for themselves what measures shall be adopted for their benefit . . . [therefore] . . . a representative government was . . . the people acting through their *agents* and hence there should be the freest and fullest representation.[67]

The next day fellow Democrat John Reynolds of Illinois followed with another classically Anti-Federalist perspective:

> If all the people of the United States could assemble together, and transact the public business, the convention would be the greatest

body of people on earth. . . . But as the whole number of people cannot assemble together, the next largest number representing the whole that can come together, and transact the public business of the whole people, must be the next greatest body! This assemblage is the House of Representatives. It is, in truth, a kind of facsimile and mirror of the people—presumed to represent them in every particular.[68]

Pennsylvanian Charles Brown conceded that large assemblies can be tumultuous and slow, but disparaged the Whig emphasis on the importance of legislative "efficiency," arguing that "there was something more than an efficient and practical government to look to . . . it was not that they should pass a certain number of laws in a certain time, but they should pass good laws."[69] These themes—the importance of deliberation and efficiency versus the creation of a facsimile of the American people in the House of Representatives—structured the ratio debate, but not particularly strongly along party lines. These conflicting visions of the House resonated with the Americans and their representatives regardless of party affiliation, just as they do today.

The single-member district debate began on April 27, and it clearly and deeply divided the parties. The districting requirement raised several avenues for support or opposition. Much of the debate centered on whether Article 1, Section 4, allowed Congress to mandate district elections. Representatives offered two interpretations of this clause. The narrow interpretation embraced by many Democrats was that it only allowed the federal government to ensure congressional elections in order to preserve its own existence.[70] The expansive interpretation supported by Whigs was that it allowed Congress to determine the means by which representatives are elected and to standardize these practices nationally. More importantly, for the Whigs the mandate was central to their survival as a political party. Despite their controlling Congress, the Whigs' political fortunes were more precarious than those of the Democrats. Beyond their own internal divisions, Democratic populist rhetoric was not easily countered by appeals to minority rights, enlightened deliberation, and efficiency in government. The district requirement would not enable the Whigs to maintain their chamber majority, but it would help ensure their survival as a political party.

Democrats based their districting arguments primarily on appeals to the state ratifying conventions, in which the Framers explained and defended the "time, place and manner" provision. New York Democratic representative

J. G. Floyd took apparent glee in subjecting Whigs to a full-bore lecture on the "time, place and manner" clause, drawing at length from the proceedings of no fewer than seven state conventions to support his contention that Congress could not infringe on how states elected their representatives.[71] His colleagues probably got the point after the second or third recitation. Representative Floyd's remarks on the Virginia convention capture the essence of this approach and merit quoting at length:

> I am sure [the chamber] . . . will listen to me with pleasure; for I am
> about to read from the proceedings of the convention of the State of
> Virginia—a convention of which . . . James Madison, James Monroe,
> Patrick Henry, John Marshall and other worthies were members. In
> the debates of that convention, Mr. Monroe asked of Mr. Madison . . .
> "information respecting the clause concerning elections." He wished
> to know why Congress had ultimate control over the time, place and
> manner of election of representatives. . . . Mr. Madison answered, "It
> was found impossible to fix the time, place and manner of the election
> of representatives in the constitution. It was found necessary to *leave
> the regulation of these, in the first place, to the state governments* as being best
> acquainted with the situation of the people subject to the control of
> the general government in order to produce uniformity and prevent its
> own dissolution.[72]

Not surprisingly, Democrats emphasized the "prevent its own dissolution" interpretation of Madison's response, and bolstered this interpretation by referring to constitutional amendments entertained by the Virginia ratifying convention that would specifically preclude congressional interference in the state-level administration of elections. Nonetheless, Madison's recognition of the importance of elections' "uniformity" and being "subject to control of the general government" did not escape the notice of the Whigs. To them, this recommended a broader understanding of congressional powers. The state ratifying conventions, like the drafting convention, left ample room for differing interpretations of the founders' intentions.

Other Democrats conceded that Congress had the authority to require the election of representatives from single-member districts,[73] but disputed that Congress could order the states to create these districts. Alabama representative W. Payne's understanding was fairly typical: "I do not intend to deny that Congress has the power, by law, to prescribe the 'times, places and manner' of holding elections; but I do deny that Congress has power to command a state legislature to district a state."[74] This is not an arcane point of constitutional law. Representative Payne's criticism captures what is known as the "anticommandeering" principle, which simply means that just because Congress has the power to do something it does not necessarily mean it has the power to order a state to do that thing for Congress.[75] Congress may require district elections but if it wants districts, so the argument goes, it must draw them itself.[76] The prospect of the federal government districting the states raised a host of potential problems, not the least of which was the sheer logistical difficulty of the national government drawing sensible House districts. As Payne's fellow Alabaman George Houston observed, it is hard enough for the statehouses to draw these districts, much less the federal government from afar.[77]

The final constitutional objection was that the bill exercised a power that heretofore had never been used. The importance of *stare antiquas via*, or deference to established practice, should not be minimized. It was a significant, perhaps the most significant, constitutional argument against the districting mandate. Constitutions are more than the words in the document; they are also the way these words have been used and interpreted. This does not mean that precedence is always binding, but it does demand considerable respect for it. Representative Clifford of Maine made this the centerpiece of his remarks, noting that "the country has gone on well for fifty years, under the laws of the states upon this subject, without inconvenience or complaint; and, in my judgment, it would be unwise in interfere."[78] Indiana representative Kennedy agreed that "here is a proposition to commence the exercise of a power by this Government, which, if it possesses the power at all, it is admitted has never been exercised, but has lain dormant for the entire period of our national existence." Anticipating this line of argument, Pennsylvania Whig George Summers cautioned against excessive deference to practice, arguing that "fifty years of past experience in the workings of the government" point to the advantages of a uniform system of House elections, and that it "is also apparent that this uniformity cannot be brought about by the actions of the states themselves."[79] The value of experience is that it brings a certain level of maturation, and with this comes the ability to adjust within the constitutional framework to improve political processes. Representative Summers's observation that the states cannot bring themselves to change electoral systems anticipated the future problem of malapportionment that ultimately led to court intervention in the 1960s.

Representative Samuel Butler of South Carolina eventually expressed exasperation with the niceties of constitutional questions, the exponents of which "very learnedly . . . convince us that four and four did not make eight."[80] He, and especially his Senate colleagues, began directing their remarks to the quality of democratic representation. In this regard, Whigs primarily spoke to three considerations: the purpose of the House of Representatives, the importance of a close connection between constituents and representatives, and the protection of political minorities, all of which, they argued, are enhanced by the single-member district system. These questions, especially those regarding the purpose of the House, elicited considerable interest in the Senate, where general ticket election was understood to foster the representation of state corporate interests, traditionally the purpose of the upper chamber. Senator John Crittenden, a Kentucky Whig, laid out the differences between the House and the Senate. The Senate, he stated, "should . . . represent the states in their sovereign capacity . . . the other branch was to represent the people—in other words there was to be a popular branch and a state branch."[81] Crittenden continued, "What will be the effect if every state shall elect its members to the House of Representatives by general ticket? Will not the representatives in both branches, be converted into representatives of the states?"[82] Representative Daniel Barnard of New York was more succinct: if the House was elected by general ticket then the national government would be nothing more than "a congress of ambassadors or ministers from sovereign powers."[83] This argument resonated in the Senate, where members were interested in safeguarding their prerogatives as spokesmen for the states in the national legislature.

Many Whigs thought that the relationship between constituents and representatives was strengthened by the single-member district system and irrevocably compromised by the general ticket. South Carolina Representative Sampson Butler exemplified this perspective by claiming, "The honest yeomanry of the country wish to know the men who seek their political confidence; and judge for themselves, and not through another, what are their qualifications. The district system affords this opportunity . . . it is the only plan by which the candidate for political favor must stand or fall—upon his own merits."[84] This was especially thought true in the new party era in which state party leaders controlled candidates' access to the general ticket and one could not run without "the endorsement of a partisan nomination." Likewise, Representative Summers argued that "the delegation . . . elected by the people, allotted into districts, come here representing the opinions of the constituency which sends them" and "the "essential feature . . . of

THE JACKSONIAN-WHIG ERA AND THE 1842 SMD MANDATE   131

representative democracy is, that the representatives shall reflect the will and know the wants of his constituents. He should live among them, be familiar with their condition, and hold with them a common political interest."[85] For Butler and Summers, single-member district elections created an intimacy between representatives and their constituents unattainable in party lists. Others argued that the district system better captured the political views and values of citizens. For example, Illinois representative McReynolds, who earlier spoke to the ratio question, endorsed districts on the grounds that "sentiments of the people will be more purely represented than by any other mode."[86] The common thread in all these remarks is that only the SMD system allows for significant familiarity and connection between representatives and constituents.

To the Whigs, the most important feature of single-member district elections was that this system protects political minorities. Connecticut senator Huntington contributed as much as anyone on this point, and his remarks reflected the sentiments of his fellow Whigs. For Huntington, "It needs no argument to prove the importance of minorities to the preservation of public liberty, and the equitable administration of government. They have rights too, which ought to be protected." Further, political minorities "ought to be fully represented, and they cannot and will not be so represented, except the election be by districts."[87] Huntington similarly argued that "the great and important benefit" that comes from the district system would be to protect minority voices otherwise lost under the general ticket. For Huntington, political minorities were a conservative power that is "watchful in their supervision of the acts and conduct of the majority. They examine carefully the measures which are proposed, and are the first to sound the note of alarm, if they perceive anything they deem injurious to national interests. They are vigilant to see that majorities are just and . . . keep themselves . . . within the limits of the constitution."[88] Huntington's belief that political minorities are a "conservative power" points to the principle that not only do political minorities provide an alternative voice in the legislative process, but in a system of dispersed political power and checks minorities often slow tyrannical majorities. As far as Senate Whigs were concerned, the single-member district system was a key institutional protection against tyranny by the majority.

Legislative action on the bill took place between early May and the middle of June. Over twenty House of Representatives votes were held on various aspects of the bill, including a concluding voice vote on the final passage.

Table 5.1. May 3rd Vote to Increase Ratio from 50,179 to 70,680

	Yes	No	
Whig	54	59	113
Democrat	21	63	84
	75	122	197

Note: Excludes two independents.
Source: Howard L. Rosenthal and Keith T. Poole, *United States Congressional Roll Call Voting Records, 1789–1990*.

Despite this, five key House of Representatives roll-call votes captured the most important aspects of legislator positions on the Apportionment Act.[89] I focus on House votes simply because only this chamber contained sufficient membership to assess patterns and trends in the support of and opposition to various aspects of the Apportionment Act. In the much smaller Senate, every individual vote of interest has a name and a relatively unique story attached to it. Three of the House votes occurred on May 3, 1842. The first was a motion to adopt a ratio of 70,680 versus 50,179.[90] The second was a motion to adopt a ratio of 68,000 again relative to 50,179. The third and most significant vote of the day was on the district amendment. This passed with a razor-thin margin of 101 to 99.[91] The final votes of significance occurred on June 17, when the Senate returned the bill to the House with a ratio of 70,680 and the previously agreed-to districting mandate. The first of these was a reconsideration of the 70,680 ratio relative to 50,179. The second and most important vote was on a motion to table the bill containing both the larger ratio and the districting requirement. This vote was effectively a vote on the entire bill because if the table motion failed the bill's passage was assured. It did fail by 95 to 111, clearing the way for the voice vote on the final passage.[92]

Table 5.2. May 3rd Vote to Increase Ratio from 50,179 to 68,000

	Yes	No	
Whig	70	47	117
Democrat	53	30	83
	123	77	200

Note: Excludes two independents.
Source: Howard L. Rosenthal and Keith T. Poole, *United States Congressional Roll Call Voting Records, 1789–1990*.

On May 3rd the first motion to increase the ratio to 70,680 was defeated 122 to 75; the second motion to adopt a ratio of 50,179 was approved 123 to 77.[93] The House voted to maintain the practice of increasing its size to keep pace with population growth. Tables 5.1 and 5.2 present simple two-by-two relationships between party affiliations—each excluding two independents—and these votes.

Together these votes reveal a core group of legislators that sought a large assembly by supporting the 50,179 ratio in both votes and another group of legislators that supported a smaller House by voting "yes" on the first question and "no" on the second. These legislators are easy enough to identify. Fifty-six representatives consistently supported a smaller chamber, and a group of 103 voted both times for a larger chamber. As one might expect, there were more Whigs in the former group, while the latter group was roughly evenly divided between Democrats and Whigs. Southerners were represented only slightly better in the smaller assembly group than one might expect from the overall membership in the chamber. At least in early May, differences on the issue of chamber size were structured by party but not overwhelmingly.

Explaining representatives' votes on districting is simple: almost all Whigs supported it and almost all Democrats opposed it. As table 5.3 shows, only eighteen Whigs opposed the single-member district mandate and only two Democrats supported it. There was relatively little commonality among the opposing Whig representatives to suggest a systematic basis for their objections.[94] Just over half were Southerners, but four of these were Georgians placed in a position of voting against their own state's electoral system.

The May votes present a reasonably clear picture of the House of Representatives prior to the final vote on the Apportionment Act. Most importantly, they show that the relevant story on chamber size was not so much

Table 5.3. May 3rd Vote to Require District Election

	Yes	No	
Whig	98	18	116
Democrat	2	80	82
	100	98	198

Note: Excludes two nonaffiliated.
Source: Howard L. Rosenthal and Keith T. Poole, *United States Congressional Roll Call Voting Records, 1789–1990.*

Table 5.4. June 17th Vote on Ratio 70,680 vs. 50,179

	Yes	No	
Whig	73	52	125
Democrat	38	52	90
	111	104	215

Note: Excludes two nonaffiliated.
Source: Howard L. Rosenthal and Keith T. Poole, *United States Congressional Roll Call Voting Records, 1789–1990.*

Whig support for reducing the size of the chamber as it was Democratic support for increasing it. In May the Whigs were fairly ambivalent about the size of the chamber. Most Whigs supported a ratio of approximately 50,000, with over half voting for the significantly larger House that came with it. Democratic support for the larger house was even stronger. At this point the Whigs were not so much united for a smaller chamber as the Democrats were for a larger chamber. However, districting clearly and sharply divided the parties. For representatives of both parties, support or opposition to the final bill depended most heavily on how representatives weighed the final ratio relative to districting. If only a few Whigs who sided with Democrats for a larger chamber considered this more important than the district mandate the bill would fail; if enough Democrats supported the district mandate the bill would pass.

The question was brought to a head on June 17 when the Senate returned its final version of the bill to the House with a ratio of 70,680 and the district requirement. This ratio reduced the House to 221 members, a difference of 82 representatives relative to the alternative ratio of 50,179. An affirmative vote to accept the bill would significantly change the House of Representatives, its selection, and the balance of federal and state authority in the conduct of elections. Table 5.4 details the vote on the ratio. It clearly shows that both Democrats and Whigs split significantly over the question of chamber size. The larger ratio was sustained, but about 40 percent of each party's members defected from their copartisans. Table 5.5 details the final roll call vote on the act, a motion to table the bill with both the higher ratio and the districting mandate. A "no" vote on the motion supported the bill while a "yes" vote opposed it. The table shows that support for the Apportionment Act was clearly structured along party lines. Only about one-fifth of all Whigs voted against the bill, and only a handful of Democrats supported it.

The received wisdom is that the Apportionment Act was a Whig party

Table 5.5. June 17th Vote to Table the Apportionment Act

	Yes	No	
Whig	24	98	122
Democrat	70	12	82
	94	110	204

Note: Excludes two independents.
Source: Howard L. Rosenthal and Keith T. Poole, *United States Congressional Roll Call Voting Records, 1789–1990.*

reform advocated most forcefully by southern Whigs. The sectional interpretation of the bill probably dates to early June, when Missouri senator
Thomas Hart Benton wrote to Martin Van Buren lamenting that the two
"movements which have made such discussion, are from the South; that
is to say, districting the States for election to the H. R. and reducing the
numbers of the H. R. These are aimed against the populous States which
are the non-slaveholding."[95] Setting aside that the districting amendment
was brought forward by a representative from New Jersey, contemporary
scholars agree. This is perfectly reasonable. Many of the principal speakers
for the bill were Southerners. However, this emphasis on sectionalism reveals a puzzle. In arguing for the act, "southerners made no overt appeals to
regional interests and their language was not sectional."[96] Southern Whigs,
like other representatives, argued for congressional and electoral reform by
appeal to the founding, not by appeal to regional interests. Further, there are
no obvious sectional grounds that explain why Southerners would strongly
support it. Their support probably reflected political conservatism; as Shields
describes it, "a pronounced commitment to eighteenth century values."[97] If
so, then there was no shortage of New Englanders and Midwesterners who
shared the same conservatism. Perhaps, as Benton suggests, districts were
more amenable to slaveholding interests. Perhaps, but Alabama governor
Bagby's advocacy of the general ticket makes this seem unlikely.

I clarify the bases for the bill's support by presenting two simple logistic
regressions of legislator votes on the bill. The first is the final vote on the
ratio. Here a "yes" vote supports the adoption of the 70,680 ratio and reduction of the chamber size. The second is on the motion to table the final
bill. A "no" vote accepts the bill with the 70,860 ratio and the districting
requirement. In table 5.6 I model these votes as a function of legislator
partisanship, whether he represented a southern state, whether the representative's state used the general ticket, and what his state's population was

Table 5.6. Regression Analysis of Votes on Chamber Size and Final Bill

Variable	Coefficient (rse)	
	Smaller Chamber	Table Final Bill
Constant	.09	0.98*
	(0.42)	(0.59)
Whig	0.75**	−3.09***
	(0.31)	(0.39)
South	1.05***	−0.05
	(0.38)	(0.43)
General Ticket State	.01	1.21**
	(0.50)	(0.56)
Population/100,000	−0.06***	0.05*
	(0.02)	(0.03)
N	215	204
LLF	−133.69	−91.84

Note: Logistic regression with robust standard errors. Dependent variable: Vote 1 on June 17 motion to adopt ratio of 70,680 instead of 50,179 (yes = 1, no = 0). Vote 2 on June 17 motion to table the final bill (yes = 1, no = 0). Robust standard errors in parentheses. *p < 0.1, **p < 0.05, ***p < 0.01.
Source: Howard L. Rosenthal and Keith T. Poole, *United States Congressional Roll Call Voting Records, 1789–1990.*

in 1840. The regression captures the differences in support of the smaller chamber and support for the overall bill. Whigs and Southerners supported the smaller chamber, while those from larger states did not. However, once the larger ratio is bundled with the districting requirement things change significantly. Partisanship becomes a much stronger predictor of the vote, and once one controls for whether the representative's state used the general ticket regional differences disappear. Finally, representatives from larger states were slightly less likely to support the act, but the influence of state size is minimal. Fundamentally, the second regression tells us little more than the corresponding two-by-two table except that controls for partisanship and whether the representative's state used the general ticket dissipates the effect of regional affiliation on the bill's outcome.

These regressions show that when push came to shove Whigs who preferred a larger chamber sacrificed this objective in favor of the far more important single-member district mandate. While it is true that most Whigs preferred both the smaller chamber and the SMD requirement, not enough representatives fell in this category to assure the bill's passage. A net shift of only nine votes on the table motion would have undoubtedly sunk the

Apportionment Act. The only feasible remedy for the Whigs would have been to placate recalcitrant Whigs with a larger chamber in order to preserve the more important districting requirement. In all likelihood such a shift would also have brought along many Democrats in support of the bill. Democratic constitutional objections notwithstanding, most Democrats preferred both a larger chamber and single-member district election, and would have set aside their constitutional scruples to achieve a chamber closer to the Anti-Federalist ideal. As it turned out, by the thinnest of margins none of this was necessary.

At the end of the day the primary explanation for the adoption of the single-member district mandate and the smaller chamber was Whig ideology, which valued the characteristics of an older understanding of the purpose of the House of Representatives and proper representation. The Whigs embraced the Federalist vision, and in 1842 had the political strength to implement it. The Democrats, like the Anti-Federalists in 1788, were not numerous or persuasive enough to change the ultimate outcome. That said, like the Federalist and Anti-Federalist debates of 1788, the Whigs and Democrats articulated distinct visions of the purpose of the House of Representatives and how best to populate it. For the Democrats the action was in the ratio. If the chamber was large enough then their primary objective was likely to be achieved, although district elections would enhance this likelihood. For the Whigs the chamber had to be small, be insulated from both internal and popular passions, and reserve a place for political minorities. This could be achieved only by a larger ratio and the single-member district mandate.

Conclusion

The drama of the Apportionment Act of 1842 did not end with these votes. On June 25 President Tyler notified Congress that he had signed the bill, but sent to Secretary of State Daniel Webster a list of his concerns about the bill to be filed in the Department of State. Tyler's was only the second presidential signing statement in history and the first one of any consequence. In it President Tyler explained that he signed the bill despite his concern about the constitutionality of the single-member district mandate. Unfortunately for President Tyler, and perhaps also for more than a few members of the House of Representatives, former president John Quincy Adams sat in the Twenty-Seventh Congress as a representative from Massachusetts. Adams took great exception to the signing statement. In principle, Adams informed the chamber that the statement by the president "approved" the bill but "destroyed the efficacy" of the act by issuing a "veto under a mask."[98] While Adams's anger over the signing statement was not widely shared by his House colleagues, he made an important point. By questioning the act's constitutionality, President Tyler opened the door to states ignoring the districting requirement on the grounds that the national government was divided on its application. The signing statement also raised the question of why the president of the United States would sign into law an act he found potentially unconstitutional. Indeed, the first presidential veto in United States history issued by George Washington was applied to the first postfounding apportionment act that implemented a formula President Washington thought unconstitutional. If President Tyler found the act questionable, then precedent recommended that he veto it rather than "attach his opinion to it."

In fact, the single-member district was not implemented by four states when they elected delegations to the Twenty-eighth Congress. This required the House to reopen the question, this time focusing on its Article 1, Section 5, authority to determine the qualifications of representatives to be seated in the chamber. The House was the final judge of the election of its membership. Despite strenuous objections from Whigs, the issue was never in doubt. The Democrats had retaken control of the chamber and voted to seat the representatives elected by general ticket. The decision to seat these representatives is best viewed as a one-time response to circumstance, and by the Thirtieth Congress all states routinely elected their representatives through single-member-district election. This became the governing rule for House elections throughout most of the balance of the nineteenth century and all of the twentieth century.

If the Apportionment Act of 1842 had simply codified existing practices in the states, then its significance would be greatly lessened, but it did not do this. It represented a wholesale establishment by law of certain principles, including that the House should be a deliberative forum for the articulation and scrutiny of ideas, the protection and representation of political minorities is a worthy and important objective, and that constituencies in the United States are defined geographically. These legislative foundations are inseparable, and in 1842 Congress decided to legislate these principles. The bill became the template for every subsequent apportionment in US history. Still, codification does not equal institutionalization. The question of districting would be revisited throughout the middle part of the nineteenth century, and once again came under scrutiny in the Progressive Era of the late nineteenth and early twentieth centuries. That said, once states districted, these practices remained in place and were only breeched temporarily, and then only under extraordinary circumstances. The ideas that recommended the districting mandate planted during the founding further established themselves in the American political mind and would never be excised.

Evidence of how clearly these ideas resonated with Americans is exemplified by how little public reaction there was to the Apportionment Act. No Democratic politician could gain political traction by railing against the Whig imposition of the single-member district system. The rapid universal adoption of the SMD system after 1842 provides testimony to the fact that constitutional objections to the act carried less weight than the idea that representatives would be drawn from local constituencies, even if these were significantly larger than those in the 1830s. This also partially reflects the new era of political parties, with voters keenly aware that congressional politics, especially in the House of Representatives, would be structured along party lines, and the Whig vision of insulated, deliberating trustees was a quaint remembrance of days gone by. In this light, the districting requirement resonated positively with citizens because it decentralized party control of representatives from the statehouse to the county courthouse. Party leaders would still control nomination and access to office, but these party leaders would now be local and accessible.

Of course, the Apportionment Act did not emerge in a political vacuum. The volatile and uncertain electoral world of the 1830s and 1840s brought the issue of electoral systems to the forefront of political debate in a way that did not occur in the early part of the nineteenth century. This uncertainty, combined with the rise of party politics and the realization that these rules could be imposed and modified for political gain, encouraged the Whigs to prioritize this legislation in the Twenty-Seventh Congress. It is important to appreciate the effect of mass enfranchisement and electoral volatility on the political contest for adoption and imposition of electoral processes. Electoral systems are not debated or changed in periods of political quiescence.

The ideas brought forward in the Apportionment Act debates in conjunction with the single-member district fostering decentralized party control of congressional elections helps explain one of the great mysteries of electoral reform in the post–Civil War era. The Progressives of the late nineteenth and early twentieth centuries devoted considerable effort to changing election practices in the United States. They brought about the secret ballot, the direct primary, voter registration, the direct election of US senators, and many other reforms. However, they never seriously challenged the single-member district system even when the principles of proportional representation were widely understood. Indeed, when the Progressives championed election reforms in city elections they did so by creating ward-based elections, which are a type of single-member district. While many Progressives opposed the SMD system, most were more ambivalent about it, and the weight of their rhetoric and reforms ultimately strengthened rather than weakened the SMD system. The following chapter explores these ideas in greater detail.

6 The Progressive Era: Consolidation and Institutionalization, 1870–1930

> The best that can be said on behalf of this traditional American system of political ideals is that it contained the germ of better things.
>
> Herbert Croly, The Promise of American Life[1]

> Of course we all believe in equal representation, but we do not all believe in adequate representation. These whispered mutterings and Solomonic expressions, accompanied by sagacious looks and suggestions of a lofty patriotic purpose . . . in good, plain, unadulterated American, is the bunk.
>
> Louisiana representative James O'Connor, in the 1928–1929 apportionment and districting debates, January 10, 1929

If Herbert Croly were alive today he would be chagrinned. On the one hand, most Americans—including many who carry copies of the constitution in their breast pocket—embrace his vision. Croly's ideal of an American political system predicated on plebiscitary politics where citizens and officeholders enjoy direct connection only modestly mediated by political parties or other institutions is the one in which we live. On the other hand, several of the reforms he championed initiated a wholesale weakening of political parties and the subsequent rise of candidate-centered, rather than party-centered, politics. The damage this did to the quality of American democratic governance is probably incalculable. Our purpose here is not to provide a complete accounting of the Progressive Era reforms but rather the narrower task of better understanding why, despite the Populist and Progressive successes in changing virtually every other election practice, the SMD system solidified and institutionalized in these years.

The great question of the Progressive Era and the Populist Era before it is why the single-member district system emerged unscathed and indeed strengthened. Almost every electoral practice was on the table for change. Despite this the House single-member district system was not challenged in any serious way. Further, unlike in the nation's early years, the alternatives to SMD election were well known. Thomas Hare's 1859 masterwork *A Treatise on the Election of Representatives, Parliamentary and Municipal* detailing the cumulative and single-transferable vote systems was widely read on this side of the Atlantic, as was John Stuart Mill's advocacy of proportional representation in *Considerations on Representative Government*.[2] Proportional representation societies emerged, debates were held, and some municipalities briefly adopted the proportional single-transferable or cumulative vote systems to elect their councils. However, these were the exceptions; the SMD system for House elections entrenched in this period.

Pennsylvania senator Charles R. Buckalew was the nation's most important early advocate for proportional representation. Buckalew introduced legislation in 1867 and 1869 mandating the use of cumulative voting in House of Representatives elections.[3] The first of these efforts was a proposed amendment to a reconstruction bill that would require Southern states to use cumulative voting upon their readmission to the Union. In 1869 he introduced a bill mandating it nationally.[4] The 1867 amendment was defeated on a procedural vote, and the 1869 bill never received a chamber vote. However, Buckalew inserted into the *Congressional Globe* his "Report on Representational Reform," which argued for proportional representation in the United States.[5] This seminal tract motivated and informed period works on proportional representation, including Simon Stern's influential *On Representative Government and Personal Representation*, which adapted Thomas Hare's treatise for an American audience.[6] That a US senator was prepared to advocate proportional representation in the immediate post–Civil War period demonstrates that the idea captured the imagination of at least some political elites.

That said, it is far too easy to overemphasize period support for proportional representation (PR). Contemporary proponents of proportional election methods sometimes point to the limited and episodic interest in single-transferable or cumulative vote processes as evidence that the Progressives and their predecessors embraced these systems. For example,

Robert Richie, director of Fairvote, an advocacy group devoted to United States electoral reform, and political scientist coauthor Steven Hill point to the "rich history" of "efforts to bring PR to American elections."[7] Likewise, Kathleen Barber contributes much to our understanding of the application of proportional systems in municipal elections, especially in Ohio, during the Progressive Era. However, these were anomalous and often ineffective advocacies for proportional elections, not the main thrust of political current. There is a natural tendency to attach undue importance to the unusual, as reflected in Barber's second chapter, titled "The Progressive Crusade for Proportional Representation," which most definitely there was not.[8] This mistakes the anomalies for the pattern, and in the process emphasizes the exceptional while discounting the major and unexceptional.

There were certainly *attempts* to bring proportional representation to American elections. One vehicle for doing so was a state constitutional amendment mandating the use of proportional methods to elect various state offices. Some of these movements were successful; more often, as in the Oregon case discussed later in the chapter, they were not.[9] Still, the closest the United States came to proportional representation was limited municipal application of at-large list proportional representation and singe-transferable vote and the use of fusion ballots. Fusion or cross-endorsement balloting is not proportional representation, but rather is an election method beneficial to minor parties in which a candidate has his or her name attached to two or more party labels. This system was fairly common in the late nineteenth century, and many of the third-party candidates elected to the House and state legislatures obtained office in this manner.[10] This practice was largely eliminated with the introduction of the secret ballot in the 1890s and never regained widespread favor.[11] As physicians are inclined to say, when one hears hoofbeats think of horses, not zebras. Highlighting a relatively few and short-lived adoptions and attempted adoptions of proportional election systems in an era when the SMD system for House elections consolidated overemphasizes zebras and underemphasizes horses.

The period between the late nineteenth and the early twentieth centuries presents two distinct electoral epochs. Its early years witnessed vigorous and closely contested elections for federal office and the most partisan and engaged electorate in US history. The period was anything but quiescent as reflected in "bloody shirt" politics, torchlight parades, and two presidential assassinations.[12] The 1868 passage of the Fourteenth Amendment counted

African Americans as whole persons for the purposes of apportionment, rather than three-fifths of a person as under the original Constitution, with significant implications for apportionment and districting. In the era's latter years women received universal suffrage, the modern regulatory structure for elections was established, and vigorous party competition and voter turnout collapsed. The House single-member district election system became routinized in these decades and its use largely unquestioned.

There are three primary considerations that help us understand why the single-member district system for House elections solidified in this period. The first is differences between Progressive Era political thought and the traditional American ideals of republican governance. As the Herbert Croly quote that opens this chapter suggests, the Progressives had no theory of republican government consonant with the American experience so could not present a compelling argument about the purpose of a representative assembly and how to best elect it. The Progressives sought to make our political system more "democratic" by increasing the avenues for direct citizen participation in electoral governance, but this left them foundering when it came to articulating a vision of the House of Representatives and how to properly staff it. Ideas and intellectual context matter greatly in shaping political institutions and processes, and nowhere is this more evident than in the Progressive Era, when those advocating changes in most established American electoral practices had little to say about the House of Representatives and its election. In addition, the traditional American preference for territorial representation became especially salient in this era. In particular, rural constituencies saw territorial representation combined with the SMD system as their best protection against the growing political power of the urban centers. Finally, the extraordinarily competitive nature of party politics in the first part of the era motivated the consolidation of the safer and more predictable SMD system. Indeed, American politics was party politics, and the old questions about state corporate interest—indeed even the concept of state corporate interest itself—faded into the background. These ideas help explain why Congress never seriously questioned the single-member district election mandate and, indeed, strengthened it by promulgating the modern standards that legislative districts should be contiguous, be compact, and contain equal population.

The chapter's next section documents the consolidation of the SMD system in the latter half of the nineteenth century and the first part of the twentieth century. It first discusses the succession of apportionment acts between 1872 and 1911 that reiterated the single-member district mandate and also codified the normative standards for districting. It was in these years that Congress formally required that House districts be contiguous, be compact, and contain approximately equal population. These principles are commonly invoked as bases for proper districting, and it is instructive to understand how Congress came to legislate these standards and their application in practice. The section then documents how completely SMD elections became the established way to elect the House of Representatives. Following this, the chapter argues that Progressive thought offered no viable alternatives to the SMD system and that the very competitive party politics of the period provided political incentives to maintain the SMD system. The chapter's fourth section details the apportionment process in the 1920s. Congress failed to pass an apportionment act following the 1920 census. Simply, Congress could not reapportion itself because the census so clearly documented the nation's urbanization that the states that stood to lose representatives effectively blocked all legislation. This log jam was cleared in 1929 with the passage of a permanent apportionment act that established a House membership of 435, transferred the apportionment process itself to the executive branch, and included a districting mandate that purposefully rescinded the compact, contiguous, and equal-population requirements of previous legislation.[13] The chapter concludes by pointing to how the politics surrounding the 1920s apportionment process made possible the malapportionment and districting problems faced by the states in the post–World War II era that ultimately led to court intervention in the 1960s.

Consolidation of the SMD System, 1870 to 1920

Compact, Contiguous, and Equal Population

At the end of Reconstruction states elected their representatives under the Apportionment Act of 1872. This act established a chamber membership of 283 and mandated that representatives be elected from "districts composed of contiguous territory, and containing as nearly as practicable an equal number of inhabitants." While equal population had long been stipulated as a goal in districting, its legal requirement was novel, as was the act's stipulation that "the Tuesday after the first Monday in November, in every second year thereafter, is hereby fixed and established as the day for election."[14] The act also explicitly prohibited multimember districts.[15] However, states that saw an increase in their House delegation could elect these additional representatives at large. This ensured that states with legislatures that would not meet before the next congressional session could elect their existing representatives from established districts and any additional representatives at large.[16] Several states exercised this prerogative. For example, Kansas elected three representatives to the Forty-Eighth Congress from single-member districts and four representatives at large. California elected two of its six representatives at large. Other states including New York, Virginia, and Georgia also selected one representative at-large. The districting language of the Apportionment Act of 1872 was carried nearly verbatim into the Apportionment Acts of 1882, 1891, 1901, and 1911, which increased the size of the House to 325, 356, 386, and 435 respectively.[17] The 1901 and 1911 acts added "compact" to these requirements, meaning districts had to look more like squares, circles, and rectangles rather than horseshoes, stars, and salamanders.

These five decades are especially important in the political history of electing United States representatives. First, unlike in 1842, the post–Civil War debates over the various apportionment acts reveal few if any serious objections to Congress specifying the method and timing of House elections. The national government was broadly recognized as having significant authority over federal elections. Congress's power to regulate "the time, place and manner" of House elections was no longer questioned. The major issue of political contention was the apportionment itself, not how the apportioned representatives were elected. Members of Congress divided over the arithmetic formulas to determine state apportionment, whether to require that new states have population equal to the apportionment ratio before admission to the Union, and whether to apply the Fourteenth Amendment's stipulation that a state's apportionment population be reduced if it denies full franchise to adult men.[18]

In these decades Congress articulated clear normative standards for drawing single-member districts. Congress codified the principle that House districts should be contiguous, be compact, and contain roughly equal population. Not that these principles were unknown prior to the late nineteenth century or subsequently taken as gospel by the state legislatures responsible for districting, but now Congress formally gave these standards its imprimatur. As a consequence, the burden of justifying their abridgement became increasingly difficult. Further, these standards required legislators to wrestle with the nuances of their application in practice. Strict adherence to the compact and equal population strictures, in particular, is difficult. Creating districts of equal population necessarily involves ignoring corporate boundaries such as county lines in drawing districts, or breaking cities into multiple districts with district boundaries sometimes dividing established neighborhoods or other "communities of interest." Equal population also necessitated that some congressional districts, especially in the western states, would be geographically immense. Finally, codification invited the participation of the judiciary in the resolution of disputes over districting.

That said, adoption of these standards proceeded without significant controversy. The equal-population requirement was rarely challenged in principle; rather, the very few objections to it centered on preserving state flexibility to district in anticipation of population shifts in the intercensus period. For example, in 1871, Michigan representative Stoughton opposed this requirement for "the very obvious reason that the northern [Michigan] districts will increase [in population] very rapidly, while the southern districts will have but a small increase in population. In order to get a fair average during the decade a discrimination must be made."[19] In other words, the southern Michigan districts should have greater population than the northern districts because population migration will gravitate toward the latter following districting. Nobody advanced explicit or implicit normative arguments against equal representation in principle as would occur in the 1920s.

Nor did the territorial implications of equal district population raise significant concerns for representatives and senators. Equal population necessarily means that districts will differ in geographic size; some will be small and some will be large. However, the speakers to this issue emphasized that this potential problem was mitigated by the era's extraordinary advances in transportation and communication technology. Representative Clarkson Potter (D-NY) observed in 1871 that "such is the condition of the country, such are the facilities of communication by railway and telegraph, and generally the various means of intercommunication now existing have become so developed, that a representative can closely represent a district containing two hundred thousand people, and maintain general and constant communication with his constituents, with far more ease than was the case when the Government was established and the constituency was but thirty thousand."[20] When representatives could travel upward of thirty miles per hour and communicate telegraphically with constituents in distant towns, concerns about the territorial extent of the district were greatly diminished.

The compactness standard is easily the most complicated districting requirement, and it is this requirement that most interested both period and contemporary observers of United States elections. This requirement, added in 1901, was easy to motivate in theory but difficult to implement in practice. This tension that shapes all contemporary debates about districting was nicely captured in an exchange between representatives John F. Rixey (D-VA) and Theodore F. Kluttz (D-NC), member of the Committee on the Census that drafted the apportionment bill:[21]

> Mr. Rixey: The words "and compact" seem to be added to this apportionment bill for the first time in the history of apportionment . . . [the bill] now provides that the territory should be "contiguous and compact." Now, what I want to know is, who is to be the judge as to when districts are sufficiently compact?
>
> Mr. Kluttz: When the committee discussed it, I will say that word "compact" was added . . . to prevent shoe-string districts; but it will raise hereafter the question which the gentleman now suggests, as to what is to be the determining authority of the meaning of that word "compact," and as to whether certain territory is or not compact.

The purpose of compactness is to prevent gerrymandering or the creation of "shoe-string" districts. However, as Representative Kluttz concedes, there is no bright-line test for determining the extent to which a district drawn into a "shoe-string" shape violates the compactness principle. It is a matter of degree. Also, adhering to a rigid compactness standard often conflicts with the attainment of other objectives such as preserving "communities of interest." Further, as the exchange makes clear, Congress itself was unsure where the authority resides to determine whether a district is or is not compact. The House of Representatives may have claim to this authority under its Article 1, Section 5, power to be the "judge of the elections" of its members, or the authority might properly reside in the courts.

The Shift in Governing Authority

Congressional action on House elections between 1870 and 1911 presents a clear and strikingly different picture from similar debates in the antebellum period. Little in the *Congressional Globe* and *Congressional Record* suggests that members questioned the right of the national government to regulate federal elections in general, and direct the states to elect their representatives from single-member districts in particular. Instead Congress seamlessly assumed this power. There was significant partisan division over the apportionment acts themselves, but these centered on the consequences of the various apportionment formulas for the party composition of the chamber. In the main, the SMD requirement and the normative standards districts should meet were widely accepted by members of Congress and implemented into the various acts. The United States appeared to reach a consensus, albeit a temporary consensus, on how to best elect representatives.

The thirty or so years following Reconstruction saw the wholesale adoption of the SMD system in accordance with federally promulgated law. No representative or senator raised significant objection either to the power exerted by the Congress or to the requirement of SMD election. The question is why. The answer is provided by the significant shift in national politics in the latter half of the nineteenth century, a change that was foreshadowed by the muted reaction to the districting mandate of the 1842 Apportionment Act. The new political era was organized around party politics, not state corporate interests. Party interest replaced state interest. This is not to suggest that the parties were especially programmatic in these years. They were not, in part because the government did not yet fulfill many of the responsibilities that motivate programmatic political parties. Nonetheless, parties and partisanship mattered greatly as a means of social and political organization, and the extraordinary close balance between the parties in national politics reinforced the SMD mandate. In particular, even though the elections were less volatile than in the 1840s, the partisan balance was significantly tauter.

In this period the states used the SMD system and rarely deviated from it. When a state deviated from SMD election it almost always followed an increase in apportionment after the decennial census. In this situation some states retained their existing House districts and elected the additional representatives at-large. To give some idea of how stable the era was, consider how Arkansas elected its representatives from the Forty-Seventh Congress, meeting in 1881, to the Fiftieth Congress, which convened in 1887. Arkansas elected its four-member delegation to the Forty-Seventh Congress from single-member districts. Following the 1881 reapportionment Arkansas received one additional representative, which it elected at large, with its remaining four representatives elected from the existing districts. Arkansas then redistricted and elected all five of its representatives to the Forty-Ninth and Fiftieth Congresses from newly drawn single-member districts. There are two changes in the Arkansas electoral system in this period: the first is from SMD election to SMD and at large, and the second is the subsequent

Table 6.1. Arkansas Election System Changes, Forty-Seventh through Fiftieth Congresses

	Forty-Seventh Congress	Forty-Eighth Congress	Forty-Ninth Congress	Fiftieth Congress
Arkansas	SMD	SMD-AL1	SMD	SMD

Source: Kenneth C. Martis, *The Historical Atlas of United States Congressional Districts: 1789–1983.*

return to SMD election. Visually, one might represent this in a four-cell matrix with these two changes highlighted.

If one considers all states and all election cycles between 1870 and 1928, there are 938 such cells.[22] Of these 55, or roughly 5 percent, capture changes in electoral systems, but almost all of these changes occurred following a reapportionment when the size of a state's congressional delegation increased and the additional representatives were elected at large. The balance were changes from SMD combined with at-large election back to SMD. More importantly, of the 938 state elections, over 90 percent, 846 to be exact, were conducted under the SMD rule. An additional 60 were conducted under a combination of SMD and at-large elections. By the time the Fiftieth Congress convened in 1887 only one representative out of 325 members was elected at large from states entitled to two or more representatives. At-large election was increasingly seen as a temporary response to circumstance, and no Congress after this saw more than a small handful of representatives elected at large, and no representatives were selected from multimember constituencies.[23]

The Progressives and Election Methods. This stability belies the extraordinary electoral changes that were imposed in the Populist and Progressive Eras. The period's lasting legacy is a collection of laws that fundamentally and irrevocably changed how elections are contested. Collectively known as the Progressive Reforms, these included the introduction of the secret ballot; the passage of the Seventeenth and Nineteenth Amendments, respectively providing for the direct election of US senators and the enfranchisement of women; primary elections and the introduction of state-level voter registration; initiative, referendum and recall elections; campaign finance regulation; nonpartisan municipal elections; and a host of other laws that structure elections to this day. Indeed, the vast corpus of current laws regulating the electoral activities of political parties, candidates, and citizens dates to these years. The Progressives had a clear political agenda; they sought to reduce the power of political parties, their leaders (or bosses if one prefers the pejorative term), and the economic interests that relied on their political protection. For the Populists and Progressives, "the only proper party was the people themselves; the only valid laws . . . were the people's truths phrased in the people's language."[24]

Perhaps less appealing to modern sensibilities, the Progressives were also deeply apprehensive of citizen engagement in the politics, especially participation by immigrants and African Americans. John R. Commons, a leading Progressive intellectual who strongly advocated abandonment of the single-member district system in favor of proportional representation, writes that a primary problem of early-twentieth-century American democracy is that "not only the original Anglo-Saxon is admitted to the suffrage, but also millions from antagonistic races."[25] For the Progressives, high, broad-based voter turnout was not a sign of a healthy and vibrant democracy so much as it was signal that electoral politics needed to be cooled and managed. They advocated a political process that was nominally more democratic in that citizens could vote more often and on more things, but also one that was more regulated and managed by elites. Voter registration, to illustrate, does not accentuate electoral participation, it detracts from it, and carries with it the need for a registrar of voters, requirements that one must meet to register, and the assumption that one can prove who one claims to be. The last consideration, as we know, carries especially significant implications for contemporary politics.[26]

The Progressives were remarkably successful. Their reforms significantly weakened political parties and with this the ability of parties to organize and contest elections. Control over elections was wrestled from parties and given to individual candidates and state bureaucracies. The consequence was the collapse of voter turnout in the first third of the twentieth century, a decline from which we have never recovered.[27] The average presidential election turnout rate between 1904 and 1932 was a full twenty points lower than it was between the end of Reconstruction and 1900.[28] Today turnout in presidential elections hovers around 60 percent of the voting eligible population, and turnout in off-year congressional elections and state and local elections ranges between low and vanishing. The reforms also increased the power and influence of special interest groups, which increasingly filled the political vacuum left by strong parties. Still, the thrust of the Progressive reforms remains exceedingly popular. Campaign finance regulation, primary elections, state-level initiative and referendum, and similar practices are embedded in our election processes even though election scholars are deeply skeptical about whether these improved United States democracy.[29] Despite these successes, the Progressives never mounted a serious challenge to the single-member district electoral system. Leading Progressive intellectuals such as Herbert Croly, John Dewey, and Charles Beard never advanced convincing intellectual challenges to it, and leading Progressive politicians such as Theodore Roosevelt never challenged it politically.[30]

This is because the Progressives had no theory of representative government consonant with the American political tradition. The Progressives never deeply engaged problems that traditionally occupied Americans, such as how to protect political minorities. Indeed, the protection of political minorities was anathema to many Progressives, as reflected in their advocacy of the initiative and referendum. For the Progressives, representative assemblies and their election were mostly an afterthought since legislative bodies were less important in a political system that centered on a stronger executive, stronger administrative agencies, and, most important, increased reliance on direct citizen input into the political process.

To the extent the Progressives had a theory of representative government, it regarded the constitution and the republican and liberal values it encapsulated as an impediment to achieving desired political objectives. So far as representative institutions are concerned, Robert Wiebe in his classic *The Search for Social Order* correctly emphasizes that the Progressives rejected "the possibility of democracy in any extralegal setting, [they] denied the legitimacy of all formal political structures."[31] For the Progressives legislatures "constituted an artificial barrier between the people and government."[32] If legislatures are an anti-democratic "barrier between the people and government," then devoting intellectual energy to determining their purpose, the qualities that define good representation, and the best way to populate an assembly is a fool's errand.

The Progressives clearly rejected Federalist ideals, but given their emphasis on privileging elites in government, expanding the scope and responsibilities of the national government, "cooling" the political process by direct and indirect barriers to political participation, and, most importantly, restricting the ability of political parties to organize and contest elections, they were hardly more accommodating to the Anti-Federalists or the later Jacksonian Democrats.[33] The upshot was that the Progressives could achieve objectives such as the direct election of senators and primary elections by appeal to our populist impulses, but could not present a cogent or compelling argument about the purpose of a representative assembly or how to elect it.

To convince oneself of this argument consider Herbert Croly's *Progressive Democracy*, which is widely regarded as a masterwork of early-twentieth-century Progressive Era political thought.[34] Here Croly develops a vision of American democracy that rejects constitutionalism and places extraordinary emphasis on public opinion as the guiding force in our government.[35] Croly dismisses exaltation of the Constitution and its associated traditions as "higher law" and instead seeks to give the government "integrity of organization and purpose" by fostering "the ability of the people to achieve some underlying unity of purpose."[36] Doing so requires replacing representation and representative bodies as the primary entry point for citizens into government. Representative bodies, according to Croly, "can hardly be entrusted with complete legal authority over the lives and property of citizens and the policy of the state."[37] Rather, according to Croly, a proper government is a "government by men rather than by law," meaning government by public opinion unconstrained by difficult-to-change laws and constitutional barriers.[38] It's hard to imagine sentiments more at odds with founding ideals, especially Federalist ideals.

The Progressives didn't believe legislatures should be abandoned; rather their importance should be diminished and they should be re-created to better capture the distribution of public opinion to supplement a political system where increased responsibility is conferred on the executive, administrative agencies, and direct citizen input into the political process.[39] The purpose of the legislature is to represent "those minor phases of public opinion which have sufficient energy of conscience to demand some vehicle of expression."[40] Legislators should represent the "minor phases of public opinion," not "districts or organized parties or the public reason or the leadership of any one class."[41] In this view the single-member district system was deficient because it failed to adequately organize the electorate around "salient and significant phases of public opinion," classes, and agitators. To effect such a representation required setting aside of the "method of representation which has passed in this country under the name of representative government."[42] Indeed, for Croly representation was made necessary only by the "primitive" "economic and social conditions" of an eighteenth- and nineteenth-century agrarian society.[43] In creating new forms of representation the maintenance of districts was only a temporary step in the "transition from the old system," and these could be eventually discarded in the expectation that constituencies will self-define themselves around "fundamental economic and social classes" and "agitators in favor of particular reforms."[44]

Croly endorses an election method proposed by the progressive Oregon People's Power League that illustrates election methods proposed in several states and their reception by the public.[45] The Oregon proposal divided the state into multimember districts with district representation proportional to population. Candidates had to affiliate with and reside in a specific district, but citizens were allowed to vote for a candidate in any district. Each citizen received a single vote. There would be no cumulation or vote transfers based on preference orders. The effect of this system would be to significantly lower the vote threshold for election. For example, a candidate receiving about one-sixteenth of the statewide vote would be elected. Since citizens might vote for a candidate in any district, political minorities, if able to coordinate, could concentrate their voting strength on one or a few candidates and be reasonably assured of their election to office.[46]

The Oregon example is instructive because it illustrates the short life cycle of attempts to introduce proportional election methods in the era. Interest in proportional representation gained traction in Oregon in the early century, and in 1908 the state approved a citizen-initiated constitutional amendment allowing, but not requiring, the state legislature to implement alternative state house election methods. At that time Oregon state representatives were elected from multimember districts where citizens cast a single vote and the top "n" vote recipients were elected where "n" is the number of district representatives. The 1908 measure identified instant runoff voting and proportional representation as possible alternative ways to elect representatives.[47] The legislature, however, retained the existing election system and in 1910 referred to voters a proposal to mandate single-member district elections. Simultaneously the People's Power League advanced an initiative that would have required election of the Oregon House of Representatives by proportional representation. Voters defeated both measures, leaving the status quo in place.[48] In 1912 the People's Power League reintroduced a ballot proposal for proportional representation coupled with abolition of the state senate.[49] This was resoundingly defeated, so in 1914 the Progressives separated the senate and proportional election questions. Both proposals were again soundly defeated, with the proportional representation mandate securing well under a quarter of the vote.[50] This was the last significant effort to introduce proportional representation for the state legislative elections.[51]

To Croly's and People's Power League's chagrin, proportional representation was rejected by the very direct democracy that they introduced and embraced. Oregonians were more deeply attached to territory and familiar political traditions than the Progressives realized, and while their Progressive ideals reflected in successful reforms appealed to our populist impulses, these were repudiated when they impinged on representative assemblies and their election. The Progressive crusade for proportional representation in Oregon lasted six years and ended in ignominious defeat.

Herbert Croly's rejection of district-based representative assemblies was not universally embraced by his fellow political travelers. Progressive John Dewey in his classic *The Public and Its Problems* comes tantalizingly close to engaging the SMD question when he raises the possibility of discarding territorial political organization in favor of "functional" or occupation bases of defining political communities. However, he eventually concludes that "there is no substitute for the vitality and depth of close and direct inter-course and attachment" found in locally defined political communities.[52] For many Progressives there was something important about community and territorially based representation.

Nationally, the demise of PR by direct democracy was not uncommon, and by the 1920s court challenges largely on equal-protection grounds and application of "Dillon's Rule" eliminated many of the remaining municipal applications of proportional representation.[53]

More generally, the consolidation of the SMD system owes much to the fact that Americans believe that the proper organization of constituency is territorial. Andrew Rehfeld notes that for the Americans "territorial con-stituencies were an institutional habit of mind so engrained in thought and practice" that we have never seriously considered any other alternative.[54] In the United States both then and today a sense of place is a sense of identity. Identity and interest were shared with neighbors and were measured in miles if not city blocks. In addition, the Populist base was rural. Rural residents were especially leery of large urban, often immigrant, workforces. Richard Hofstadter most clearly focuses on the American rural and urban divide in the period, emphasizing the antipathy rural citizens felt for their urban counterparts and the reciprocity of these feelings by urban dwellers. In doing so he captures the salient differences between the Populists and the Progressives in that the former was "overwhelmingly rural and provincial" while the latter was "urban, middle-class and nationwide."[55] Those who lived in the provinces thought territorial representation was their best bulwark

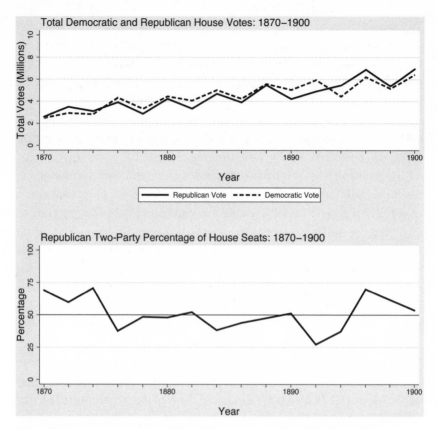

Figure 6.1. Party House Competition: 1870–1900. Source: Michael J. Dubin, United States Congressional Elections, 1788–1997: The Official Results, and Gerald G. Rusk, A Statistical History of the American Electorate.

in protecting their interests against the urban middle classes, and believed they would be swamped in any system other than single-member, territorially defined districts. This reasoning was carried to extremes by Southern whites, who were especially opposed to any system other than SMD election with districting firmly controlled by the state house, anticipating the effect of losing such control should African Americans ever regain the limited franchise they enjoyed during Reconstruction. Geography and location matters to Americans.

The final part of the explanation for the consolidation of the SMD system in the Populist and early Progressive Eras centers on the nature of period party politics and the introduction of the secret ballot. National politics was party politics, and it was exceedingly competitive in the first part of this era.

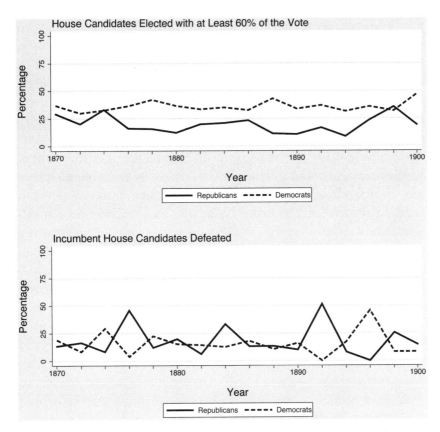

Figure 6.2. House Candidate Electoral Security: 1870–1900. Source: Michael J.
Dubin, United States Congressional Elections, 1788–1997: The Official
Results, *and Gerald G. Rusk,* A Statistical History of the American
Electorate.

Figure 6.1 captures this by graphing the Democratic and Republican vote
totals for House elections between 1870 and 1900.[56] The top panel shows
that the national shares of the two-party House vote have only the slightest
separation, with overall advantage changing twice in the series. The bottom
panel displays the Republican two-party share of House seats. Throughout
much of the era the Democrats and Republicans maintained a tight partisan
balance in the chamber, but as the periods 1872–1876 and 1890–1898 illustrate, the chamber's party composition could change quickly. Figure 6.2 digs
a little deeper by graphing the percentage of House candidates winning with
at least 60 percent of the vote—what we would call today a "safe seat"—and
the percentage of incumbents defeated in these years. The Democrats enjoy

more safe seats than the Republicans, but the percentage of candidates who win with safe margins is well below 50 percent for almost all Congresses. By comparison, the percentage of today's safe seats is about 80 percent.[57]

The SMD system when combined with the newly introduced Australian, or secret, ballot presented legislators with the opportunity to cultivate a personal vote that insulated them from the rigors of national partisan politics.[58] A "personal" vote is district support that owes to the actions of the representative on behalf of the district and that is independent of party or national political trends. It is cultivated by performing services for constituents, bringing federal largess and pork to the district, and similar activities. Since the secret ballot often required voters to cast ballots for each office rather than cast a straight party vote, a representative's candidacy was decoupled from the party to some extent. This separation insulated representatives against the partisan political winds. As Katz and Sala argue, these late-nineteenth-century "ballot changes raised the interest of members of Congress in . . . [building] personal reputations."[59] There is considerable evidence that period legislators indeed cultivated such a vote. For example, Jill N. Wittrock and coauthors report that between 1885 and 1901 representatives elected under the office-bloc version of the Australian ballot increasingly sought to obtain committee assignments relevant to their constituent's interests and were less likely to vote with their partisan colleagues in the chamber.[60] In addition, those representatives elected by Australian ballot brought more pork back to their districts.[61]

The secret ballot reinforced legislator support of the single-member district system because in combination they provided opportunities to obtain electoral support that was removed from the highly competitive partisan politics of the era. Rather than party preservation as in 1842, the motivation was representative preservation. While it is true that legislators can cultivate a personal vote under alternative electoral arrangements, the single-member district system is far superior in this regard. One can more easily separate oneself from one's party when needed, and there is no need to share credit with other legislators for the services and largess returned to the constituency. Simply, when the secret ballot was introduced into the United States in the last years of the 1880s, it significantly reinforced legislators' and constituents' preference for the single-member district system. Further, the compact, contiguous, and equal-population requirements were more manageable in that if one had a clearly defined and stable district, one could devote the necessary time and energy needed to cultivate a personal vote even if the partisan makeup of the district was not as one would design with more fungible districting parameters.

In some ways, this recitation captures a relatively brief and anomalous period in American politics. With the electoral defeat of William McKinley and the Democratic Party more generally in 1896, the United States entered a new period of Republican Party dominance and electoral quiescence. The Apportionment Acts of 1901 and 1911 were passed without significant controversy, and the districting standards of compact, contiguous, and equal population were codified in law. However, within a decade this consensus and the electoral processes that came with it would be discarded. So far as election processes, especially with respect to the House of Representatives, were concerned, party politics faded into the background as the new fault line was urban versus rural areas. This division would shape congressional election processes for several decades, and the place where this division played out most clearly was the battle to reapportion the House of Representatives in 1921.

Failed Apportionment and the Permanent Apportionment Act of 1929

The year 1920 was pivotal for the political demographics of the United States. For the first time more Americans lived in urban than rural areas.[62] This threshold had extraordinarily significant implications for apportionment and districting. If the House membership remained at 435, relative changes in state population meant that ten states would lose at least one representative and Missouri would lose two representatives.[63] Further, population shifted within states. Rural areas lost significant numbers relative to urban industrial centers, greatly complicating districting within states. The size of the House, the census and following apportionment, and the subsequent state-level districting are inexorably linked. Rural areas faced a double loss. First, rural states would lose representation to more urbanized states, and second, rural areas within states would lose representation to the states' urban centers. This created a political quagmire that required a decade and one foregone apportionment cycle to resolve.

To unravel this problem, Congress had to proceed in order. First, the size of the chamber had to be established, then the reapportionment, then the districting requirements given the apportionment. Overlaid on all of this was deep disagreement over the accuracy of the 1920 census. Representatives from rural areas simply didn't believe the numbers, or if conceding their accuracy, believed that much of the upsurge in urbanization was a temporary aberration due to the exigencies of World War I. Mississippi Democratic representative John Rankin spoke for many rural representatives when he reflected on his opposition to reapportionment in accordance with the 1920 census:

> I was opposed to the reapportioning of the House under the census of 1920 for several reasons . . . first . . . America was still in the World War . . . when thousands and thousands were away from home and were not counted where they should have been counted . . . owing to war activities, the population of a good many states had been drawn away from home and concentrated in the large industrial centers of the country. . . . As a result, [the census] showed . . . an unreasonable gain . . . in the large, congested, industrial centers and at the same time an unreasonable falling off in the agricultural sections.[64]

Many believed, like former Speaker James "Champ" Clark (D-MO), that "the flow of people to the great cities is going to come back. The agricultural states proper will increase in population in the next ten years as compared with these great cities."[65] Mr. Clark was wrong. America's sons and daughters never returned to their towns and villages, and the population shift to the cities accelerated.

Even if population was irrevocably shifting to the cities, some representatives advanced normative arguments for maintaining rural representation even at the expense of malapportionment and abrogation of the equal-population principle. These centered on protecting traditional American ideals that idolize rural values and distrust urban morality and lifestyles.[66] Vermont Republican Frank L. Greene appealed to these ideals maintaining that rural constituencies provide an important "moral influence" on the nation.[67] The less savory manifestation of these sentiments linked rural virtues to national birth and citizenship. Representative Milton Romjue (D-MO) conceded the accuracy of the census but lamented the enumeration of immigrants. In doing so, he linked nativist sentiment to Jefferson's praise of agricultural labor and life:

> The rural sections of the country already have too little power and influence and too small a number of representatives. . . . Thomas Jefferson . . . never ceased to praise the rural sections of our country,

and that particularly devoted to agriculture, as the one most moral and ennobling. . . . The constitution . . . in providing for the apportionment of representatives . . . takes into consideration the whole and entire population of the United States . . . without regard to whether the population consists of American citizens or people of foreign birth . . . [reapportionment] . . . would . . . take away from some states that are populated with a highly American citizenship and add to the states . . . which there are a much higher percentage of people of foreign birth.[68]

Kansas Republican Edward C. Little was more direct, claiming that strict adherence to population-based apportionment would "turn this government over to the cities where ignorance, poverty, vice and crime are staring you in the face." The Kansan argued that "it is not best for America that her councils be dominated by semicivilized colonies in Boston, New York [and] Chicago."[69] Representatives were well aware that "semicivilized colonies" was a euphemism for immigrant communities. They were also aware that the United States was becoming an urban nation and that rural representatives would use every possible means to protect their constituencies and themselves.[70]

Recognizing that the census would eventually have to be taken seriously and reapportionment proceed, Congress attempted to solve the problem through the tried and true approach of increasing the size of the chamber. The most serious of these proposals put forth a House with 483 members, which if adopted would guarantee that no state lost representation. Even this size chamber was hardly comforting to rural states. To preserve the twelve small state seats lost under the extant chamber size, the more populous states would gain an additional thirty-six seats. New York alone would increase its delegation by three. Nonetheless, in January 1921 the House voted to maintain the existing membership of 435. This figure was approved over the strained objections of several rural representatives and the recommendation of the chamber's own Census Committee, and served notice that the practice of placating states poised to lose representation had run its course.[71] However, standing firm on the chamber size did nothing to further reapportionment, and by the end of the year it was clear that the House could not pass legislation, and even if the House could muster the votes there were sufficient senators to block passage. No additional action was taken on apportionment until the latter part of the decade, and all elections in the 1920s were conducted under the 1911 Apportionment Act and its districting provisions.

The apportionment question reemerged in 1927 in anticipation of the 1930 census. By this time it was clear that the urbanization that derailed the 1921 process would only be magnified in the 1930s. This motivated legislation that proved to be the genesis of the modern apportionment, which was shifted to the executive branch. Specifically, in the Sixty-Ninth Congress, Census Committee chair Edward Fenn (R-CT) introduced a bill that charged the secretary of commerce with reapportioning the House following the census while retaining the districting language of the 1901 and 1911 acts. The delegation of the apportionment to the secretary of commerce was decried as "ridiculous" and "revolutionary" because it transferred a heretofore congressional prerogative to the executive branch.[72] The Census Committee refused to endorse the bill, but in March Fenn moved to suspend the rules to force a vote in the chamber. This motion failed 197–183, killing the bill for the remainder of the Congress. Despite this, the idea of shifting apportionment to the executive branch gained interest.

The legislative battle for reapportionment resumed in spring 1928, and a political understanding was forged that provided the foundation for the eventual passage of a permanent apportionment act. The compromise admitted population-based reapportionment for a House of 435 members while providing districting concessions to rural constituencies, or at least the legislators that represented rural constituencies. The principals outlining this idea were Democratic representative Ralph Lozier and Republican George Scott Graham. Representative Lozier was elected from Missouri's north-central Second District and spoke for rural interests, while Representative Graham represented the densely populated and immigrant-heavy central Philadelphia Second District.[73]

The key to furthering the bill was removal of its third section, which reiterated the compact, contiguous, and equal-population requirements from previous acts.[74] The finally enacted Permanent Apportionment Act of 1929 established executive-led decennial reapportionment and eliminated all districting standards. States had to elect their representatives from single-member districts, but the construction of these districts was left entirely to the states.

This concession took two congressional sessions to play out, and key chamber speeches by Representatives Fenn, Lozier, and Graham trace its evolution. Read in its entirety, the chamber discussion elucidates why representative Fenn unilaterally removed section 3 from the bill on the House floor without debate, objection, or a vote. The exchanges illuminate the final form the bill took the following year. To see this, it is necessary to detail some of the congressional debate surrounding legislative action on the apportionment bill in May 1928 and in the subsequent January 1929 session.

In this debate Representative Lozier returned to the 1842 script, arguing that the national government had no authority to dictate how the states elected their representatives. In his words the bill

> embodies a proposition that is clearly invalid. The bill provides that the congress shall allocate to the several states the number of representatives to which they are entitled according to their population. When that act is done the power of congress ends. The power of congress does not exist to determine how and in what manner the states shall elect their representatives *or in what form the states shall [create] . . . their congressional districts.* . . . There is no power in Congress to in any way determine or direct how the states shall elect the Members of Congress to which they are entitled.[75]

Lozier then introduced an amendment to strike out the section 3 districting requirements, which was rejected.[76] However, Representative Fenn equivocates when responding to questions about the extent of state discretion in determining how to elect their House delegations. When asked whether states could elect some representatives at large following increases in representation, he responds, "That is a matter for the state itself to determine."[77] Fenn then tepidly justifies the compact, contiguous, and equal-population requirement by stating that "these are the same sections that have been carried in previous apportionment bills," offering no further defense.[78] Following the debate and the failure to strike section 3, the chamber voted to recommit the bill to the Committee on the Census, and there was no further action on it in the session.[79] Nonetheless, the May exchanges made clear that section 3's districting standards were an obstacle to reapportionment.

The House returned to apportionment in early 1929. Representative Graham enters the discussion by arguing for reapportionment in accordance with the Fenn bill, but also wonders "if the third and fourth paragraphs" are "really necessary."[80] He reminds the chamber that "under the constitution the power rests with the states to regulate [elections] except so far as congress may enact legislation; the whole power is with the state."[81] In other words, Congress is not required to legislate standards for congressional districts. Immediately following, Representative Lozier reiterates that no

> man . . . will contend for one moment that sections 3, 4 and 5 have any binding force or effect whatever. The gentleman from Pennsylvania [Representative Graham], one of the ablest lawyers in this body . . . [agrees that] . . . the only power that Congress is given . . . is to apportion the representation. . . . That duty done, the power of congress ends, and Congress has no power to determine in what manner the several states exercise their sovereign rights in selecting their representatives, and I was glad to hear the gentlemen from Pennsylvania [Mr. Graham] indorse what I said on this subject.[82]

The next day, Representative Fenn removed the compactness, contiguous, and equal-population requirements from the bill on the floor and without a murmur of regret. After a subsequent motion to recommit the bill failed, it was passed by voice vote and was sent to the Senate.[83]

The Senate was unable to complete action on the apportionment act before the end of the session, but early in the Seventy-First Congress the bill picked up a powerful advocate in Michigan Republican senator Arthur Vandenberg, who rewrote portions of it to make the process automatic in that the president would initiate a reapportionment that would take place following every census. The Senate bill maintained a House membership at 435 and did not reinsert the compact, contiguous, and equal-population requirements. Indeed, the districting requirements were never discussed or considered by the Senate. The upper chamber passed the Vandenberg bill on May 29th and the House followed suit on June 6th.[84] After a conference to iron out modest differences in the House and Senate versions of the bill it was signed into law by President Hoover June 19, 1929, and the modern apportionment process was established. The act mandated that representatives be elected from single-member districts, but was silent on any standards for those districts. There was no legal requirement that districts be compact, be contiguous, and contain roughly equal population.[85]

These debates outline a political arrangement that enabled passage of the Permanent Apportionment Act of 1929. Understanding this arrangement is important because it drives the subsequent state-level malapportionment that ultimately invited court intervention in the districting process in the 1960s. For urban representatives the apportionment was the principal issue, and the districting language, even if widely supported, was a card that could be traded away to secure this greater objective. Rural representatives were increasingly resigned to the likelihood that some sort of reapportionment would happen in the early 1930s. Public sentiment was heavily building in this direction, and it was inconceivable that the nation would go thirty years without reapportionment. If Representative Robert Clancy (R-MI) was correct that the "real reason" legislators oppose reapportionment is to "save their own political hides," then the most obvious way to rectify interstate malapportionment was to allow intrastate malapportionment.[86] This way incumbent representatives from states that would lose representation could hope that their colleagues in the state houses would redistrict in a manner that would preserve their districts and those of their allies as much as possible. Such redistricting was not implausible since many state houses were weighted toward rural interests. Scholars who have studied this apportionment have lamented the lack of congressional debate surrounding the elimination of districting requirements, describing the decision as "inexplicable."[87] In fact, it is perfectly explicable. Without the compact, contiguous, and equal-population requirement the bill created an opportunity for representatives from rural areas to coalesce with representatives from populous states with large urban areas for their mutual benefit by increasing the overall representation of these states while preserving the possibility that these states could protect rural interests through creative districting. For a sufficient number of legislators the removal of section 3 enabled them to support the reapportionment bill, ensuring its passage.[88]

Two House votes provide evidence that the elimination of section 3 paved the way for eventual passage of the reapportionment act. These were the May 18, 1928, and January 11, 1929, motions to recommit the bill to committee. These motions were effectively votes on the bill itself because failure to recommit would demonstrate there was sufficient support for it to proceed. The May vote passed 186–164, killing the bill for the session. The January recommit vote failed with 135 "yes" votes to 227 "no" votes. Following this the apportionment bill was immediately passed by a voice vote and sent to the Senate. The only difference between the May and January versions of the bill was the former included sections 3, 4, and 5; in particular the compact, contiguous, and equal-population districting requirements, while these were eliminated from the January legislation. Three hundred representatives voted on both motions, so those who changed from opposing to supporting the bill between May 1928 and January 1929 are the key legislators for whom removal of districting standards was sufficient to overcome their opposition

Table 6.2. May and January Votes to Recommit the Apportionment Bill
to the Census Committee*

	May 18, 1928			January 11, 1929		
	Dem.	Rep.	Total	Dem.	Rep.	Total
Recommit (Yes)	113	73	186	94	41	135
Do Not Recommit (No)	41	120	161	65	159	224
	154	193	347	159	200	359

*Two minor party representatives are not included.
Source: *Congressional Record.*

to population-based apportionment. To see this, and to better understand the progression of the apportionment act, it is useful to consider the votes on these two motions in more detail.

Table 6.2 presents the votes on the May and January motions by representative party affiliation. Both votes show that Republicans were more likely to support the bill and Democrats to oppose it. The May vote recommitted the bill to the Census Committee by a narrow margin, with most Democrats opposing the bill and most Republicans supporting it.[89] However, almost 40 percent of Republicans voted to kill the bill. Following removal of section 3 the chamber vote shifted decisively in favor of the apportionment act. Eighty percent of Republicans voted in favor of the bill, and it was the Democrats that divided, with about 40 percent favoring reapportionment when decoupled from districting. The January nearly two-to-one margin meant a reapportionment act was very likely to pass by the end of the year, provided it did not contain districting standards.

To substantiate the argument that stripping the compact, contiguous, and equal-population districting requirements facilitated passage of the permanent apportionment act, it is useful to analyze the votes on the motions to recommit the bill to committee. To do so, consider the subset of legislators who voted on both the May 1928 and January 1929 motions. There are 300 such representatives. For these legislators there are only four possible voting patterns. One could vote "yes" on both motions, "no" on both, "yes" on the first motion and "no" on the second, or "no" on the first motion and "yes" on the second. As one expects, the majority of legislators fall into the first two categories by consistently voting for or against the reapportionment act.[90] Specifically, 115 representatives consistently opposed the bill by voting "yes" on both motions, while 137 consistently supported the bill by voting "no."

Table 6.3. Legislator Characteristics and Votes on the Motions to Recommit the Apportionment Act of 1929

	Chamber Average	Vote to Recommit in May and January	Vote against Recommit in May and January	Vote to Recommit in May and Vote against Recommit in January
State Population (Millions)	3.93	2.71	4.48	5.60
Urban Population (Percentage)	54.1	38.1	64.1	65.8
N	300	115	137	45

Note: The table excludes three representatives who voted against recommittal in May and for recommittal in January. All differences from the chamber average are statistically significant at the 0.001 level (one tail t-test).
Source: *Congressional Record.*

However, 45 representatives who supported recommittal in May switched their votes and opposed recommittal in January. By changing their votes these legislators provided the margin for eventual passage of the Permanent Apportionment Act of 1929. Their characteristics, especially with respect to their states' population and urbanization, most clearly show that the removal of the districting provisions drove reapportionment.

Table 6.3 presents the average state population and the average percentage of state urbanization for these 300 representatives. It also presents the corresponding averages for those who consistently voted for recommittal, those who consistently voted against recommittal, and the 45 representatives who voted to recommit in May and then against recommittal in January. It is this last group of representatives for whom removal of the districting provisions appears sufficient to obtain their support for the bill that was otherwise identical to the May version. As expected, those who consistently sought to kill the bill disproportionally came from states with small populations, while those who consistently supported it came from the larger states. More interesting is that representatives who initially voted to recommit the bill and then later supported it came from the most populous states. These representatives' states are significantly larger than even the states of those who twice voted against recommittal.[91] The same pattern exists for urbanization. Those who consistently opposed the bill come from less urbanized states. Those representatives who consistently supported it came from more urbanized states, although these states are no more urbanized than those of representatives who switched their votes.

That the representatives who changed their votes in favor of the apportionment act came from the most populous states tells us much about how the districting stipulations affected the final vote. Of these 45 representatives, over half came from just three states: 7 from New York, 8 from Pennsylvania, and 10 from Illinois. New York, Pennsylvania, and Illinois, in that order, were the most populous states in the nation. This net shift of 25 representatives was sufficient to ensure passage of the apportionment act. The question is why they would initially oppose the act with districting stipulations and then support it when these are removed.

These representatives came from exactly the types of states where relaxing districting standards should be a key consideration in changing votes. Specifically, they came from populous states that would benefit from population-based reapportionment, but also states that were deeply divided between populous urban centers and geographically large rural and agricultural areas. The politics in each state is often described in terms of an "in-state versus outstate" conflict between the major metropolitan centers and rural areas. It was precisely these legislators who, should there be no districting provisions, could simultaneously further the interests of their states, potentially their own interests, and those of political allies, or simply reach an accommodation with politicians with different interests. For example, of the 10 Illinois legislators who switched votes, 9 represented agricultural districts. For New York and Pennsylvania the switchers came from both rural and urban areas. Most of the New York representatives who eventually supported the reapportionment act came from the New York City metropolitan area, while the Pennsylvania switchers were roughly evenly divided between those representing rural areas and those representing urban constituencies. The removal of the compact, contiguous, and equal-population requirements from the apportionment act furthered the interests of both urban and rural legislators. The urban legislators benefited from reapportionment and the rural representatives benefited from state-level ability to district without significant constraints. This is what a political deal looks like.

Conclusion

This chapter traced the near universal mid-nineteenth century adoption and institutionalization of the single-member district electoral system for

House elections. By about 1880 the only exceptions to the SMD House elections occurred when a state changed its apportionment and was unable to redistrict for the first election or two following reapportionment. Further, by the early 1900s the now widely accepted normative standards of compact, contiguous, and equal population were codified into federal election law. It is remarkable in and of itself that the single-member district institutionalized in this period because the Populist and Progressive Eras affected virtually all other aspects of the conduct of US elections, including the use of SMD elections at the local level. The most compelling explanation for the lack of period interest in changing the SMD system for House elections was that the Progressives had little to say about republican governance, hence had no serious alternative vision of the House of Representatives or its election to offer in place of SMD election. In addition, SMD election, when combined with the secret ballot, primary elections, the direct election of senators, and other Progressive reforms, was an acceptable means to staff the House of Representatives.

This brief period of stability and acceptance of the normative standards for districting came to an end with the First World War and the subsequent urbanization revealed by the 1920 census. With a fixed House membership of 435 the decade of the 1920s demonstrated convincingly that Congress was incapable of reapportioning itself in the presence of significant population shifts across and within states. The only potential remedy to gross malapportionment across states was passage of the Permanent Apportionment Act of 1929, which removed control of the apportionment process from Congress and admitted the possibility of malapportionment within states.

This legislation had momentous consequences for districting practices. The Apportionment Act effectively returned the legal framework for districting to the pre-1900 period. The apportionment would mirror state-level population, but the states could elect representatives as they chose. Missouri, to take the exemplar state in these debates, lost three representatives after the 1930 reapportionment. This was more than the anticipated two, but less than the worst-case scenario of four. The state did not redistrict for the first congressional cycle following reapportionment and elected thirteen representatives at large, including Representative Lozier. However, after this election Missouri created thirteen single-member congressional districts, and Representative Lozier's worst fear materialized. His rural north-central Missouri district was carved up, with parts ending up in three redrawn districts. He declined to seek reelection and retired from national politics.

The bill itself was an admission that Congress was incapable of reapportioning itself when states, and their incumbent representatives, would lose seats. By delegating this power to the president the representational chips would simply fall where they might, and no legislator would be placed in a position of voting against his own state's interest in the name of equal protection. However, by solving this one problem Congress created another problem that would fester for thirty years before the courts ultimately had to intervene. The following chapter discusses the single-member districting process in the court era, but it is important to keep in mind this history and politics to fully understand how we came to a position where the courts had to intervene in state-level malapportionment. The possibility of such malapportionment was a price large-state legislators were willing to pay in 1929 for national reapportionment, and it was a coalition of representatives from both rural and urban districts in the large, industrial, northern states that set this process in motion. Further, the compact, contiguous, and equal-population standards were well known and advocated in the early nineteenth century, not created whole cloth by the courts in the middle nineteenth century. Representatives from populous state urban districts in the 1920s paid a steep price for reapportionment. The states received their representatives, but within two apportionment cycles these were so malapportioned as to create stunning differences in the populations contained within urban and rural districts in the same state. Further, since the control of redistricting lies in the statehouse, these constituents and their representatives had few congressional-level cards to play to cajole the state houses to district in accordance with population density within states. The districting problem was removed from Congress and would eventually prove insoluble at the state house level. That is the subject of the next chapter.

7 The Court Years, 1960–Present

> Mr. Speaker—my point of order is against the
> Senate amendment to the bill H.R. 2275. . . . [As]
> the other body has done so many times in the
> past, they have taken a bill of no great merit and
> of interest probably to one Member of Congress,
> and have attached to that bill an amendment which
> would affect practically every member of Congress
> and each one of the 200 million inhabitants of the
> United States. . . . I know as well as anything that
> I am standing here today engaging in an act of
> futility. I know that I am up here battling against
> windmills.
>
> Representative Paul C. Jones (D-MO)[1],
> November 28, 1967

Certainly only a handful of Americans have ever heard of Dr. Ricardo Vallejo Samala. Dr. Samala was born in the Philippines in 1931 and quietly practiced medicine in the Florida panhandle for most of his adult life. His name, however, provides the title for the current law requiring the election of US representatives from single-member districts. The SMD mandate was attached as an amendment to a 1967 bill certifying that Dr. Samala was a legal resident of the United States.[2] That the law stipulating how federal representatives are elected was part of a bill clarifying one man's immigration status suggests the political complexity of elections following the Court's one-person one-vote jurisprudence and passage of the Voting Rights Act. When the chambers debated the Act for the Relief of Dr. Ricardo Vallejo Samala, not one minute was devoted to Dr. Samala or his residency status. As Representative Jones knew, the outcome was a foregone conclusion. Congress reaffirmed the SMD requirement in the new era of vote value equality and emphasis on obtaining "fair and effective" representation for racial minorities. These considerations were deeply intertwined. The greatest friends of voting rights were also the strongest proponents of the SMD system and saw it as the best vehicle through which the goal of representational fairness could be advanced.

This final era solidifying the House of Representatives single-member district system began in the early 1960s and continues through the present day. In these years the federal courts responded to state-level malapportionment fostered by the 1929 Apportionment Act's lack of districting standards. Congressional districts became increasingly malapportioned as rural areas lost population relative to the urban centers, while legislative district boundaries remained static. The Supreme Court eventually ruled that legislative districts must contain equal population, an area of jurisprudence it had been reluctant to enter because of its traditional distaste for adjudicating "political questions." In addition, the pursuit of minorities' civil and voting rights introduced race as a factor in districting, with the Court seeking to ensure that legislative districts were not drawn for discriminatory effect and admitting the possibility that districting might be used to ameliorate deficiencies in minority representation.

This overview is well known and has been detailed in many sources. This chapter shifts the focus from narrating the trajectory of judicial involvement in legislative elections to highlighting how the period further established the SMD system as the way we elect our representatives. As in previous eras, it was franchise expansion, in this case the increased enfranchisement of African Americans following passage of the Voting Rights Act of 1965, that reinforced the SMD system. In the civil rights era many believed that the single-member district system could be harnessed to secure the voting rights and political influence of underrepresented populations. The courts and Congress recognized the importance of the single-member district system in the corpus of American republican thought and believed that properly used it could advance the political representation and voice of racial minorities. In the twenty-first century this is deeply disputed as many believe that other election processes are better suited to achieve this objective. But when the United States most fully pursued the enfranchisement of racial minorities and the protection of their political interests, those most closely involved in this struggle supported SMD plurality elections.

The judiciary embraced the holy trinity of legislative districting: compact, contiguous, and equal population, but unlike in the Blessed Trinity, the Court established a first or priority element. The equal representational value of votes is sacrosanct, and all other objectives are secondary to it. That the Court insulated equal vote value even when it was sympathetic to advancing other goals says much about the ideals that most deeply resonated in the judiciary. Justices paid proper respect to the representation of communities of interest and corporate entities, but the electoral equality of *individuals* was inviolable, even if it sometimes forced the Court into strained jurisprudence. The court years illustrate that for electoral systems in general and districting in particular, the achievement of some normative objectives always comes at the expense of other normative objectives.

The stipulation of equal vote value along with the need to advance the representational presence of racial minorities forced the Court to address a number of complex legal and political questions. For example, how much can district populations differ while still being considered "equal"? How does one know if a particular plan dilutes the vote of minority populations? Should the courts intervene to prevent gerrymandered districts? Should they treat different types of gerrymanders differently, for example, partisan or incumbency gerrymanders as opposed to racial gerrymanders for the purpose of creating majority-minority districts? Is there a meaningful distinction between a racial gerrymander and a party gerrymander if there is a strong partisan direction to the racial vote? How does one reconcile districting practices that secure greater minority representation in Congress but simultaneously reduce the overall influence of minorities in the political process? Indeed, how can one even tell if a district is gerrymandered? These and related questions provide few clear answers and continue to occupy the attention of the federal courts and scholars.

The Supreme Court pursued a line of jurisprudence that increasingly privileged the SMD system. This primarily owed to deference to Congress's 1967 SMD mandate and the importance of the SMD system in American political thought and history. In doing so, the Court sought to advance the Fourteenth Amendment's commitment to electoral equality, the Fifteenth Amendment's guarantee that the electoral process was open to all, and the Voting Rights Act's reaffirmation of that commitment. The courts thought that the SMD could further these objectives while respecting Congress and *stare antiquas via*. It is undeniable that the Court sometimes struggled to find consistency in accommodating and balancing the republican and liberal values that inform the American political tradition. This is understandable; justices are not political theorists, and they worked within the constraints imposed by sanctifying equal vote value so that other goals could be advanced only so far as they did not compromise this principle. The judiciary continued the political discussion on electing the House in light of renewed emphasis on political equality generally and racial equality in particular. The inherent tension of achieving some normative objectives at the expense of other objectives assures us that the Court will never fully extricate itself from Justice Frankfurter's political thicket, nor should it.

This chapter provides an overview of the mid-twentieth-century legislative and judicial foundations underpinning contemporary House of Representatives elections and advancing the electoral rights of racial minorities. The next section details the congressional malapportionment that motivated court intervention in districting. I discuss the enactment of the 1967 federal law reiterating the single-member district mandate. This illuminates the context within which the Court worked and shaped its responses to House election methods. The chapter then discusses court responses to the Voting Rights Act and its treatment of race so far as these affect the election of the House of Representatives. In doing so, it discusses the federal court cases that most directly establish the parameters governing House election methods. These cumulatively created a jurisprudence that favored the single-member district system. Civil rights–era jurisprudence and, more importantly, the ideals underlying it reinforced the SMD system. The postwar era produced hundreds of federal apportionment and districting cases, which can be mind-numbing in their detail. We will not enter the legal weeds. There is a core group of about a dozen Supreme Court rulings that elucidate the Court's thought on these questions. These are grouped into three sometimes overlapping categories: equal vote value, gerrymandering, and the protection of racial minority voting rights and representation. These cases present the ground rules for the single-member district system, and their trajectory increasingly recommended the single-member district system as the election method best suited for ensuring general political equality and protecting minority political interests in a manner consistent with the republican and liberal values that most deeply shaped the United States.

The Court's entry into House election processes in the 1960s was unavoidable when the pursuit of civil and voting rights accelerated; these movements are inseparable. The Supreme Court's "one-person one-vote" jurisprudence was about equality at the ballot box, as was the Voting Rights Act of 1965. There is certainly a fundamental difference between determining the value of one's vote based on where one lives and denying one the right to vote on the basis of race. There may be good reasons to weight votes differently.

Senate votes, for example, are weighted unequally across states because we recognize the federal component of US government. In contrast, denial of the right to vote is not simply the most extreme case of weighting votes differently; it is profoundly different. Such denial strikes at core republican values by abandoning the social and political advantages that come with living in a self-governing political community. The period's jurisprudence recognized the importance of the founding era's embrace of republican values buttressed and given effect by the Fourteenth Amendment's guarantee of equality before the law and the Fifteenth Amendment's promise of racial equality at the polls. These foundations supported and reinforced each other and in doing so strengthened the SMD electoral system for House of Representatives elections.

Electing the House in the 1960s

The Apportionment Act of 1929 was silent on the compact, contiguous, and equal-population districting requirements of previous apportionment acts, but it did not explicitly repeal them either. The states generally discarded these principles in post-1930 reapportionments that often accompanied significant changes in the size of state congressional delegations. The first challenge to a state's failure to follow districting standards came in *Wood v. Broom* (1932), brought by Mississippi voters who objected to a gerrymandered district drawn following a reduction in the state's congressional delegation from eight to seven. The petitioners asked the Court to require that Mississippi's congressional delegation be elected at large. There was no question that the districts were not especially compact, nor did they contain equal population. All parties agreed they were gerrymandered and malapportioned. The question was whether the compact, contiguous, and equal-population standards of the 1901 and 1911 Apportionment Acts carried forward through the Permanent Apportionment Act of 1929. The Supreme Court unambiguously declared that they did not. On behalf of the majority, Chief Justice Hughes reasoned that "the terms of the act, and its legislative history shows that the omission was deliberate. The question was up, and considered" and the districting standards were eliminated by an affirmative act of Congress. They "expired by their own limitations."[3] So far as the federal courts were concerned, Mississippi could draw congressional districts in any shape it chose because Congress permitted it to do so.

Importantly, the *Wood* decision directly addressed only the gerrymandering question. The Court bypassed the malapportionment issue, allowing the possibility that such districts could be challenged on Fourteenth Amendment equal protection grounds. This distinction is significant because it foreshadowed differences in the way the courts would address gerrymandering and district population later in the twentieth century. *Colegrove v. Green* (1946) presented the first opportunity for the federal judiciary to pursue the question of unequal district populations. Here the Court established the jurisprudence that would guide it until the early 1960s. The *Colegrove* question was similar to that in *Wood*: congressional districts in Illinois were grossly gerrymandered and malapportioned. Again, there was no disputing the facts. Illinois congressional districts at midcentury contained as many as 914,000 persons and as few as 112,000 persons, meaning that a congressional vote in the latter district carried eight times the representational value of a vote in the former district. The difference was the *Colegrove* plaintiffs explicitly challenged malapportionment on equal protection grounds. The Court was asked to decide whether the Constitution allows the representational value of a congressional vote to differ across citizens.

The Supreme Court again declined to answer the question, and in doing so served notice that under the extant composition of the Court such issues would be considered "political questions" beyond the competency of the Court to adjudicate. Chief Justice Felix Frankfurter wrote the plurality opinion in an unusual 3–1–3 decision, stating that the "remedy for unfairness in districting is to secure State legislatures that will apportion properly, or to invoke the ample powers of Congress."[4] Justice Frankfurter offered no insight as to how one would secure a state legislature that would "apportion properly" by abandoning a politically favorable districting pattern of its own volition, or why one would expect members of Congress to district themselves out of a job in the name of political equality. Nonetheless, the Court's opinion was not entirely unexpected. The judiciary is reluctant to directly confront the elected branches because, as is often said, it possesses neither the power of the purse nor the power of the sword to enforce its decisions. The Court's legitimacy is often best protected by avoiding direct confrontation with the legislature and the executive branches, and in this view discretion is often the better part of valor.[5] The deeply divided Court declined to intervene in districting. Justice Frankfurter and dissenting Justices Hugo Black and William O. Douglas would have the opportunity to reargue the question when it returned to the Supreme Court in the early 1960s. In the meantime, the states were free to district as they saw fit without fear of court intervention.

Malapportionment

The application of *Wood* and *Colegrove* to postwar demographic changes ensured the accelerating malapportionment of congressional and statehouse districts. Table 7.1 presents the House of Representatives district malapportionment, sorted from the least to the most malapportioned states on the eve of the 1960s Court's "one-man one-vote" jurisprudence. The figures are for the Eighty-Seventh Congress, meeting in 1961, with the House district population obtained from the 1960 census. For each state, the table lists the minimum House district population, the maximum district population, the average district population, the representational value of a vote cast in the least populous district relative to one cast in the most populous district, and average relative deviation in district populations in the state. The representational value of a vote, sometimes called the "ratio of inequality," is simply the population of the most populous district divided by the population of the least populous district. This figure is the representational value of a vote cast in the lesser-populated district relative to one cast in the most populous district. Relative deviation is calculated as:

Relative Deviation
$$= \{[abs(\text{district populastion} - \text{ideal district polulation})]$$
$$\div (\text{ideal district population})\} \times 100$$

where ideal district population is simply the state's population divided by its apportionment. This figure is the percentage population deviation across districts relative to that which would be obtained through equal population districting. This is the more informative measure of the extent of state malapportionment because it is based on all of a state's districts rather than just the least and most populated districts as in the representational value figure. Consequently, there are states such as Ohio that have particularly egregious differences in the representational value of votes cast in largest and smallest districts that are significantly less malapportioned, on average, than many other states.

The figures in table 7.1 are striking. In 1961 the difference between the least and the most populated districts in a moderately malapportioned state such as Kentucky was a factor of two. At the upper end of the scale, Minnesota's Ninth District in the northwest part of the state counted approximately 266,000 residents while its Third District on the northern side of the Minneapolis and Saint Paul area had nearly 700,000 residents.

Table 7.1. State-Level Malapportionment in the Eighty-Seventh Congress (1961–1963)

State	Min. CD Population	Max. CD Population	Average CD Population	Vote Value Difference	Relative Deviation (%)
Arizona	638,651	663,510	651,081	1.04	1.91
Maine	304,984	349,291	323,088	1.15	5.41
Rhode Island	399,782	459,706	429,744	1.15	6.97
Washington	342,540	510,512	407,602	1.49	8.62
New Hampshire	275,103	331,818	303,461	1.21	9.34
Arkansas	182,314	360,183	297,712	1.98	12.92
Nebraska	296,592	421,198	352,833	4.42	13.61
Virginia	312,890	539,618	396,695	1.73	14.51
Massachusetts	272,361	474,691	367,756	1.74	14.71
West Virginia	268,334	421,085	310,070	1.57	15.71
North Carolina	253,511	487,159	379,680	1.92	16.12
Louisiana	263,850	536,029	407,128	2.03	16.19
New York	260,235	906,187	390,286	3.48	17.12
South Carolina	272,220	531,555	397,099	1.95	17.29
Mississippi	237,887	460,100	363,024	1.93	17.73
Montana	274,194	400,573	337,384	1.46	18.72
Pennsylvania	260,767	553,154	377,312	2.12	18.74
Missouri	301,098	568,029	392,710	1.89	19.18
Indiana	290,596	697,567	423,864	2.40	19.21
Kentucky	303,431	610,947	379,770	2.01	20.00
Oregon	265,164	522,813	442,172	1.97	20.02
Minnesota	266,075	697,572	379,318	2.62	21.17
Iowa	236,585	465,828	344,692	1.97	21.23
Ohio	236,288	726,156	422,017	3.07	21.44
Wisconsin	236,870	530,316	395,178	2.24	22.10
Idaho	257,242	409,949	333,596	1.59	22.89
Tennessee	223,387	627,019	396,343	2.81	23.29
Illinois	235,202	905,761	403,246	3.85	23.93
Alabama	236,216	634,864	362,971	2.69	24.13
Connecticut	318,942	689,555	507,047	2.16	25.96
Georgia	272,154	823,680	394,312	3.03	26.05
Oklahoma	227,692	552,863	388,047	2.42	27.08
California	253,360	1,014,460	523,907	4.00	27.47
New Jersey	255,165	667,906	433,342	2.62	27.56
Utah	317,973	572,654	445,314	1.80	28.60
Kansas	212,520	580,124	363,102	2.73	29.02
Colorado	195,551	653,954	438,487	3.34	30.89
Michigan	177,431	802,994	434,622	4.53	31.31
Florida	239,992	982,968	618,945	4.10	32.74
Texas	216,371	951,527	435,440	4.40	34.00
Maryland	243,570	711,045	442,956	2.92	39.52
South Dakota	182,845	497,669	340,257	2.72	46.26
US Average	269,475	602,490	403,181	2.36	17.82

Note: Excludes states that elect a single representative and North Dakota and New Mexico, which each elected two representatives at large.
Source: 1960 Census.

In the most extreme case, Detroit, with a population of over 800,000, was effectively Michigan's Sixteenth Congressional District while the Upper Peninsula's Twelfth District had only 177,000 residents. A vote cast in Detroit carried about one-quarter the representational value of one cast in the Upper Peninsula. In California, districts differ on average from those obtained by equal-population districting by about 27 percent. Only a handful of states had relative deviations from perfect apportionment in the single digit range; the US average deviation is over 15 percent. Congressional malapportionment was not confined to a handful of states, nor was it a regional problem. Even the least malapportioned states had significant differences in the populations of their congressional districts. There is no obvious geographic or regional pattern to these figures.[6] That malapportionment existed nationally created significant roadblocks to the expectation that Congress's "ample powers" would be applied to ameliorate malapportionment. Too many representatives from too many states would have to gore their own ox to legislate voter equality.

One-Person One-Vote

The Court revisited the malapportionment question in 1961 when it allowed Memphian Charles W. Baker to bring a Fourteenth Amendment challenge to Tennessee's statehouse districts. These were created under a turn-of-the-century law that in application provided disproportionate representation to rural areas of the state. The 1961 Court differed significantly from that which heard *Colegrove*, as did the political world. The Court still counted Felix Frankfurter in its membership but he was no longer chief justice; Californian Earl Warren held that position. In addition, *Colegrove* dissenters Hugo Black and William O. Douglas, both of whom argued in 1946 that the Constitution was "intended to make illegal a nationwide 'rotten borough' system," remained on the Court.[7] Civil rights were also beginning to structure how the Court approached electoral jurisprudence. The Court had already entered the political thicket of race and districting in *Gomillion v. Lightfoot* (1960) by declaring unconstitutional a Tuskegee Alabama districting that removed virtually all African Americans from the city by defining the city limits according to race.[8]

The intensely divisive *Baker v. Carr* (1962) required two oral arguments and generated a 6–2 decision that produced a remarkable five opinions: a majority decision written by Justice Brennan and signed by Chief Justice Warren and Justice Black; three separate concurring opinions written by

Justices Douglas, Clark, and Stewart respectively; and a dissenting opinion written and signed by Justices Frankfurter and Harlan.[9] *Baker's* importance stems not from righting the wrong of unequal Tennessee votes; indeed, the Court declined to do so. Rather, it is significant for the more important reason that the Court ruled that districting questions could be brought to the federal courts. Justice Frankfurter watched the jurisprudence that he constructed nearly twenty years earlier discarded, and in a scathing dissent accused the Court of blithely ignoring precedent by "revers[ing] a uniform course of decision established by a dozen cases" and repudiating "the experience of our whole past."[10] Somewhere in the *ménage-a-cinq* of affirmative Baker opinions, the insulation that the states enjoyed from federal court intervention in districting began to dissipate.

Two years later in two separate cases and on two distinct legal foundations, the Court ruled that legislative districts must contain equal population. The first of these, *Wesberry v. Sanders* (1964), originated in Georgia and applied specifically to the House of Representatives. Here the Court found that the Article I constitutional requirement that representatives be elected by the people of the United States necessitated that all votes must count equally.[11] In *Reynolds v. Sims* (1964) the Court reached the same conclusion with respect to the Alabama state house on the grounds of the Fourteenth Amendment's equal protection clause. The gravity and political implications of these cases were not lost on the Court. Equal-population districting would shift representatives and political power from rural areas to urban and suburban locations.[12] Privately in chambers, Justice Potter Stewart admonished his colleagues to proceed with caution, reminding them that "we are hitting Congress where it lives. Their jobs are involved." He urged them to "go slow" and "delay" in pursuing equal vote value.[13] Chief Justice Warren, however, would book no delay: in his words "legislators represent people, not trees or acres," and this standard would be promulgated immediately.[14] States would have to redistrict, with an inevitable shifting of political power and influence.

These cases capture how seriously the Court took founding-era understandings of republican governance. In the *Wesberry* oral arguments US attorney Bruce J. Terris, speaking on amicus basis, appealed to Madison, Mason, Randolph, and *The Federalist* in support of vote value equality and encouraged the justices to base their deliberations on the republican principles encapsulated in Article I, Section 2, and the Fourteenth Amendment's "equal protection" and "privileges and immunities" clauses.[15] The majority of justices affirming equal vote value agreed, and engaged in an intramural debate with those opposed to interference in state districting over the applicability of these ideals to the most significant representational question of the twentieth century. Justice Hugo Black's majority opinion held that "construed in its historical context, the command of Art. I, § 2 that Representatives be chosen 'by the People of the several States' means that, as nearly as is practicable, one man's vote in a congressional election is to be worth as much as another's." Black substantiated this conclusion with a lengthy recitation of the underlying principles of the revolution, the Constitutional Convention, and the ratification conventions, capturing how deeply the republican ideals that resonated at the founding drove the modern jurisprudence. Summarizing, Justice Black ensured that the relevancy of founding thought to modern districting was not lost to anyone:

> The debates at the Convention make at least one fact abundantly clear: that, when the delegates agreed that the House should represent "people," they intended that, in allocating Congressmen, the number assigned to each State should be determined solely by the number of the State's inhabitants. The Constitution embodied Edmund Randolph's proposal for a periodic census to ensure "fair representation of the people," an idea endorsed by Mason as assuring that "numbers of inhabitants" should always be the measure of representation in the House of Representatives. . . . It would defeat the principle solemnly embodied in the Great Compromise—equal representation in the House for equal numbers of people—for us to hold that, within the States, legislatures may draw the lines of congressional districts in such a way as to give some voters a greater voice in choosing a Congressman than others. The House of Representatives, the Convention agreed, was to represent the people as individuals, and on a basis of complete equality for each voter.[16]

Dissenting justice John Harlan responded by pointing to the "dubious propriety in turning to the 'historical context' of constitutional provisions," by which he meant founding-era thought to elucidate the meaning of the Constitution. However, he argued, if one insists on appealing to "historical context" then "whatever the dominant political philosophy at the Convention . . . it is in the last degree unlikely that most or even many of the delegates would have subscribed to the principle of 'one person, one vote.'"[17] In the end, court majority rejected Justice Harlan's reading of the Constitution and its ideals, and agreed that the republican values reflected in the Constitution demanded nothing less than equal representation.

Wesberry and *Reynolds* created an inescapable foundation to remedy legislative malapportionment. Equal vote value was no longer a political question; it was a constitutional right that citizens could petition the Court to secure. If a legislative body represented people, then the republican principles of Article I combined with the Fourteenth Amendment's guarantee that people are equal before the law required that all votes count equally in the selection of representatives. This meant that if representatives were elected from districts, then these must contain equal population. The details would center on how equal is sufficiently equal and whether the population in question was the number of people living in the district or the number of voting-eligible persons in the district.[18] In addition, the Court and others would soon come to recognize that the stipulation of equal district population would complicate efforts to achieve other representational objectives. With these rulings, however, the Court unequivocally established vote equality as the paramount constitutional protection, and all other considerations are secondary to it.

The SMD Mandate of 1967

The quest for equal vote value came when the nation pursued electoral equality generally. President Johnson signed the Voting Rights Act of 1965 soon after the *Wesberry* and *Reynolds* decisions; in just eighteen months the courts invalidated districting plans that had been in effect for more than a generation and Congress enacted potentially the greatest increase in electoral franchise since ratification of the Nineteenth Amendment. Further, the ideas motivating the Twenty-Sixth Amendment enfranchising eighteen- to twenty-one-year-olds were on the horizon. The 1967 SMD mandate was Congress's response to the "one-person one-vote" decisions and the expected increase in the electoral participation of African Americans.

The current single-member district requirement emerged from several bills introduced between 1965 and 1967, most notably House Resolution (H.R.) 5505, introduced in 1965 by House Judiciary Committee chairman Emanuel Celler.[19] These eventually crystalized into two bills: H.R. 2508, advocated by those seeking to frustrate the Court's one-person one-vote rulings, and H.R. 2275, ultimately passed by a coalition of southern Republicans and northern Democrats that anticipated a benefit from equal population districting. In the South equal population districting would increase the voting strength of suburban and urban areas where Republicans were beginning to erode Democratic strength. In the North equal population districting was anticipated to shift political power to urban areas with larger concentrations of African Americans, increasing their political influence and congressional representation. H.R. 2508 benefited those advantaged by malapportionment, while H.R. 2275 advantaged those benefiting from the equal population districting.

It was H.R. 2275, beginning life as Dr. Salama's humble immigration bill, that ultimately passed, but H.R. 2508 occupied the vast majority of congressional attention; it was around this bill that the two opposing congressional groups organized. As introduced, H.R. 2508 required SMD elections but allowed district populations to differ by as much as 15 percent, though subsequent amendments allowed for a 30 percent difference, which could persist through the Ninety-Second Congress. Thereafter it permitted a 10 percent difference in district populations.[20] It also absolved the states from redistricting until after the 1970 census, making the 1972 election the first election in which more restrictive population variances could take effect.[21] H.R. 2508 also allowed New Mexico and Hawaii to continue to elect their representatives at large until the Ninety-Third Congress, after which time no state could elect representatives at large. It was well understood that at-large elections provide no protection for political or racial minorities, but for legislators unsympathetic to racial equality at the polls this restriction was palatable since single-member district elections, especially if allowed generous population differences, could also be used for discriminatory effect.[22] The bill's principal supporters included House Judiciary Committee chairman Emanuel Celler of New York and Republican senator Everett Dirksen of Illinois.[23] The northern-southern bipartisan coalition opposing H.R. 2508 was led by Michigan Democratic representative John Conyers, Tennessee Republican senator Howard Baker, and Democratic senator Edward "Ted" Kennedy of Massachusetts. These legislators and their like-minded colleagues saw H.R. 2508 as an attempt to "oust the federal courts of all jurisdiction over congressional redistricting."[24] The bill's supporters certainly did hope that the Court would acquiesce to its districting parameters rather than challenge Congress's authority to establish the acceptable limits of representational equality. Justice Stewart's admonishment to his colleagues to "delay" redressing malapportionment suggests this outcome was not inconceivable.

The legislative path of these bills took most of a year to complete. H.R. 2508 was introduced in April 1967, amended and passed by the Senate in June, and went through two conference committees because of House and Senate disagreements over the bill. The Senate was unwilling to accept significant differences in district populations or delay in redistricting even when these provisions were agreed to by their own conferees. The bill ultimately died on November 8 when the Senate would not support the final conference report. Within minutes of disposing of H.R. 2508, the chamber took up the Act for the Relief of Dr. Ricardo Vallejo Samala, H.R. 2275, to which Senator Baker attached an amendment requiring that the House of Representatives be elected by SMD elections effective with the upcoming Ninety-First Congress.[25] Senator Baker's amendment said nothing about district population, compactness, or contiguity. By mid-November it was clear that no precise parameters on district populations or compactness language could pass both chambers, and the proponents of equal-population districting were satisfied that the courts would achieve what Congress could not. The Senate allotted just thirty minutes for debate, and then approved the retitled Act for Relief of Doctor Ricardo Vallejo Samala and to Provide for Congressional Redistricting. The House took up the bill on November 28 and, Representative Paul Jones's procedural objections notwithstanding, passed it with language that allowed Hawaii and New Mexico to retain at-large elections until the Ninety-Second Congress. The Senate accepted the bill on November 30, and President Johnson signed the bill into law in the second week of December.

It is difficult to separate the influence of the one-person one-vote jurisprudence, the movement to secure voting rights, increases in effective franchise on the two bills, and the congressional motivations for passing the 1967 SMD mandate. The overwhelming majority of debate centered on responses to *Wesberry* and the other decisions on equal vote value.[26] Regardless, all of these considerations were in the background of the conversation and occasionally in the foreground. That Representative Celler and Senator Dirksen supported H.R. 2258 suggests the complexity of the relationship between racial equality in voting and these bills. Both Celler and Dirksen were advocates of civil and voting rights. Representative Celler was chairman of the House Judiciary Committee that moved both the Civil Rights Act of 1964 and the Voting Rights Act of 1965 through the chamber. Further, there is evidence that Representative Celler supported equal population districting in principle, but supported H.R. 2258 as a matter of political expediency for the purpose of getting a districting bill through the chamber. Specifically, with respect to the compactness standard, a handwritten note in the H.R. 2508 file at the National Archives Center for Legislative Archives that was presumably written by Representative Celler references possible amendments to H.R. 2508. In it Celler states that the committee should strike out the compactness requirement to make the bill acceptable to the chamber, which would otherwise "fight it tooth and nail."[27] All legislators understood the respective implications of these considerations for these two bills, and the strongest proponents of racial equality at the polls and the increased representation of these groups in Congress rallied behind an SMD mandate with little room for population differences across districts.

As early as the 1965 debate over H.R. 5505, legislators linked the SMD mandate to voting rights. As *Congressional Quarterly Weekly Report* records "opposition to the amendment (allowing at-large House elections) was that southern states might use at-large elections to dilute the strength of the Negro vote."[28] Similarly, the Harlem Democrats for Action appealed to Representative Celler to oppose the 30 percent population deviation allowed under the amended H.R. 2805 because such difference "smacks of the invidious conformation Negros face too often in dealing with the everyday realities of life in America today."[29] For this and other civil rights groups, the interests of African Americans were best served by single-member district elections where districts contain equal population. The relationship between race and elections, however, was most directly addressed in the Congress in a June 8, 1967, exchange between Senator Robert F. Kennedy of New York and Senator Edward "Ted" Kennedy. On this day the Senators Kennedys dominated the floor debate on H.R. 2508, arguing against it. Robert Kennedy spoke most directly to the relationship between districting and voting rights, and motivations for some to support the bill.

> Let me add a word about the political realities which are also behind H.R. 2508. Existing apportionment patterns—both in terms of population variations and the way in which district lines are drawn—cause underrepresentation of the latest immigrants to our great cities: Negros, Puerto Ricans, Mexican Americans, and other groups who have moved to our inner cities in recent years. Court-supervised adherence to the principles of equal representation all across our nation would probably increase significantly the number of Congressmen who are closer to and more responsive to the interests of large urban minority groups.[30]

In Robert Kennedy's view, supporters of H.R. 2508 sought to thwart the representation of these groups and their acquisition of political influence. He emphasized the relationship between race and districting, further arguing that the Voting Rights Act and the equal vote value jurisprudence were part of a single trend "moving in the direction of guaranteeing the value of one's vote" and that the malapportionment allowed under H.R. 2508 deferred this "constitutional right."[31] The supporters of SMD elections combined with vote value equality agreed, while opponents recognized that Robert Kennedy was probably correct. Taking all of this into consideration, it becomes clear that the friends of minority representation linked the SMD elections, especially when combined with compactness and contiguousness, to voting rights, and did so in a manner that argued SMD elections would advance the objectives of increased minority participation, political influence, and representation.

With enactment of the 1967 SMD requirements, every state entitled to more than one seat in the House from the Ninety-Second Congress forward elected their representatives from single-member districts. The legislative movement toward SMD election, beginning with Representative John Nicholas's 1800 proposal for a constitutional amendment, reached fruition. While there have been subsequent efforts to disestablish the SMD system for House elections, often in the name of voting rights and minority representation, these appear very unlikely to succeed.[32] Congress and the courts have established the ground rules for House elections; they will take place in single-member districts containing equal population. However, these legal and political principles accelerated the Court's role in determining how House elections would function in practice, especially with respect to furthering the representational presence and influence of minorities in the House of Representatives. The outline of this jurisprudence, which occupies the chapter's next section, completes the foundation for contemporary legislative elections.

The Courts Clarify the Rules

The combination of the one-person one-vote jurisprudence, the Voting Rights Act of 1965, and the SMD mandate of 1967 establishes the basic parameters in which contemporary congressional elections are contested. Since that time the courts have clarified how these principles work in application. The equal vote requirement, while refined by the Court in successive years, was least subject to interpretation because the courts tolerate only very minor differences in district populations. Further, it became abundantly clear that the courts considered at-large elections a questionable means of electing representatives, ruling as early as 1969 in *Allen v. State Board of*

Elections that such elections diluted the votes of minorities and this election method was unlikely to survive judicial scrutiny.[33] This shifted court attention to district shape.

Gerrymandering is complicated terrain, and the Court remains cautious about adjudicating for good reasons. Consider first the question of how the Court might determine whether a district is gerrymandered. Gerrymandered districts are typically defined by how irregular or bizarrely shaped they are. There are certainly mathematical principles that can be applied to assess whether a district is compact. For example, one can consider the ratio of the district boundary to the area contained within the district. Schools teach these formulas for circles, rectangles, triangles, and other shapes, and one might imagine some deviation from these ratios beyond which the Court might define a district unconstitutional.[34] I discuss these principles in the following chapter, but the Court has declined to rely on such formulaic approaches, providing little guidance for those drawing legislative districts. Further, it is unclear how useful this approach would be, given that the one-person one-vote requirement guarantees districts cannot be such regular shapes. If districts must contain equal population and if people are distributed in a lumpy manner—let's call these lumps cities, towns, villages, hamlets, and crossroads—then district geography will not be circular or square or triangular. If one further seeks to preserve "communities of interest" or corporate boundaries such as county lines, then district shapes will be even less regular.

Still, gerrymandering exists, and as Patrick Henry's presumably evil attempt to district a George Mason victory over James Madison in the first federal election illustrates, the practice is as old as the republic itself. Elbridge Gerry's famous salamander-shaped district that gives the practice its name dates from 1812. Gerrymandering probably reached its peak in the late nineteenth century when states would sometimes redistrict two or three times in an apportionment cycle, depending on which party controlled the statehouse.[35] As Erik Engstrom shows, there was a noticeable decline in gerrymandering in the first half of the twentieth century. This is because the migration of citizens to urban areas, combined with static district boundaries, achieved the same objectives.[36] The increasing malapportionment in the twentieth century combined with stable district lines naturally created what representatives wanted: safe, predictable districts. So long as the Court tolerated malapportionment, population migration accomplished the same objective as gerrymandering: the creation of demographically and politically homogeneous districts.[37] When the Court promulgated its one-person one-vote rulings, the states had to move district boundaries to create such districts. Gerrymandering accelerated noticeably in the late twentieth century because of the one-person one-vote rulings. The accommodation of one normative objective—the equal representational value of votes—created new incentives for politicians to draw district boundaries in increasingly bizarre shapes.

In the current era, two primary types of gerrymanders have been brought before the Court: political and demographic. There are two main types of political gerrymanders. The first is the standard partisan gerrymander. This is the practice of drawing district boundaries to benefit a political party and its candidates. Its objective is to place a sufficient majority of partisans in as many districts as possible to ensure party control of the associated legislative seats without placing too many of its partisans in any one district, thereby creating an unnecessarily large electoral majority. If done properly, one's party will win many legislative seats by small but safe margins, while the opposing party will win a few seats by overwhelming margins. The second type of political gerrymander is the incumbency gerrymander. These are created by bipartisan agreement to district in a manner that preserves the electoral safety of incumbents by maintaining the boundaries of their existing districts as much as possible. Political gerrymanders admit several variations. For example, districts may be drawn to force two incumbents into the same district, necessitating that one will lose, or they may be drawn to remove the residence of an incumbent or potential strong challenger from the district.[38]

As a general statement, political gerrymandering is the sole part of Justice Frankfurter's thicket that remains standing. In two recent cases the Court established that partisan gerrymanders are largely immune from federal court intervention. In the first of these, *Vieth v. Jubelirer* (2004), the Supreme Court found that partisan gerrymanders are largely beyond the competency of the Court because there is no agreeable judicial standard for assessing the extent of a partisan gerrymander. This ruling partially overturned the earlier *Davis v. Bandemer* (1986) decisions in which the Court, at least in principle, reserved the right to address districting disputes. More definitively, in the closely watched *League of Latin American Citizens v. Perry*, the Court affirmed in 2006 that partisan gerrymanders are judiciable, but the legal threshold for establishing an unconstitutional gerrymander is exceedingly high. The Court also reaffirmed states' right to redistrict in the middle of census cycles, as was common in the nineteenth century. The cumulative effect of *Vieth* and

League of Latin American Citizens was to effectively place run-of-the-mill political gerrymanders—whether partisan, incumbency, or some combination of these—beyond the reach of the federal courts.[39] There may conceivably be a partisan gerrymander that the Court would rule unconstitutional based solely on the shape of the district, but one has not yet been produced; given the extraordinary gerrymanders presently existing, it is hard to imagine what such a district would look like. [40]

Gerrymandering to secure greater minority voices in Congress presents a much more complex jurisprudence. The Voting Rights Act sought to provide minorities "fair and effective" representation in the political process. While it is unclear what constitutes fair and effective, the act, especially as amended in 1982, presented considerable legal foundations for challenging racially discriminatory election practices and to advance the ability of minority groups to elect one of their own to Congress.[41] The amended VRA came to the Court in *Thornburg v. Gingles* (1986), in which the Supreme Court established a three-part test for proving vote dilution in at-large and multimember district elections.[42] *Gingles* confirmed the direction of the *Allen* decision that at-large House elections will not withstand court scrutiny, and in doing so promulgated standards under which majority-minority districts may be created for the purpose of electing more racial minorities to Congress. Shortly thereafter, the US Department of Justice ordered several states to create such districts following the 1990 census. To create districts containing majority African American or Hispanic populations while simultaneously satisfying the equal population requirement typically necessitated that these districts be very gerrymandered. The exemplar of this was the North Carolina Twelfth District, which snaked from the north of the state to the far south, at times no wider than a freeway, in order to contain sufficient numbers of African Americans to form an electoral majority. I further discuss the North Carolina Twelfth in the next chapter, and while it may have been one of the most extremely gerrymandered majority-minority districts, virtually all such districts, such as the Texas Thirtieth District, were comparably gerrymandered because drawing a majority-minority gerrymander is fundamentally no different than drawing a partisan gerrymander. These districts demonstrate how complicated it is to draw majority-minority districts even when a sufficient population of relevant voters is available. Indeed, it is probably more difficult to draw a district containing a majority of African Americans or Hispanics than to encompass a majority of Democrats or Republicans as in a traditional gerrymander.

The *Thornburg* decision and the majority-minority districts created in its wake initiated a series of court decisions that sought to resolve the extent to which race can be used to determine legislative district boundaries. The Court holds to very strict standards that limit the legitimate purposes for which the government can classify citizens by race. This heightened standard—known as strict scrutiny—comes from *Brown v. Board of Education* (1954), and presumes that any government classification of citizens by race is unconstitutional unless the government can show that doing so fulfills a compelling public interest that cannot be achieved in any other manner. Advocates of majority-minority districting argue that electing minorities to Congress satisfies a compelling interest and that the election of minorities will not generally be possible in the absence of such districting. Therefore the government is justified in classifying its citizens by race and using this information to draw legislative districts.

The opponents of majority-minority districting argue that the Fourteenth Amendment's equal protection clause requires that government treat all citizens equally regardless of race, and the stated purpose of majority-minority districting does not present a sufficient justification to satisfy the strict scrutiny standards. In 1993 this argument was brought to the Court in *Shaw v. Reno*, which challenged the constitutionality of North Carolina's Twelfth District. In *Shaw* the Court ruled in a 5–4 decision that excessive use of race in determining legislative district boundaries may violate the Fourteenth Amendment's equal protection clause and ordered North Carolina to redraw the district. According to the Court, racially gerrymandered districts can create an "expressive harm" by minimizing other constitutional values in districting. Writing for the majority in the closely related *Bush v. Vera* (1996) case that centered on the Texas Thirtieth District, Justice Sandra Day O'Connor concluded that if "the promise of the Reconstruction amendments, that our nation is to be free of state-sponsored discrimination, is to be upheld, we cannot pick and choose . . . in our efforts to eliminate unjustified racial stereotyping by government actors."[43] In other words, when the government classifies citizens by race for the purpose of drawing legislative district boundaries—which for some bears an uncomfortable resemblance to government using race to draw school district boundaries or, as in Tuskegee, city limit boundaries—it is likely violating the equal protection provisions of the Constitution. In successive cases—*Miller v. Johnson* (1995), *Shaw v. Hunt* (1996), and *Bush v. Vera* (1996)—the Court confirmed that race cannot be the predominate factor in districting and the excessive use of race in drawing legislative districts is likely to fail the strict scrutiny test.

In the current millennium the courts have relaxed their standard for assessing the constitutionality of racially gerrymandered districts. In *Easley v. Cromartie* (2001) it established a high standard for concluding that race was the predominant factor in drawing district boundaries relative to political considerations such as partisanship. Districts that appear racially gerrymandered may be constitutional if it can be shown that political considerations are the predominant factor in drawing district boundaries. *Easley* points to the difficulty of distinguishing a racial gerrymander from a partisan gerrymander when there is a strong partisan direction to the vote.[44] While excessive use of race in districting may be unconstitutional, the heavy reliance on partisanship is not. The Court furthered the ability of states to use race in districting in *Georgia v. Ashcroft* (2003) when it established the standard of "effective exercise of electoral franchise." Here the Court recognized the importance of both "substantive" representation and "descriptive" representation in assessing whether election processes contribute toward fair and effective representation. The Court also recognized "safe," "coalitional," and "influence" districts, and outlined how these contribute to fair and effective representation.

These types of districts are discussed in the following chapter, but the cumulative direction of these decisions points to the benefits of majority-minority districting that has clearly facilitated the election of minority representatives, but also the primary concern raised about racially driven districting: majority-minority districting can be used to dilute the overall influence of minorities in the political process. In particular, such districting can approximate the practice of "packing" a district if populated by a proportion of minority voters to the extent necessary to elect a member of this group to Congress. In addition, minority voters placed in majority-minority districts have to come from other districts, thereby "bleaching" the surrounding districts by increasing the percentage of white voters in them, with correspondingly less influence for the remaining minority voters. The laudable normative objective of increasing minority representation in Congress through majority-minority districting may come at the expense of the reduced overall political influence of minorities in American government.

Conclusion

If American political development is properly understood in terms of shifts in governing authority, then the courts era captures such a change within the national government. In the late nineteenth century the national government wrestled control of House elections from the states, but this authority resided entirely within Congress. The courts repeatedly confirmed this principle in the mid-twentieth century. The judiciary recognized congressional authority to specify the manner of House elections and the right of Congress to determine what powers in this regard were delegated to the states. In the 1960s the Court began to erode congressional authority, and by the 1990s the judiciary was primarily responsible for determining the institutional framework in which Americans elect their representatives. The courts, inter alia, would not tolerate deviations from equal vote value, greatly restricted the use of at-large elections, and established guidelines the executive branch could follow to compel states to advance minority representation in Congress. The courts also protected political parties and statehouse ability to draw districts as they saw fit, but this protection was granted at the pleasure of the Court.

The process of the judiciary asserting control over House elections reveals the complicated problems the Court faces when called on to adjudicate district geography. If representatives are elected from single-member districts, and if these must contain equal population, then districts will be irregularly shaped. Some level of what we call gerrymandering is inevitable if we elect representatives from geographic districts, single-member or otherwise, where districts must contain equal population. The extent of gerrymandering only increases if we add additional requirements that districts must satisfy. Irregularities in district shape are exacerbated if districts are drawn to encompass particular classes of people: Democrats, Republicans, African Americans, or tall people. Further, in the absence of reliance on a formulaic rule, determining the limits of acceptable and unacceptable gerrymandering is a very subjective enterprise. The popular politics of districting is equally subjective; one person's gerrymander is often protecting another person's community of interest. The limits of gerrymandering are even more uncertain if it is permissible for some purposes—say, protecting incumbents or Republicans—but subject to extra scrutiny if they appear designed to encompass a particular demographic group. There can be no geographically perfect district, and the benefits of district elections and the achievement of particular representational objectives have to be weighed against one's tolerance for odd geography.

The book's concluding chapter returns to these normative arguments, but before this discussion the following chapter assesses the House SMD system by standards often used to assess the performance of electoral systems. In doing so, the chapter focuses on aggregate-level considerations that help us assess the application of the single-member system to House of Representatives elections. These include whether SMD elections are responsible for the American two-party system, whether gerrymandering significantly detracts from the quality of American democracy, and whether the system tends to fairly reward parties with House seats given their vote shares. In doing so, the chapter assesses whether there are significant biases in this votes-to-seats translation that favor one or the other party, and whether the system is responsive to shifts in the popular vote. The chapter argues that by these largely empirical standards, the House of Representatives single-member district electoral system performs well. It turns out that there are several considerations that drive the two-party system. In addition, in the United States the party vote shares and seat shares often match quite well. There are certainly particular elections in which the Democrats or the Republicans have secured more chamber seats than their vote shares merit, but over the long term these biases are modest and fleeting. Further, the introduction of such biases—generally through redistricting and gerrymandering—tends to increase the responsiveness of the system to shifts in the vote. This suggests that a districting plan that produces partisan advantage also often contains the seeds of its own destruction. Parties that live by the gerrymander can die by the gerrymander. In addition, the decennial census-induced redistricting invariably makes the political system more responsive to changing political opinion. This further balances the short-run advantages of gerrymandering. The following chapter also considers more deeply the SMD system in light of efforts to increase the influence of racial minorities and their presence in Congress. In doing so, it argues that, as anticipated by the supporters of the system in the civil rights era, it is actually quite beneficial to furthering these objectives and that many of the proposed alternatives to SMD election are likely to have a detrimental effect in this regard. We now turn to these considerations.

8 The Performance of the US SMD System

> We would say, Your Honor, that an incompetent
> gerrymander is no less a gerrymander when
> it unequally apportions the population than a
> competent gerrymander that obtained the partisan
> objective.
>
> *Attorney Mark F. Hearn II*[1]

This chapter assesses the performance of the US House of Representatives single-member district system in contemporary House elections. Doing so requires traversing complicated terrain. Some criticisms of House elections are largely criticisms of Congress in general, and while these critiques may have aspects that owe to elections, some derive from other sources, including chamber rules and processes. I am concerned only with the SMD system, not the overall workings of the House of Representatives. In addition, the chapter's starting point is that for reasons rooted in political thought and historical development the single-member district electoral system best fits the US polity and its constitutional architecture. Therefore its performance is properly judged according to standards appropriate for this election method. The performance of any electoral system is necessarily relative to some set of benchmarks or ideals. Political scientists have well-established standards for evaluating electoral systems in general and the SMD system in particular. This chapter is empirical and as such focuses on relevant empirical standards. I defer discussion of the deeper ideals relevant to the single-member district system to the concluding chapter. Together, these chapters provide both supporters and detractors of the SMD system a foundation for discussing and evaluating the merits of this election method.

I first consider the relationship between the single-member district system and the American two-party system. Many believe that the SMD plurality-rule system axiomatically produces a two-party system. It is true that the SMD plurality-rule system favors the two-party system, but the connection between election method and the Democratic and Republican Parties' dominance is more subtle and nuanced than suggested by a simple causal linkage. The United States has two major political parties in part because of the unique historical development of these parties and the nature of American partisanship. Unlike the European democracies, the United States witnessed the emergence of modern mass political parties commanding deep attachment before the full onset of industrialization and urbanization. This had profound consequences for the number of parties, their organizational characteristics, and their relationships with the mass electorate. This helps explain why the single-member district system operates quite differently in the United States than it does in other nations.

The third section considers districting and, in particular, gerrymandering. The controversial practice of gerrymandering recalls the Federalist and Anti-Federalist dispute over whether legislative districts should be homogeneous or heterogeneous. The Federalists advocated heterogeneous districts without a dominant political interest or constituency. The Anti-Federalists preferred homogeneous districts encompassing clearly defined political communities. The second and third chapters explained the reasons for these Federalist and Anti-Federalist differences that hearken back to their respective understandings of the purpose of the House of Representatives and its proper election. Reminding ourselves about the founding-era discussions of districting helps us make better sense of contemporary disputes over the drawing of legislative districts. Still, the founding-era debate does not map perfectly to the current discussion because of the emergence of modern political parties. US political parties are politically heterogeneous; each is comprised of many, often rather distinct, groups. Consequently, even in a district dominated by a single party a constituency can speak with many voices.

Americans are convinced that irregularly shaped districts are undesirable. That said, most political scientists would argue that gerrymandering is not as significant a problem for US electoral democracy as is generally thought. This stems in part from the nature of American political parties while in other respects it owes to the mathematics of drawing districts and the limits of partisan geography. This section discusses standards for assessing gerrymandering, the relationship between gerrymandering and the votes-to-seats translation, whether gerrymandering contributes to political polarization, and the effects of racial gerrymandering on minority representation and political efficacy in Congress. This discussion emphasizes the inherent tradeoffs in gerrymandering. Effective gerrymanders increase electoral responsiveness, so that parties that live by the gerrymander risk dying by the gerrymander. There is little or no evidence that gerrymandering contributes significantly to US political polarization. Finally, racial gerrymanders demonstrably increase the representation of racial minorities in Congress, but these may also reduce the overall electoral influence of minorities writ large. These tradeoffs must be recognized and accommodated.

The final section evaluates the partisan fairness and responsiveness of the vote-seat translation in House of Representatives elections. Scholars commonly invoke two considerations to assess the performance of the single-member district system. The first is partisan fairness. A fair system should not put a thumb on the electoral scale favoring one party over another party. Second, the election system should respond to shifts in the vote. It is unclear what level of responsiveness is desirable. Surely election results should reflect shifts in the vote, but one would not want a system that changed party control of the House of Representatives in response to every small and transient shift in public opinion. Many election observers would agree that a properly responsive election system would translate a given shift in the aggregate vote to a somewhat larger change in the partisan composition of Congress. Still, there is no "best" level of electoral responsiveness. Some have a high toleration for political change while others might prefer a translation that privileges stability and continuity.

I begin this section by estimating the vote-seat translation curve for contemporary US elections. Beginning in the 1970s, the United States witnessed a fairly significant pro-Democratic bias in this translation that lasted until the 1990s, and a modest pro-Republican bias thereafter. The 2002–2010 apportionment era witnessed little partisan bias in the votes-to-seats translation, while a pro-Republican bias emerged in 2012 that largely dissipated by 2014. On balance, the current empirical performance of the US single-member district system by the standards that are commonly invoked to evaluate electoral systems is satisfactory. The SMD system returns vote-seat shares that are surprisingly proportional, display only modest and episodic partisan bias, and are responsive to the vote. In addition, the theoretical and empirical limits of gerrymandering confirm that while we may find oddly drawn legislative districts aesthetically displeasing, these districts are not the bane of American electoral democracy.

SMD Elections and the US Two-Party System

It is useful to begin with the relationship between SMD plurality elections and the two-party system. There is a nearly reflexive belief among some that the SMD system creates the Democratic and Republican Party duopoly. This follows from Duverger's Law, which describes the apparent empirical regularity with which SMD plurality elections produce two-party systems.[2] "Apparent" is the operative word because this relationship seems to exist only in the United States. Other nations that use SMD plurality elections to select their legislators regularly see viable third- and lower-ranking parties, as evidenced by the United Kingdom's Liberal Democrats, who forced a minority collation government in 2010 by winning 23 percent of the national vote and fifty-seven seats in the House of Commons. Likewise, multiple parties have received nontrivial vote shares and legislative seats in Canada and India. These nations' experiences show that the relationship between electoral system and party system is far from deterministic.[3]

One explanation for the viability of minor parties under SMD elections is that they enjoy graphically concentrated support. Duverger's Law describes a district-level, not national-level, relationship. So, for example, the Scottish National Party secures parliamentary seats because it is viable in Scottish constituencies where it often competes against Labour candidates. While this explanation has merit, it does not account for the existence of truly national third parties such as the Liberal Democrats. Likewise, the Canadian Conservatives, Liberals, and New Democrats are all national parties. These parties have elected parliamentarians from multiple provinces with each party heading or serving as the official opposition in recent governments.[4] Similarly, India has witnessed at least three parties securing at least 5 percent of the national vote in recent elections.

This leads one to explore the foundations of Duverger's Law and why the United States is anomalous among nations that use the single-member district system. Two mechanisms underlie Duverger's Law. The first is the psychological effect that postulates that in SMD plurality elections voters have an incentive to support one of the two leading parties regardless of whether their most preferred party is among them. This is because in winner-take-all elections the difference between first and second place determines the election outcome, whereas the difference between second and third (and lower) finishes does not. One expects instrumental voters—those whose primary purpose in casting a ballot is to affect the election outcome—to vote for their favored party of the two leading parties. This is illustrated by the example of an election contested by Democratic, Republican, and Green Party candidates. A liberal voter who prefers the Green Party candidate to the mainstream Democrat still has an incentive to vote Democratic because the Green Party candidate is unlikely to win, and voting for her advantages the presumptively least favored Republican candidate by taking votes that would otherwise be cast for the Democrat. In this example, voting one's sincere preferences increases the likelihood of one's least-desirable outcome.

A problem with the behavioral underpinning of Duverger's Law is that there is little evidence that US citizens vote strategically. Extant research finds only modest levels of strategic voting in mass elections, insufficient in scale to have an appreciable effect on aggregate election results.[5] One reason for this is that strategic voting requires the presence of three or more parties.[6] The only period when one might witness such voting is the later nineteenth and early twentieth centuries when the Populists, Greenbacks, and Progressives provided a potential alternative to the Republican and Democratic Parties. The evidence, however, suggests that the demise of these parties had little to do with strategic voting; instead, these parties evaporated because their support was undercut by the Democratic Party's move to the political left in the New Deal Era.[7]

A second reason for the dearth of strategic voting in the United States is that voters are not simply instrumental; a vote is also an expressive act of partisan identity. This is certainly true in the United States, where partisanship is especially strong, with Democratic or Republican affiliation often established early in life and generally quite stable. Further, partisans make up a large share of the electorate.[8] All of this argues against a strong psychological effect driving the US two-party system. The absence of viable third parties owes less to strategic voting than it does to the history and role of political parties in the United States. The United States is unique in the depth, breadth, and stability of partisan identification centered on two parties that have existed in their modern forms for generations. In the United States most people think of themselves as a Democrat or a Republican and vote accordingly.

While the evidence casts doubt on the strength of Duverger's psychological effect, the discrepancy in the 2010 United Kingdom Liberals' vote-seat share of 23 percent and their seat share of 9 percent is considerable and results from the way the single-member district system translates votes into legislative seats. This is Duverger's mechanical effect, which describes the pattern that in SMD systems parties are underrepresented in legislative

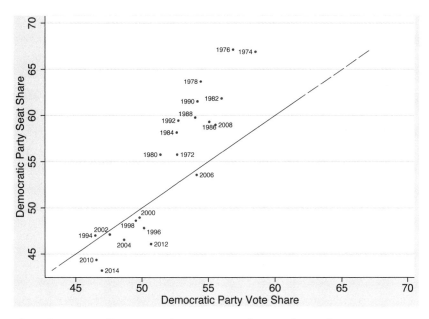

Figure 8.1. House of Representatives Party Vote Shares and Seat Shares: 1972–2014. Gerald G. Rusk, A Statistical History of the American Electorate, and the Office of the Clerk of the US House of Representatives.

seats for vote shares below 50 percent and overrepresented for vote shares in excess of 50 percent. For example, if two parties split the vote 45 percent to 55 percent, one might expect the party that received 55 percent of the vote to win about 60 percent of the seats. This is generalizable; parties that fall farther down in the vote order receive successively smaller seat shares relative to their vote shares, and parties that receive higher vote shares receive disproportionally higher seat shares.[9]

The mechanical effect shapes the distribution of legislative seats in the United States and abroad. Still, the House of Representatives party seat shares align tolerably well with their vote shares. Figure 8.1 graphs the Democratic Party's national share of the two-party vote against its two-party share of seats in the House of Representatives from 1972 to 2014.[10] I begin the series in 1972 because this was the first post-reapportionment election following passage of the Voting Rights Act and the court's one-person/one-vote rulings. The graph superimposes a 45-degree line indicating perfect proportionality. If party vote and seat shares matched, then all observations would fall on this line. They do not, but they do tend to cluster around it, especially after 1990. For example, in 1982 the Democrats received about 56 percent of the national vote and about 62 percent of the House seats. In 2002 the Democrats received about 48 percent of the national vote and a nearly equivalent 47 percent of the chamber seats. The 1970s witnessed the greatest disproportionality, which worked to the benefit of the Democratic Party. Parity increased in the post-2000 era, with a more modest Republican Party advantage during much of this period. Most of the post-2000 observations fall near the proportionality axis with the exception of 2008, which shows a significant Democratic Party advantage in the votes-to-seats translation, and 2012 and 2014, which demonstrate a comparable Republican advantage.

If proportionality is defined as the correspondence between vote share and legislative seat share, then the United States is surprisingly proportional.[11] Indeed, its votes-to-seats correspondence compares quite favorably with polities that apply proportional election methods to multimember constituencies. One reason for this is there are only two parties and the House of Representatives is a large assembly. The United States has no equivalent of the United Kingdom's Liberal Democratic Party or Canada's New Democratic Party. As a consequence for legislative constituencies one is averaging a large number of binary outcomes—Democratic or Republican victory—and this will to a greater or lesser extent approximate the national party vote shares. When one aggregates 435 disproportionate outcomes—and winner-take-all is clearly disproportionate—one can obtain a proportional outcome.[12]

None of this diminishes the importance of Duverger's Law, but rather provides context and nuance for understanding how it operates in the United States. To argue that the SMD plurality-rule system produces a two-party system is to misread Maurice Duverger's actual characterization that "the simple majority single-ballot system favors the two-party system" and this relationship "approaches most nearly perhaps to a true sociological law."[13] Duverger's unfortunate use of the word law belies the extraordinary disciplinary disagreement over the extent to which Duverger's proposition approaches law-like status and wrongfully suggests that there is a deterministic mechanism by which SMD elections produce two-party systems.[14] Duverger himself points to the importance of historical and societal characteristics in shaping party systems: "The historical explanation is more worthy of consideration. The age-long habit of dualism in England and America is obviously a factor in its present strength. It remains to be discovered why this habit has taken such firm root. . . . Only individual investigation of the circumstances in each country can determine the real origins of the two-party system."[15]

On balance, it is simply not the case that the SMD plurality system produces two-party systems. Indeed, nations with geographically concentrated ethnic, religious, or linguistic minorities, multiple dimensions of political competition, and similar divisive fault lines will generally host multiple political parties regardless of electoral system. The United States, however, is a relatively simple polity. Our linguistic and cultural lines of cleavage do not approach the saliency of those in Canada or India. Our regional differences, while important, do not have the political significance of those in the United Kingdom.[16] In the United States political competition revolves around a single liberal-to-conservative spectrum.[17] Duverger compares the effect of the election system on the number of political parties to a "brake or an accelerator" on a car.[18] It is these other polity features that are the engine. In combination with the unique nature of US partisanship, these present obstacles to third parties, but obstacles that would exist regardless of the electoral system. Duverger's Law applies so well to the United States because the pump is primed for it to do so.

Gerrymandering

Gerrymandering is the amorphous defect of American electoral politics. We attribute many of the ills of American government to gerrymandering even if we can't precisely define what makes a gerrymandered district gerrymandered. Any discussion of gerrymandering has to begin with the legal and practical constraints on districting. Politicians may not draw districts however they please; districts must contain equal population and be drawn to nondiscriminatory effect in accordance with the Voting Rights Act, exhibit deference to local political subdivisions, and adhere to a host of other constraints. Districts are certainly drawn for partisan advantage or incumbency protection, but these objectives are often incommensurable; optimal partisan gerrymanders may make some incumbents more vulnerable, and protecting incumbents often reduces the efficacy of partisan districting. Finally, districting is an inherently uncertain activity. Despite the use of geographic information systems and knowledge of constituents' past electoral behaviors, map drawers cannot easily forecast the future. Left to their own devices, politicians would prefer stable districts in which they can create supportive constituencies through contact, service, and legislating rather than attempting to design sympathetic constituencies through districting.

To understand the relationship between gerrymandering and the House SMD election system, it is useful to review the basics of territorial districting. One can then assess how gerrymandering affects the vote-seat translation, representation, and related considerations.[19] How does one know if a district is gerrymandered? Representative Richard L. Roudebush once colorfully described gerrymandered districts as looking like "octopi in mating season."[20] The first task, then, is to formalize the appearance of amorous octopi.

To begin, consider the simple geometry of area. A circle is the shape that contains the largest area relative to its perimeter. The area of a circle is $A = \pi r^2$ with radius r and perimeter $P = 2\pi r$, so if a circle encloses an area of 10 then its radius is 1.78 and its perimeter is approximately 11.20. Compare this with a square containing the same area. The area of a square is $A = s^2$ the length of a side squared, and its perimeter is four times the length of a side. So a square containing an area of 10 has a side of $s = 10^{1/2} \approx 3.16$ and a perimeter of 12.65. With this in mind, the most common definition of district compactness is area relative to its boundary. Districts that enclose larger areas relative to their perimeters are more compact than those that enclose smaller areas relative to their perimeters. The more compact a district is, the less it looks like an octopus in mating season. If one accepts this definition, then district shapes can be compared to the circular benchmark. For example, the ratio of the square perimeter to the circle perimeter is 12.65/11.20 = 1.13, the ratio for an equilateral triangle is 1.29, and so forth. This motivates the conceptually simple Polsby-Popper compactness measure, which compares the ratio of the area in a legislative district to the area contained in a circle with the same perimeter. To illustrate, consider a district that has an area of 10 contained in a perimeter of length 20. Since the perimeter of the corresponding circle is 11.20, the Polsby-Popper measure is 11.2/20.0 = 0.56. This measure ranges from 0 to 1, with values near 0 returned by districts with lengthy perimeters relative to their areas and values close to 1 for nearly circular districts. Customarily, one subtracts the ratio value from 1 and multiplies by 100 to create a gerrymander scale ranging from approximately 0 for circular districts to near 100 for very irregularly shaped districts.[21]

A problem with this measurement approach is that districts that are bounded by natural topographical features such as rivers and mountains are inevitably less compact than otherwise comparable districts drawn without reference to these features, yet we often prefer that districts follow natural boundaries. Kentucky House districts aren't very compact, but the Ohio River forms the northern boundary of six of its congressional districts. There is little one can do to make these districts more compact given the state's irregular border. Likewise, Washington has some districts that appear quite gerrymandered, but these are hemmed in by the densely populated Puget Sound region on the west and the Cascade Mountains on the east. Most Washingtonians would probably agree that the sparsely populated eastern two-thirds of the state is politically distinct from the western third and should have congressional districts that do not reach into the Seattle metropolitan area. One could ignore the Puget Sound and Cascade Mountains and draw districts that perform better by Polsby-Popper standards, but this would be castigated as unfair or even ridiculous. Such topographical challenges to compact districting exist to one extent or another in all states.

Geometry and topography aside, district shape does not determine whether a district is gerrymandered—the drawer's purpose does. House Judiciary Committee chairman Emanuel Celler made this clear when he defined gerrymandering as drawing a district "in an unnatural and unfair way with the *purpose* of giving special advantage to one group."[22] Likewise, Representative Richard Poff, also a member of the Judiciary Committee, argued that "the heart of the definition (of gerrymandering) is an evil political purpose or a wicked intent." If it is political intent that gives rise to a gerrymander, then there arises a considerable obstacle to defining a gerrymander because:

> [A] district which might be a perfect square, while geographically compact, may be the result of an evil political purpose or a wicked intent associated with the definition of gerrymandering. And by the same token a district which follows a natural geographical boundary as the lines meander may appear to anything but compact geographically, but because it was the result of a proper purpose and good intent it would not be a gerrymander and therefore would not violate the definition of compactness as the word is used in this bill.[23]

If the definition of a gerrymander includes the purpose or intent of its designer, then shape is less relevant to determining whether a district is gerrymandered. A square district may be an egregious gerrymander while a serpentine district may be perfectly acceptable. Adjectives such as "unnatural," "unfair," "evil purpose," and "wicked intent" are subject to the same definitional problems Justice Potter Stewart encountered in watching racy films when he articulated his "I know it when I see it" test for obscenity, and amenable to the same level of precision.[24]

The designer's objective, not the district's shape, determines whether it is gerrymandered. Shape is certainly an indicator of purpose; we often suspect that oddly shaped districts are drawn with "evil political purpose" and "wicked intent," meaning political advantage. However, the same district may also be drawn with proper purpose and good intent. District shape alone reveals little about the author's intention.

The difficulty of divining the drawer's intent notwithstanding, there is no doubt that legislative districts are drawn for political advantage. If so, "wicked intent" resides in the state legislatures, which are largely responsible for drawing congressional districts. In most states the state house majority party decides on legislative district boundaries in the same manner as ordinary legislation.[25] Gerrymandering requires the majority party to district so that it has "an electoral majority in a large number of districts while concentrating the voting strength of the opposition in as few districts as possible."[26] The goal is to create as many safe districts as possible without placing an unnecessarily large number of party support-ers in these districts. The opposing party's districts, in contrast, should be packed with as many of its supporters as possible. Such districting indicates "evil purpose" because it increases the likelihood that the gerrymandering party will win seats well beyond what its popular support would appear to justify. It is quite possible for one party to win a majority of the state-level House vote and the gerrymandering party to win a majority of the state's House seats. Aggregated to the national level, one party can win control of Congress while the other party wins most of the national congressional vote, as occurred in 2012.

Table 8.1 presents the average state-level Polsby-Popper scores for states that elect at least four representatives.[27] The state average, not individual district scores, speaks most directly to gerrymandering. Any state can contain an irregularly shaped district or two, but effective partisan gerrymandering requires winning small but safe margins in as many districts as possible. Further, in the face of the equal-population constraint, it is mathematically impossible to draw one district's bound-aries without affecting all district boundaries. Every district's zigs must be offset by corresponding zags in other districts. The table is sorted from the highest scores (states with the most irregular districts) to lowest scores (states with the least irregular districts). I do not include

Table 8.1. Average District Compactness, Party Seats, and Party Votes—112th and 113th Congresses

State	Polsby-Popper	112th Congress				113th Congress			
		Dem. Seats	Rep. Seats	Dem. Vote Share	Rep. Vote Share	Dem. Seats	Rep. Seats	Dem. Vote Share	Rep. Vote Share
Maryland	88.73	7	1	65.4	34.5	7	1	58.1	41.9
North Carolina	87.53	4	9	50.6	49.4	3	10	44.2	55.8
Louisiana	85.92	1	5	23.9	76.1	1	5	28.3	71.7
Virginia	84.20	3	8	49.0	51.0	3	8	42.5	57.5
Illinois	83.66	12	6	55.4	44.6	10	8	51.4	48.6
Pennsylvania	83.62	5	13	50.8	49.2	5	13	44.5	55.5
Ohio	81.68	4	12	47.9	52.1	4	12	40.0	60.0
Kentucky	81.60	1	5	40.0	60.0	1	5	36.4	63.6
Alabama	81.10	1	6	36.0	64.0	1	6	32.0	68.0
Tennessee	80.59	2	7	36.8	63.2	2	7	34.6	65.4
Texas	80.51	12	24	40.0	60.0	11	25	35.4	64.6
New Jersey	80.47	6	6	55.6	44.4	6	6	51.0	49.0
Arkansas	80.36	0	4	32.3	67.7	0	4	33.3	66.7
South Carolina	79.61	1	6	41.0	59.0	1	6	33.9	66.1
Massachusetts	78.37	9	0	74.9	25.1	9	0	82.7	17.3
California	76.81	38	15	62.0	38.0	39	14	58.0	42.0
Colorado	76.41	3	4	48.6	51.4	3	4	48.4	51.6
Oklahoma	75.14	0	5	32.4	67.6	0	4	27.6	72.5
Georgia	74.35	5	9	40.8	59.2	4	10	41.5	58.5
Missouri	73.92	2	6	43.3	56.7	2	6	38.0	62.0
Mississippi	73.72	1	3	36.9	63.1	1	3	41.1	58.9
Connecticut	73.52	5	0	64.3	35.7	5	0	59.3	40.7
Utah	73.20	1	3	33.4	66.6	0	4	34.3	65.7

(continued on next page)

Table 8.1. (continued)

State	Polsby-Popper	112th Congress				113th Congress			
		Dem. Seats	Rep. Seats	Dem. Vote Share	Rep. Vote Share	Dem. Seats	Rep. Seats	Dem. Vote Share	Rep. Vote Share
Washington	72.99	6	4	54.4	45.6	6	4	51.6	48.4
Wisconsin	72.27	3	5	50.8	49.2	3	5	47.2	52.8
Michigan	71.46	5	9	52.7	47.3	5	9	50.9	49.1
Arizona	70.73	5	4	45.6	54.4	4	5	41.4	58.6
Oregon	70.70	4	1	60.9	39.1	4	1	57.2	42.8
Florida	70.11	9	16	47.0	53.0	9	14	44.0	56.0
Minnesota	68.95	5	3	56.3	43.7	5	3	51.9	48.1
New York	66.72	22	5	69.2	30.8	19	8	60.2	39.8
Iowa	65.05	2	2	51.5	48.5	1	3	46.1	53.9
Kansas	59.28	0	4	20.9	79.1	0	4	36.6	63.4
Indiana	56.42	2	7	45.8	54.2	2	7	38.9	61.1
Nevada	49.35	2	2	49.8	50.2	1	3	40.8	59.2
Average	75.11								

Source: Polsby-Popper scores from Christopher Ingraham, "America's Most Gerrymandered Congressional Districts." Washington Post, May 15, 2014.

Table 8.2. Potentially Gerrymandered States, 2012 and 2014

2012	2014
Alabama	Arkansas
Arkansas	Maryland
Arizona	Michigan
Kentucky	North Carolina
Massachusetts	Oklahoma
Maryland	
Michigan	
North Carolina	
Ohio	
Oklahoma	
Pennsylvania	
South Carolina	
Virginia	
Wisconsin	

states that elect three or fewer representatives because these states cannot be easily gerrymandered. One cannot gerrymander a state that elects a single representative, and it is difficult to gerrymander a couple of districts because population distribution largely determines district boundaries. Four or more districts give mapmakers sufficient discretion to district for political advantage. The table also presents the number of Democratic and Republican representatives elected to the 112th and 113th Congresses from each state, and the corresponding Democratic and Republican Party House vote shares. These data tell us much about House district gerrymandering and its effects.

I assess the extent to which a state is gerrymandered by considering its Polsby-Popper score in combination with evidence of districting-induced political advantage. A high score combined with significant discrepancy between a party's vote share and its House seat share indicates gerrymandering. If the majority statehouse party wins a significantly larger share of House seats than its congressional votes would appear to justify, then one might reasonably suspect partisan gerrymandering. However, one has to approach these figures with some caution. First, a fair SMD vote-seat translation can turn a majority vote share into an even larger seat share. In addition, unlike vote shares, legislative seats are a lumpy quantity. Most states have only a handful of representatives, making the seat share ratio rather coarse. With this in mind, I identify potentially gerrymandered states as those meeting the threshold of (1) a Polsby-Popper score above the national average of 75.11 *and* a 20-point or greater gap between a party's statewide House vote share and its seat share, *or* (2) a state in which the party that won the majority of the statewide vote failed to win a majority of the state's congressional seats regardless of its Polsby-Popper score. Fourteen states met this standard in 2012 and five met it in 2014.

The 2012 election to the 112th Congress saw five states in which the party that won the majority of the statewide House vote failed to win a majority of seats: Arizona, Michigan, North Carolina, Pennsylvania, and Wisconsin. Arizona, however, cannot be properly considered gerrymandered. It uses a nonpartisan commission to draw districts, returns a low Polsby-Popper score, and is electorally competitive, and its vote share–seat share discrepancy is driven by the allocation of a single seat. Wisconsin and Michigan's Polsby-Popper scores are below the national average, but each presents vote share–seat share reversals favoring the Republican Party. The average winning vote margin for Wisconsin Democrats was only slightly greater than those for Republicans, casting doubt on how heavily the state is gerrymandered. In contrast, the average victory margin for Michigan Democrats was three times that for Republican winners, providing evidence for Representative Poff's contention that gerrymandered districts can be geographically compact.[28] North Carolina and Pennsylvania present strong cases for gerrymandering. These states have high Polsby-Popper scores, and Democratic candidates in each state won a slim majority of the statewide vote but only about one-third of the seats. In both states the average Democratic margin of victory was substantially higher than that for Republican winners.

Several other states saw significant discrepancies between vote shares and seat shares. Virginia and Ohio stand out in this regard. Both states were electorally competitive, with the statewide party vote shares separated by only a few points, but the Republican Party won lopsided seat shares in each state. South Carolina and Kentucky fit this profile, albeit to a lesser extent. Maryland contains the nation's least compact districts, and its Democratic candidates turned two-thirds of the vote into all but one of the state's eight House seats. Massachusetts Democrats and Oklahoma and Arkansas Republicans won overwhelming shares of the House vote and all of their respective state's seats. However, it is not clear how much of this owes to gerrymandering and how much to the SMD vote-seat translation. Arkansas and Oklahoma Republican candidates won over 67 percent of their states' votes and all of the seats. Similarly, Massachusetts Democrats swept the board with approximately three-quarters of the vote. It is unclear whether any SMD districting could have elected a minority party representative in these states because there is no obvious geographic concentration of minority party supporters sufficient to support a congressional district. If such a district could be created, its geography would have to be highly irregular.

The number of states meeting the potential gerrymandering threshold in 2014 was greatly reduced; only Michigan saw a vote share–seat share reversal. Maryland presents perhaps the most egregious example of gerrymandering. In this cycle, Republicans increased their vote share to nearly 42 percent but still won only a single seat. North Carolina's discrepancy between party vote shares and seat shares was about the same as in 2012. Republican candidates in Arkansas and Oklahoma continued to hold all seats, with Oklahoma Republicans again winning over 70 percent of the vote, suggesting that no alternative districting could have elected a Democrat in 2014. The difference between 2012 and 2014 is illuminating because the districts remained unchanged. Following the 2012 election a number of national media figures decried what a *New York Times* op-ed writer described as "The Great Gerrymander of 2012."[29] If there was a great gerrymander in 2012, then there must have been a great gerrymander in 2014 because the districts did not change. However, there were few critiques of districting in 2014 because it did not appear to be as significant in driving election outcomes. It was vote-seat translation, not gerrymandering, that drove much of the Republican Party's magnified seat share in 2014.

The politics of gerrymanders is usefully illustrated by more fully considering the Maryland and North Carolina districts. Maryland and North Carolina present remarkable partisan symmetry; Maryland's gerrymanders benefited Democratic officeholders and North Carolina's benefited Republicans. These states illustrate complexities and nuances in assessing gerrymanders.

In 2014 Maryland Democratic House candidates won 57.4 percent of the statewide popular vote and seven of eight House seats. Representative Andrew Harris was the sole elected Republican, winning the Eastern Shore First District with 70.4 percent of the vote compared to the average Democratic winning plurality of 62 percent.[30] The most gerrymandered district is the western Sixth, which encompasses Maryland's Appalachian panhandle and snakes as far south as Montgomery County just outside of Washington, DC. The Sixth District returns a Polsby-Popper score of 92, making it among the most gerrymandered in the nation. The rural western part of the district leans Republican, and it becomes more Democratic as it progresses eastward toward the Washington, DC, area. In 2014 the Sixth was Maryland's only competitive House district. In this election all winning House candidates secured at least 60 percent of the vote except in the Sixth, where no candidate won a majority of the vote. Incumbent Democrat John Delany defeated Republican challenger Dan Bongino with a 49.7 percent plurality. However, Bongino secured a very respectable 48.3 percent of the vote, nearly upsetting the Democratic incumbent. Given its Polsby-Popper score, there is little doubt that Maryland's Sixth District could be modestly adjusted to produce a district in which Republicans could compete more effectively.[31]

North Carolina presents the mirror image of Maryland. It is heavily gerrymandered, but to Republican advantage. In 2014 Republicans won 55.8 percent of the statewide vote and ten of thirteen House seats. The average winning Democratic margin was 74.4 percent, while that for Republican candidates was 61.3.[32] This leaves little doubt that the Republican-controlled state legislature districted for partisan advantage. However, the worthy objective of electing more African Americans to Congress also contributed to gerrymandering. In *Thornburg v. Gingles* (1986) the Supreme Court established standards that could be used to justify the creation of majority-minority legislative districts.[33] In response to *Gingles* the Department of Justice, acting under authority derived from the Voting Rights Act, ordered North Carolina to create two majority-minority House districts. These became the First and Twelfth Districts. Currently, these districts respectively contain approximately 50 and 45 percent black residents and return Polsby-Popper scores of 96 and 97, making them perhaps the most gerrymandered districts in the nation. The Twelfth District is so extraordinarily irregular that the *Wall Street Journal* once described it as "political pornography"; it is depicted in textbooks as, well, the textbook example of gerrymandering. The Supreme Court eventually declared these districts unconstitutional in *Shaw v. Reno* (1993) because race was the primary factor in determining their boundaries, effectively limiting the reach of the *Gingles* decision. However, modest boundary changes survived court challenge until February 2016, when the US District Court for the Middle District of North Carolina concluded that First and Twelfth Districts were drawn for wicked intent, ruling that they were created for the purpose of packing African Americans into these districts for the purpose of advantaging Republicans in other districts and were therefore unconstitutional.[34] Still, these two districts also elected the first African Americans to the House of Representatives from North Carolina in a century.[35] The Twelfth District

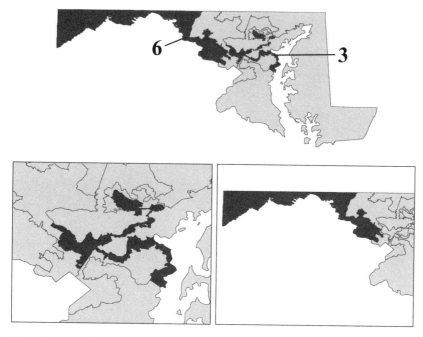

Figure 8.2. *Maryland Congressional Districts: 2014. Source: Jeffrey B. Lewis et al.,* Digital Boundary Definitions of United States Congressional Districts, 1789–2012.

elected Representative Melvin Watt in 1992 and is currently represented by Representative Alma Adams. Current chair of the House Black Caucus G. K. Butterfield represents the First District.[36] One can agree with the federal district court that these districts were drawn with "wicked intent" because they sought to secure Republican advantage by geographically concentrating African American voters, but they also advanced the laudable objective of increasing the racial diversity of Congress.[37] A districting can simultaneously serve shameful and worthy objectives.

It is important to understand that the courts embrace a holistic definition of compactness that recognizes the lumpiness of population distributions, common political history, and the extent to which citizens are "close enough" in terms of geography and their political and economic interests to justify inclusion in a single legislative district. They also defer to the preservation of local political subdivisions.[38] The extent to which these other things matter was brought to the forefront in *Miller v. Johnson* (1995), where the court struck down a highly irregular Georgia majority-minority

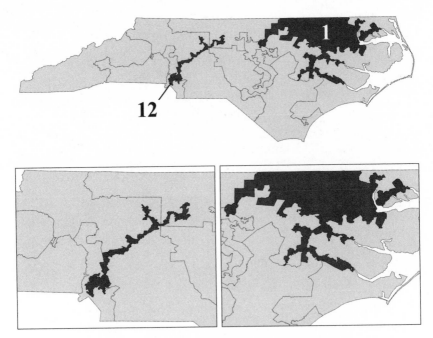

Figure 8.3. North Carolina Congressional Districts: 2014. Source: Jeffrey B. Lewis et al., Digital Boundary Definitions of United States Congressional Districts, 1789–2012.

district on the grounds that these districts ignored traditional districting principles such as "compactness, contiguity, [and] respect for political subdivisions or communities defined by actual shared interests." Race was the only consideration that could explain its shape. However, the court simultaneously recognized that "traditional districting principles" could drive irregularly shaped districts. Districts crafted according to these principles will not necessarily fare well by Polsby-Popper standards. In the United States deference to traditional districting principles means that districts will be irregularly shaped, and whether they are too irregularly shaped is in the eye of the political beholder.

Stipulating the presence of gerrymandering, does it present a serious problem for the quality of US representative democracy? Many political scientists are skeptical that gerrymandering ranks among the most crucial defects in American electoral democracy. Gerrymandering for the purpose of diluting the voting power of racial minorities clearly does present a serious threat to the quality of American democracy. The other major alleged gerrymandering harms including that it increases political polarization and diminishes electoral responsiveness fail to survive close scrutiny.

The United States is politically polarized. The question is to what extent polarization owes to gerrymandering and to what extent it emerged from other sources. The causal mechanism linking districting to polarization is parsimonious; homogeneous partisan districts allow ideological extremists to win election because they do not have to appeal to moderates. This tendency is reinforced by the primary system because it requires candidates to appeal to the more extreme wings of their respective parties to secure nomination for office. Once nominated, they are assured victory because of the partisan composition of the district.

The empirical evidence, however, does not support this explanation; instead, political polarization owes to partisan changes that are quite independent of districting. The United States became increasingly polarized during the civil rights era and the associated Republican "Southern Strategy" to court white voters away from the Democratic Party. The resulting southern realignment transformed a solid Democratic south represented by conservative Democrats to a nearly solid Republican south. More liberal northeastern Republicans withered until they were eventually replaced by Democrats, and in the rural west the "Sagebrush Rebellion" advantaged conservative Republicans. The result was the parties aligned on their ideological bases. The Democrats became more liberal when their conservative southern brethren left the party, and Republicans, with the loss of their more liberal northeastern and western members, became more conservative. This secular trend, not districting, drove polarization. The extent to which representatives have become more ideologically extreme is a consequence of this realignment, combined with political parties that are too weak to structure elections or congressional chamber behaviors.[39]

Even if districting does not cause polarization, one might reasonably expect it to entrench or even exacerbate it. The evidence for this proposition is also weak.[40] First, there has been a comparable polarization increase in the Senate, which is not subject to gerrymandering. Second, if the causal story is correct then gerrymandering itself constrains the ideological extremism of the majority party. A proper gerrymander leaves majority party districts more heterogeneous than minority party districts. Consequently, majority party legislators should be more moderate than minority party legislators, which does not appear to be the case. In perhaps the most extensive and methodologically sophisticated study of the relationship between gerrymandering and political polarization, Nolan McCarty, Keith T. Poole, and Howard Rosenthal conclude that in their "search to uncover the smoking gun [of districting-induced political polarization], the case has crumbled."[41] These scholars argue that legislative polarization instead owes to differences in how Democratic and Republican representatives view their responsibilities and their respective roles in the party organization, how they pursue legislative career paths, and similar considerations. Even if elected from heterogeneous districts, representatives will deviate from the preferences of the median citizen in the normal course of events. James Campbell's recent and exhaustive study of American political polarization is unequivocal in claiming that "polarization is a much broader phenomenon than gerrymandered redistricting could possibly explain."[42] District gerrymandering does not contribute in any significant way to legislative or broader political polarization.

The North Carolina First and Twelfth Districts raise questions about whether districting to facilitate the election of racial minorities to Congress is beneficial as a matter of principle. This introduces, as Vincent L. Hutchings and Nicholas A. Valentino succinctly put it, the question of whether the most effective approach to protecting and advancing the political interests of racial minorities "requires maximizing the number of black representatives in Congress . . . or whether racial minorities acting in concert with like-minded white Americans can achieve genuine representation for blacks."[43] There is little doubt that the election of racial minorities to Congress requires districts with a heavy concentration of minority voters.[44] Purposeful districting to achieve this objective is often necessary.

The benefits of descriptive representation—of creating a chamber that looks more like the United States—certainly exist, especially if one subscribes to the Anti-Federalist preference for mirroring representation. Minority communities are also benefited by better substantive representation; the evidence shows that racial minorities represent their constituents better than white representatives. This is reflected in representatives' roll-call voting, committee work, constituency service, and other legislative activities.[45] Minority representation also appears to increase constituents' feelings of political efficacy and engagement. Further, minority representatives elected from majority-minority districts also appear to do a good job of representing the interests of their white constituents.[46] This chain of reasoning argues that the election of minorities to the House that requires noncompact districting is beneficial on both descriptive and substantive grounds.

The critique of this argument as reflected in the continual litigation over the North Carolina districts is that such districts draw minority populations from surrounding districts, making these whiter and more likely to elect representatives unsympathetic to the priorities of racial minorities. This so-called bleaching of districts is posited to negatively affect racial minorities because these legislators negate the substantive representational gains achieved by minority populations through racial districting. This is sometimes called the "perverse effects thesis" in that the overall effect of electing more racial minorities to Congress may be to diminish the overall efficacy of these groups in the political process. Evidence for this proposition is mixed. On one hand, studies in the 1990s seemed to support the thesis.[47] Looking at legislative voting in the first Congress after the 1990 reapportionment and redistricting, Marvin Overby and Kenneth Cosgrove argue that there was "a significant, quantifiable, trade-off between descriptive and substantive representation afforded by majority-minority districts."[48] Likewise, David Epstein and Sharyn O'Halloran argue that the effect of racial gerrymandering is to "dilute rather than enhance substantive minority representation."[49] More recently, scholars such as Bernard Groffman, David Canon, and Kenneth Shotts express skepticism that such effects are pronounced, and even if they exist they are insufficient to offset the beneficial effects of electing more racial minorities to Congress. As Kenneth Shotts concludes, "Racial gerrymandering for southern House districts promotes liberal policy outcomes" presumably desired by and beneficial to minority communities.[50] On balance, the "perverse effects thesis" enjoys only mixed support, and any diminution of overall political efficacy for minorities' communities from purposeful districting appears to be compensated by other benefits derived from increased descriptive representation.

The Bias and Responsiveness of the US SMD System

The figure 8.1 vote share to seat share graph motivates considering more deeply whether there are any systematic biases in the US House vote-to-seat translation and the responsiveness of this translation. A fair electoral system should translate 50 percent of the vote into 50 percent of the legislative seats for both parties, and any other vote share into the same seat share for both parties. If Democrats receive 55 percent of the vote and win 60 percent of the House seats, then Republicans should also turn 55 percent of the vote into 60 percent of the House seats. A fair system turns equivalent vote shares into equivalent seat shares for both parties.

Districting affects the votes-to-seats translation. The packing of one party's supporters into a few districts enables the other party to win a majority of a state's legislative seats with less than a majority of the statewide vote. Districting can also affect the responsiveness or "swing ratio" of the votes-to-seats translation, which captures how a percentage change in the vote translates into a change in the distribution of legislative seats. A large number of competitive districts produces a higher swing ratio than a districting with few competitive districts. If a party gerrymanders so that its supporters are spread thinly across districts in an attempt to win as many seats as possible, one would expect a greater swing ratio than in an alternative districting with safer margins in fewer districts. That said, the mere act of redistricting as is required following the decennial census, regardless of whether the redrawn districts are gerrymandered or not, tends to increase system responsiveness and reduce partisan bias compared with leaving districts stagnant. Redistricting in and of itself has beneficial effects even if we blanch at the shapes of the new districts.[51]

To assess the fairness of the US single-member district system in this regard, I estimate a vote-seat curve for US House elections between 1972 and 2014. The vote-seat curve captures the translation of party vote shares into legislative seat shares in a two-party system elected under the SMD plurality-rule system. The votes-to-seats translation follows a functional form first proposed by M. G. Kendall and A. Stuart in 1950.[52]

$$\text{Seat Share}_i/(1\text{-Seat Share}_i) = [\text{Vote Share}_i/(1\text{-Vote Share}_i)]^{\beta}$$

This specification relates the ratio of party seat shares to the ratio of their vote shares. The subscript "i" denotes one of the political parties, which throughout this section is the Democratic Party. Thus defined, the right-hand term is the ratio of the Democratic Party's vote share to the Republican Party's vote share. The left-hand side is defined analogously for House of Representatives seat shares. The parameter β is the system's responsiveness or "swing ratio." If β equals one, then a shift of 1 percent in the vote ratio produces an identical shift in the seat ratio. If β is greater than one, then the vote-to-seat translation is described by a sigmoid curve with responsiveness increasing in this parameter.[53] Because the curve is S-shaped, a given shift in roughly equal party vote shares produces a substantially larger change in the seat ratio than an equivalent change when the vote shares are highly unequal. Kendall and Stewart dubbed this votes-to-seats relationship the

"Law of Cubic Proportions" because β equal to 3 appeared to fit observed vote and seat ratios. However, this is yet another "law" that isn't a law. For the United States, scholars have generally found that the votes-to-seats translation is more often characterized by values closer to 2.[54]

One can estimate the votes-to-seats translation from House of Representatives election returns. Logging both sides of the equation gives:

$$\ln[\text{Seat Share}_i/(1\text{-Seat Share}_i)] = \beta \times \ln[\text{Vote Share}_i/(1\text{-Vote Share}_i)]$$

A regression of the logged vote share on the seat shares produces:

$$\ln[\text{Seat Share}_i/(1\text{-Seat Share}_i)] = \widehat{\ln\lambda} + \hat{\beta} \times \ln[\text{Vote Share}_i/(1\text{-Vote Share}_i)]^\beta$$

where the estimated $\hat{\beta}$ is the responsiveness of the vote-seat translation and $\widehat{\ln\lambda}$ is the partisan bias in the translation. Specifically, captures whether or not the parties receive equal seat shares for equal vote shares. If $\widehat{\ln\lambda}$ is zero, then neither party is advantaged by the translation. A value larger than zero means that party "i" receives more legislative seats than the other party would with the same vote share. The converse is true if $\widehat{\ln\lambda}$ is less than zero; party "i" receives fewer legislative seats than the other party would with the same vote. It is important to understand that bias has nothing to do with Duverger's mechanical effect. An unbiased vote-to-seat translation turns equivalent vote shares into equivalent seat shares. This means that the vote-seat curve must pass through the 50-50 point on a graph that plots vote shares against seat shares. Before and after this point, the extent of the mechanical effect depends solely on the swing ratio. A perfectly unbiased system can translate 52 percent of the vote into 55 percent of the seats; it must simply do so for both parties.

A nonzero $\widehat{\ln\lambda}$ may indicate gerrymandering since such districts are won by smaller margins than districts won by the other party. Gerrymandering is further suggested if $\widehat{\ln\lambda}$ is accompanied by a larger $\hat{\beta}$ since gerrymandering increases the responsiveness of the system. This is because more districts are won with thin margins, so that a shift in the vote produces a larger change in seats. Still, there may be other reasons why $\widehat{\ln\lambda}$ differs from zero, including incumbency advantage that results from activities that have nothing to do with districting such as constituency service, so this parameter should be interpreted with care informed by political context.

One can calculate vote-seat curves for historic House elections. I do this by first estimating the following equation for the figure 8.1 national House vote and seat shares:

$$\ln[\text{Seat Share}_i/(1\text{-Seat Share}_i)] = \ln\lambda + \beta \times \ln[\text{Vote Share}_i/(1\text{-Vote Share}_i)]$$

Table 8.3 presents these estimates. The first column presents the estimate for the above equation, and the second column presents estimates for a model that calculates separate biases for periods before and after the 1994 election that led the Republican Party to control the House of Representatives for the first time since 1952.

The first-column estimates suggest that for the 1972 to 2014 period the House SMD system was heavily biased in favor of the Democratic Party, with a responsiveness coefficient approaching 2. The estimated bias parameter $\widehat{\ln\lambda} = 0.64$ so $\lambda = 1.9$; over this period the Democratic Party enjoyed an extraordinary 15 percent advantage in the House votes-to-seats translation. The Republicans had to win about 65 percent of the vote to win a majority of chamber seats. However, this partisan advantage owes to the 1970s and 1980s confluence of Watergate and sticky southern districts that continued to benefit Democratic candidates through the 1980s. As late as 1980 the Democrats held over two-thirds of House seats based on approximately 54 percent of the national vote.[55] Many Republican candidates won respectable vote receipts, but these were still insufficient to translate into seats. Re-estimation of the model separating the pre- and post-1994 elections reduces estimated responsiveness by about 20 percent, and produces more sensible

Table 8.3. Bias and Responsiveness in House Elections, 1972–2014

	Model 1	Model 2
Intercept (Bias)	0.64**	
	(0.11)	
Intercept (1972–1994)		0.43**
		(0.08)
Intercept (1996–2014)		−0.10**
		(0.02)
Vote Ratio (Responsiveness)	1.92**	1.52**
	(0.17)	(0.12)
N	22	22
Adj-R²	0.86	0.95

**p < 0.01

bias estimates of approximately 10 points in favor of the Democratic Party prior to 1996 and about 2.4 percent in favor of the Republican Party thereafter. These figures comport well with our understanding of congressional elections in this period.[56]

National-level aggregation obscures important state-level aspects of this translation and severely limits the number of observations on which one bases inferences. Consequently, I reestimated the same model for the 2002–2010 period, and the 2012 and 2014 elections using state-level observations on vote and seat shares. Specifically, I estimated:

$$\ln[\text{Seat Share}_{ist}/(1\text{-Seat Share}_{ist})] = \ln\lambda + \beta \times \ln[\text{Vote Share}_{ist}/(1\text{-Vote Share}_{ist})]$$

The unit of analysis is the state election with the new indices "s" and "t" denoting the state and election respectively. The dependent variable is the proportion of state-level House seats won by the Democratic Party in state "s" in election "t," and the independent variable is the corresponding proportion of the House vote won by the Democratic Party. Thus for any election we have fifty observations.[57] I first estimated the model for the combined 2002–2010 period because this encapsulates an entire apportionment cycle. I then reestimated the model for the 2012 and 2014 elections separately. The increased number of observations allows exploration of the vote-to-seat curve in detail, including the extent to which particular states drive any biases in the translation. However, estimation is complicated by the fact that a substantial number of state-level seat shares are either 0 or 1 because some states elect an entirely Democratic or an entirely Republican delegation. This is necessarily true for the seven states that elect a single representative. Because of this, ordinary least squares estimation is no longer appropriate. Consequently, I used a method proposed by Leslie Papke and Jeffrey Wooldrich to estimate the vote-to-seat translation.[58] The logistic specification obtains estimates with desirable properties, but the returned coefficients are no longer interpretable in the same manner as those in table 8.3. I therefore used graphical methods to illustrate the vote-seat translation for these elections.

The 2002 and 2012–2014 House of Representatives votes-to-seats translation shows a responsiveness coefficient significantly greater than zero. However, since the substantive interpretation of the intercept and swing ratio cannot be ascertained directly from the estimated coefficients, I present votes-to-seats curves for these elections in Figures 8.4 and 8.5.

Table 8.4. Bias and Responsiveness in House Elections, 2002–2010, 2012, and 2014

	2002–2010	2012	2014
Intercept	−5.94**	−7.57**	−7.65**
	(0.38)	(0.85)	(0.81)
Vote Ratio	11.90**	14.83**	15.38**
	(0.78)	(1.65)	(1.64)
N	249	50	50
Wald Chi-Square	231.42	81.02	87.67

Figure 8.4 shows that for the 2002–2010 apportionment cycle the estimated vote-to-seat translation is unbiased and has a swing ratio of just over
two at the 50-50 point on the graph. This is not surprising. In these five elections, two (2002 and 2006) produced nearly proportional vote-seat shares,
while one (2008) of the remaining three elections presented a significant
Democratic Party advantage, and two (2004 and 2010) produced smaller
Republican Party advantages. Averaging over these elections across all
states produces a nearly symmetric and responsive vote-to-seat translation.

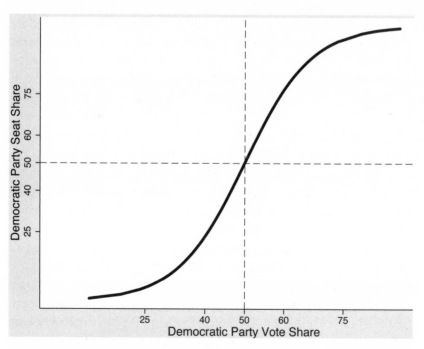

Figure 8.4. Vote-Seat Curve, 2002–2010

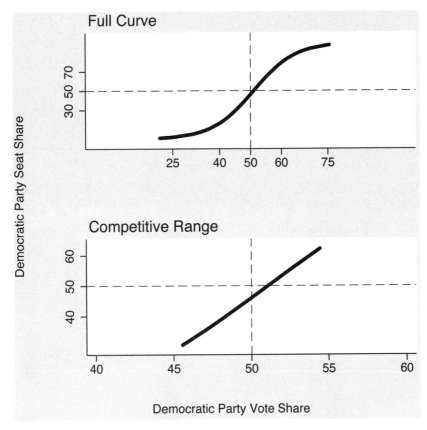

Figure 8.5. Vote-Seat Curve, 2012

Figure 8.5 graphs the 2012 vote-seat curve that displays a pronounced Republican bias. The top panel displays the entire curve and the bottom panel focuses on the electorally competitive range of between 45 and 55 percent party vote shares. The latter panel shows that the curve is shifted to the right, so that if the Democratic Party won 50 percent of the House vote they would win about 46 percent of the chamber seats. Figure 8.6 shows that by 2014 this pro-Republican bias largely dissipates. For comparison purposes, in *Gerrymandering in America*, which is the most current and comprehensive study of congressional gerrymandering in the post–*Vieth v. Jubelirer* era, Anthony J. McGann, Charles Anthony Smith, Michael Latner, and Alex Keena use a different statistical method to estimate the 2002–2010 vote-seat translation and the 2012 vote-seat translation.[59] They find a modest pro-Republican bias in the 2002–2010 period, and their estimated 2012 vote-seat curve is nearly

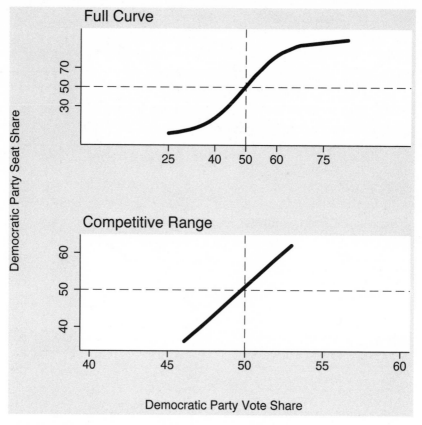

Figure 8.6. Vote-Seat Curve, 2014

identical to that reported here.[60] Both McGann et al.'s and my analyses tell similar stories: the vote-seat translation from 2002 to 2010 was either unbiased or only modestly biased, and there was a significant pro-Republican bias in the 2012 vote-seat translation. However, consistent with expectations, this bias is significantly reduced in the subsequent election cycle.[61]

This does not change the fact that in 2012 and 2014 the Republicans turned smaller aggregate vote shares into chamber majorities. In 2012 Democratic candidates secured approximately 59.2 million votes, while Republican candidates won about 57.6 million votes. Despite this, the Republicans won 234 House seats while the Democrats won 201 seats; this provides corroborating evidence that the vote-seat curve really shifted to the right in 2012, favoring the Republican Party, and that this shift resulted from the state-level redistricting that followed the 2010 census. In

2014 Democratic candidates won just over 35 million votes to the nearly 40 million won by Republican candidates, producing significant Republican gains in the House of Representatives. The final 242 to 193 Republican to Democratic seat division did not result from a biased vote-to-seat translation. The Republicans did better than their vote percentage because they were high enough on the vote-seat curve for Duverger's mechanical effect to reward them with disproportionally large seat shares. Had the electoral gods been more evenhanded, in 2014 then one would have expected a more closely divided House of Representatives.

The US SMD plurality system is fair in the sense that if each party receives a given vote share it will receive the same corresponding seat share. That does not mean it is fair in every election cycle, nor does it mean that the vote-to-seat translation is linear and proportional. Even when the vote-to-seat translation is unbiased, at vote shares above 50 percent parties will be rewarded with a disproportionate share of legislative seats. The US single-member district electoral system displays episodic electoral bias, but this tends to be modest, depends on the party in power, and has diminished in recent decades. When the SMD system produces partisan advantage it typically does so not from bias in the vote-to-seat translation but rather from rewarding disproportionate legislative seats to parties that secure significantly more than 50 percent of the legislative vote. That was certainly the case in several recent House election cycles. Whether this is a good thing depends on how much importance one places on elections returning chamber majorities sufficiently large to govern. Turning 53 percent of the vote into a chamber majority of 56 percent takes a modest margin of victory and produces a chamber membership probably sufficient to enact a legislative program. A proportional vote-seat share that turns a small vote majority to a comparably small seat majority leaves little room for error or defection in pursuing a legislative agenda.

Conclusion

This chapter evaluates the performance of the US single-member district system by considering whether it produces the two-party duopoly, whether districting significantly biases political outcomes or drives other detrimental effects in the political process, and whether its votes-to-seats translation is fair and responsive. The general theme in all of these topics is that while the SMD system may be rightfully subject to indictment, there is little ground for conviction.

The US single-member district system advantages the two-party system, but it does not create it. There are several reasons why the United States has a two-party system, and many of these have little to do with single-member district elections. The two-party system is advantaged by the nature of political competition in a large, heterogeneous nation in which parties were formed early in our political history in a polity with few linguistic, religious, or similar fault lines. To the extent that these cleavages exist, corresponding political conflict takes place within the two-party framework. This is exemplified by sectional politics, which the United States has most certainly observed, characterized by the historic one-party Democratic south and the contemporary Republican Party strength in the same region. Similarly, racial politics is captured, at least to some extent, by the disproportionate support African Americans provide the Democratic Party. In the main, the two-party system was created and is maintained for reasons that center on the historical circumstances of party building in the preindustrial age, and is maintained because US partisan identification is exceptionally broad and deep.

Some argue that different electoral institutions will foster a broader menu of parties and corresponding partisan affiliation. The difficulty with this argument is that it requires one to speculate on the current support base for third parties and what it would be under alternative electoral arrangements. While a significant proportion of Americans express dissatisfaction with the two-party system, the evidence indicates that this is more talk than a serious expression of advocacy for an increased number of party alternatives. Despite polarization, US political parties are heterogeneous, which arguably makes them especially well suited for a large, diverse nation. For all our reservations, US political parties perform functions that smaller, more homogeneous parties are unlikely to fulfill as well. These include brokering political compromise, especially internal compromise within parties; mobilizing the electorate; organizing Congress; and structuring national and state government relations. Given the decentralized constitutional structure of the United States, the size and heterogeneity of our polity, and the ideological traditions that resonate in the American experience, the US two-party system encouraged by the single-member district system fits its resident nation well.

Taking all of this into consideration, the US two-party system is probably not a major source of representational disenfranchisement. As seen previously, the aggregate US vote share and seat share relationship is often proportional, and this is especially true in the post-2000 era. Still, to argue that on average Democrats and Republicans are represented according to their national party strengths is to sympathize with the idea of virtual representation that the American tradition rejects. However, the American rejection of virtual representation has to be tempered by the development of modern political parties. While colonial-era Americans were quite correct that no Briton shared a commonality of interest with those on this side of the Atlantic and therefore no Briton could represent them in Parliament, this argument carries less weight in the presence of political parties that carry consistency in orientation across constituencies. To the extent that this is correct, the contemporary vote-to-seat translation for House elections appears fair. The discrepancies in vote share–seat share ratios often derive from the Duvergerian mechanical effect, which is intrinsic to the single-member district system.

Finally, some of the most strenuous objections to the SMD system center on gerrymandering. Any districting system can be gerrymandered, including multimember constituencies that apply proportional formulas. Gerrymandering is a function of the district, not the vote aggregation rule. That said, this chapter supports the very conventional argument that gerrymandering does not cause the dire effects that the most strenuous objectors to SMD election attribute to it. Districts can be drawn for political advantage, and some are certainly created for this purpose. They can also be drawn to advance socially desirable goals. However, there are significant limitations on districting, redistricting makes elections more rather than less responsive, and the effects of districting are often dwarfed by the overall ebb and flow of the vote. This is not to suggest that districting can be ignored as a source of political malfeasance, but rather to place districting in the context of the many considerations relevant to electing a democratic assembly. Just because irregular districts are often visually objectionable does not mean that they are the most significant deficiency in American politics. There are sometimes very good reasons to draw highly irregular legislative districts.

The most important conclusion drawn from this chapter is that there is no perfect district and any given districting requires balancing multiple objectives. Most Americans probably believe in the abstract that we should increase the number of heterogeneous districts and by extension the number of competitive districts. However, this would require placing less emphasis on respecting communities of interest, including those defined by race and ethnicity, income, political history, and other considerations. Conversely, respecting communities of interest probably produces less-competitive elections. Most favor more-heterogeneous districts up to the point where it is their neighborhood that is divided into multiple districts. More generally, districting is a political process subject to a number of legal, social, and mathematical constraints. Parties will gerrymander, but overly aggressive gerrymandering sometimes produces what Bernard Grofman and Thomas Brunell call a "dummymander," in which the districting party extends its reach so far that it loses an inordinate number of seats when the electoral winds shift.[62] This mathematical limit is hard to estimate, and every ten years the census resets the chessboard. On balance, there will be districts that justifiably produce concern, but if one considers the larger span of history or even the short span of a census cycle, and considers the inherent tradeoffs in any districting plan and the fact that the United States elects a large assembly, then the disagreeable effects of particular districting are placed in proper perspective and are of less concern.

The next chapter addresses the intellectual foundation for the US single-member district system, the political history of its adoption and institutionalization, and the assessment of its contemporary performance to make a comprehensive argument about its place in the US conception of representative democracy. All of these elements are needed to form a more complete assessment of how we elect our representatives. The chapter's argument focuses on the place of single-member district elections within the broader constitutional architecture and American political thought surrounding elections and representation. One of the chapter's key points is that changes in electoral processes propagate out to affect other aspects of constitutional design; electoral institutions cannot be evaluated in isolation. With this in mind, one can accept or reject the argument of the chapter that the single-member district system is a well-functioning and well-placed feature of US constitutional democracy, but whatever assessment one makes about it should be predicated on this broader corpus of considerations.

9 An Affirmative Argument for SMD Elections

> The decision to rely on single member
> geographical districts as a mechanism for
> conducting elections is merely a political choice—
> and one that we might reconsider in the future.
>
> *Associate USSC Justice Clarence Thomas in*
> Holder v. Hall (1994) *Concurrence*

Richard Katz begins his *Democracy and Elections* with the observation that democratic theorists have focused "on the 'true' meaning of democracy and the impact of elections in general on its achievement, with little attention devoted to the possibility that some democratic values may be better achieved, or more seriously undermined, by one variety of electoral system rather than another."[1] His lament that "democratic theory and the study of elections are two fields of inquiry that ought to be connected intimately but that, in fact, have tended to proceed independently" is significant because democratic ideals underlie the success and failure of electoral methods, helping to explain why a given method sometimes performs admirably in one nation and is an abject failure in another nation.[2] This book fills some of this gap for the American experience by focusing on the place of single-member district plurality elections in the context of American political thought and development. The United States is a relatively simple, heterogeneous polity in which republican and liberal values transcend its history. The universal adoption and institutionalization of the SMD system says much about the democratic values that define the United States, and the performance of the SMD system informs us whether this election method continues to further the normative values that resonate in the American experience.

The chapter synthesizes criticisms of the single-member district system in House of Representatives elections and presents an affirmative argument in its defense. I first place contemporary critiques of the SMD system within the context of the Federalist and Anti-Federalist debates over the House of Representatives and its election. The most persuasive of these are grounded in distinctly Anti-Federalist visions of the chamber and the purpose of elections. Harvard Law professor Lani Guinier's *The Tyranny of the Majority* is perhaps the best known of these challenges to the US single-member district system, and I am certainly not the first to notice that she and those writing in a similar vein often recall arguments made by the Anti-Federalists.[3] These criticisms of SMD elections and proposals for alternative election methods are firmly based in American ideals, and this is precisely why they must be taken seriously. This also means these critiques come with much of the intellectual and normative foundation that underlies this thought.

I then turn to the probable political implications of alternative electoral arrangements relative to the single-member district system. Advocates of proportional election methods rightfully maintain that proportional methods will encourage the emergence of niche and issue parties. Less convincingly, they often maintain that the SMD system privileges conservative politics and that proportional alternatives will benefit the politically disadvantaged.[4] This argument parallels the conventional belief that increased voter turnout advantages the political left. We've known this argument is wrong for a very long time.[5] Instead, proportional voting methods will likely produce a rightward shift in American politics and an increase, rather than decrease, in political polarization. This is primarily because US political parties are weak, and the operation of proportional election methods in combination with weak political parties advantages those most capable of mustering the increased organizational resources needed to compete effectively in these systems. This will not be the downtrodden. In addition, many of our most ideologically strident citizens are sympathetic to the populist right and are precisely those likely to be benefited by alternative election methods. Proportional representation in the United States is more likely to produce an American Marine Le Pen than advance the electoral fortunes of political progressives. Electoral systems are overlaid on a particular polity at a particular time, and proportional representation will not produce European social democracy in the United States.

Finally, I offer proposals for reforming the US single-member district system to better capture the promise of American constitutional ideals. I am clearly sympathetic to the Federalist understanding of the House of Representatives and its proper election, but I also believe the current SMD system does not achieve the Madisonian vision. This is because House districts are too homogeneous, seemingly placing me in league with those who believe the most significant failure of our electoral system is gerrymandering. However, the primary problem lies not with districting but rather the size of the chamber. The Madisonian ideal requires returning to the original Federalist understanding of the House of Representatives as a deliberative assembly in which representatives were entrusted to search for a greater public good. This requires a much smaller House and a less direct connection between representatives and the represented.

The House of Representatives is most certainly not a deliberative assembly and hasn't been one in a very long time; the business of Congress takes place behind closed doors in committees. There are few great debates, and most members of the House of Representatives have little conception of a broadly national good or, more charitably, believe their constituents' good is the national good. Size was problematic for Madison because it encouraged passions. In this regard he misjudged the most important consequence of a large House. The primary problem with chamber size, especially in a great, diverse polity where government exercises substantial responsibilities, is precisely the opposite; it promotes the tranquility of legislators who quietly go about their work in a hierarchical, rules-based chamber that is primarily organized by specialized committees. The contentious partisan flare-ups that entertain us on the evening news are the exception, not the rule, in the daily business of Congress. Its daily business is interest-group liberalism, and this is what most directly affects our lives. Representatives advocate, work, and trade on behalf of their constituents and other special interests and in doing so produce a "public good" that is weighted toward those most capable of organizing effectively. These advantages are magnified by the size of the chamber and will be further magnified by any electoral system that requires increased resources and organizational capacity to compete effectively.

Restoration of the Madisonian ideal of legislating for a broadly conceived national good requires first and foremost keeping narrow interests out of the chamber, not finding more reliable ways to bring them into Congress. Reducing the size of the chamber necessarily makes districts more heterogeneous, and with this comes the election of legislators with broader perspectives who pursue more moderate politics. Such districts also encourage a more politically informed and engaged public. This, more than some other way of electing the House, will best secure and advance all voices, including those of underrepresented citizens. I save this discussion for later in the chapter. Here I focus placing the critiques of the single-member district system in the context of the arguments that shaped the book and assess their implications for contemporary American electoral politics.

The Founding Legacy and Current Debates over the US SMD System

Criticisms of the single-member district system rarely get beyond representation to the underlying purpose of the House of Representatives and its role in the constitutional system, and they are seldom situated in American political thought and a system of government characterized by the dispersion of political power and mutual checks. In the third chapter I stated that one reason for this is that most Americans believe the purpose of the House is to legislate. The House is where representatives gather to press their constituents' interests in the legislative process. By now it is clear that at the founding this vision was deeply disputed. The Anti-Federalists understood that a properly constructed House would be a forum where interests are pressed, brokered, and reconciled. Out of this presumably emerges legislation encapsulating the public will or good. For the Federalists, legislating was *a* purpose of the House but not *the* purpose of the House. The Federalist House was principally a forum for the public discussion of ideas. Only those that withstood scrutiny would be legislated. The House had to fulfill this role in order for the broader constitutional architecture to make sense. Compelling ideas that resonated were likely to withstand senatorial, presidential, and judicial checks, while those driven by momentary, unreflective passions would not.

Two influential criticisms of the SMD system and calls for proportional representation, Professor Lani Guinier's *The Tyranny of the Majority* and Professor Douglas J. Amy's *Real Choices / New Voices*, offer modest attempts to ground themselves in political thought. However, these are tepid, and neither explicitly discusses founding-era understandings of the House. Still, like the Anti-Federalists, these authors see the House as a venue for the brokering of interests. Guinier is quite explicit, devoting large portions of her core chapter to arguing that the principal problem with the SMD system is that it does not adequately facilitate the "higher goal" of interest representation.[6] This leads her to recommend the adoption of voting mechanisms that better advance the "representation of interests, not just of voters."[7] For her, as for the eighteenth-century British proponents of virtual representation, it is interests—understood to be conceptually distinct from citizens—that should receive representation. Likewise, Amy argues for the desirability of "negotiation democracy" centered on the "give-and-take between different political, economic, racial, and religious groups."[8] This is possible only if all groups and their interests are at "the political table."[9] Like the Anti-Federalists from whom they draw possibly unrecognized inspiration, they hold that the House should primarily be a venue for the expression, advancement, and brokering of well-defined and disparate interests.

If the purpose of the House is to serve as the venue for the brokering of interests, then the purpose of elections is to bring these interests into the chamber. Most critics of SMD, winner-take-all elections believe their major shortcoming is that the system does a poor job of doing so, especially the interests of racial and political minorities. Amy argues that "one of the most serious defects of single-member plurality systems . . . is that large numbers of voters come away from these elections without any representation, and thus go without any say in government."[10] The Anti-Federalists, of course, opposed Federalist districting on precisely these grounds. In particular, they believed that Federalist districting primarily advantaged elite interests at the expense of those of the middling class. This is the same argument that opponents of the SMD system make today: districting is deficient because it fails to bring all interests into the chamber. This, in the view of contemporary critics, recommends replacing the SMD system with an election method presumably more capable of doing so to the benefit of underrepresented interests. The Federalists—whether successful or not—sought to balance and reconcile interests in the constituency and to expose representatives to a variety of political perspectives that would inform their ability to comprehend and pursue a broad national good. In their view, elections, as much as possible, should inhibit the transmission of well-defined interests to the chamber.

This points to one of the primary perceived deficiencies of the single-district system, namely that it generates "wasted" votes. Amy, for example, defines wasted votes as votes that are cast for candidates or parties that are not elected to office.[11] Put simply, voting for a candidate that does not win office "wastes" a vote because those casting these votes "come away from elections without any representation."[12] Voting in elections where it is possible for citizens to vote for candidates or parties that do not win office "gives only the illusion of democracy."[13] Proportional representation is preferred because such systems "are explicitly designed to maximize the number of voters who are able to elect a representative."[14] In essence, everybody should be able to influence the election outcome and vote for a winner, and this is presumably more likely in proportional systems than in single-member district systems.

This is a very peculiar criticism. First, while groups certainly matter in electoral politics, voting is an individual act. We give votes to people, not groups or corporate entities. Given this, as an empirical statement, in most elections most of the time individual votes have no influence on the outcome.[15] The probability of an individual influencing the outcome of a mass election, even one conducted under proportional representation, is nearly zero. Thus it is very hard to say what a "wasted" vote means when individually they have minimal effect.[16] Second, as a normative principle, votes *should* have little effect. When individual votes influence election outcomes, this means that some citizen or group of citizens possesses the ability to exercise tyrannical authority over others. One foundation of democracy is precisely that no citizen or small group of citizens should be able to dictate collective political decisions. As political theorist Andrew Rehfeld asks, "Why should we design [electoral] systems whose value is to increase the likelihood that everyone can be a dictator over a communal choice?"[17] Despite what is taught in high school civics, one's vote generally doesn't matter, nor should it.

While opponents of the SMD system do not generally share with the Anti-Federalists a normative preference for a homogeneous and largely undifferentiated polity, they do share a preference for and a reliance on the homogeneity of constituencies and their interests. The notion of "group" or interest representation presumes homogeneity.[18] In homogeneous constituencies fewer votes are "wasted" in the sense understood by Douglas Amy. In her call for alternatives to SMD elections, Guinier predicates her argument on the assumption that both white and black interests are homogeneous and largely distinct.[19] The raison d'être for her preferred remedy, cumulative voting, is that this system allows a political minority with well-defined, distinct, and intense preferences to advance these electorally. This election method has few representational advantages in the absence of considerable political homogeneity in the relevant population that is distinguishable from other societal interests.[20] More generally, a primary perceived benefit of any semiproportional or proportional election system is that subgroups of voters can organize around niche or single-issue parties focusing on, for example, race, the environment, or, for that matter, guns. For the Federalists this is the antithesis of what elections should encourage, which is precisely why they emphasized the desirability of societal *and* constituency heterogeneity.

Where critics of SMD elections often part company with the Anti-Federalists is in the electoral institutions best suited to bring desired interests into the chamber. The Anti-Federalists advocated electing officials using majoritarian processes applied to small, homogeneous districts. This also motivates contemporary majority-minority districting to increase black and Hispanic legislative representation. It also recommends instant-runoff voting as an alternative to first-past-the-post plurality elections.[21] However, some critics of SMD elections reject purposeful districting to increase the representation of minority interests. Guinier, for example, argues that the "subdistricting strategy marginalizes minority legislative presence."[22] In her view, majority-minority districting "segregates" political and racial minorities to their detriment in the legislative process.[23] This creates "an especially thin version of pluralism that allows a racially homogeneous majority disproportional representation at the expense of an historically oppressed racial minority."[24] Likewise, many critics of SMD elections are often disposed against instant-runoff voting precisely because it is a winner-take-all, majoritarian system that may dilute the voices of political minorities by combining these with other voters.[25] In "a pluralist society, a winner-take-all approach legitimated by majority rule actually exacerbates marginalization of minorities."[26] It is unclear if these arguments would maintain their currency if the House were significantly enlarged, thereby naturally creating smaller and more homogeneous constituencies.[27] Regardless, in this view pluralism or "negotiation democracy" is desirable, but what is needed is a more-robust version of pluralism achieved through proportional representation.

Perhaps the best-known critique of the single-member district system is that it does not promote a legislative chamber that looks like the United States. In particular, it is presumably biased against women and minorities in a way that proportional systems are not.[28] The current (114th) Congress counts forty-four African American and thirty-two Hispanic voting representatives. There are eighty-four women in the chamber.[29] Blacks are modestly underrepresented relative to their proportion of the population, while Hispanics and women are significantly underrepresented.[30] In *Real Choices / New Voices* Amy argues that "the notion that legislatures should reflect the political desires of the public as accurately as possible is central to most Americans' conceptions of democracy."[31] He appeals to John Adams's *Treatise* and well-known constitutional convention remarks by James Wilson to buttress his argument that "elections should produce legislatures that mirror the political preferences of the public."[32] Likewise, Jonathan Still, another prominent critic of the SMD system, argues that the "legislative body ought to be a microcosm of the electorate, so each group ought to be represented in the same relative numbers as it would be if the entire electorate were to meet."[33] For Guinier, representatives should be "politically, psychologically, and culturally" similar to their constituents.[34] These sentiments are indistinguishable from the Federal Farmer's admonishment that "it is deceiving a people to tell them they are electors, and can choose their legislators, if they cannot, in the nature of things, choose men from among themselves, and genuinely like themselves."[35]

The importance that this line of argument places on descriptive representation says much about its advocates' underlying views of republican government. Recall that the Anti-Federalists considered representative democracy intrinsically inferior to direct democracy and advocated "mirroring" representation in part because it offered a potential solution to the deficiencies they associated with the act of representation. For them, descriptive representation presented a solution to the agency problem of directing the actions of distant legislators. It does so because representatives will think, feel, and reason like those on whose behalf they legislate. In this view, a primary benefit of descriptive representation is that it limits legislator independence and discretion. As Hanna Pitkin argues, descriptive representation "does not allow for an activity of representing, except in the special and restricted sense of . . . giving information. It has no room for any kind of representing as acting for, or on behalf of, others, which means that in the political realm it has no room for the creative activities of a representative legislature, the forging of consensus, the formulating of policy, the activity we roughly designate by 'governing.'"[36]

Instead, descriptive representation encourages the legislature to act as if the entire nation were assembled.[37] Descriptive or "mirroring" representation seeks to approximate direct democracy and in doing so constrains the ability of representatives to pursue "the creative activities of a representative legislature."[38] It also implies a "delegate" conception of the relationship between the representative and his or her constituent.[39] To the extent that representatives think, feel, and reason like their constituents, it is unclear what exercising discretion even means. Contemporary critics of SMD elections often share this sentiment, one that is distinctly Anti-Federalist and that stands in stark contrast to the Federalists, who advocated "trustee" representatives who enjoyed considerable autonomy in pursuing the "creative activities" of government.

These criticisms of SMD elections provide ample evidence that the Anti-Federalist ideals that animated the founding transcend American history and still gain purchase in contemporary America. Proportional representation advocates view the chamber as a forum for the brokering of interests and embrace a "delegate" conception of representation that is reinforced by electoral processes that foster homogeneous, self-defined constituencies. Regardless of how constituencies are created, they should "mirror" the nation and govern in a manner similar to what would happen if all assembled for this purpose. There is nothing revolutionary or un-American about any of this; it is as old as the republic and as American as apple pie.

With this comes the political ideals that resonate in this tradition. Viewing the House of Representatives as a forum for the brokering of disparate interests implies a very particular conception of the public good, one that is limited and less national than that envisioned by the Federalists. Congress amply demonstrates that a broad public good does not easily emerge from negotiation and logrolling. This conception also places considerable emphasis on the quality of electoral democracy, both to convey constituent interests and to thwart government-promulgated tyranny. If there is anything that the social choice literatures exemplified by work of Arrow, Downs, Riker, Hinich, and others have clearly demonstrated, it is that one should be deeply skeptical of the ability of votes to carry this kind of weight. Elections are very blunt instruments for conveying the political sentiments of the electorate, and to rely on them to transmit interests and prevent tyranny is a risky proposition at best. These considerations are especially salient to those who seek greater political voice for political and racial minorities. If the representational goal is to mimic or correspond to governance in which the entire nation assembled, then there are few obvious protections for minorities.[40]

This all assumes that alternative election methods will bring more voices to the table and in doing so increase the political strength of underrepresented groups. To say the least, this is doubtful. Proportional election methods are just that, proportional. They do not affect only a single segment of society. More proportional election methods may increase the representation of racial minorities, but just as easily these may increase the representation of Tea Party supporters. More importantly, electoral system effects are not politically neutral. They tilt the political scales in favor of those most capable of leveraging these processes for advantage. Election methods such as cumulative voting, instant-runoff voting, or something as exotic sounding as d'Hondt proportional representation applied to multimember districts are not overwhelmingly complicated, but they are more complicated than SMD plurality rule. To be effective, cumulative voting requires like-minded voters to coordinate their ballots on one or a few candidates; instant-runoff voting requires voters to present a preference ranking of candidates; divisor or quotient proportional methods applied to multimember constituencies require voters to consider the likely implications of their vote on the total distribution of seats in the district.[41] None of this is especially daunting, but at the margins it advantages citizens and interests best positioned to invest the time and resources to engage a less transparent election system. While underrepresented minorities may increase representation through these methods, these are not the first groups one would anticipate being advantaged by election methods that require increased resources to compete effectively. These methods more likely increase the extant political advantages enjoyed by older, wealthier, and whiter citizens relative to younger, poorer, and browner citizens. The old saw about being careful about what you wish for applies especially well to election methods.

The main reason proportional election methods will likely exacerbate, rather than ameliorate, the political advantages enjoyed by those already advantaged by the electoral process is that US political parties are weak. Throughout the democratized world, political parties are the principal agents for contesting elections and coordinating like-minded voters. Political parties, inter alia, recruit candidates, mobilize voters, and organize legislatures. However, US political parties do not do any of these things especially well. Despite a generally recognized resurgence in party strength in the 1990s and 2000s, US parties are still weak by world standards, and especially so in electoral politics. The direct primary ensures parties have little or no control over the nomination of candidates; they are heavily regulated in their ability to raise and spend money; and they have very limited ability to enforce party discipline in the legislature. Instead, self-selected candidates seek nomination with or without party support, and while we have greatly limited the ability of parties to raise and spend money, there are few corresponding restrictions on individuals and organized groups; finally, representatives enjoy considerable legislative autonomy. US political parties cannot easily do the things that parties do in other Western democracies.

For this reason, proportional representation is unlikely to function here as it does abroad. Alternatives to the SMD system require increased organizational capacity to achieve the goals its proponents advocate, and the existence of weak US parties advantages special interests and political entrepreneurs in the electoral process. Increasing the complexity of the electoral system furthers these advantages, and there is little reason to believe this will benefit those presently disadvantaged in the political process.

In addition, United States parties are decentralized and built from the local constituency up. This stands in stark contrast to parties in other Western democracies, which are typically centralized, top-down organizations. The importance of territory and location to Americans fostered the adoption and institutionalization of the single-member district system, but in turn the single-member district system furthered the development of decentralized, locally built, political parties. In a heterogeneous polity such as the United States there is much that recommends decentralized, locally oriented political parties. What it means to be a Republican in Orange County, California, differs considerably from what it means to be a Christian County, Missouri, Republican; likewise Democrats in Oregon's upper Willamette Valley differ in important ways from their partisan brethren in Philadelphia. While legally enfeebled parties present numerous disadvantages for democratic governance, decentralized parties present important benefits in a heterogeneous nation such as the United States. In particular, such parties help accommodate and integrate the divergence of political preferences that one expects in a large, diverse, nation. However, it is precisely this decentralization that makes such parties ill-suited for the kind of disciplined, programmatic politics necessary for proportional representation systems to achieve the outcomes their strongest advocates desire.

If proponents of proportional alternatives wish these to effectively implement their preferred notion of electoral democracy, then these proposals have to be coupled with political reforms that strengthen US parties. These characteristics of US politics, however, are largely fixed. The Progressives won our hearts and minds and convinced Americans that strong, well-organized political parties are the bane of democratic governance. The Progressives' victory culminated in the streets of Chicago during the 1968 Democratic Convention, where party activists resolved to strip the bosses' ability to control the nomination of candidates for national office.[42] Almost simultaneously, the Court in its well-known *Buckley* decision guaranteed that individuals spending money on behalf of candidates enjoy First Amendment speech protections. This line of jurisprudence culminated in *Citizens United*, which guarantees that citizens who band together for this same purpose enjoy equivalent speech protections in their collective capacity, while in the same period Congress passed laws that legally prohibited political parties from raising large contributions from individual donors.[43] This political reality is unlikely to change. We take the First Amendment seriously, and the courts are extremely reluctant to reconsider extant speech and association protections. Further, members of Congress have few incentives to strengthen political parties at the expense of their own autonomy and careers.

Finally, there is considerable evidence that the SMD system promotes policy moderation relative to proportional systems. In previous studies I provide empirical evidence that the electoral positions of political parties in majoritarian electoral systems are more moderate than the positions of parties in proportional systems. There is nothing that resembles the "cheek and jowl" convergence suggested by the median voter result, but the electoral positioning of parties in SMD systems is noticeably more moderate than that of parties in proportional systems.[44] Scholars such as Arend Lijphart and G. Bingham Powell may well be correct that proportional electoral systems produce more moderate policy outcomes from their legislative processes, but again this transpires in polities that have the strong political parties necessary to forge consensus and ensure that individual representatives are held to these agreements.[45] This is not the case in the United States. In the United States weak political parties mean that moderation has to be achieved at the electoral stage, and here electoral and policy outcomes are likely to be more convergent under SMD rules than under proportional rules.

All of this raises serious doubts about how alternatives to the SMD system would function in practice and who would benefit from these alternatives. The primary beneficiaries would be those advantaged by resources and organizational capacity. In a nation where political parties have limited control over elections and actions of affiliated legislators, and narrowly defined interests can mobilize large numbers of supporters, these systems will advantage already-privileged interests. Further, it will reward the most ideologically strident, including those supporting single issues such as guns, abortion, or whatever, thereby increasing the politics of extremism at the expense of moderation. Electoral systems operate on a particular polity at a particular time. The weakness of US political parties—including new ones that might emerge—argues that proportional representation will function quite differently here than elsewhere in the world. These differences will come at the expense of precisely those that the strongest advocates of proportional rules seek to strengthen politically. In all likelihood, proportional representation would be an unmitigated disaster for politically marginalized groups.

Strengthening and Improving the US SMD System

The continued use of the single-member district system in House elections is nearly certain. First, Americans are deeply attached to territory. For many, location provides a sense of identity. Congressional districts have been becoming more homogeneous over the past few decades because people self-select where to live and often choose locations populated by similar citizens.[46] Our impression that we are a highly mobile, transient society is easily exaggerated. The truth is that mobility and relocation have declined in recent decades, and nearly 60 percent of Americans live in the state in which they were born.[47] Perhaps the most endearing indication of how important place is to our lives is the fact that most Americans live within just a few miles of their mothers.[48] The republican tradition views territorial representation as something intrinsically good. With territorial representation we share something with our neighbors, whereas self-defined constituencies are often physically isolated constituencies. A primary justification for republican government is that it helps build political and social communities, and physical proximity and the interaction it fosters form the foundation of these communities.[49] In an influential work on representation, The Blue Guitar, Nancy Schwartz makes a compelling case for territorial representation, arguing that

> political representation structured on local geographic districts provides suitable arenas in which the ideal of the citizen might be approximated. . . . In the local district . . . people come to know each other over time . . . people's characters develop from personhood to citizenship as individuals enact, enrich, and understand the rules of the political game . . . in competing among friends and neighbors to choose one candidate, and then one representative, the people as citizens develop standards of judgment about public character.[50]

While perhaps a bit idealized, these sentiments are intrinsic to the conception of government that has informed the American experience. The benefits of people coming to know each other and the development of informed citizenship cannot be overstated. There are compelling reasons to believe that the single-member district system is the best-equipped election method to further these objectives. The question is how to strengthen and improve the performance of the US SMD system.

The Federalist and Anti-Federalist understandings of single-member district elections transcend American history, and either could be adapted to fit the contemporary political environment and potentially meet our political and social objectives. The Anti-Federalist vision argues for the creation of homogeneous constituencies and application of highly majoritarian election processes, and views interest bargaining in the House favorably. This would argue for a significantly larger House of Representatives and recommend rejection of plurality rule for majority runoff or instant-runoff voting methods. A larger House would by construction make constituencies more homogeneous simply because there would be more of them. A current congressional constituency contains just over 700,000 citizens, making it difficult to create homogeneous districts, whether defined by race or political inclinations, without gerrymandering. If the number of representatives were doubled, then constituencies would shrink to 350,000, and it is relatively easy to draw homogeneous districts that encapsulate like-minded citizens without heroic cartography. This could assuage concerns about majority-minority districting because such districts would be crafted much more naturally. The application of majority voting rules—especially to such small and homogeneous districts—assures that representatives will have a clear understanding of their constituents' interests, and for their part constituents can be reasonably assured that representatives will faithfully promote these interests. A larger chamber better facilitates the creation and maintenance of constituencies of interest whether these interests are defined racially, economically, or by something else, and foster a more robust interest-group liberalism. If this is what we want, then American political thought and history is more supportive of this representational universe than one crafted outside the single-member district tradition. Still, while such reforms may produce a richer pluralism, at the end of the day it's still just interest liberalism.

Alternatively, the Federalist vision recommends a significantly smaller House of Representatives. No deliberative assembly can host 435 members; half this number is more plausible. To decide whether this is reasonable, it is tempting to compare the 1789 constitutional apportionment to corresponding figures today. However, there is no sensible comparison. Changes in transportation, communications, and related considerations make early republic apportionments, or even those in 1842 or 1911, incomparable to a modern apportionment. However, the Federalist spirit argues for staffing the chamber with representatives drawn from large, heterogeneous constituencies. The question is what constitutes a large, heterogeneous constituency in the twenty-first century?

Currently, a House of 250 members would require constituencies of approximately 1.5 million persons. This figure nearly guarantees heterogeneity. For example, the Los Angeles metropolitan area currently hosts eleven congressional districts. This would shrink to about six or seven districts, with the near inevitability that any Southern California district would include a mixture of ethnicities, income ranges, economic foundations, and similar considerations.[51] Similarly, Chicago would probably collapse to three or four districts, and these districts would inevitably mix affluent, less affluent, urban, and suburban neighborhoods. In Missouri a decrease from eight to five representatives would require extending the current St. Louis– and Kansas City–area congressional districts well into suburban communities and possibly large swaths of rural areas. Simply reducing the number of representatives guarantees that they will be drawn from significantly more heterogeneous districts and they will have to engage a larger range of constituents.

Larger constituencies make it difficult for a permanent majority to establish itself in a district. Electoral majorities would be more fluid, and representatives would have to respond to a broader range of voices. One probable effect would be a reduction of the reelection rate of incumbent legislators. Representatives are reelected at a rate well in excess of 90 percent. There is nothing inherently wrong with high reelection rates; presumably we want representatives to enjoy their support of their constituents and to be rewarded for effectively representing them. High reelection rates do not exist because of corruption and malfeasance, but primarily because representatives do such a good job of responding to their constituents. It's easy for them to do so. Extant districts are sufficiently homogeneous to have fixed, stable majorities to which representatives can respond. By way of comparison, senators represent more heterogeneous constituencies, have to address a larger diversity of constituents and interests, and enjoy reelection rates that, while still high, run about 10–15 points lower than rates for representatives. One reason senatorial reelection rates aren't even lower is that senators are advantaged by their six-year terms, which gives them sufficient time to address the interests of a variety of constituencies and explain their legislative behaviors to a wide audience. A smaller House will require representatives to face broader, more fluid coalitions of voters over the course of a brief two-year term. The consequence would likely be a significant reduction in their electoral security. The most successful representatives would be those most capable of effectively representing diverse constituencies. Representatives' perspectives will be broadened to the benefit of national governance. Finally, the boundaries of congressional districts would inevitably be more compact simply because of the geometry of drawing fewer districts within a state. The degrees of freedom afforded mapmakers declines in proportion to the decrease in districts, and they would be unable to exercise significant discretion. Such districting would do much to level the partisan playing field tilted by gerrymandering. It would be difficult for Maryland to district in a manner that didn't give Republicans a fighting chance in most districts, and likewise for Michigan and North Carolina Democrats.

A smaller chamber promises significant changes for the way the House works. Members would necessarily be less specialized. Some representatives from urban areas would have to learn about rural concerns, and conversely for representatives from rural areas. They would be better equipped to do so because of the increase in the diversity of voices they hear in the normal course of their work. Committees in Congress would likely diminish in importance, while floor activity would become more important. This alone would move the chamber toward a more deliberative forum with more of its business conducted in public, with corresponding benefits for civic awareness and engagement. It may well also improve the quality of legislation because more ideas would be exposed to chamber and public scrutiny rather than being crafted in committees out of the spotlight. Simply, the norms and practices of the House would gravitate more toward those presently in the Senate, which tends to be a more collegial and less hierarchical body that places greater premium on the good-faith exchange of ideas, where compromises are more readily obtained because senators have a broader political perspective and deeper personal relationships, and where more of the Senate's business is conducted on the floor of the chamber. The House, of course, is not supposed to be the Senate, and there are good reasons for the differences in the chambers. That said, even a significant reduction in the size of the House would preserve much of its distinct character and role in the legislative process while making it conform more closely to its original constitutional purpose.

The nineteenth- and early-twentieth-century disputes over the size of the House of Representatives demonstrate how unlikely it is that the size of the chamber will be reduced. The only reduction in chamber membership occurred in 1842, and that was a modest reduction. Chamber size, however, is determined by common legislation, so it is a political reform that does not demand the extraordinary efforts of constitutional amendment. Still, assuming there is never a significant reduction in the chamber, population growth will accomplish some of these objectives so long as the membership remains fixed. The US population is expected to crest at approximately 400 million by the middle years of this century. It addition, its demographic composition will shift significantly. In the next few decades the proportion of white Americans will decline from about 77 percent of the population to about 68 percent, while Hispanics will increase from about 17 percent to just over a quarter of the total population.[52] This means House constituencies will approach a million residents, and the composition of these constituencies, even with demographic sorting by locations, will be more diverse. More districts will have more people of different backgrounds, means of livelihood, and political preferences. These changes will have profound implications for American politics over the next century. It would be difficult for representatives to be accountable only to a relatively narrow spectrum of their district residents. That said, few of the chamber processes associated with a smaller House of Representatives will be realized by the natural growth in constituency size, leaving a significant gap between the House envisioned at the framing and that likely to exist in the near future.

Conclusion

In the republic's early years the primary question of representative democracy was how to elect representatives. The states experimented with election methods, but by the Jacksonian era most settled on the single-member district system, and in 1842 Congress mandated it for all states. With few exceptions, it has been so ever since. The political history of the US single-member district system is the history of the nationalization of elections and, in particular, the nationalization of the single-member district system. Election authority granted to the states gravitated to the national government in the nineteenth and twentieth centuries, and now firmly resides with the national government. Within the national government this authority over federal elections witnessed a shift from the Congress to shared authority between Congress and the judiciary, with a lesser role played by the executive. There remains little room for the states in determining federal election processes, and the system is so engrained in our political consciousness that many mistakenly believe it has been in continuous use since the founding and is required.

The nationalization of the single-member district system initially came at the behest of the states and later the state-level party leaders. The states' early-nineteenth-century petitions to constitutionally mandate SMD elections were motivated by a recognition of the superiority of the single-member district system for legislative elections, coupled with a recognition that unless all states adopted the method, the states that used single-member districts to elect their congressional delegations would be politically vulnerable to states that elected by general ticket. Much of this pressure to require single-member district elections evaporated in the Era of Good Feelings, but the Jacksonian-era franchise expansion and massive increases in voter turnout led leaders of the new parties to pursue the single-member district system as a device to manage a rapidly changing and volatile political world. Just as Madison and the Federalists believed the SMD system promised to solve the problem of tyranny of the majority under the expectation of full enfranchisement, so too did the Whigs in the 1840s, the Republican-controlled congresses of the 1920s, and electoral rights advocates in the 1960s. A properly constructed single-member district system is a solution to, and not a cause of, the problem of majority tyranny. The adoption and institutionalization of the SMD system cannot be understood apart from franchise and electoral participation, and its current congressional mandate and court oversight derives from the politics of electoral participation and the right to vote.

The US single-member district electoral system was adopted and institutionalized because it fits so comfortably within the constitutional architecture and the political thought from which that architecture emerged. At the broadest level, US politics continues to revolve around the underlying the tension between liberalism and republicanism. As a nation, we embrace the idea of rights and protections from government-promulgated tyranny, especially for political minorities. We also aspire to a greater national good and the development of citizenship and political community. Majority rule and minority protection are worthy standards, but require political institutions capable of balancing these ideals and giving them effect. The single-member district system is among those institutions, and its preferred standing comes from its relationship to the other institutions.

A properly constructed single-member district system best contributes to the overall functioning of US government when it returns knowledgeable representatives who are responsive to their constituents. Such a system conveys differing perspectives and broad sentiment to Congress, encouraging thoughtful public consideration. This should be the House's primary contribution to American government, and unless it does so effectively the balance of the constitutional system will not function properly.

The single-member district system is especially important to contemporary US politics because it encourages the development of civic communities and citizenship. Madison was correct that "different opinions concerning religion, concerning government, and many other points . . . have . . . divided mankind into parties, inflamed them with mutual animosity, and rendered them much more disposed to vex and oppress each other than to co-operate for their common good."[53] Political differences naturally repel us from seeking engagement with others. However, citizenship is not enhanced when we interact with only the politically like-minded. Political segregation by districting or by an election method that permits self-defined constituencies defeats, rather than enhances, the republican aspirations and foundations of our constitution. The Federalist spirit recommends districting so that citizens of different backgrounds and political interests are placed in the same political community and have to engage these differences locally rather than nationally. Nothing is more important and touches our lives more directly than where we live. Sufficiently broad districting driven by a smaller House of Representatives demands that those of different incomes, social orientation, life situations, and similar considerations will have to share their political fortunes with those of different orientations. It also means that different subconstituencies within these districts can more easily upset the apple cart and cannot be overlooked.

I am not so naive as to believe that larger districts are sufficient to drive face-to-face interactions among people of different political and social orientation. I claim only they are necessary and will create incentives for such interactions. Larger districts will demand that political elites, including legislators and those who seek to be legislators, engage the diversity of their constituents. The Anti-Federalists and Federalists raised legitimate concerns about districts being too large, and therefore precluding legislators from deep acquaintance with their constituents. However, given the ease of transportation and the ubiquity of instant communication in the modern era, even constituencies double the current size pose few significant problems in this regard. A representative can interact with any political community at his or her discretion and even in the most geographically dispersed of districts can present himself or herself to constituents in a matter of hours. Likewise, constituents can easily know the fine details of candidates' and representatives' lives, and can be made aware of legislative activity in the House in real time. Today significantly more-populous districts pose none of the logistical or familiarity programs that so concerned the founding generation. Simply, the Anti-Federalist concern that such districting would create "a government of strangers" bears little weight today.

I have argued that electoral systems have to be assessed according to the standards they were intended to fulfill. The US SMD system was intended to keep narrowly defined and transient interests out of the chamber and to bring the best and brightest into it to deliberate the most pressing political and social problems faced by the nation. In this regard, the extant SMD is lacking. The exceptionally large chamber, the lack of strong political parties—especially parties that can influence nomination for office—and the specialization of Congress and its members in response to increasing demands placed on government make the current SMD system insufficiently robust to completely fulfill its constitutional purpose. That said, it performs well on many dimensions. In particular, it tends to be unbiased and responsive to the vote. Its deficiencies do not recommend selecting an alternative House election system as much as they recommend rethinking the framing ideas of how an electoral system should function, given the United States' constitutional design and our contemporary polity. This recommends a smaller chamber and the fewer, more heterogeneous districts that will come with it.

The advantages of the SMD could be magnified if we revisit the early-nineteenth-century movement to constitutionally require the selection of presidential electors from congressional districts with each state's two remaining electors selected at large. Americans are dissatisfied with the Electoral College because it focuses presidential campaigns on only a handful of states. Unlike in House selection, the presidential selection by state-level winner-take-all processes is detrimental to the quality of US electoral democracy. The requirement that presidential electors be selected at the district level will expand the number of competitive areas considerably, especially if this is coupled with fewer congressional districts. This selection method would dovetail presidential selection with the selection of the House and Senate, as was arguably originally intended, with positive consequences for governability. It is true that states could institute this method, as Nebraska and Maine have, by simple state legislation. However, as the early republic debates illustrate, any state that does this unilaterally without a guarantee that other states will follow suit will leave itself at a disadvantage in influencing the outcome of presidential elections. Consequently, constitutional amendment seems to be the only possible path to this reform.

Justice Thomas is correct that "the decision to rely on single member geographical districts as a mechanism for conducting elections is merely a political choice," as is its current implementation. The historic decisions to implement and require single-member district elections were all political. His suggestion that we may reconsider this decision in the future seems unlikely, but political decisions can always be reconsidered. As Lipset and Rokkan argued in 1967, political leaders select election methods most advantageous to their own interests. This means that the most likely scenario is that little will change. In addition to the weight of 150 years of single-member district elections on a national scale, politicians and citizens are risk-averse. Rolling the political dice does not come easily to us. Nonetheless, every electoral system rests on underlying predicates and advances some normative values at the expense of others. One must recognize these assumptions and values privileged by the SMD plurality-rule system relative to its potential alternatives in US application. There is no perfect way to elect a representative assembly, and public discourse is best served by considering the trade-offs across systems rather than searching for the nonexistent "best" system, and to do so within a deeper context than a perceived simple division of the political pie. It is not centrally important that I am correct in my diagnosis and remedy, but rather that those understandably concerned with election methods look beyond the surface to better appreciate the place of electoral methods in the broader constitutional design, historical circumstances, and deepest values that we wish to advance.

CASES CITED

Allen v. State Board of Elections (1969)

Baker v. Carr, 369 U.S. 186 (1962)

Brown v. Board of Education (1957)

Bush v. Vera, 517 U.S. 952 (1996)

Clinton v. The Cedar Rapids R.R. Co. (1868)

Colegrove v. Green, 328 U.S. 549 (1946)

Davis v. Bandemer (1986)

Easley v. Cromartie (2001)

Evenwel v. Abbott (2016)

Georgia v. Ashcroft (2003)

Gomillion v. Lightfoot, 364 U.S. 339 (1960)

Harris v. Arizona Independent Redistricting Commission (2016)

Harris v. McCrory (2016)

Jacobellis v. Ohio, 378 U.S. 184 (1964)

League of Latin American Citizens v. Perry (2006)

New York v. United States, 505 U.S. 144 (1992)

Miller v. Johnson, 515 U.S. 900 (1995)

Printz v. United States, 521 U.S. 898 1997)

Reynolds v. Sims, 379 U.S. 870 (1964)

Shaw v. Hunt, 517 U.S. 899 (1996)

Shaw v. Reno (1993)

Tennant v. Jefferson County, 567 U.S.___ (2012)

Thornburg v. Gingles, 478 U.S. 53 (1986)

Vieth v. Jubelirer (2004)

Wesberry v. Sanders, 376 U.S. 1 (1964)

Wood v. Broom, 287 U.S. 1 (1932)

Worchester v. Georgia, 31 U.S. 515 (1832)

NOTES

Chapter 1. House of Representatives Elections and American Political Development

1. Ira Katznelson and John S. Lapinski, "At the Crossroads: Congress and American Political Development," *Perspectives on Politics* 4, no. 2 (June 2006): 243.

2. Seymour M. Lipset and Stein Rokkan, "Cleavage Structures, Party Systems, and Voter Alignments: An Introduction," in *Party Systems and Voter Alignments: Cross-National Perspectives*, ed. Seymour M. Lipset and Stein Rokkan (London: Free Press, 1967), 30.

3. Stein Rokkan, *Citizens, Elections, Parties: Approaches to the Comparative Study of Study of the Processes of Development* (New York: David McKay, 1970) 155–158.

4. Walter Dean Burnham, "The Changing Shape of the American Political Universe," *American Political Science Review* 59, no. 1 (March 1965): 24. Beyond its contribution to our understanding of American political development, Dean Burnham's "Changing Shape" study is notable because it cast doubt on the theoretical reach of the influential "Michigan School" model of political behavior by providing evidence that voter behavior in the nineteenth century differed significantly from that observed in the mid-twentieth century.

5. E. E. Schattschneider, *Party Government* (New York: Farrar and Rinehart, 1942), xxvii.

6. For an overview see Robert C. Lieberman, "Ideas, Institutions, and Political Order: Explaining Political Change," *American Political Science Review* 96, 4 (December 2002): 697–712.

7. The classic argument rejecting the Beardian thesis is found in Forrest McDonald, *We the People: The Economic Origins of the Constitution* (Chicago: University of Chicago Press, 1958).

8. George Thomas, "What Is Political Development? A Constitutional Perspective," *Review of Politics* 73, no. 2 (Spring 2011): 275–294; Karen Orren and Stephen Skowronek, "Have We Abandoned a 'Constitutional Perspective' on American Political Development?," *Review of Politics* 73, no. 2 (Spring 2011): 295–299. See also George Thomas, "Political Thought and Political Development," *American Political Thought* 3, no. 1 (Spring 2014): 114–125.

9. One side of this debate is nicely summarized by my alma mater's motto, *mens agitat molen*, which is Latin for "the mind moves the mass" or, more simply, ideas matter, but which has been misinterpreted by generations of students to mean "men against moles."

10. Thomas, "Political Development," 276.

11. Ibid., 280.

12. Orren and Skowronek, "Constitutional Perspective," 297.

13. Ibid., 296.

14. Lieberman, "Ideas, Institutions, and Political Order," 698.

15. John W. Kingdon, *Agendas,*

Alternatives and Public Policies (Glenview IL: Scott, Foresman, 1984), quoted in Leiberman, "Ideas, Institutions and Political Order," 697.

16. James W. Ceaser, "Foundational Concepts and American Political Development," in *Nature and History in American Political Development*, ed. James W. Ceaser (Cambridge, MA: Harvard University Press, 2006), 5.

17. Ibid., 5, 10.

18. In this spirit, Jeremy D. Bailey, *James Madison and Constitutional Imperfection* (New York: Cambridge University Press, 2015) provides an outstanding example of recent scholarship on Madison's political thought, and in particular, reconciling the Federalist Madison with the James Madison who aligned so closely with Thomas Jefferson in the republic's early years.

19. This point is made perhaps most forcefully by Richard S. Katz, who provides an explicitly theoretical treatment of the relationship between the values of various strains of democratic theory and election methods. See Richard S. Katz, *Democracy and Elections* (New York: Oxford University Press, 1997).

20. Lani Guinier, *The Tyranny of the Majority: Fundamental Fairness in Representative Democracy* (New York: Free Press, 1994).

21. Michael Kammen, *Deputies and Liberties: The Origins of Representative Government in Colonial America* (New York: Knopf, 1969), 54.

22. Only Delaware and Georgia established their assemblies in the 1700s. See Peverill Squire and Keith E. Hamm, *101 Chambers: Congress, State Legislatures and the Future of Legislative Studies* (Columbus: Ohio State University Press, 2005), Chapter 1, Table 1-1.

23. This idea survived well into the twentieth century. Until the "reapportionment revolution" of the 1960s and the court's rulings that all legislative districts must contain approximately equal population, many states allocated legislative seats, particularly state senate seats, by county.

24. J. R. Pole, *Political Representation in England & the Origins of the American Republic* (Berkeley: University of California Press, 1971), 38–39, 52.

25. Alison G. Olson, "Eighteenth-Century Colonial Legislatures and Their Constituents," *Journal of American History* 79, no. 2 (September 1992): 543–567.

26. Pole, *Political Representation*, 200.

27. Ibid.

28. Ibid., 54.

29. This idea of representation incorporates the notion of virtual representation, in which representatives are expected to speak on behalf of the interests of the corporate entity because there is no distinction in interest between those who have the franchise and those who do not. In the early to middle colonial period virtual representation "was widely practiced" and fell out of favor only with the rise of popular sovereignty and actual representation in the late colonial and revolutionary period.

30. In practice, this meant about 1 representative for every 120 citizens. Boston through much of this period sent four representatives. See Pole, *Political Representation*, 173–175.

31. The Massachusetts senate has had a membership of forty since its creation in the 1780 Massachusetts constitution, which required electoral districts but based representation from these districts on taxes paid. Elbridge

Gerry's famous 1812 gerrymander was, in fact, possible only because Massachusetts senators were elected from districts, but some districts could elect multiple senators.

32. Three additional towns were entitled to one representative. Peverill Squire, *The Evolution of American Legislatures: Colonies, Territories and States, 1619–2009* (Ann Arbor: University of Michigan Press, 2014), 69.

33. Ibid., 15–16, See also Peverill Squire, *The Rise of the Representative: Lawmakers and Constituents in Colonial America* (Ann Arbor: University of Michigan, forthcoming).

34. Rogers M. Smith, "Beyond Tocqueville, Myrdal, and Hartz: The Multiple Traditions in America," *American Political Science Review* 87, no. 3 (September 1993): 558.

35. Maurice Klain, "A New Look at the Constituencies: The Need for a Recount and a Reappraisal," *American Political Science Review* 49, no. 4 (December 1955): 1105–1119.

36. Gary W. Cox, "Strategic Electoral Choice in Multi-Member Districts: Approval Voting in Practice?," *American Journal of Political Science* 28, no. 4 (1984): 722–738.

37. See Malcolm Jewell, "The Consequences of Single and Multi-Member Districting," in *Representation and Redistricting*, ed. Bernard Grofman et al. (Lexington MA: Lexington Books, 1982), and Bernard Grofman, Lisa Handley, and Richard G. Niemi, *Minority Representation and the Quest for Voting Equality* (New York: Cambridge University Press, 1992).

Chapter 2. Founding-Era Thought and the Selection for Office

1. The direct election of US senators commenced with the passage of the Seventeenth Amendment in 1913.

2. Gordon S. Wood, *The Creation of the American Republic, 1776–1787* (Chapel Hill: University of North Carolina Press, 1969), 48–49.

3. J. R. Pole, *Political Representation in England and the Origins of the American Republic* (Berkeley: University of California Press, 1971), 1.

4. As Ralph Ketcham argued "In profound tension with the Lockean emphasis on limited government, Americans of the founding era, schooled in classical language and lore, also accepted Aristotle's argument that "a state exists for the sake of the good life, and not for the sake of life only. . . . Political society exists for the sake of noble actions, and not merely companionship." Ralph Ketcham, *Framed for Posterity: The Enduring Philosophy of the Constitution* (Lawrence, Kansas: University Press of Kansas, 1993), 47.

5. Simply, *Federalist Paper No. 10* and *Federalist Paper No. 51* are inseparable and cannot be understood in isolation. See, for example, Robert J. Morgan, "Madison's Theory of Representation in the Tenth Federalist," *Journal of Politics* 36, no. 4 (November 1974): 852–885

6. David F. Epstein, *The Political Theory of the Federalist* (Chicago: University of Chicago Press, 1984), 60. See Ketcham, *Framed for Posterity*, chapters 6 and 7, for discussions of the Framers' conceptions of liberty and the public good. The Framers took very seriously the notion that there is a public or collective good and that the government and its powers existed to advance the

public good, including the protection of liberties necessary for the civic life necessary to identifying and advancing it. These positive aspects, the existence of a collective good and the liberty to engage in both personal and community affairs, had to be balanced against the possibility of "tyrannies and restraints of government," especially that promulgated by majorities. Ketcham, *Framed for Posterity*, 43.

7. Epstein, *Political Theory*, 60–64.

8. *Federalist No. 10.*

9. Carter Braxton, *Address to the Convention of Virginia; on the Subject of Government* (1776), quoted in Wood, *Creation of the American Republic*, 96.

10. Quoted in Ketcham, *Framed for Posterity*, 47.

11. Epstien, *Political Theory*, 147.

12. Charles de Montesquieu, *Montesquieu: The Spirit of the Laws*, trans. and ed. Anne M. Cohler, Basla Carolyn Miller, and Harold Samuel Stone (New York: Cambridge University Press, 1989), Book XI, chapter 6, especially 160.

13. *Federalist No. 39.* "The first question that offers itself is, whether the general form and aspect of the government is strictly republican. It is evident that no other form would be reconcilable with the genius of the people of America; with the fundamental principles of the revolution; or with that honorable determination which animates every votary of freedom, to rest all our political experiments on the capacity of mankind for self-government. If the plan of the convention, therefore, be found to depart from the republican character, its advocates must abandon it as no longer defensible."

14. *Federalist No. 10*; Epstein, *Political Theory*, 5–6

15. *Federalist No. 1.*

16. *Federalist No. 9.*

17. Alexander Hamilton, John Jay, and James Madison, *The Federalist: The Gideon Edition*, ed. George W. Cary and James McClellan (Indianapolis: Liberty Fund, 2001), xlv–xlvi.

18. Thomas Jefferson letter to Samuel Kercheval (1816), quoted in Lorraine Smith Pangle and Thomas L. Pangle, *The Learning of Liberty: The Educational Ideas of the American Founders.* (Lawrence: University Press of Kansas, 1993), 3.

19. Carter Braxton, *Address to the Convention of Virginia on the Subject of Government* (1776), as quoted in Wood, *American Republic*, 96.

20. Wood, *American Republic*, 68; Saul Cornell, *The Other Founders; Anti-Federalism and the Dissenting Tradition in America, 1788–1828* (Chapel Hill: University of North Carolina Press, 1999), 103.

21. Wood, *American Republic*, 415–425; Herbert J. Storing, *What the Anti-Federalists Were For: The Political Thought of the Opponents of the Constitution* (Chicago: University of Chicago Press, 1981), 20–21

22. Letter John Jay to Thomas Jefferson, Feb. 9, 1787; Theodore Sedgwick, *A Memoir of the Life of William Livingston* (N.Y. 1833); both quoted from Wood, *American Republic*, 424–425.

23. Wood, *American Republic*, 416–417.

24. See Cornell, *The Other Founders*, 86–87, on the Anti-Federalists' agreement that virtue was necessary for successful republican governance.

25. Storing, *What the Anti-Federalists Were For*, 48.

26. *Federalist No. 51.*

27. *Federalist No. 57.*

28. Federal Farmer, *Essay 7.*

29. Ibid.

30. George Washington, "On Recruiting and Maintaining an Army," 1776, in *The Writings of George Washington*, vol. 4 (1776), ed. and coll. Worthington Chauncey Ford (New York: G. P. Putnam's Sons, 1889), http://oll.libertyfund.org/titles/2402.

31. *Federalist No. 10*; Wood, *American Republic*, 237.

32. Cornell, *The Other Founders*, 40; Wood, *American Republic*, 479–480.

33. Philip B. Kurland and Ralph Lerner, eds., *The Founders' Constitution* (Chicago: University of Chicago Press, 1987), vol. 1, chapter 13, document 36.

34. *Federalist No. 37*.

35. Federal Farmer, *Essay 7*.

36. Ibid.

37. Storing, *What the Anti-Federalists Were For*, 20.

38. Cornell, *The Other Founders*, 57.

39. Storing, *What the Anti-Federalists Were For*, 21–22. Strictly speaking, this is a generalization that applies to most, but not all, Anti-Federalist writers. "Elite" Anti-Federalists, including George Mason, believed that civic virtue principally resided in constitutional opponents such as themselves. See Cornell, *The Other Founders*, chapter 2.

40. Thomas Jefferson, *Notes on the State of Virginia* (1787), chapter 19. Despite this, the most persuasive Anti-Federalist writings on virtue are often more liberal than republican in that they stress the different social elements that comprise the United States and the close connection between virtue and the interests of these classes. Cornell, *The Other Founders*, 97–98.

41. Pangle and Pangle, *The Learning of Liberty*, 209–210.

42. Cornell, *The Other Founders*, 40; Centinel, *Essay 1*.

43. Cornell, *The Other Founders*, 102–103.

44. Centinel, *Essay 8*, quoted in Cornell, *The Other Founders*, 102–103. See also Pangle and Pangle, *The Learning of Liberty*, 203.

45. Cornell, *The Other Founders*, 102–103.

46. Ibid., 97.

47. Wood, *American Republic*, 55.

48. Ibid., 58.

49. The republican thought of the Framers is distinct from "classical" republican teachings in one very important respect. In the classical republican tradition inherited from ancient Greece and Rome there is no conflict between the public will as articulated through direct citizen participation in the political process, or in legislative assemblies, and the public good. Public good and public opinion are synonymous. In the classical tradition, this understanding justifies the censoring of dissenters who speak out against the actions of a majority of citizens, or their representatives, precisely because one is opposing the collective good.

50. *Federalist No. 10*.

51. *Federalist No. 23*.

52. *Federalist No. 31*.

53. Storing, *What the Anti-Federalists Were For*, 7.

54. Brutus, *Essay 7*.

55. Brutus, *Essay 10*.

56. Quoted in Gary J. Schmidt and Robert H. Webking, "Revolutionaries, Anti-Federalists, and Federalists: Comments on Gordon Wood's Understanding of the American Founding," *Political Science Reviewer* 9, no. 1 (Fall 1979): 195–229.

57. Brutus, *Essay 1*.

58. Continuing in his fifth essay, Brutus details his objections to these constitutional provisions: "The legislature having every source from which money can be drawn under their direction, with a right to make all laws necessary and proper for drawing forth all resource of the country, would, in fact, have all power. . . . This power given to the federal legislature, directly annihilates all the powers of the state legislatures."

59. Wood, *American Republic*, 58.

60. Epstein, *Political Theory*, 66.

61. Thomas Paine, *Dissertations on Government*, quoted in Schmidt and Webking, "Gordon Wood and the American Founding," 201.

62. As Madison states in *Federalist No. 48*, "The legislative department is everywhere extending the sphere of its activity and drawing all power into its impetuous vortex." In *Federalist No. 51*: "In Republican Government, the legislative authority necessarily predominates." Likewise, in *Federalist No. 71* Hamilton points to "the tendency of the legislative authority to absorb every other."

63. *Federalist No. 48*. Reflecting revolutionary sentiment that there be "no taxation without representation," the Constitution (Article I, Section 7) requires that tax measures originate in the House of Representatives.

64. I would suggest that a reasonable understanding of contemporary American government would argue the same is true today. The Fifth Congress passed the Alien and Section Acts. The Patriot Act was legislated by the 107th Congress.

65. Carl J. Richard, "The Classical Roots of the US Congress: Mixed Government Theory," in *Inventing Congress:*

The Origins and Establishment of the First Federal Congress, ed. Kenneth R. Bowling and Donald R. Kennon (Athens: Ohio University, 1999), 12–13.

66. John Adams is generally considered the leading constitutional-era proponent of balanced government or its United States variant in separation of powers and functions. The Anti-Federalist Centinel in his first essay offers one of the strongest objections to balanced government and in doing so most clearly defines and advocates for its alternative simple government: "if, imitating the constitution of Pennsylvania, you vest all the legislative power in one body of men (separating the executive and judicial) elected for a short period, and necessarily excluded by rotation from permanency, and guarded from precipitancy and surprise by delays imposed on its proceedings, you will create the most perfect responsibility for then, whenever the people feel a grievance they cannot mistake the authors, and will apply the remedy with certainty and effect, discarding them at the next election. This tie of responsibility will obviate all the dangers apprehended from a single legislature, and will the best secure the rights of the people." In his advocacy for simple government, however, Centinel was almost alone, as nearly all Anti-Federalist writers supported separation of functions and powers.

67. This is reflected in the bicameral legislature in which the Senate was expected to check the House, the president's possession of the legislative veto, and the court's power to interpret the constitutionality of law. Madison devotes the forty-seventh to fifty-first papers to defending this complexity.

68. Storing, *What the Anti-Federalists Were For*, 56

69. *Federalist No. 47.*

70. *Federalist No. 48.*

71. *Federalist No. 51.*

72. Centinel, *Essay 1.*

73. This idea survived well into the twentieth century. Until the "reapportionment revolution" of the 1960s and the court's rulings that all legislative districts must contain approximately equal population, many states allocated legislative seats, particularly state senate seats, by county.

74. Luther Martin was perhaps the most personally objectionable member of the founding generation. Edward J. Larson and Michael P. Winship describe him as "a bad-mannered, slovenly, heavy-drinking Princeton graduate who succeeded as a lawyer in Maryland." Presumably there is nothing about being a Princeton graduate or a successful Maryland lawyer that makes one objectionable. Nonetheless, his personal characteristics likely contributed to his dying alone and broke in New York City and being buried in an unmarked grave. Edward J. Larson and Michael P. Winship, *The Constitutional Convention: A Narrative History from the Notes of James Madison* (New York: The Modern Library, 2005), 172.

75. Luther Martin, Speech to the Maryland House of Delegates, November 29, 1787.

76. Luther Martin delivers the canonical Constitutional Convention speech advocating state corporate capacity on June 26th and 27th. Roger Wilson summarizes, but strongly opposes, "the leading argument of those who contend for equality of votes among the states, is, that the states, as such, being equal,

and being represented, not as districts of individuals, but in their political and corporate capacities, are entitled to an equality of suffrage," June 28, 1787. See James Madison, *Notes of Debates in the Federal Convention of 1787*, 2nd ed., ed. Adrienne Koch (New York: W. W. Norton, 1985). Hereafter all speaker remarks from the Constitutional Convention are obtained from Madison's *Notes of Debates*.

77. Roger Wilson, Constitutional Convention, June 30, 1787.

78. In his June 29 speech William Johnson of Connecticut noted the extraordinary difficulty of bridging the gap between those who supported representation based on population and those who advocated state corporate capacity, but also pointed toward a possible compromise. "The controversy must be endless whilst gentlemen differ in the grounds of their arguments: those on one side considering the states as districts of people composing one political society, those on the other considering them as so many political societies. The fact is, that the states do exist as political societies, and a government is to be formed for them in their political capacity, as well as for the individuals composing them." The Great or Connecticut Compromise was fully drafted and approved by the convention in late July.

79. John Dickinson, Constitutional Convention, June 7, 1787.

80. James Madison, Constitutional Convention, June 26, 1787.

81. *Federalist No. 63.*

82. John Dickinson, Constitutional Convention, June 7, 1787; *Federalist No. 63.*

83. John Dickinson, Constitutional Convention, June 7, 1787.

84. George Mason, Constitutional Convention, June 7, 1787. James Madison, despite disagreeing with Dickinson, Mason, and other proponents of state legislative selection, faithfully, albeit briefly, presents their arguments in *Federalist* 62, capturing the theme, if not the depth, of the Convention debate: "[The Senate] is recommended by . . . giving to the state governments such an agency in the formation of the federal government, as must secure the authority of the former, and may form a convenient link between the two systems."

Chapter 3. The Founding-Era House of Representatives and the SMD System

1. George Mason, Constitutional Convention, May 31, 1787.

2. George Mason, Constitutional Convention, September 15, 1787.

3. George Mason, "Objections to the Constitution of Government Formed by the Convention (1787)," in *The Essential Antifederalist*, 2nd ed., ed. W. B. Allen and Gordon Lloyd (Lanham, MD: Rowman & Littlefield, 2002), 16–18.

4. George Mason, Constitutional Convention, June 6, 1787, and July 17, 1787. In sharp contrast to his views on the House of Representatives, Mason wanted the people to have nothing at all to do with the selection of president, the popular election of whom he thought as "unnatural" as referring "a trial of colors to a blind man."

5. *Federalist No.* 10.

6. Ibid.

7. Melancton Smith, Speech at the New York Ratifying Convention, June 20–21, 1788, in *The Founders' Constitution*, ed. Philip B. Kurland and Ralph Lerner (Chicago: University of Chicago Press, 1987), vol. 1, chapter 13, document 37; John Adams, "Thoughts on Government," April 1776.

8. Gordon S. Wood, *The Creation of the American Republic, 1776–1787* (Chapel Hill: University of North Carolina Press, 1969), 485–499, especially 487. See also Saul Cornell, *The Other Founders: Anti-Federalism and the Dissenting Tradition in America, 1788–1828* (Chapel Hill: University of North Carolina Press, 1999), 96–99.

9. *Federalist No.* 10. Emphasis added. See discussion in David F. Epstein, *The Political Theory of the Federalist* (Chicago, IL: University of Chicago Press, 1984), 9.

10. Hanna F. Pitkin, *The Concept of Representation* (Berkeley: University of California Press, 1967), 195.

11. Epstein, *Political Theory*, 176–178.

12. Jean Yarbrough, "Representation and Republicanism: Two Views," *Publius* 9, no. 2 (1979): 77–98. See also Allen and Lloyd, *Essential Antifederalist*, 147.

13. Allen and Lloyd, *Essential Antifederalist*, 147.

14. *Federalist No.* 10. See also Epstein, *Political Theory*, 94.

15. *Federalist No.* 10.

16. The Athenian Assembly approximated direct democracy rather than a representative assembly as understood in the founding. See *Federalist* 55.

17. *Federalist No.* 10.

18. Epstein, *Political Theory*, 94.

19. *Federalist No.* 10.

20. Ibid.

21. Ibid.

22. According to Madison's *Federalist No.* 10, the most common and durable source of faction was the various and unequal distribution of property.

23. Ibid.

24. As Federalist Noah Webster argued: "Virtue, patriotism, or love of country, never was and never will be, till mens' natures are changed, a fixed, permanent, principle and support of government." Quoted in Herbert J. Storing, *What the Anti-Federalists Were For: The Political Thought of the Opponents of the Constitution* (Chicago: University of Chicago Press, 1981), 46.

25. *Federalist No. 10*.

26. Andrew Rehfeld, *The Concept of Constituency* (New York: Cambridge University Press, 2005), 97.

27. *Federalist No. 10*.

28. Rehfeld, *Concept of Constituency*, 129.

29. Ibid., 97.

30. *Federalist No. 10*.

31. Ibid.

32. Melancton Smith, New York Ratifying Convention, June 20, 1788, in *The Founder's Constitution*, vol. 1, chapter 13, document 37.

33. Ibid., emphasis added.

34. Ibid.

35. Yarbrough, "Representation and Republicanism," 96.

36. Federal Farmer, *Essay 7*, emphasis added.

37. Storing, *What the Anti-Federalists Were For*, 56.

38. Federal Farmer, in his second essay, argues for election processes that will "allow professional men, merchants, traders, farmers, mechanics, etc. to bring a just proportion of their best informed men respectively into the legislature." It is important to note that, as a general statement, the Anti-Federalists did not often explicitly advocate representing the poor. Their focus was on representing the middle classes in the Congress. See also Cornell, *The Other Founders*, 97.

39. Federal Farmer, *Essay 7*.

40. Allen and Lloyd, *Essential Antifederalist*, 147.

41. Cornell, *The Other Founders*, 98.

42. Edmund S. Morgan, *Inventing the People: The Rise of Popular Sovereignty in England and America* (New York: W. W. Norton, 1988), 239–240.

43. James Hogan, *Election and Representation* (Cork, Ireland: Cork University Press, 1945), quoted in Pitkin, *Concept of Representation*, 172. See also Morgan, *Inventing the People*, 240, 271–272.

44. Edmund Burke. "Letter to Langriche," quoted in Pitkin, *Concept of Representation*, 173.

45. Pitkin, *Concept of Representation*, chapter 8, especially 172–183.

46. Wood, *American Republic*, 175–177.

47. *Federalist No. 14*.

48. Alexander Hamilton's *Federalist No. 35* addresses Anti-Federalist objections that "the house of representatives is not sufficiently numerous for the representation of all the different classes of citizens; in order to combine the interests and feelings of every part of the community, and to produce a due sympathy between the representative body and its constituents." Here he counters with passages that echo themes of virtual representation that "the idea of an actual representation of all classes of the people, by persons of each class, is altogether visionary" but this is not problematic because "mechanics and manufacturers . . . know that the merchant is their natural patron and friend" and "wealthiest landlord, down to the poorest tenant" will be properly represented by landowners in general.

49. Edmund Burke thought the Americans were ill served by virtual

representation in parliament, as exemplified by his 1774 speech "On American Taxation," which castigated British colonial taxation policy.

50. Alexander Keyssar, *The Right to Vote: The Contested History of Democracy in the United States* (New York: Basic Books, 2000), chapter 1 and especially 24. See also Gordon S. Wood, *The Radicalism of the American Revolution* (New York: A. A. Knopf, 1992).

51. See, for example, H. T. Dickinson, "The Representation of the People in Eighteenth-Century Britain" in *Realities of Representation: State Building in Early Modern Europe and European America*, ed. Maija Jansson (New York: Palgrave Macmillan, 2007), 20. Dickinson estimates that approximately 23 percent of the English and Welsh men possessed franchise in this period.

52. Property and taxpaying requirements were typically modest in the early republic, and these disappeared quite quickly in the first third of the nineteenth century. See Keyssar, *The Right to Vote*, tables A1, A2 and A3. Several jurisdictions enforced compulsory voting for white males in the late colonial and early republic eras. See J. R. Pole, *Political Representation in England and the Origins of the American Republic* (Berkeley: University of California Press, 1971), 293.

53. Yarbrough, "Representation and Republicanism," 86. This raised a similar problem for the Anti-Federalists. The importance of the chamber "mirroring" the population notwithstanding, what many Anti-Federalists primarily wanted was increased representation of the great yeomanry. This class, however, was largely enfranchised, and broader franchise raised the disquieting prospect that the chamber might truly "mirror" the population.

54. Ibid., 90.

55. This argument is essentially the same as the Federalist argument against a plural executive. If the United States instituted, for example, an executive council instead of a single president, the executives would "split the community into violent and irreconcilable factions, adhering differently to the different individuals who composed the magistracy." Alexander Hamilton, *Federalist No. 70*.

56. Federal Farmer, Essays 2, 3, and 12.

57. Herbert J. Storing, ed., *The Anti-Federalist: An Abridgement, by Murray Dry, of the Complete Anti-Federalist* (Chicago: University of Chicago Press, 1985), 341.

58. Federal Farmer, Essay 12. If Madison uses the phrase "the public good" repeatedly in *Federalist No. 10*, the Federal Farmer more than matches this repetitiveness in the use of *majority* in his 12th Essay, which argues for majority rule. Here the Federal Farmer invokes *majority* more than twenty times to ensure the reader does not miss the point.

59. *Federalist No. 56*, emphasis added.

60. Rehfeld, *Concept of Constituency*, 98.

61. *Federalist No. 56*.

62. *Federalist No. 57*; Epstein, *Political Theory*, 151–153.

63. Edmund Burke, "Speech to the Electors of Bristol," November 3, 1774, in *The Founders' Constitution*, ed. Philip B. Kurland and Ralph Lerner (Chicago: University of Chicago Press, 1987), vol. 1, ch. 13, document 7. See Joel A. Johnson, "Disposed to Seek Their True Interests: Representation and Responsibility in

Anti-Federalist Thought," *Review of Politics* 66, no. 4 (Fall 2004). Also, Kurland and Lerner, *The Founder's Constitution*, vol. 1, 386.

64. Letter from George Washington to Bushrod Washington, November 15, 1786, in Kurland and Lerner, *The Founders' Constitution*, vol. 1, document 16, 399.

65. *Federalist No. 35.*

66. *Federalist No. 57.*

67. Allen and Lloyd, *Essential Antifederalist*, 147.

68. Cato, *Essay 7.*

69. Federal Farmer, *Essay 2.*

70. Federal Farmer, *Essay 9.*

71. Cato, *Essay 5.*

72. Amicus, "A Plea for the Right of Recall," *Columbia Herald*, August 28, 1788. As a practical matter the feasibility of instructing representatives had largely fallen out of favor among Anti-Federalists by this time. Still, many Anti-Federalists were sympathetic to the principle while aware of the practical difficulties of its use.

73. Richard Katz, *Democracy and Elections* (New York: Oxford University Press, 1997), chapter 1.

Chapter 4. House of Representatives Elections in the Early Republic, 1788–1824

1. Election Ordinance of September 13, 1788.

2. Merrill Jensen and Robert A. Becker, eds., *The Documentary History of the First Federal Elections: 1788–1790*, vol. 1 (Madison: University of Wisconsin Press, 1976), 438, 477. Hereafter FFE.

3. This illustrates the more general point that even some of our most revered patriots and founders were not above malevolent acts when elections were involved. For a contrary view see Thomas

Rogers Hunter, "The First Gerrymander? Patrick Henry, James Madison and James Monroe, and Virginia's 1788 Congressional Districting," *Early American Studies* 9, no 3 (Fall 2011). The Madison and Monroe contest makes this the only House election to feature two future US presidents as candidates.

4. Throughout this and subsequent chapters I do not distinguish between the block vote and the general ticket as the only difference between the two is whether the names of those voted for appear on a single ballot or on multiple ballots. The Pennsylvania method of voting described in the following paragraph is a block vote even though I classify it as general ticket.

5. See, for example, Thomas Herty, *A Digest of the Laws of Maryland Being An Abridgment Alphabetically Arranged of All the Public Acts of Assembly Now in Force and of General Use*, 1799, 230, http://heinonline.org.

6. *The Statutes at Large of Pennsylvania*, 1788.

7. Kenneth Lockridge, *Literacy in Colonial New England* (New York: W. W. Norton, 1975).

8. Maryland Election Law of 1805, 7. The penalty for opening ballots prematurely was a substantial $50 fine.

9. The public nature of voting was one of the justifications for property requirements in the early republic. The argument was that those who were economically dependent on others could be pressured to vote in the same manner as those on whom they were dependent, and consequently the votes of those without property were subject to the influence of economic elites. The property or taxpaying requirement ensured that the electorate consisted of the economically

independent, thus ensuring that elections were less susceptible to corruption.

10. To provide a specific example, early state historian Jeremy Belknap provided the following description of the New Hampshire election process:

> Representatives to Congress are chosen by the inhabitants in town meetings, and the vote of each town are returned to the Secretary's office and laid before the General Court. Those who have a majority of the votes are declared duly elected; but if there be a deficiency, the General Court make a list of such persons as have the highest number of votes, equal to double the number wanting; this list is sent to the towns, and out of it they make the choice. The votes then are returned as before; and the person or persons who have the highest number are elected. (Jeremy Belknap, The History of New-Hampshire, vol. 3 [Dover, NH: 1812], accessed through Internet Archive, https://archive.org, Library of Congress).

Jeremy Belknap is one of the first American historians and is known for his History of New Hampshire.

11. See Jensen and Becker, FFE, 1:510, for a discussion of the Massachusetts electoral process.

12. Article 1, Section 2. By constitutional amendment the states cannot deny franchise on the basis of race (Fifteenth Amendment) or gender (Nineteenth Amendment), or those between the ages of eighteen and twenty-one (Twenty-Sixth Amendment).

13. The second question centered on whether representatives should be required to live in the district they represent. Today we understand that such a restriction introduces an unconstitutional qualification to be a representative. The Constitution simply requires, inter alia, that representatives be a resident of the state they represent; the states may not impose additional qualifications to serve. However, this principle was not clear in 1788, and some states passed residency requirements as part of their election law. These states included Georgia, Maryland, North Carolina, and Virginia.

14. Although there was never serious consideration given to allowing these to be cast cumulatively.

15. Pennsylvania Mercury, September 16, 1788, in Jensen and Becker, FFE, 1:274, emphasis in the original.

16. Gordon DenBoer, ed., The Documentary History of the First Federal Elections: 1788–1790, vol. 3 (Madison: University of Wisconsin Press, 1986), 233.

17. Ibid.

18. Jensen and Becker, FFE, 1:469.

19. Ibid., 1:470.

20. Civis, Maryland Journal (Baltimore), July 11, 1788, in Gordon DenBoer, ed., The Documentary History of the First Federal Elections: 1788–1790, vol. 2 (Madison: University of Wisconsin Press, 1984), 108.

21. Jensen and Becker, FFE, 1:246.

22. Those favoring the general ticket sometimes made the opposite argument—that the "consequence" of a freeman's ballot is increased by the number of allocated votes. For example, Massachusetts writer Honorius writes that at-large election in Massachusetts "gives every elector EIGHT-FOLD CONSEQUENCE." Jensen and Becker, FFE, 1:470, emphasis in the original.

23. DenBoer, FFE, 3:211.

24. Edward Carrington letter to James Madison, Richmond, VA, November 9–10, 1789, in DenBoer, FFE, 2:367. Carrington was elected to the House of Representatives from Virginia's first district.

25. Jensen and Becker, FFE, 1:302.

26. Ibid., 1:147–148, 155–162.

27. Rosemarie Zagarri, The Politics of Size: Representation in the United States, 1776–1850 (Ithaca, NY: Cornell University Press, 1987), chapter 5.

28. Pennsylvania elected two of its thirteen representatives from a dual-member district and the rest from single-member districts.

29. Zagarri, The Politics of Size, 108. See also Gordon S. Wood, Empire of Liberty: A History of the Early Republic, 1789–1815 (New York: Oxford University Press, 2009), 57.

30. Zagarri, The Politics of Size, 118–119.

31. Including the dual-member fourth district.

32. Kenneth C. Martis, The Historical Atlas of Parties in the United States Congress: 1789–1989 (New York: Macmillan, 1989).

33. For example, Tennessee used the general ticket through the third apportionment (Eighth through Twelfth Congresses) when its apportionment was three representatives. It then changed to SMD election when its apportionment increased to six in the fifth apportionment. Likewise, Ohio adopted SMD elections when its apportionment increased from one representative to six representatives between the third and fourth apportionments.

34. This calculation does not hold in majority runoff systems, in which a vote for a favored candidate who is unlikely to win is not "wasted" so long as no candidate receives a majority.

35. This is known as the Cube Law of Legislative Proportions, which notes that if two parties complete in an SMD system the ratio of the two-party party vote shares cubed is the ratio of their seat shares in the legislature. In my contrived example, the ratio is $(55/45)^3 = 1.83$. In a 100-seat legislature we would expect the party that received 55 percent of the vote to obtain 65 percent of the chamber seats. See chapter 8.

36. One would normally expect one more candidate than the number of elected representatives from a given district to stand for election. See Gary Cox, Making Votes Count (New York: Cambridge University Press, 1997), chapter 5.

37. V. O. Key Jr., Southern Politics in State and Nation (New York: Knopf, 1949). This is equally true, perhaps especially true, if a state is dominated by a single faction or party. In this case affiliation with the dominant faction carries with it the assurance that one's political competitors are often allies. This encourages individuals to stand for election and potentially crowd the field. Even if several like-minded candidates split the vote, the elected are likely to be ideological friends rather than adversaries.

38. Endorsing documents including letters, pamphlets, and broadsheets were common. For an example of a coordinating document in a more complex electoral setting see "Address of the District Delegates to the Democratic Citizens of the County of Philadelphia," [Philadelphia, 1810], which endorsed six Democratic House of Representatives candidates. Accessed at the American Antiquarian Society, Worcester, MA, March 2016.

39. *A New Nation Votes: American Election Returns, 1787–1825,* http://elections .lib.tufts.edu. (Note: This is an online data archive.) All data used in this section are obtained from the *A New Nation Votes* project.

40. In all calculations I discarded candidates who received less than 100 votes. I calculated the maximum number of votes possible as the total number of votes cast in the election divided by the number of elected seats.

41. In 1816 there were four primary candidates for Delaware's two seats, all of whom secured pluralities of between 46 and 48 percent of the votes. Two additional candidates, Federalists Thomas Clayton and Thomas Cooper, received modest vote shares of approximately 6 percent.

42. This law also explicitly enfranchised (single) women, making New Jersey the first state to formally extend franchise to women. In the early nineteenth century, however, this provision was repealed by the New Jersey Assembly and franchise was restricted to white, property-owning men.

43. John G. Kolp, "The Dynamics of Electoral Competition in Pre-Revolutionary Virginia," *William and Mary Quarterly* 49, no. 4 (October 1992): 652–674.

44. Ibid., figure IV.

45. Martis, *Atlas of United States Congressional Districts.*

Chapter 5. The Jacksonian-Whig Era and the 1842 SMD Mandate

1. As discussed in following chapters, the SMD was mandated in most but not all subsequent apportionment cycles. The Apportionment Act following the 1850 census (9 Stat L. 433) did not require districting, but those following the 1860 and 1870 censuses (12 Stat. L. 572 and 17 Stat. L. 28) did require states to district, with the latter allowing for the at-large election of one representative. Legislation following the next seven censuses from 1880 to 1940 required states to district (22 Stat. L. 5., 26 Stat. L. 735, 31 Stat, L. 733, 37 Stat. L. 13, 46 Stat. L. 13, and 54 Stat. L. 162). However, these acts differed in their language regarding whether districts had to be contiguous and have as near as possible equal population. In the twentieth century the trend was to ignore these latter considerations; no such requirements were written into these acts after 1929. For a compilation of these laws prior to World War II see Lawrence F. Schmeckebier, *Congressional Apportionment* (Washington, DC: Brookings Institution, 1941), 132–135.

2. When Alaska and Hawaii were admitted to the union in 1959 the House temporarily increased its membership to 437, then subsequently reduced it back to 435 in the apportionment following the 1960 census.

3. James Monroe, whose presidency (1817–1825) epitomized the era, was elected with only nominal opposition since Federalists could not agree on an opposition candidate, nor could they have competed nationally had they done so.

4. Martin H. Quitt, "Congressional (Partisan) Constitutionalism: The Apportionment Act Debates of 1842 and 1844," *Journal of the Early Republic* 28, no. 4 (Winter 2008): 628.

5. Many believe that the Whigs emerged from the Federalist Party following its demise in the early nineteenth century. This view has been discredited. The Whigs, while sympathetic

to many Federalist ideals, emerged from a schism among the Jeffersonian Republicans that centered on acceptance or rejection of Hamiltonian ideals about economic development and a stronger national government. While the Whigs embraced these ideals, they also rejected the most stringent forms of Federalist elitism. See Michael F. Holt, *The Rise and Fall of the American Whig Party* (New York: Oxford University Press, 1999), 2–3.

6. Ibid., 39.

7. The amendment proposed by Nicholas was introduced in the Sixth Congress, 1st session (3/14/1800), and the final committee report on the bill was issued in the 2nd session (1/22/1801). 10 Annals of Cong. 628, 785, 941–946 (1800, 1801).

8. Other states petitioning during this period for constitutional amendment to require SMD election of representatives include Vermont, North Carolina, Massachusetts, New York, and New Hampshire. See Herman V. Ames, *The Proposed Amendments to the Constitution of the United States during the First Century of Its History* (Washington, DC: Government Printing Office, 1897) 56–57.

9. Thomas Jefferson, letter to James Monroe, January 12, 1800. Jefferson advocated district election on the familiar Anti-Federalist grounds that this method produces a more "exact representation of [the nation's] diversified sentiments."

10. Today only Nebraska and Maine select presidential electors by district, with the two remaining at-large electors determined by the statewide vote.

11. Ames, *Proposed Amendments to the Constitution*, 57.

12. 33 Annals of Cong. 139 (1819).

13. Ibid.

14. Ibid.

15. 31 Annals of Cong. 185 (1818). Dickerson's remarks are also notable because of his early use of the term "gerrymander" indicating that this word came into common political use before 1820. Specifically he states: "This system of defeating every purpose of a fair election, has become an art and a science; and is known by the technical term of *gerrymandering*." 31 Annals of Cong. 181 (1818).

16. 33 Annals of Cong. 139 (1819).

17. Ibid.

18. 31 Annals of Cong. 185–186 (1818). On the reasonableness of this interpretation, see the *Records of the Federal Convention*, August 9, 1787, especially remarks by James Madison and Rufus King.

19. 33 Annals of Cong. 151–154 (1819).

20. Ibid., 154.

21. Ames, *Proposed Amendments to the Constitution*, 57.

22. In 1824 no candidate received a majority in the Electoral College, so selection of the president fell to the House of Representatives. Andrew Jackson had the leading vote share among the candidates, but speaker Henry Clay threw his support to John Quincy Adams, who was selected to be president by the House. Adams subsequently made Clay his secretary of state, suggesting to many that there had been a "corrupt bargain" in the form of a deal between Clay and Adams that produced this outcome.

23. For the single most complete discussion of this period, especially with respect to the birth of modern political parties and voter mobilization, see Holt, *The Rise and Fall of the American Whig Party*, especially chapters 1 and 5.

24. Walter Dean Burnham, with

Thomas Ferguson and Louis Ferleger, *Voting in American Elections: The Shaping of the American Political Universe since 1788* (Bethesda, MD: Academic Press, 2010).

25. Alexander Keyssar, *The Right to Vote: The Contested History of Democracy in the United States* (New York: Basic Books, 2000), 39.

26. Ibid., especially table A.2. See also Holt, *The Rise and Fall of the American Whig Party*, 8.

27. Sources: Burnham, *Voting in American Elections*, tables 2 and 10. On page 29 and in note 14 Burnham describes the difficulty of calculating the size of the eligible electorate in this era. For a detailed discussion on how Burnham arrives at these figures consult his "Those High Nineteenth Century American Voting Turnouts: Fact or Fiction?," *Journal of Interdisciplinary History* 16, no. 4 (Spring 1986). To convince the reader that the size of the potential electorate and hence the turnout figures are accurate, consider the following "back of the envelope" calculations based on the census: according to the 1820 census, the US population was 9,638,453, of whom 1,538,128 were enslaved blacks. The free white male population of voting age is recorded as approximately 2 million. The 1830 census lists the US population as nearly 13 million, of whom approximately 2 million were enslaved. The 1840 population was just over 17 million, of whom approximately 2.4 million were enslaved. A plausible estimate of the white, male, voting-age population during this period is about one-fifth of the total US population. This would produce estimates of the potential electorate of about 2 million in 1820, 2.6 million in 1830, and 3.4 million in 1840. These are close to Burnham's more

carefully researched figures presented in figure 4.1, and they tell exactly the same story: the size of the potential electorate increased at an extraordinary pace in these two decades.

28. See Holt, *The Rise and Fall of the American Whig Party*, 9.

29. Ibid,, 48, table 2.

30. W. Dean Burnham, Jerome M. Clubb, and William Flanigan, State-Level Congressional, Gubernatorial and Senatorial Election Data for the United States, 1824–1972, *ICPSR Find and Analyze Data*, 1991, http://www.icpsr.umich .edu/icpsrweb/ICPSR/studies/4.doi.org /10.3886/ICPSR00075.v1; Lyn Ragsdale, *Vital Statistics on the Presidency* (Washington, DC: Congressional Quarterly Press, 1998).

31. Holt, *The Rise and Fall of the American Whig Party*, 12–13, 50–53, 58.

32. I use the Pedersen (1983) measure of party system volatility: This is the most common measure of electoral volatility in relevant research. If a party's vote share in a given election is the same as its vote share in the next election, then volatility is zero. If party vote shares in the current election differ significantly from those in the subsequent election, then volatility is high. Mogens N. Pedersen, "Changing Patterns of Electoral Volatility in European Party Systems, 1948–1977: Explorations in Explanation," in *Western European Party Systems: Continuity and Change*, ed. Hans Daalder and Peter Mair (London: Sage, 1983), 29–66.

33. For example, in the election cycle for the Twenty-Second Congress in 1830 and 1831, the Anti-Masons secured approximately 12.6 percent of the vote and sometimes more than 18 percent in northern areas. Burnham, *Voting in*

American Elections, table 3.4. For the basis for Anti-Mason support see Holt, *The Rise and Fall of the American Whig Party*, 46–47 and 52.

34. Michael F. Holt, *Political Parties and American Political Development from the Age of Jackson to the Age of Lincoln* (Baton Rouge: Louisiana State University Press, 1992), 153.

35. Holt, *Political Parties and American Political Development*, 163.

36. This section builds heavily on ibid., chapter 4.

37. Ibid., 188.

38. Ibid.

39. Ibid., 181.

40. President Harrison was sixty-eight years old when he assumed office, making him the oldest US president up to that point. The average male life expectancy for a man born in 1773, conditional on being alive at age fifty, was about twenty years. In other words, Harrison probably had two good years left in him absent any intervention, divine or otherwise. (Life expectancy source: Clarence Pope, "Adult Mortality in America before 1900: A View from Family Histories," in *Strategic Factors in Nineteenth Century American Economic History: A Volume to Honor Robert W. Fogel*, ed. Claudia Goldin and Hugh Rockoff (Chicago: University of Chicago Press, 1991).

41. Holt, *Political Parties and American Political Development*, 190.

42. This section builds on Jeffrey A. Jenkins, "Partisanship and Contested Election Cases in the House of Representatives, 1789–2002," *Studies in American Political Development* 18, no. 2 (2004): 112–135.

43. If these seats were awarded to the Democrats, then the Democrats would have a majority in the chamber. If the Whigs won the seats, then no party would command a majority of seats.

44. Speech delivered by Tennessee representative Aaron Brown on March 18, 1840, printed in *Volume of Speeches Delivered in Congress, 1840* (Washington, DC Globe Office, 1840). See also Cong. Globe, 26th Cong., 1st Sess. 278 (1840).

45. Chester H. Rowell, *A Historical and Legal Digest of All the Contested Election Cases in the House of Representatives from the First to the Fifty-Sixth Congress, 1789–1901*, H.R. Doc. No. 510-56 (1901).

46. Ibid.

47. Milo B. Howard Jr., "The General Ticket," *Alabama Review* 19, no. 3 (July 1966): 163–166.

48. Ibid., 164.

49. Ibid., 163.

50. David I. Durham, *A Southern Moderate in Radical Times: Henry Washington Hilliard, 1808–1892* (Baton Rouge: Louisiana State University Press, 2008), 65.

51. Quoted in ibid., 66.

52. Howard, "The General Ticket," 170, 172–173. The referendum was narrowly decided: of 42,717 votes cast, the districting option won by 665 votes.

53. These states and their delegation composition were: Georgia (nine Whig), New Jersey (six Whig), Rhode Island (two Whig), Alabama (five Democratic), New Hampshire (five Democratic), Mississippi (two Democratic), and Missouri (two Democratic).

54. Quitt, "Congressional (Partisan) Constitutionalism," 628.

55. James Albert Woodburn, *The American Republic and Its Government* (New York: G. P. Putnam's Sons, 1903): 248–50.

56. Quitt, "Congressional (Partisan) Constitutionalism," 627.

57. Ibid., 636; Johanna Nicol Shields, "Whigs Reform the 'Bear Garden': Representation and the Apportionment Act of 1842," *Journal of the Early Republic* 5, no. 3 (Autumn 1985): 379.

58. The *Congressional Globe* Appendix contains over eighty pages of remarks by members of both chambers on the Apportionment Act. These are the primary sources on which this section is based.

59. Michele Rosa-Clot, "The Apportionment Act of 1842: 'An Odious Use of Authority,'" *Parliaments, Estates & Representation* 31, no. 1 (April 2011): 33–52, 34.

60. Cong. Globe, 27th Cong., 2d Sess. 437 (1842). See also Rep. Stokely's remarks on the same day.

61. Shields, "Whigs Reform the 'Bear Garden,'" 355–382, 363.

62. Cong. Globe, 27th Cong., 2d Sess. 437 (1842).

63. Ibid.

64. Cong. Globe app., 27th Cong., 2d Sess. 884 (1842).

65. As an example, fellow Kentuckian Joseph Underwood "believed that less than half of the present number of representatives would do more business, and do it better, than the existing number. [He] depreciated any large increase of members, as tending toward a mob government, by confusion, crowing like cocks, braying like asses, shuffling with feet, coughing, and other similar expedient now pursued in the House of Commons in England." Cong. Globe, 27th Cong., 2d Sess. 436 (1842).

66. Ibid., 621.

67. Ibid., 443, emphasis added.

68. Cong. Globe app., 27th Cong., 2d Sess. 345 (1842).

69. Ibid., 436.

70. The most restrictive interpretation of this clause was offered by Georgia representative Colquitt and Virginia representative Summers, each of whom went beyond denying this power in toto but extended this to argue that the general ticket was the only constitutional means to elect representatives. These representatives argued that having representatives selected by the people of the states meant that the enfranchised had the right to vote for all members of the state's congressional delegation, either by general ticket or in a manner similar to the founding-era methods used by Maryland and Georgia. At least as far as this argument was concerned, Colquitt and Summers were viewed as cranks. See, for example, remarks by Representatives Davis and Barnard, Cong. Globe app., 27th Cong., 2d Sess. 338, 380 (1842).

71. But just to make sure, Representatives Clifford of Maine, Atherton of New Hampshire, and others made similar speeches.

72. Remarks by Representative Floyd, Cong. Globe app., 27th Cong., 2d Sess. 320–321 (1842), emphasis in original.

73. Indeed, many if not most members of the Twenty-Seventh Congress seemed to agree that Congress could determine the times of elections in order to standardize the congressional calendar.

74. Cong. Globe app., 27th Cong., 2d Sess. 360 (1842).

75. Recent applications of this principle include *New York v. United States* (505 US 144) 1992, in which the court ruled that "the federal government may not compel the states to enact or administer a federal regulatory program"; and *Printz v. United States* (521 US 898) 1997, which ruled that the federal government cannot compel state officers to execute

federal firearms background checks. For discussion of this constitutional principle in the context of the Apportionment Act of 1842, see David P. Currie, *The Constitution in Congress: Democrats and Whigs 1829–1861* (Chicago: University of Chicago Press, 2005), 260–264.

76. For a clear statement on this point see the remarks of Representative Kennedy of Indiana, Cong. Globe app., 27th Cong., 2d Sess. 316–318 (1842). Kennedy favored districts but not the act. In his words, the "pending amendment proposes to issue an order to the Legislatures of the different state of this union, *directing* them *how*, and *commanding* them, *to* . . . form their respective states into different congressional districts." According to Kennedy, "This [drawing districts] you must do yourselves."

77. Quitt, "Congressional (Partisan) Constitutionalism," 639. Cong. Globe app., 27th Cong., 2d Sess. 341–343, 369 (1842).

78. Ibid., 348.

79. Ibid., 351–353.

80. Ibid., 519.

81. Ibid., 458. Also see the June 3rd remarks by Senator Graham (W-KY), Ibid., 749.

82. Ibid.

83. Ibid., 379.

84. Ibid., 320.

85. Ibid., 353, 354.

86. Ibid., 346.

87. Ibid., 493.

88. Ibid., 490.

89. All roll call data used in this section were obtained from "United States Congressional Roll Call Voting Records, 1789–1998," ICPSR *Find and Analyze Data*, 2010, http://www.icpsr.umich.edu/icpsrweb/ICPSR/studies/4, doi:10.3886/ICPSR00004.v3.

90. Ibid., Variable 504.

91. Ibid., Variable 506.

92. These characterizations of votes on the act are substantiated by personal communication with the Office of the Historian, United States House of Representatives on January 12, 2015. See also the *House Journal*, June 17, 1842.

93. "United States Congressional Roll Call Voting Records, 1789–1998," Variable 505.

94. Among the eighteen Whigs who voted against the districting requirement, five were from the North, two from the border state of Kentucky, and the remaining eleven from the South. Of these eleven, four represented Georgia, which used the general ticket.

95. Benton to Martin Van Buren, June 3, 1842, *Martin Van Buren Papers*, quoted in Shields, "Whigs Reform the 'Bear Garden,'" 371.

96. Shields, "Whigs Reform the 'Bear Garden,'" 379.

97. Ibid., 359.

98. Cong. Globe, 27th Cong., 2d Sess. 872 (1842).

Chapter 6. The Progressive Era: Consolidation and Institutionalization, 1870–1930

1. Herbert Croly, *The Promise of American Life* (New York: Macmillan, 1909), 51. Croly was a Progressive Era leader and ranks among the most influential of the Progressive intellectuals; he cofounded the *New Republic*.

2. Thomas Hare, *A Treatise on the Election of Representatives, Parliamentary and Municipal* (London: Longman, Brown, Green, Longmans & Roberts, 1859). John Stuart Mill, *Considerations on Representative Government* (London: Parker, Son, and Bourn, 1861)

3. Senator Buckalew was no egalitarian. In a speech foreshadowing the perspectives of many Progressives, he strongly opposed the Fourteenth Amendment clause that permits a reduction in a state's apportionment if it restricts adult male suffrage. See Speech of Senator Charles R. Buckalew, Cong. Globe, 39th Cong., 1st Sess. 957–965, esp. 961–962 (1866).

4. For the 1867 amendment see the Cong. Globe, 40th Cong., 1st Sess. 573–575 (1867). This proposed amendment was voted out of order by the chamber. The 1869 bill is S.B. 772, which was referred to a select committee on January 13, 1869, and reported back to the chamber on March 2, 1869. See the Cong. Globe, 40th Cong., 3d Sess. 320, 1769.

5. Cong. Globe, 40th Cong., 3d Sess. Appendix 268–279.

6. Simon Sterne, *On Representative Government and Personal Representation: Based in Part upon Thomas Hare's Treatise, Entitled "The Election of Representatives, Parliamentary and Municipal"* (Philadelphia: J. B. Lippincott, 1871). A useful compilation of Senator Buckalew's writing and speeches on proportional representation was done by John G. Freeze, ed,. *Proportional Representation* (Philadelphia: John Campbell & Son, 1872).

7. Robert Richie and Steven Hill, *Reflecting, All of US: The Case for Proportional Representation* (Boston: Beacon Press, 1999), 23.

8. Kathleen Barber, *A Right to Representation: Proportional Representation Systems for the Twenty-First Century* (Columbus: Ohio State University Press, 2000).

9. A short list of states and territories that seriously entertained constitutional amendments requiring proportional representation for state legislative and other offices in the early 1870s includes Illinois, West Virginia, the Utah Territory in anticipation of statehood, and Pennsylvania. See Freeze *Proportional Representation*, 219, 226–228.

10. Importantly, this method aided the election of southern African American representatives including North Carolinians George White and Henry Cheatham in the immediate post–Civil War era. "Black Americans in Congress, 1870–2007: Elections," *History, Art and Archives, US House of Representatives*, Office of the Historian (Washington, DC: US Government Printing Office, 2008), http://history.house.gov/Exhibitions-and-Publications/BAIC/Historical-Essays/Temporary-Farewell/Elections/.

11. Peter H. Argersinger, *Structure, Process and Party: Essays in American Political History*. (Armonk, NY: Routledge, 1992), 56–57.

12. Presidents Garfield and McKinley were assassinated in 1881 and 1901 respectively. It is unclear whether Garfield assassin Charles J. Guiten is wholly responsible for the president's death. Garfield was gravely wounded by Guiten, but his medical care, even by the standards of the times, was deficient. One can make a plausible argument that Garfield would have survived had his physicians only remained in the next room. Later in the era there were also attempts on the lives of William Howard Taft in 1909 and Theodore Roosevelt in 1912, although in the former case it was unclear whether the assassin sought to kill Taft, Mexican president Diaz, or both. In the latter case Roosevelt was running for a third term under the Progressive Bull Moose label,

not sitting as president. Still, he took a bullet in the chest, slowed by a folded speech he planned to deliver later in the day. True to form Roosevelt delivered the speech on schedule, displaying to the audience both the bullet hole through the paper and the blood on his shirt. Despite this, he lost the election to Woodrow Wilson.

13. For reasons that will become clearer in the next chapter, it is important to understand that the US Supreme Court believed that Congress "purposely" abandoned the "compact, contiguous, and equal-population" requirements when it held these were not applicable in post-1930 districting disputes. See *Wood v. Broom*, 287 US 1 (1932).

14. 17 Stat. L. 28.

15. Two other important aspects of this act were that it (1) prohibited the admission of new states unless these contained the minimum quota for a representation under the 1872 apportionment formula and (2) that each state's population for apportionment purposes be reduced if the state violated the Fourteenth Amendment's second section prohibiting the abridgement of voting rights to men age 21 or older. Neither of these sections proved enforceable. The ratio question improperly bound subsequent Congresses and the Fourteenth Amendment question proved politically intractable. For a complete discussion see Laurence F. Schmeckebier, *Congressional Apportionment* (Westport, CT: Greenwood Press, 1941), 94–96, 118–119.

16. See the explanation of this provision offered by the amendment's author, Representative John Farnsworth (R-IL), in an exchange with Representative Eugene Hale (R-ME). Cong. Globe, 42nd Cong., 2d Sess. 62–63 (1871).

17. The 1911 apportionment act initially established a House of 433 members but contained a clause that would automatically increase the chamber size to 435 upon admission of Arizona and New Mexico to the union, each of which would receive a single representative.

18. Fourteenth Amendment, Section 2, reads in part "[W]hen the right to vote at any election . . . is denied to any of the male inhabitants of such state, being twenty-one years of age, and citizens of the United States, or in any way abridged . . . representation therein shall be reduced in the proportion which the number of such male citizens shall bear to the whole number of male citizens twenty-one years of age in such state." See remarks by Representative Charles Willard (R-VT), Representative Michael Kerr (D-IN), and Representative Samuel Cox (D-NY) . Cong. Globe, 42nd Cong., 2d Sess. 64, 105–107, 108–110 (1871). For a complete discussion see Schmeckebier, *Congressional Apportionment*, 94–96.

19. Cong. Globe, 42nd Cong. 2d Sess. 141 (1871).

20. Ibid., 115. Representative Clarkson was actually speaking to a potentially smaller chamber, which would have the same effect of increasing the territorial extent of districts.

21. 34 Cong. Rec. 605–606 (1901).

22. The state-election is the unit of analysis with each state's first election in the period eliminated from the matrix because this election is the starting point from which electoral system change is measured. These figures are based on state elections to the Forty-Seventh through Seventieth Congresses inclusive.

23. The election cycle that saw the

greatest number of representatives elected at large from states entitled to two or more representatives was the Sixty-Third Congress, meeting in 1913, which counted 12 so elected representatives out of a membership of 435. More typical during this period is 4 or fewer so-elected members in any given cycle.

24. Quoted in Robert H. Wiebe, *The Search for Order: 1877–1920* (New York: Hill and Wang, 1967), 61.

25. John R. Commons, *Proportional Representation*, 2nd ed. (New York: Macmillan Company, 1907), 31. Commons was an academic economist who contributed much to the study of economic history and the study of labor.

26. Voter ID laws are meaningless in the absence of registration.

27. Walter Dean Burnham, "The Changing Shape of the American Political Universe," *American Political Science Review* 59, no. 1 (March 1965): 7–28, esp. 11 and 24–27.

28. The average turnout based on the voting eligible population between 1876 and 1900 inclusive was 78.7 percent. No election in this period saw less than a 73 percent turnout rate. The average voter turnout for presidential elections between 1904 and 1932 inclusive was 58 percent. No election in this period saw a turnout rate greater than 65.7 percent. Source: *United States Election Project*, http://www.electproject.org/national-1789-present, with data compiled by University of Florida professor Michael P. McDonald.

29. A primary marker of democratic health is electoral participation. This was clearly diminished by the Progressive weakening of US political parties. Political parties are the primary mobilizer of the electorate and are most capable of doing so when strong and vibrant. The Progressive reforms and later reforms in this spirit sapped this vibrancy. To provide one example, the 2002 passage of the Bipartisan Campaign Finance Reform Act, which prohibited large, unregulated, contributions to political parties most certainly helped spur the growth of the "527" organizations that now receive and spend these resources. In effect, BCFRA fostered the transfer of political resources from broad-based parties to narrower special-interest groups.

30. Theodore Roosevelt's Progressive Party never formally endorsed proportional representation, as reflected in the notable absence of a PR plank in its 1912 platform, which endorsed several other electoral reforms, including direct election of US senators, primary elections, and the short ballot. See Barber, *A Right to Representation*, 42.

31. Wiebe, *The Search for Order*, 61.

32. Ibid.

33. An important caveat to this is the admiration of many progressives for Alexander Hamilton. Croly, for example, goes to great pains in his writings to express admiration for Hamilton, especially his truly national vision of the United States and a government with powers commensurate to the responsibilities entrusted to it.

34. Herbert Croly, *Progressive Democracy* (New York: Macmillan Company, 1914).

35. To this end, Croly regards the difficulty in amending the constitution as "the most formidable legal obstacle in the path of progressive democratic fulfilment." Ibid., 230, 227–230.

36. Ibid., 227.

37. Ibid., 236.

38. Ibid., 274.

39. Ibid., 275, 277–279, 282–283.

40. Ibid., 301.

41. Ibid.

42. Ibid., 273.

43. Ibid., 238, 263–264.

44. Ibid., 299–300.

45. For an excellent discussion of the Oregon People's Power League and the Progressive movement in Oregon, see James D. Barnett, "Reorganization of State Government in Oregon," *American Political Science Review* 9, no. 2 (May 1915): 287–293.

46. In the Oregon case about 1/16th of the vote would be sufficient to elect a candidate.

47. Oregon Measure 15, 1908. The ballot proposal wording is confusing as it simultaneously recommends the legislature consider the majoritarian instant runoff voting process and proportional representation. For a discussion of this proposal see the *Oregonian*, May 21, 1908, 8. All Oregon election descriptions and results are obtained from *Ballotpedia*, accessed February 24, 2016, https://www.ballotpedia.org.

48. Oregon Measures 4 and 31, 1910.

49. Oregon Measure 31, 1912.

50. Oregon Measures 25 and 26, 1914. The proportional representation mandate was supported by 22.5 percent of the electorate.

51. Barnett, "Reorganization of State Government in Oregon," 290.

52. John Dewey, *The Public and Its Problems* (New York: Henry Holt, 1927), 212–213.

53. Dillon's Rule is the constitutional principle that local governments enjoy only those powers granted to them by their states. It was most clearly

articulated in 1868 by federal judge John R. Dillon in *Clinton v. The Cedar Rapids R.R. Co.* See Barber, *A Right to Representation*, 38, 55–61. See also [author unknown], "Minority or Proportional Representation," 21 *Columbia Law Review*, 182–186 (1921). The unattributed author of this article may be John R. Commons, author of the 1907 Progressive treatise *Proportional Representation*.

54. Andrew Rehfeld, *The Concept of Constituency: Political Representation, Democratic Legitimacy, and Institutional Design* (New York: Cambridge University Press, 2005), 56. However, Peter H. Argersinger in *Structure, Process and Party*, 73, correctly notes that questions were raised about the propriety of geographic representation in the late nineteenth century.

55. Richard Hofstadter, *The Age of Reform* (New York: Alfred A. Knopf, 1955), 131.

56. Michael J. Dubin, *United States Congressional Elections, 1788–1997: The Official Results* (Jefferson, NC: McFarland & Company, 1998), and Gerald G. Rusk, *A Statistical History of the American Electorate* (Washington, DC: CQ Press, 2001), tables 5-15 and 5-16.

57. See, for example, David Wasserman, The Cook Political Report Partisan Voter Index, 2014. By their calculation a partisan voter index of greater than 5 for either party denotes a safe congressional district. The Cook Report estimates that there were 345 such House districts in 2014.

58. Most states introduced some form of the secret ballot between 1885 and 1890.

59. Johnathon N. Katz and Brian R. Sala, "Careerism, Committee Assignments and the Electoral Connection,"

American Political Science Review 90, no. 1 (March 1996): 21–33.

60. Initially there were two types of ballots: the "party bloc" ballot designed to encourage citizens to cast a party vote and the "office bloc" ballot that required voters to cast a ballot for each office individually. The party bloc ballot eventually fell out of favor.

61. Jill Wittrock, Stephen C. Nemeth, Howard Sanborn, Brian DiSarro, and Peverill Squire, "The Impact of the Australian Ballot on Member Behavior in the US House of Representatives," *Political Research Quarterly* 61, no. 3 (September 2008): 434–444.

62. Specifically, the census recorded that more Americans lived in cities with populations of 25,000 or more than lived in towns and villages with smaller population.

63. 69 Cong. Rec. 9001 (1928).

64. Ibid., 9005.

65. Quoted in Charles W. Eagles, *Democracy Delayed: Congressional Reapportionment and Urban-Rural Conflict in the 1920s* (Athens: University of Georgia Press, 1990), 39. Former Speaker Clark was speaking as a private citizen, not as a member of the chamber, as he was not reelected in 1920. He did not live long enough to recognize the extent of mass urban migration as he died a few weeks after speaking these words.

66. If one doubts whether these values continue to resonate, consider Stanly Fish's (July 1, 2007) *New York Times* Opinionator Column in which he writes: "The dominant tone [in contemporary country music] is an unapologetic celebration of country—life virtues (honesty, loyalty, friendship, piety) in the company of a nostalgia for the days, now vanished, when those virtues really

flourished," or, like Fish, just listen to a country radio station for an hour or two. This nostalgia for the simple, agrarian, virtues of days gone by was just as prevalent in 1929 as it is today. See Stanley Fish, "Country Roads," *New York Times*, July 1, 2007, accessed March 21, 2016, http://opinionator.blogs.nytimes.com/2007/07/01/country-roads/.

67. Eagles, *Democracy Delayed*, 38.

68. 69 Cong. Rec. 9092 (1928). Many, like Representative Romjue, were resigned to urbanization and constitutional enumeration, but hopeful that a 1930 census would be more generous to rural areas and their congressional representation.

69. Quoted in Eagles, *Democracy Delayed*, 38.

70. An as example, Representative Romjue notes that "it is apparent to anyone conversant with the present condition existing in the country that there is a very rapid drifting of power and population into the large cities of our country and away from the rural sections and agricultural people." 69 Cong. Rec. 9092 (1928).

71. H.R. 11725. 70th Congress, 2nd Sess. This horse trading also eliminated the fourth section, which permitted the at-large election of any additional representatives a state received in reapportionment, and the fifth section, which allowed at-large election of all of a state's representatives should the state lose representation following reapportionment.

72. Eagles, *Democracy Delayed*, 59–62. This bill was introduced in the Sixty-Ninth Congress, Second Session, in January 1927 (H.R. 13471).

73. To say the least, Representative Lozier had a dog in the apportionment

fight. Prior to the 1930 reapportionment Missouri had 16 representatives; following reapportionment Missouri decreased its chamber membership by 3 to 13 representatives. Representative Lozier was elected from the (pre-1930) Missouri Second District in the rural north-central part of the state. He was elected to the House for the final time in the 1932 election at large when Missouri failed to redistrict. The 1934 election was again contested in newly drawn single-member districts, but significant sections of the Lozier's former Second District were redrawn into the new Missouri First, Third, and Ninth Districts. Pennsylvania's situation was less certain. It was not expected to lose a seat under the 1920 apportionment, but did lose two representatives following the 1930 census, with its delegation declining from 36 to 34.

74. Eagles, *Democracy Delayed*, 72.

75. 69 Cong. Rec. 9104 (1928). Emphasis added.

76. Ibid., 9105.

77. Ibid.

78. Ibid.

79. Ibid., 9106.

80. 70 Cong. Rec. 1496 (1929).

81. Ibid.

82. Ibid.

83. Ibid., 1602–1605 (1929).

84. 71 Cong. Rec. 2443–2458 (1929).

85. *Wood v. Broom*, 287 US 1 (1932). Chief Justice Charles Hughes wrote for the majority that the removal of the compact, contiguous, and equal-population requirements from the apportionment act was "deliberate" and states were under no legal obligation to create such districts.

86. 69 Cong. Rec. 9090 (1928).

87. Eagles, *Democracy Delayed*, 72.

88. To further support this interpretation it is useful to note that Representative Lozier took special care to preserve both the relevant *Congressional Record* and newspaper clippings in his personal papers. He wished his actions that contributed to the removal of the districting requirements to be remembered, not forgotten. Lozier papers accessed at the Missouri State Historical Society, Columbia, Missouri.

89. The relationship between legislator party affiliation and votes on both motions is statistically significant at the 0.01 level.

90. There were 115 representatives who consistently supported recommittal and 137 who consistently opposed recommittal. Three representatives opposed recommittal in May but supported it in January, suggesting that for these representatives the compact, contiguous, and equal-population requirements were so important that they would not support an apportionment act without them.

91. The one tail t-test is significant at the 0.05 level.

Chapter 7. The Court Years, 1960–Present

1. 113 Cong. Rec. 34032–34033 (1967). Representative Jones was objecting to the addition of the single-member district mandate to an immigration bill affecting only Dr. Ricardo Samala of Pensacola, Florida. This quote combines two statements made by Representative Jones, interrupted by remarks by the speaker pro tempore.

2. H.R. 2275, 90th Cong.: An Act for the Relief of Dr. Ricardo Vallejo Samala and to Provide for Congressional Redistricting, Pub. L. No. 90-196, 81 Stat. 581 (1967).

3. *Wood v. Broom* majority decision, 287 US 1 (1932).

4. Chief Justice Felix Frankfurter plurality decision in *Colegrove v. Green*, 328 US 549 (1946). Justices Reed and Burton voted with Chief Justice Frankfurter, while Justice Rutledge concurred but also thought there were circumstances under which the Court might enter the political thicket. Justices Black, Douglas, and Murphy dissented. Justices Jackson and Stone did not participate since Justice Jackson was prosecuting the Nuremburg War Crimes Trial and Justice Stone died shortly after oral arguments.

5. The canonical story that motivates this observation comes from *Worchester v. Georgia*, 31 US 515 (1832), in which Chief Justice John Marshall and a majority of the Supreme Court upheld certain aspects of Native American sovereignty against abrogation by white settlers. It may be apocryphal, but President Andrew Jackson is understood to have responded to the court ruling by remarking, "John Marshall has made his decision, now let him enforce it." The result was the removal of the Cherokee People from Georgia and the infamous Trail of Tears. The lesson for the federal judiciary was that it would need either executive or legislative support to enforce its decisions, and it challenged these branches at its own risk.

6. See Michael Altman, "Traditional Districting Principles: Judicial Myths vs. Reality," *Social Science History* 22, no. 2 (Summer 1998): 159–200, esp. figures 3 and 4, for a graphical breakdown of historical malapportionment by region from the early republic to the court era. With the possible exception of particularly high malapportionment in the middle Atlantic region driven by New York, the extent of malapportionment does not differ by regions.

7. *Colegrove v. Green*, 328 US 549 (1946). Dissent written by Justice Hugo Black and signed by Justice William O. Douglas.

8. This districting effectively drew city boundaries according to the racial composition of the neighborhoods so that only a small handful of African Americans remained within the city limits. *Gomillion v. Lightfoot*, 364 US 339 (1960).

9. "Baker v. Carr, 369 US 186 (1962)," *Oyez Project at IIT Chicago-Kent College of Law*, accessed April 10, 2015, http://www.oyez.org/cases/1960-1969/1960/1960_6. Justice Whittaker did not participate for health reasons.

10. *Baker v. Carr*, 369 US 186 (1962). Justice Frankfurter retired from the bench shortly thereafter due to poor health and died in 1965.

11. *Wesberry v. Sanders*, 376 US 1 (1964). Article 1, Section 2, of the Constitution requires that "the House of Representatives shall be composed of members chosen every second year by the people of the several states."

12. For an overview of the effects of malapportionment see Stephen Ansolabehere and James M. Snyder, *The End of Inequality: One Person, One Vote and the Transformation of American Politics* (New York: W. W. Norton, 2008); and Mathew McCubbins and Thomas Schwartz, "Congress, the Courts, and Public Policy: Consequences of the One Man One Vote Rule," *American Journal of Political Science* 32, no. 2 (1988): 388–415.

13. Del Dickson, ed., *The Supreme Court in Conference (1940–1985)* (New York: Oxford University Press, 2001), 853.

14. *Reynolds v. Simms*, 379 US 870 (1964). Importantly, the court applied this reasoning to all state legislative districts including state senates, thus rejecting the principle that state political units such as counties enjoyed the same corporate standing and representation as states in the US Senate.

15. "Wesberry v. Sanders," *The Oyez Project at IIT Chicago-Kent College of Law*, accessed June 3, 2015, http://www.oyez .org/cases/1960-1969/1963/1963_22.

16. *Wesberry v. Sanders*, 376 US 1, Opinions, accessed June 12, 2015, https://www.law.cornell.edu/.

17. Ibid.

18. The US Supreme Court in *Evenwel v. Abbott*, 578 US (2016) ruled that states may use total population, rather than voting-eligible population, in drawing district boundaries for the purpose of fulfilling the "one person, one vote" constitutional requirement. The *Evenwel* decision strongly suggests that the court would rule that states must use total population in such districting should the question reach the court. On at least three previous occasions in the contemporary era the Court declined to hear such challenges, consistently basing its equal vote value requirement on persons in the district.

19. These include H.R. 5505 (1965), H.R. 2508 (1967), and the eventually passed H.R. 2275 (1967), most of which were introduced by New York Democratic representative Emanuel Celler. See also H.R. 3149, 3654, 5333, 10258, 13618, and 13691, 90th Cong., 1st Sess., alone.

20. These differences were measured from the mean district population. For example, after 1970 the least populated district could have a population 5 percent below the average district

population and the most populated district could have a population 5 percent greater than the average district population.

21. Specifically, H.R. 2508, as reported from the Judiciary Committee on April 13, 1967, permitted 30 percent district population differences through the Ninety-Second Congress, allowed New Mexico and Hawaii to elect representatives at large, and prohibited more than one redistricting in a decennial census cycle. Thereafter all representatives had to be elected from single-member districts with no more than 10 percent difference in their populations. The House Judiciary Committee report accompanying the bill contained a majority statement and a minority dissent authored by William L. Hungate (D-MO). See Judiciary Committee Report to Accompany H.R. 2508, April 13, 1967. H.R. Rep. No. 191, 90th Cong., 1st Sess.

22. H.R. 2275 as passed did allow for the New Mexico and Hawaii exceptions.

23. In addition, Senator Dirksen was Senator Howard Baker's father-in-law, suggesting that debates over these bills continued at the Sunday dinner table.

24. Remarks by Representative Conyers, 113 Cong. Rec. 30249 (1967).

25. The final SMD mandate bill (H.R. 2275) was largely negotiated behind closed doors with little record of its progress. The immigration portion of the bill was brought to the floor of the Senate on November 8, 1967, under a unanimous-consent agreement limiting debate to one-half hour. Almost immediately two SMD amendments were proposed to be added to the bill. The first by Senator Birch Bayh (D-IN), seeking to preserve the essential features of H.R. 2508, was defeated in favor of an

amendment by Howard Baker (D-TN), which was approved and became the final act.

26. For example, the June 1 Senate Judiciary report on H.R. 2508 specifically states that the "primary purpose of H.R. 2508 . . . is to provide congressional guidelines to state legislatures implementing the one-man one-vote doctrine of Wesberry v. Sanders"; S. Rep. No. 291, at 2 (June 1967).

27. Document recovered at the National Archives Center for Legislative Archives, July 2015.

28. *Congressional Quarterly Weekly Report*, week ending March 19, 1965, 419.

29. Letter from Harlem Democrats for Action dated June 6, 1967 to Representative Emanuel Celler. Recovered at the National Archives Center for Legislative Archives, July 2015.

30. Senator Robert F. Kennedy, Remarks in the Senate, June 8, 1967. 113 Cong. Rec. 15238 (1967)

31. Senator Edward Kennedy, Remarks in the Senate, June 8, 1967. 113 Cong. Rec. 15239 (1967).

32. Most notably, Georgia Representative Cynthia McKinney introduced the Voter Choice Act, which would allow states to elect their representatives using proportional representation in the 104th–107th Congresses. These bills never made it out of committee and obtained only a handful of cosponsors.

33. This was especially true after the Court addressed revisions to Article 2 of the Voting Rights Act as amended in 1982 where, in *Thornburg v. Gingles*, 478 US 53, discussed below, the Court reduced the legal threshold for showing that at-large elections dilute the minority vote to the demonstration that the jurisdiction in question experiences "racially polarized" bloc voting that systematically thwarts the election of minority candidates.

34. For a survey of the several possible ways of measuring district compactness see Richard G. Niemi, Bernard Grofman, Carl Carlucci, and Thomas Hofeller, "Measuring Compactness and the Role of a Compactness Standard in a Test for Partisan and Racial Gerrymandering," *Journal of Politics* 52, no. 4 (November 1990): 1155–1181. Such measures will be explored more fully in the following chapter.

35. This frequent redistricting illustrates that gerrymandering does not guarantee political control of a legislature. Statehouse control shifted often in the late nineteenth century despite heavy gerrymandering because of significant swings in votes and because gerrymandered districts were often created with relatively thin majorities, guaranteeing significant seat shifts with only modest shifts in aggregate vote. Erik J. Engstrom, *Partisan Gerrymandering and the Construction of American Democracy* (Ann Arbor: University of Michigan Press, 2013), 130–135. More is said on this point in the following chapter.

36. Ibid., 170–175.

37. In addition, the mid-twentieth century districting stasis also helped develop the congressional career because legislators could plan for their future on the assumption that their districts were fixed. Congressional activities such as developing a personal vote, bringing federal largess to the district, and related activities are significantly more attractive when district boundaries are stable. Ibid., 186.

38. The former type of districting often occurs following a decrease in

apportionment, as occurred in Missouri following the 2010 census. In this case, two predominately Democratic districts represented by William Lacy Clay Jr. and Russ Carnahan respectively were combined so that both incumbents had to compete for the same seat in an election won by William Clay. The latter occurred in Chicago in 2000 when a largely unknown Democratic state senator named Barack Obama garnered a respectable 35 percent of the primary election vote in south Chicago's First Congressional District represented by fellow Democrat Bobby Rush. Following the 2001 redistricting, Mr. Obama's home was placed in the Second Congressional District although the state senate district in which he lived was extended to the Chicago loop area. Mr. Obama was elected to the Illinois state senate, and this ultimately aided his election to the US Senate in 2004.

39. In an important but isolated case, a federal appellate court attempted to bypass the judiciary reluctance to judge the shape of districts by ruling that a clearly pro-incumbency West Virginia gerrymandered districting was unconstitutional because the populations of two districts differed—by a single voter. This case was resolved by the US Supreme Court, *Tennant v. Jefferson County*, 567 US___ (2012), which allowed the original districting to stand and provided a strong indication that the Court would consider partisan and incumbency gerrymanders as political questions.

40. In November 2016 the United States District Court for the Western District of Wisconsin ruled in *Whitford v. Gill* that Wisconsin's state legislative districts were unconstitutionally gerrymandered to give the Republican party electoral advantage. If this ruling is upheld by the United States Supreme Court it would represent a major revision to the court's previous jurisprudence on political districting.

41. An important change in the amended Voting Rights Act is that one does not have to demonstrate that electoral processes were created to intentionally dilute the minority vote, but instead meet the lower standard that the process has this effect whether intended or not.

42. The components of this test are (1) whether there is a compact enough minority population to create a single-member majority-minority district, (2) whether this minority group is politically cohesive, and (3) whether white voters regularly vote as a block to thwart the election of minority candidates to office. If these conditions are met, then the courts may require the disbandment of multimember constituencies. In addition, the *Gingles* standards appeared to provide legal guidance under which the government could construct majority-minority districts that would withstand court challenge.

43. Majority Opinion, *Bush v. Vera*, 517 US 952 (1996).

44. For discussion of legal attempts to disentangle acceptable political gerrymanders from unacceptable racial gerrymanders based on *Shaw* and the "children of Shaw" cases (*Miller v. Johnson*, 515 US 900 (1995) and *Bush v. Vera*, 517 US 952 (1996)), see Howard A. Scarrow, "Vote Dilution, Party Dilution, and the Voting Rights Act: The Search for Fair and Effective Representation," in *The US Supreme Court and the Electoral Process*, 2nd ed., ed. David K. Ryden

(Washington, DC: Georgetown University Press, 2002), 42–59.

Chapter 8. The Performance of the US SMD System

1. Hearn was explaining to USSC Associate Justice Ruth Bader Ginsburg why his Arizona Republican clients were suing to invalidate a districting plan that advantaged Republican candidates. *Harris v. Arizona Independent Redistricting Commission* (USSC 14-232), Oral Arguments, December 8, 2015.

2. For an overview of Duverger's Law and the development of our understanding of it see William H. Riker, "The Two-Party System and Duverger's Law: An Essay on the History of Political Science," *American Political Science Review* 76, no. 4 (December 1982): 753–766. For a more detailed overview of the disciplinary understanding of Duverger's law See Gary W. Cox, *Making Votes Count* (New York: Cambridge University Press, 1997), chapter 2.

3. In an important contribution, Pradeep Chhibber and Ken Kollman argue that fiscal federalism is an important determinant of whether the SMD system produces two parties. Nations with highly nationalized fiscal control provide incentives to coalesce into two parties, while decentralized fiscal policy encourages the establishment and maintenance of regional parties even under the SMD system. See Pradeep Chhibber and Ken Kollman, "Party Aggregation and the Number of Parties in India and the United States," *American Political Science Review* 92, no. 2 (June 1998): 329–342. See also Pradeep Chhibber and Ken Kollman, *The Formation of National Party Systems: Federalism and Party Competition in Canada, Great Britain,*

India and the United States (Princeton, NJ: Princeton University Press, 2004).

4. As of this writing the Canadian Parliament (41st) is led by the Conservative Party with the New Democratic Party serving as the official opposition. The Tories also led the previous government with the Liberal Party serving as the official opposition.

5. One reason for this is that strategic voters must be minority party supporters. Given the breadth and depth of major party voter identification, this is a relatively small subset of the electorate. So, for example, D. S. Hillygus reports (table 1) that about one-quarter of all Nader supporters in 2000 voted for Al Gore, suggesting about a 25 percent strategic voting rate among these citizens, but this would amount to a much smaller percentage of the total electorate. See D. S. Hillygus, "Stand by Your Man?: Assessing the Strategic Behavior of Nader Supporters in Election 2000," presented at the Annual Meeting of the Midwest Political Science Association, Chicago, IL, 2003.

For an argument that strategic voting in the United States is episodically more widespread see P. R. Abramson, J. H. Aldrich, P. Paolino, and D. W. Rohde, "Third-Party and Independent Candidates in American Politics: Wallace, Anderson, and Perot," *Political Science Quarterly* 110, no. 3 (1995): 349–361.

6. Barry C. Burden, "Minor Parties and Strategic Voting in Recent US Presidential Elections," *Electoral Studies* 24, no. 4 (2005): 603–618.

7. Shigeo Hirano and James M. Snyder Jr., "The Decline of Third Party Voting in the United States," *Journal of Politics* 69, no. 1 (2007): 1–16.

8. For a complete overview of US partisanship in the contemporary era see Michael S. Lewis-Beck, William G. Jacoby, Helmut Norpoth, and Herbert F. Weisberg, *The American Voter Revisited* (Ann Arbor: University of Michigan Press, 2008). Their figures suggest that nearly 90 percent of the US electorate can be described as partisan identifiers of various strengths (table 6.1), partisanship is generally established early in life (tables 7.1 and 7.2), and partisanship tends to be stable (p. 142 and table 7.3).

9. This relationship is sometimes described as following the Law of Cubic Proportions, which states that the cubed ratio of the two leading parties' vote shares is equal to the cubed ratio of their respective seat shares. This pattern was first identified by M. G. Kendall and A. Stuart in "The Law of Cubic Proportions in Election Results," *British Journal of Sociology* 1, no. 3 (1950): 183–196. For a classic discussion of the vote-seat relationship in two-party systems and approaches for estimating this translation see Edward R. Tufte, "The Relationship between Seats and Votes in Two-Party Systems," *American Political Science Review* 67, no. 2 (1973): 540–554.

10. I use the two-party vote share because only a trivial proportion of House votes are cast for minor party candidates.

11. Scholars have proposed several measures of disproportionality. For a partial listing see Arend Lijphart, *Electoral Systems and Party Systems: A Study of Twenty-Seven Democracies, 1945–1990* (New York: Oxford University Press, 1994), 58–62. The standard measure is $D = (1/2)\sum_{i=1}^{n}|S_i - V_i|$, which is simply one-half the absolute value of the difference

between vote shares and seat shares summed over all parties. A widely used variation of this measure was proposed by Michael Gallagher, and uses the quadratic form of the seat-vote differential to weight greater deviations more heavily in the calculation. See Michael Gallagher, "Disproportionality in a Proportional Representation System: The Irish Experience," *Political Studies* 23, no. 4 (1975): 501–513.

12. This is especially true for majoritarian systems such as the United States. See Lijphart, *Electoral Systems and Party Systems*. To illustrate, consider the following coin-flip analogy. If one flips a coin, the outcome is binary winner take all (heads or tails). If one flips a fair coin 435 times, then one expects about 50 percent heads and 50 percent tails. Likewise, if one flips a weighted coin (60 percent likelihood of heads, 40 percent likelihood tails) 435 times then one expects about 60 percent heads and 40 percent tails. Think of the coin weight as the relative national support for the Democratic and Republican parties.

13. Maurice Duverger, *Political Parties: Their Organization and Activity in the Modern State*, trans. Barbara and Robert North, with a foreword by D. W. Brogan (New York: John Wiley and Sons, 1954) , 217, emphasis added.

14. Cox, *Making Votes Count*, 14–27.

15. Ibid. See also ibid., 80–98, especially 95–97.

16. Nearly 45 percent of Scots voted in favor of independence from the United Kingdom in 2014. In 1995 nearly half of all Quebecois voted for independence from Canada. No matter how distinct one considers the various regions of the United States, it is preposterous to think that today any region or state

experiences such support for separation from the rest of the Union.

17. See Arend Lijphart, *Patterns of Democracy: Government Forms and Performance in Thirty-Six Countries* (New Haven, CT: Yale University Press: 1999), 78–87, for a cross-national treatment of dimensions of political competition. Lijphart argues that the United States is characterized by socioeconomic and cultural-racial dimensions of political organization, but empirical studies such as that in James M. Enelow and Melvin J. Hinich, *Introduction to the Spatial Theory of Voting* (New York: Cambridge University Press, 1984), provide evidence that the socioeconomic dimension is significantly more salient than any secondary axes of political organization.

18. Maurice Duverger, "Factors in a Two-Party and Multiparty System," in *Party Politics and Pressure Groups*, ed. Maurice Duverger (New York: Thomas Y. Crowell, 1972), 23–32.

19. It is important to note that gerrymandering is not confined to the single-member district system. Any geographic district can be gerrymandered, including multimember constituencies that elect representatives using proportional formulas, although the prospects for effective gerrymandering diminish in constituencies that elect a large number of representatives.

20. "Congressional District Standards Set by House," in *CQ Almanac 1965*, 21st ed. (Washington, DC: Congressional Quarterly, 1966), 603–605.

21. There are many definitions of compactness. Two dozen (!) of these are discussed in Richard G. Niemi, Bernard Grofman, Carl Carlucci, and Thomas Hofeller, "Measuring Compactness and the Role of a Compactness Standard in a Test for Partisan and Racial Gerrymandering," *Journal of Politics* 52, no. 4 (1990): 1155–1181. The Polsby-Popper measure falls under their classification of district area compared with the area of compact figure. Their conclusion "that compactness has multiple components and that no single measure can adequately assess all of them" points to the extraordinary difficulty of even classifying districts as gerrymandered by mathematical or geometrical formulas. For a discussion of the Polsby-Popper and related measures of district compactness see Anthony J. McGann, Charles Anthony Smith, Michael Latner, and Alex Keena, *Gerrymandering in America: The House of Representatives, the Supreme Court, and the Future of Popular Sovereignty* (New York: Cambridge University Press, 2016), 82–87.

22. "Congressional District Standards Set by House," emphasis added. It is important to note that New York representative and House Judiciary Committee chairman Emanuel Celler was an expert on apportionment and districting long before the courts entered the apportionment and districting process. See, for example, Emanuel Celler, "Congressional Apportionment—Past, Present, and Future," *Law and Contemporary Problems* 17, no. 2 (1952): 268–275.

23. Ibid.

24. This well-known quip by Justice Potter Stewart comes from the case of *Jacobellis v. Ohio*, 378 US 184 (1964), which centered on the showing of the allegedly pornographic movie *Les Amants*. Justice Stewart stated in his concurrence that while he could "never succeed in intelligibly [defining pornography]. . . . I know it when I see it, and the motion picture involved in this case is not that."

25. As of this writing, thirty-seven

states that elect more than one representative have district boundaries created by the state legislature in a process identical to ordinary law, including the possibility of gubernatorial veto, veto overrides, and similar law-making considerations.

26. "Congressional District Standards Set by House." See also Gary W. Cox and Johnathan N. Katz, *Elbridge Gerry's Salamander: The Electoral Consequences of the Reapportionment Revolution* (New York: Cambridge University Press, 2002), 33.

27. These scores were obtained from Cristopher Ingraham, "America's Most Gerrymandered Congressional Districts," *Washington Post*, May 15, 2014, accessed November 19, 2015, https://www.washingtonpost.com/news/wonk/wp/2014/05/15/americas-most-gerrymandered-congressional-districts/ and http://www.washingtonpost.com/wpsrv/special/politics/gerrymandering/.

28. In Wisconsin the average Democratic House candidate margin of victory was 31.3 percent, while the average Republican margin was 26.3 percent. The greatest margin of 43.4 percent was returned in the Democratic Fourth District, suggesting that this district contains an excessive number of Democratic voters. However, Republican Jim Sensenbrenner won the Fifth District with a 39.1 percent margin. In Michigan the average Republican winning margin was 17.2 percent, while the average winning Democratic margin was an extraordinary 48.1 percent. "United States House of Representatives Elections, 2012," *Ballotpedia*, https://ballotpedia.org/United_States_House_of_Representatives_elections_2012, accessed March 1, 2016.

29. Sam Wang, "The Great Gerrymander of 2012," *New York Times Sunday Review*, Opinion, February 2, 2013.

30. The only truly competitive district in the state is the western Sixth District. The average Democratic winning plurality was 64.2 percent if one excludes the Sixth District from this calculation.

31. The Polsby-Popper score for the Maryland Sixth District is 92.92.

32. The Republican average excludes the North Carolina Ninth District, which in 2014 did not feature a Democratic challenger.

33. The test's first component required determining whether there was a sufficiently numerous and compact minority community to encapsulate a district, while the remaining two standards centered on the political cohesiveness of the minority population relative to majority voters.

34. *Harris v. McCrory* (2016) argued in United States District Court for the Middle District of North Carolina.

35. This line of jurisprudence is exceptionally long and complicated and includes a series of post-Shaw cases that refined this decision, including *Miller v. Johnson* (1995), *Shaw v. Hunt* (1996), *Bush v. Vera* (1996), and *Easley v. Cromartie* (2001). This last case upheld the redrawn North Carolina Twelfth on the grounds that it is drawn on the basis of the political cohesiveness of the community rather than race itself. For an overview of the Shaw lineage see Howard A. Scarrow, "Vote Dilution, Party Dilution, and the Voting Rights Act: The Search for Fair and Effective Representation," in *The US Supreme Court and the Electoral Process*, 2nd ed., ed. David K. Ryden (Washington DC: Georgetown University Press,

2002), 42–59. An important recent case is *League of United Latin American Citizens v. Perry* (2006), which considers a racial group's "needs and interests" in determining whether districts are sufficiently compact.

36. Source: US Congressional Directory. https://www.gpo.gov/fdsys/browse /collection.action?collectionCode =CDIR. Accessed November 1, 2016.

37. Majority-minority districting certainly increased black and Hispanic representatives in Congress. Indeed, nineteen additional black and Hispanic representatives were elected to Congress in 1992 following reapportionment and the creation of several majority-minority districts.

38. Richard L. Engstrom, "The Political Thicket, Electoral Reform, and Minority Voting Rights," in *Fair and Effective Representation? Debating Electoral Reform and Minority Voting Rights*, ed. Mark E. Rush and Richard L. Engstrom (New York: Rowman and Littlefield Publishers, 2001), esp. 24. For a more detailed understanding of districting constraints see note 34.

39. James E. Campbell, *Polarized: Making Sense of a Divided America* (Princeton, NJ: Princeton University Press, 2016), 134–44.

40. See Alan I. Abramowitz, Brad Alexander, and Matthew Gunning, "Incumbency, Redistricting, and the Decline of Competition in U.S. House Elections," *Journal of Politics* 68, no. 1 (2006): 75–88, who provide evidence that redistricting has contributed little to the decline in the number of safe districts and hence polarization. Likewise, Thomas Mann argues that redistricting probably is not a major cause of polarization; instead, it is

"more of an effect of polarization." Thomas Mann, "Polarizing the House of Representatives: How Much Does Gerrymandering Matter?," in *Red and Blue Nation? Characteristics and Causes of America's Polarized Parties*, ed. Pietro Nivolo and David W. Brady (Washington, DC: Brookings Institution Press, 2006), 266. For an argument that gerrymandering contributes to political polarization see Jamie L. Carson, Michael H. Crespin, Charles J. Finocchiaro, and David W. Rohde, "Redistricting and Party Polarization in the U.S. House of Representatives," *American Politics Research* 35, no. 6 (2007): 878–904, but even these authors concede the effect of districting on party polarization in Congress is "modest."

41. Nolan McCarty, Keith T. Poole, and Howard Rosenthal, "Does Gerrymandering Cause Polarization?" *American Journal of Political Science* 53, no. 3 (2009): 666–680.

42. Campbell, *Polarized*, 135.

43. Vincent L. Hutchings and Nicholas A. Valentino, "The Centrality of Race in American Politics," *Annual Review of Politics* 7, no. 1 (2004): 383–408, at 396.

44. See Lisa Handley and Bernard Grofman, "The Impact of the Voting Rights Act on Minority Representation: Black Office Holding in Southern State Legislatures and Congressional Delegations," in *Quiet Revolution in the South: The Impact of the Voting Rights Act 1965–1990*, ed. Chandler Davidson and Bernard Grofman (Princeton, NJ: Princeton University Press, 1994), esp. 336–337 and 343–350.

45. Michael D. Minta, *Oversight: Representing the Interests of Blacks and Hispanics in Congress* (Princeton NJ: Princeton University Press, 2011). See also David T.

Canon, *Race, Districting and Representation: The Unintended Consequence of Black Majority Districts* (Chicago: University of Chicago Press, 1999), chapter 4.

46. See, for example, Canon, *Race, Districting and Representation*.

47. An important early contribution that makes this argument is David Lubin, *The Paradox of Representation: Racial Gerrymandering and Minority Interests in Congress* (Princeton, NJ: Princeton University Press, 1997).

48. Marvin Overby and Kenneth Cosgrove, "Unintended Consequences? Racial Redistricting and Representation of Minority Interests," *Journal of Politics* 58, no. 2 (May 1996): 540–550.

49. David L. Epstein and Sharyn O'Halloran, "Measuring the Electoral and Policy Impact of Majority-Minority Voting Districts," *American Journal of Political Science* 43 (1999): 367–395, at 393.

50. K. W. Shotts, "Does Racial Redistricting Cause Conservative Policy Outcomes? Policy Preferences of Southern Representatives in the 1980s and 1990s," *Journal of Politics* 65, no. 1 (2003): 216–226.

51. Andrew Gelman and Gary King, "Enhancing Democracy through Legislative Redistricting," *American Political Science Review* 88, no 3 (1994): 541–559.

52. Kendall and Stuart, "The Law of Cubic Proportions."

53. Generically, one can represent the votes-to-seats translation as a sigmoid curve written as Seat Share$_i$ = 1/ [1 + exp(–b Vote Share$_j$)].

54. Tufte, "The Relationship between Seats and Votes." Gary King and Andrew Gelman argue that incumbency advantage biases estimates of the swing ratio downward, and if one accounts for this, then estimates of the swing ratio will be closer to that postulated under the cube rule. They find evidence for this in the 1970s through 1980s period, and also show that the U.S. swing ratio has been declining in recent decades. See Gary King and Andrew Gelman, "Systemic Consequences of Incumbency Advantage in U.S. House Elections," *American Journal of Political Science* 35, no. 1 (February 1991): 110–138, especially figures 9 and 10.

55. This figure is for the Ninety-Sixth Congress, elected in 1978.

56. The large pro-Democratic bias before 1994 and smaller pro-Republican bias thereafter is confirmed by Jonathan P. Kastellec, Andrew Gelman, and Jamie P. Chandler, "Predicting and Dissecting the Seats-Votes Curve in the 2006 U.S. House Election," *PS: Political Science and Politics* 41, no. 1 (2008): 139–145. See figure 1.

57. With the exception of Vermont in 2008, in which no Republican contested the congressional election.

58. Leslie E. Papke and Jeffrey M. Wooldridge, "Econometric Methods for Fractional Response Variables with an Application to 401 (K) Plan Participation Rates," *Journal of Applied Econometrics* 11, no. 6 (1996): 619–632.

59. Anthony J. McGann, Charles Anthony Smith, Michael Latner, and Alex Kenna, *Gerrymandering in America: The House of Representatives, the Supreme Court, and the Future of Popular Sovereignty* (New York: Cambridge University Press, 2016). For a discussion of the statistical methodology see Appendix 3B. This methodology is originally proposed in Andrew Gelman and Gary King, "A Unified Method of Evaluating Electoral Systems and Redistricting Plans," *American Journal of Political Science* 38, no. 2 (1994): 514–554.

60. These authors report a 2002–2010 pro-Republican bias of less than 2 percent. For 2012 they estimate that if Democrats won 50 percent of the vote they would win about 45 percent of the seats. *Gerrymandering in America*, 71–72.

61. McGann et al. argue that there still exists a pro-Republican bias in the vote-seat translation in 2014, but cannot confirm this because their data analysis does not extend to the 2014 election cycle. That the Republicans turned 53 percent of the House vote and 57 percent of the House seats in this cycle can be produced by a biased or an unbiased vote-seat translation. My analysis suggests the latter interpretation is correct. *Gerrymandering in America*, 232–234.

62. Bernard Grofman and Thomas Brunell, "The Art of the Dummymander: The Impact of Recent Redistrictings on the Partisan Makeup of Southern House Seats," in *Redistricting in the New Millennium*, ed. Peter F. Galderisi (Lanham, MD: Lexington Books, 2005), 183–199.

Chapter 9. An Affirmative Argument for SMD Elections

1. Richard S. Katz, *Democracy and Elections* (New York: Oxford University Press, 1997), 3.

2. Ibid., 4

3. Lani Guinier, *The Tyranny of the Majority: Fundamental Fairness in Representative Democracy* (New York: Free Press, 1994). *The Tyranny of the Majority* includes essays composed from articles published in academic outlets in the early 1990s. In some instances I draw on these essays, but maintain focus on material presented in the book. In his "Conflicting Representations: Lani Guinier and James Madison on Electoral Systems," *Constitutional Commentary*

13, no. 3 (1996): 291–307, Mark Graber details how the premises underlying Guinier's rejection of the single-member district system in favor of cumulative voting derive from a distinctly Anti-Federalist understanding of the House and its election. The first part of this chapter is deeply indebted to Graber's insights.

4. Guinier, *Tyranny*, 44.

5. James DeNardo (1980) first provided empirical evidence that increased voter turnout did not advantage Democratic Party candidates. See James DeNardo, "Turnout and the Vote: The Joke's on the Democrats," *American Political Science Review* 74, no. 2 (1980): 406–420. Subsequent studies, including Harvey J. Tucker and Arnold Vedlitz ("Does Heavy Turnout Help Democrats in Presidential Elections?," *American Political Science Review* 87, no. 4 [1986]: 1291–1298), Jack H. Nagle and John E. McNulty ("Partisan Effects of Voter Turnout in Presidential Elections," *American Politics Quarterly* 28, no. 3 [2000]: 408–429, and "Partisan Effects of Voter Turnout in Senatorial and Gubernatorial Elections," *American Political Science Review* 90, no. 4 [1996]: 780–793), and Bernard Grofman, Guillermo Owen, and Christian Collet ("Rethinking the Partisan Effects of Higher Turnout: So What's the Question?," *Public Choice* 99, no. 3 [1999]: 357–376), largely confirm that there is not a partisan direction to the vote associated with increased voter turnout. Jack Citrin, Eric Schickler, and John Sides ("What if Everyone Voted? Simulating the Impact of Increased Turnout in Senate Elections," *American Journal of Political Science* 47, no. 1 [2003]: 75–90), in contrast, provide evidence for a Democratic Party advantage in higher-turnout Senate elections,

although these effects are too modest to change election outcomes. See Karen M. Kaufman, John R. Petrocik, and Daron R. Shaw, *Unconventional Wisdom: Facts and Myths about American Voters* (New York: Oxford University Press, 2008), chapter 7, for an overview.

6. Guinier, *Tyranny*, 71, 94–117.

7. Ibid., 155.

8. Douglas J. Amy, *Real Choices / New Voices: How Proportional Representation Elections Could Revitalize American Democracy*, 2nd ed. (New York: Columbia University Press, 2002), 169–77.

9. Ibid., 170.

10. Ibid., 26.

11. Ibid., 7, 25–31.

12. Ibid., 26.

13. Ibid., 27.

14. Ibid., 29.

15. Anthony Downs, *An Economic Theory of Democracy* (New York: Harper and Row, 1957); William H. Riker and Peter C. Ordeshook, "A Theory of the Calculus of Voting," *American Political Science Review* 62, no. 1 (1968): 25–42.

16. Andrew Rehfeld, *The Concept of Constituency* (New York: Cambridge University Press, 2005), 22–23, 195–197.

17. Ibid., 197.

18. Ibid., 33, 235–236. See also, for example, Jane Mansbridge, "Should Blacks Represent Blacks and Women Represent Women? A Contingent 'Yes,'" *Journal of Politics* 61, no. 3 (1999): 628–657.

19. See, for example, Guinier, *Tyranny*, 73, 77, 82.

20. Cumulative voting is a voting system in which candidates are elected from multimember districts and voters receive as many votes as there are positions to be filled. The top "n" vote recipients win office where "n" is the number of positions filled. Voters may cast their votes however they wish, including cumulating or "plumping" their multiple votes on one or two candidates. Hence it is "cumulative" voting. In this manner, a minority population can focus its voting strength on one or a few candidates and increase the likelihood that their preferred candidate is elected.

21. Instant-runoff voting is effectively a series of runoff elections such that if no candidate receives a majority in the first round, the last-place finisher is eliminated and votes for him or her are redistributed among the remaining candidates in order of preference stipulated by the voter. This process continues until one candidate has a majority of the vote. See Amy, *Real Choices*, 217–219. Instant-runoff voting is currently used in San Francisco and Minneapolis municipal elections.

22. Guinier, *Tyranny*, 82, chapter 5.

23. Kathleen L. Barber, *A Right to Representation: Proportional Representation Systems for the Twenty-First Century* (Columbus: Ohio State University Press, 2000), 137.

24. Guinier, *Tyranny*, 82, see also chapter 5.

25. Amy, *Real Choices*, 215–219, especially 217.

26. Guinier, *Tyranny*, 82, chapter 5.

27. Ibid., 75–76. Guinier points to legislative processes and rules that disadvantage the expression of minority interests in Congress even if minorities are elected from majority-minority districts, and suggests that these legislative processes must also be changed for proper representation to be achieved. Guinier, *Tyranny*, 101–109, especially 107.

28. See, for example, Amy, *Real Choices*, chapter 5.

29. Jennifer E. Manning, *Membership of the 114th Congress* ([Washington, DC]: Congressional Research Service, 2015).

30. African Americans comprise about 13 percent of the US population and about 10 percent of the chamber membership. Hispanics compose about 17 percent of the population and about 7 percent of the chamber membership.

31. Amy, *Real Choices*, 32.

32. Ibid.

33. Jonathan W. Still, "Political Equality and Election Systems," *Ethics* 91, no. 3 (1981): 375–394.

34. Guinier, *Tyranny*, 56.

35. Federal Farmer, *Essay* 7.

36. Hanna Fenichel Pitkin, *The Concept of Representation* (Berkeley: University of California Press, 1967), 90.

37. Ibid., chapter 3. See also Anne Phillips, *The Politics of Presence* (Oxford: Clarendon Press, 1995), 34.

38. Pitkin, *Concept of Representation*, 90.

39. Graber, "Conflicting Representations," 239.

40. Recognition of this fact perhaps motivates coupling calls for proportional representation with proposals for a minority veto over policy. See Guinier, *The Tyranny of the Majority*, 260, n. 19.

41. Proportional rules applied to multimember districts rules may pit like-minded candidates against each other rather than those advocating other political perspectives. See Jay K. Dow, "A Spatial Analysis of Candidate Competition in Dual Member Districts: The 1989 Chilean Senatorial Elections," *Public Choice* 97, no. 3 (1998): 451–474.

42. This manifest in the McGovern-Fraser report established processes for Democratic Party presidential nomination in the 1972 election, which relied heavily on primary elections. This tradition has been maintained since, and the Republican Party uses similar rules.

43. The Bipartisan Campaign Finance Reform Act of 2002 prohibited parties from raising large "soft-money" contributions. The effect has been to hamstring party ability to control the flow of resources to candidates relative to individuals and 527 groups that spend "on behalf" of candidates.

44. Jay K. Dow, "A Comparative Spatial Analysis of Majoritarian and Proportional Elections," *Electoral Studies* 20, no. 1 (2001): 109–125; Jay K. Dow, "Party System Extremism in Majoritarian and Proportional Electoral Systems," *British Journal of Political Science* 41, no. 2 (2011): 341–361. See also Lawrence Ezrow's response in this same issue.

45. Arend Lijphart, *Democracies: Patterns of Majoritarian and Consensus Government in Twenty-One Countries* (New Haven, CT: Yale University Press, 1984); G. Bingham Powell Jr., *Elections as Instruments of Democracy: Majoritarian and Proportional Visions* (New Haven, CT: Yale University Press, 2000), especially chapters 7, 8, and 9.

46. Bill Bishop and Robert G. Cushing, *The Big Sort* (New York: Houghton Mifflin, 2008).

47. United States Census Bureau, "Lifetime Mobility in the United States: 2010," in *American Community Survey Briefs* (Washington, DC United States Census Bureau, 2011).

48. Robert Putnam, *Bowling Alone* (New York: Simon & Schuster, 2000), 204–205; Quoctrung Bui and Claire Cain Miller, "The Typical American Lives Only 18 Miles from Mom," *New York Times*, December 23, 2015.

49. Putnam, *Bowling Alone*, 214–215.

50. Nancy L. Schwartz, *The Blue Guitar: Political Representation and Community* (Chicago: University of Chicago Press, 1988), 13.

51. Such districting would also likely produce one or more majority-minority districts because white citizens constitute approximately 43 percent of the Los Angeles basin population. Large-scale districting would likely produce one or more majority Hispanic districts, with the residual population drawn from white, black, and Asian communities. Similar majority Hispanic districts could be expected in Texas and other southwest states.

52. United States Census Bureau, *Projections of the Size and Composition of the US Population: 2014–2060*, https://www .census.gov/content/dam/Census/library /publications/2015/demo/p25-1143.pdf.

53. Madison, *Federalist No. 10*.

BIBLIOGRAPHY

Abramowitz, Alan I., Brad Alexander, and Matthew Gunning. "Incumbency, Redistricting, and the Decline of Competition in US House Elections." *Journal of Politics* 68, no. 1 (2006): 75–88.

Abramson, P. R., J. H. Aldrich, P. Paolino, and D. W. Rohde. "Third-Party and Independent Candidates in American Politics: Wallace, Anderson, and Perot." *Political Science Quarterly* 110, no. 3 (1995): 349–361.

Allen, William B., and Gordon Lloyd. *The Essential Antifederalist.* 2nd ed. Lanham, MD: Rowman and Littlefield, 2002.

Altman, Michael. "Traditional Districting Principles: Judicial Myths vs. Reality." *Social Science History* 22, no. 2 (1998): 159–200.

Ames, Herman V. *The Proposed Amendments to the Constitution of the United States during the First Century of Its History.* Washington, DC: Government Printing Office, 1897.

Amicus. "A Plea for the Right of Recall." *Columbia Herald,* August 28, 1788.

Amy, Douglas J. *Real Choices / New Voices: How Proportional Representation Elections Could Revitalize American Democracy.* 2nd ed. New York: Columbia University Press, 2002.

Ansolabehere, Stephen, and James M. Snyder. *The End of Inequality: One Person, One Vote and the Transformation of American Politics.* New York: W. W. Norton, 2008.

Argersinger, Peter H. *Structure, Process and Party: Essays in American Political History.* Armonk, NY: Routledge, 1992.

Bailey, Jeremy D. *James Madison and Constitutional Imperfection.* New York: Cambridge University Press, 2015.

Baker v. Carr, 369 US 186 (1962). *Oyez Project at IIT Chicago-Kent College of Law.* Accessed April 10, 2015. http:// www.oyez.org/cases/1960-1969/1960/1960_6.

Barber, Kathleen. *A Right to Representation: Proportional Representation Systems for the Twenty-First Century.* Columbus: Ohio State University Press, 2000.

Barnett, James D. "Reorganization of State Government in Oregon." *American Political Science Review* 9, no. 2 (May 1915): 287–293.

Belknap, Jeremy. *The History of New-Hampshire.* Vol. 3. Dover, NH: Routledge, 1812.

Bishop, Bill, and Robert G. Cushing. *The Big Sort.* New York: Houghton Mifflin, 2008.

"Black Americans in Congress, 1870–2007: Elections." *History, Art & Archives, US House of Representatives.* Office of the Historian. Washington, DC: US Government Printing Office, 2008. http://history.house.gov/Exhibitions-and-Publications/BAIC/Historical-Essays/Temporary-Farewell/Elections/.

Bui, Quoctrung, and Claire Cain Miller. "The Typical American Lives Only 18 Miles from Mom." *New York Times,* December 23, 2015.

Burden, Barry C. "Minor Parties and Strategic Voting in Recent US Presidential Elections." *Electoral Studies* 24, no. 4 (2005): 603–618.

Burnham, Walter Dean. "The Changing Shape of the American Political Universe." *American Political Science Review* 59, no. 1 (March 1965): 7–28.

———. "Those High Nineteenth Century American Voting Turnouts: Fact or Fiction?" *Journal of Interdisciplinary History* 16, no. 4 (Spring 1986): 613–644.

Burnham, W. Dean, Jerome M. Clubb, and William Flanigan. "State-Level Congressional, Gubernatorial and Senatorial Election Data for the United States, 1824–1972." ICPSR Find and Analyze Data. 1991. http://www.icpsr.umich.edu/icpsrweb/ICPSR /studies/4. doi.org/10.3886/ICPSR00075.v1.

Burnham, Walter Dean, with Thomas Ferguson and Louis Ferleger. *Voting in American Elections: The Shaping of the American Political Universe since 1788*. Bethesda, MD: Academic Press, 2010.

Campbell, James E. *Polarized: Making Sense of a Divided America*. Princeton, NJ: Princeton University Press, 2016.

Canon, David T. *Race, Districting and Representation: The Unintended Consequence of Black Majority Districts*. Chicago: University of Chicago Press, 1999.

Carson, Jamie L., Michael H. Crespin, Charles J. Finocchiaro, and David W. Rohde. "Redistricting and Party Polarization in the US House of Representatives." *American Politics Research* 35, no. 6 (2007): 878–904.

Ceaser, James W. "Foundational Concepts and American Political Development." In *Nature and History in American Political Development*, edited by James W. Ceaser, 1–90. Cambridge, MA: Harvard University Press, 2006.

———. *Nature and History in American Political Development*. Cambridge, MA: Harvard University Press, 2006.

Celler, Emanuel. "Congressional Apportionment—Past, Present, and Future." *Law and Contemporary Problems* 17, no. 2 (1952): 268–275.

Chhibber, Pradeep, and Ken Kollman. *The Formation of National Party Systems: Federalism and Party Competition in Canada, Great Britain, India, and the United States*. Princeton, NJ: Princeton University Press, 2004.

———. "Party Aggregation and the Number of Parties in India and the United States." *American Political Science Review* 92, no. 2 (June 1998): 329–342.

Citrin, Jack, Eric Schickler, and John Sides. "What if Everyone Voted? Simulating the Impact of Increased Turnout in Senate Elections." *American Journal of Political Science* 47, no. 1 (2003): 75–90.

Cohler, Anne M., Basia C. Miller, and Harold S. Stone, eds. *Montesquieu: The Spirit of the Laws*. Cambridge: Cambridge University Press, 1989.

Commons, John R. *Proportional Representation*. 2nd ed. New York: Macmillan Company, 1907.

"Congressional District Standards Set by House." In *CQ Almanac 1965*, 21st ed., 603–605. Washington, DC: Congressional Quarterly, 1966.

Cornell, Saul. *The Other Founders; Anti-Federalism and the Dissenting Tradition in America, 1788–1828*. Chapel Hill: University of North Carolina Press, 1999.

Cox, Gary W. *Making Votes Count*. New York: Cambridge University Press, 1997.

———. "Strategic Electoral Choice in Multi-Member Districts: Approval Voting in Practice?" *American Journal of Political Science* 28, no. 4 (1984): 722–738.

Cox, Gary W., and Johnathan N. Katz. *Elbridge Gerry's Salamander: The Electoral Consequences of the Reapportionment Revolution.* New York: Cambridge University Press, 2002.

Croly, Herbert. *Progressive Democracy.* New York: Macmillan Company, 1914.

———. *The Promise of American Life.* New York: Macmillan Company, 1909.

Currie, David P. *The Constitution in Congress: Democrats and Whigs 1829–1861.* Chicago: University of Chicago Press, 2005.

DeNardo, James. "Turnout and the Vote: The Joke's on the Democrats." *American Political Science Review* 74, no. 2 (1980): 406–420.

DenBoer, Gordon, ed. *The Documentary History of the First Federal Elections: 1788–1790.* Vol. 2. Madison: University of Wisconsin Press, 1984.

———. *The Documentary History of the First Federal Elections: 1788–1790.* Vol. 3. Madison: University of Wisconsin Press, 1986.

Dewey, John. *The Public and Its Problems.* New York: Henry Holt, 1927.

Dickinson, H. T. "The Representation of the People in Eighteenth-Century Britain." In *Realities of Representation: State Building in Early Modern Europe and European America,* edited by Maija Jansson, 19–44. New York: Palgrave Macmillan, 2007.

Dickson, Del, ed. *The Supreme Court in Conference (1940–1985).* New York: Oxford University Press, 2001.

Dow, Jay K. "A Comparative Spatial Analysis of Majoritarian and Proportional Elections." *Electoral Studies* 20, no. 1 (2001): 109–125.

———. "Party System Extremism in Majoritarian and Proportional Electoral Systems." *British Journal of Political Science* 41, no. 2 (2011): 341–361.

———. "A Spatial Analysis of Candidate Competition in Dual Member Districts: The 1989 Chilean Senatorial Elections." *Public Choice* 97, no. 3 (1998): 451–474.

Downs, Anthony. *An Economic Theory of Democracy.* New York: Harper and Row, 1957.

Dubin, Michael J. *United States Congressional Elections, 1788–1997: The Official Results.* Jefferson, NC: McFarland & Company, 1998.

Durham, David I. *A Southern Moderate in Radical Times: Henry Washington Hilliard, 1808–1892.* Baton Rouge: Louisiana State University Press, 2008.

Duverger, Maurice. "Factors in a Two-Party and Multiparty System." In *Party Politics and Pressure Groups,* edited by Maurice Duverger, 23–32. New York: Thomas Y. Crowell, 1972.

———. *Political Parties: Their Organization and Activity in the Modern State.* Translated by Barbara and Robert North, with a foreword by D. W. Brogan. New York: John Wiley and Sons, 1954.

Eagles, Charles W. *Democracy Delayed: Congressional Reapportionment and Urban-Rural Conflict in the 1920s.* Athens: University of Georgia Press, 1990.

Enelow, James M., and Melvin J. Hinich. *Introduction to the Spatial Theory of Voting.* New York: Cambridge University Press, 1984.

Engstrom, Erik J. *Partisan Gerrymandering and the Construction of American Democracy.* Ann Arbor: University of Michigan Press, 2013.

Engstrom, Richard L. "The Political Thicket, Electoral Reform, and Minority Voting Rights." In *Fair and Effective Representation? Debating Electoral Reform and Minority*

Voting Rights, edited by Mark E. Rush and Richard L. Engstrom, 3–68. New York: Rowman and Littlefield, 2001.

Epstein, David F. *The Political Theory of the Federalist.* Chicago: University of Chicago Press, 1984.

Epstein, David L., and Sharyn O'Halloran. "Measuring the Electoral and Policy Impact of Majority-Minority Voting Districts." *American Journal of Political Science* 43, no. 2 (1999): 367–395.

Ezrow, Lawrence. "Reply to Dow: Party Positions, Votes, and the Mediating Role of Electoral System?" *British Journal of Political Science* 41, no. 2 (2011): 448–452.

Fish, Stanley. "Country Roads." *New York Times*, Opinionator Column, July 1, 2007. Accessed March 21, 2016, http://opinionator.blogs.nytimes.com/2007/07/01/country-roads/.

Fleischacker, Samuel. "Adam Smith's Reception among the American Founders, 1776–1790." *William and Mary Quarterly*, 3rd series, 59, no. 4 (October 2002): 897–924.

Ford, Worthington Chauncey, ed. *The Writings of George Washington.* Vol. 4 (1776). New York: G.P. Putnam's Sons, 1889. http://oll.libertyfund.org/titles/2402.

Freeze, John G., ed. *Proportional Representation.* Philadelphia: John Campbell & Son, 1872.

Gallagher, Michael. "Disproportionality in a Proportional Representation System: The Irish Experience." *Political Studies* 23, no. 4 (1975): 501–513.

Gardner, James A. "Madison's Hope: Virtue, Self-Interest, and the Design of Electoral Systems." *Iowa Law Review* 86, no. 1 (October 2000): 87–171.

Gelman, Andrew, and Gary King. "Enhancing Democracy through Legislative Redistricting." *American Political Science Review* 88, no. 3 (1994): 541–559.

———. "A Unified Method of Evaluating Electoral Systems and Redistricting Plans." *American Journal of Political Science* 38, no. 2 (1994): 514–554.

Graber, Mark. "Conflicting Representations: Lani Guinier and James Madison on Electoral Systems." *Constitutional Commentary* 13, no. 3 (1996): 291–307.

Grofman, Bernard, and Thomas Brunell. "The Art of the Dummymander: The Impact of Recent Redistrictings on the Partisan Makeup of Southern House Seats." In *Redistricting in the New Millennium*, edited by Peter F. Galderisi, 183–199. Lanham, MD: Lexington Books, 2005.

Grofman, Bernard, Lisa Handley, and Richard G. Niemi. *Minority Representation and the Quest for Voting Equality.* New York: Cambridge University Press, 1992.

Grofman, Bernard, Guillermo Owen, and Christian Collet. "Rethinking the Partisan Effects of Higher Turnout: So What's the Question?" *Public Choice* 99, no. 3 (1999): 357–376.

Guinier, Lani. *The Tyranny of the Majority: Fundamental Fairness in Representative Democracy.* New York: Free Press, 1994.

Hamilton, Alexander, John Jay, and James Madison. *The Federalist: The Gideon Edition.* Edited by George W. Carey and James McClellan. Indianapolis: Liberty Fund Press, 2001.

Handley, Lisa, and Bernard Grofman. "The Impact of the Voting Rights Act on Minority Representation: Black Office Holding in Southern State Legislatures and Congressional Delegations." In *Quiet Revolution in the South: The Impact of the Voting*

Rights Act 1965–1990, edited by Chandler Davidson, and Bernard Grofman, 336–350. Princeton, NJ: Princeton University Press, 1994.

Hare, Thomas. *A Treatise on the Election of Representatives, Parliamentary and Municipal.* London: Longman, Brown, Green, Longmans & Roberts, 1859.

Hillygus, D. S. "Stand by Your Man?: Assessing the Strategic Behavior of Nader Supporters in Election 2000." Annual meeting of the Midwest Political Science Association, Chicago, IL, 2003.

Hirano, Shigeo, and James M. Snyder Jr. "The Decline of Third Party Voting in the United States." *Journal of Politics* 69, no. 1 (2007): 1–16.

Hofstadter, Richard. *The Age of Reform.* New York: Alfred A. Knopf, 1955.

Holt, Michael F. *Political Parties and American Political Development from the Age of Jackson to the Age of Lincoln.* Baton Rouge: Louisiana State University Press, 1992.

———. *The Rise and Fall of the American Whig Party.* New York: Oxford University Press, 1999.

Howard, Milo B. Jr. "The General Ticket." *Alabama Review* 19, no. 3 (July 1966): 163–166.

Hunter, Thomas Rogers. "The First Gerrymander? Patrick Henry, James Madison and James Monroe, and Virginia's 1788 Congressional Districting." *Early American Studies* 9, no. 3 (Fall 2011): 781–820.

Hutchings, Vincent L., and Nicholas A. Valentino. "The Centrality of Race in American Politics." *Annual Review of Political Science* 7, no. 1 (2004): 383–408.

Ingraham, Cristopher. "America's Most Gerrymandered Congressional Districts." *Washington Post*, May 15, 2014. http://www.washingtonpost.com/news/wonk/wp/2014/05/15/americas-most-gerrymandered-congressional-districts/ and http://www.washingtonpost.com/wp-srv/special/politics/gerrymandering/

Jefferson, Thomas. *Notes on the State of Virginia* (1787). Printed for M. Carey, Philadelphia, 1794.

Jenkins, Jeffery A. "Partisanship and Contested Election Cases in the House of Representatives, 1789–2002." *Studies in American Political Development* 18, no. 2 (2004): 112–135.

Jensen, Merrill, and Robert A. Becker, eds. *The Documentary History of the First Federal Elections: 1788–1790.* Vol. 1. Madison: University of Wisconsin Press, 1976.

Jewell, Malcolm. "The Consequences of Single and Multi-Member Districting." In *Representation and Redistricting*, edited by Bernard Grofman, Arend Lijphart, Robert McKey, and Howard Grofman Scarrow, 129–135. Lexington, MA: Lexington Books, 1982.

Johnson, Joel A. "Disposed to Seek Their True Interests: Representation and Responsibility in Anti-Federalist Thought." *Review of Politics* 66, no. 4 (2004): 649–673.

Kammen, Michael. *Deputies and Liberties: The Origins of Representative Government in Colonial America.* New York: Knopf, 1969.

Kastellec, Jonathan P., Andrew Gelman, and Jamie P. Chandler. "Predicting and Dissecting the Seats-Votes Curve in the 2006 US House Election." *PS: Political Science and Politics* 41, no. 1 (2008): 139–145.

Katz, Johnathon N., and Brian R. Sala. "Careerism, Committee Assignments and the Electoral Connection." *American Political Science Review* 90, no. 1 (March 1996): 21–33.

Katz, Richard S. *Democracy and Elections.* New York: Oxford University Press, 1997.

Katznelson, Ira, and John S. Lapinski. "At the Crossroads: Congress and American Political Development." *Perspective on Politics* 4, no. 2 (2006): 243–260.

Kaufman, Karen M., John R. Petrocik, and Daron R. Shaw. *Unconventional Wisdom: Facts and Myths about American Voters.* New York: Oxford University Press, 2008.

Kendall, M. G., and A. Stuart. "The Law of Cubic Proportions in Election Results." *British Journal of Sociology* 1, no. 3 (1950): 183–196.

Ketcham, Ralph. *Framed for Posterity: The Enduring Philosophy of the Constitution.* Lawrence: University Press of Kansas, 1993.

Key, V. O. Jr. *Southern Politics in State and Nation.* New York: Knopf, 1949.

Keyssar, Alexander. *The Right to Vote: The Contested History of Democracy in the United States.* New York: Basic Books, 2000.

King, Gary, and Andrew Gelman. "Systemic Consequences of Incumbency Advantage in US House Elections." *American Journal of Political Science* 35, no. 1 (1991): 110–138.

Kingdon, John W. *Agendas, Alternatives and Public Policies.* Glenview, IL: Scott, Foresman, 1984.

Klain, Maurice. "A New Look at the Constituencies: The Need for a Recount and a Reappraisal." *American Political Science Review* 49, no. 4 (December 1955): 1105–1119.

Kolp, John G. "The Dynamics of Electoral Competition in Pre-Revolutionary Virginia." *William and Mary Quarterly*, 3rd series, 49, no. 4 (October 1992): 652–674.

Kurland, Phillip, and Ralph Lerner, eds. *The Founder's Constitution.* Vols. 1–5. Chicago: University of Chicago Press, 1987.

Lange, Stephen J. "Civic Virtue, the American Founding, and Federalism." IFIR Working Paper 2008-01, IFIR Working Paper Series, 2007.

Larson, Edward J., and Michael P. Winship. *The Constitutional Convention: A Narrative History from the Notes of James Madison.* New York: Modern Library, 2005.

Lewis, Jeffrey B., Brandon DeVine, Lincoln Pitcher, and Kenneth C. Martis. *Digital Boundary Definitions of United States Congressional Districts, 1789–2012.* 2013. [Data file and code book.] http://cdmaps.polisci.ucla.edu.

Lewis-Beck, Michael S., William G. Jacoby, Helmut Norpoth, and Herbert F. Weisberg. *The American Voter Revisited.* Ann Arbor: University of Michigan Press, 2008.

Lieberman, R. C. "Ideas, Institutions, and Political Order: Explaining Political Change." *American Political Science Review* 96, no. 4 (December 2002): 697–712.

Lijphart, Arend. *Democracies: Patterns of Majoritarian and Consensus Government in Twenty-One Countries.* New Haven, CT: Yale University Press, 1984.

———. *Electoral Systems and Party Systems: A Study of Twenty-Seven Democracies, 1945–1990.* New York: Oxford University Press, 1994.

———. *Patterns of Democracy: Government Forms and Performance in Thirty-Six Countries.* New Haven, CT: Yale University Press, 1999.

Lipset, Seymour M., and Stein Rokkan. "Cleavage Structures, Party Systems, and Voter Alignments: An Introduction." In *Party Systems and Voter Alignments: Cross-National Perspectives*, edited by S. M. Lipset, and S. Rokkan, 1–64. London: Free Press, 1967.

Lockridge, Kenneth. *Literacy in Colonial New England.* New York: W. W. Norton, 1975.

Lubin, David. *The Paradox of Representation: Racial Gerrymandering and Minority Interests in Congress.* Princeton, NJ: Princeton University Press, 1997.

Madison, James. *Notes of Debates in the Federal Convention of 1787.* Athens: Ohio University Press, 1987.

———. *Notes of Debates in the Federal Convention of 1787.* Introduction by Adrienne Koch. Athens: Ohio University Press, 1985.

Mann, Thomas. "Polarizing the House of Representatives: How Much Does Gerrymandering Matter?" In *Red and Blue Nation? Characteristics and Causes of America's Polarized Parties,* edited by Pietro Nivolo and David W. Brady, 263–283. Washington, DC: Brookings Institution Press, 2006.

Manning, Jennifer E. *Membership of the 114th Congress.* [Washington, DC]: Congressional Research Service, 2015.

Mansbridge, Jane. "Should Blacks Represent Blacks and Women Represent Women? A Contingent 'Yes.'" *Journal of Politics* 61, no. 3 (1999): 628–657.

Martis, Kenneth C. *The Historical Atlas of Parties in the United States Congress: 1789–1893.* New York: Macmillan, 1989.

———. *The Historical Atlas of United States Congressional Districts: 1789–1983.* New York: Free Press, 1982.

Mason, George. "Objections to the Constitution of Government Formed by the Convention (1787)." In *The Essential Antifederalist,* 2nd ed., edited by W. B. Allen and Gordon Lloyd, 16–18. New York: Rowman and Littlefield, 2002.

McCarty, Nolan, Keith T. Poole, and Howard Rosenthal. "Does Gerrymandering Cause Polarization?" *American Journal of Political Science* 53, no. 3 (2009): 666–680.

McCubbins, Mathew, and Thomas Schwartz. "Congress, the Courts, and Public Policy: Consequences of the One Man One Vote Rule." *American Journal of Political Science* 32, no. 2 (1988): 388–415.

McDonald, Forrest. *We the People: The Economic Origins of the Constitution.* Chicago: University of Chicago Press, 1958.

McDonald, Michael P. *United States Election Project.* http://www. electproject.org.

McGann, Anthony J,, Charles Anthony Smith, Michael Latner, and Alex Keena. *Gerrymandering in America: The House of Representatives, the Supreme Court, and the Future of Popular Sovereignty.* New York: Cambridge University Press, 2016.

Mill, John Stuart. *Considerations on Representative Government.* London: Parker, Son, and Bourn, 1861.

[Author unknown]. "Minority or Proportional Representation." *Columbia Law Review,* 21, no. 2 (1921): 182–186.

Minta, Michael D. *Oversight: Representing the Interests of Blacks and Hispanics in Congress.* Princeton, NJ: Princeton University Press, 2011.

Mitchell, J. T., H. Flanders, J. W. Martin, and H. L. Carson. *The Statutes at Large of Pennsylvania from 1682 to 1801.* Vol. 6, no. 1759–1765. [Harrisburg]: Clarence M. Busch, State Printer of Pennsylvania, 1899.

Morgan, Edmund S. *Inventing the People: The Rise of Popular Sovereignty in England and America.* New York: W. W. Norton, 1988.

Morgan, Robert J. "Madison's Theory of Representation in the Tenth Federalist." *Journal of Politics* 36, no. 4 (November 1974): 852–885.

Nagle, Jack H., and John E. McNulty. "Partisan Effects of Voter Turnout in Presidential Elections." *American Politics Quarterly* 28, no. 3 (2000): 408–429.

———. "Partisan Effects of Voter Turnout in Senatorial and Gubernatorial Elections." *American Political Science Review* 90, no. 4 (1996): 780–793.

A New Nation Votes: American Election Returns, 1787–1825. http://elections.lib.tufts.edu. Accessed February 10, 2015.

Niemi, Richard G., Bernard Grofman, Carl Carlucci, and Thomas Hofeller. "Measuring Compactness and the Role of a Compactness Standard in a Test for Partisan and Racial Gerrymandering." *Journal of Politics* 52, no. 4 (1990): 1155–1179.

Niemi, Richard, Jeffrey Hill, and Bernard Grofman. "The Impact of Multimember Districts on Party Representation in US State Legislatures." *Legislative Studies Quarterly* 10, no. 4 (1985): 441–455.

Olson, Alison G. "Eighteenth-Century Colonial Legislatures and Their Constituents." *Journal of American History* 79, no. 2 (1992): 543–567.

Oregonian, May 21, 1908. Ballotpedia. http://www.ballotpedia.org.

Orren, Karen, and Stephen Skowronek. "Have We Abandoned a 'Constitutional Perspective' on American Political Development?" *Review of Politics* 73, no. 2 (Spring 2011): 295–299.

Overby, Marvin, and Kenneth Cosgrove. "Unintended Consequences? Racial Redistricting and Representation of Minority Interests." *Journal of Politics* 58, no. 2 (1996): 540–550.

Pangle, Lorraine Smith, and Thomas L. Pangle. *The Learning of Liberty: The Educational Ideas of the American Founders.* Lawrence: University Press of Kansas, 1993.

Pangle, Thomas. *The Spirit of Modern Republicanism: The Moral Vision of the American Founders and the Philosophy of Locke.* Chicago: University of Chicago Press, 1988.

Papke, Leslie, and Jeffrey M. Wooldridge "Econometric Methods for Fractional Response Variables with an Application to 401 (K) Plan Participation Rates." *Journal of Applied Econometrics* 11, no. 6 (1996): 619–632.

Pedersen, Mogens N. "Changing Patterns of Electoral Volatility in European Party Systems, 1948–1977: Explorations in Explanation." In *Western European Party Systems: Continuity and Change*, edited by Hans Daalder and Peter Mair, 29–66. London: Sage, 1983.

Phillips, Anne. *The Politics of Presence.* Oxford: Clarendon Press, 1995.

Pitkin, Hanna F. *The Concept of Representation.* Berkeley: University of California Press, 1967.

Pole, J. R. *Political Representation in England and the Origins of the American Republic.* Berkeley: University of California Press, 1971.

Pope, Clarence. "Adult Mortality in America before 1900: A View from Family Histories." In *Strategic Factors in Nineteenth Century American Economic History: A Volume to Honor Robert W. Fogel*, edited by Claudia Goldin and Hugh Rockoff, 267–296. Chicago: University of Chicago Press, 1991.

Powell, G. Bingham Jr. *Elections as Instruments of Democracy: Majoritarian and Proportional Visions*. New Haven, CT: Yale University Press, 2000.

Putnam, Robert. *Bowling Alone*. New York: Simon & Schuster, 2000.

Quitt, Martin H. "Congressional (Partisan) Constitutionalism: The Apportionment Act Debates of 1842 and 1844." *Journal of the Early Republic* 28, no. 4 (Winter 2008): 627–651.

Ragsdale, Lyn. *Vital Statistics on the Presidency*. Washington, DC: Congressional Quarterly Press, 1998.

Rehfeld, Andrew. *The Concept of Constituency*. New York: Cambridge University Press, 2005.

Richard, Carl J. "The Classical Roots of the US Congress: Mixed Government Theory." In *Inventing Congress: The Origins and Establishment of the First Federal Congress*, edited by Kenneth R. Bowling and Donald R. Kennon, 3–28. Athens: Ohio University Press, 1999.

Richie, Robert, and Steven Hill. *Reflecting All of US: The Case for Proportional Representation*. Boston: Beacon Press, 1999.

Riker, William H. "The Two-Party System and Duverger's Law: An Essay on the History of Political Science." *American Political Science Review* 76, no. 4 (1982): 753–766.

Riker, William H., and Peter C. Ordeshook. "A Theory of the Calculus of Voting." *American Political Science Review* 62, no. 1 (1968): 25–42.

Rokkan, Stein. *Citizens, Elections, Parties: Approaches to the Comparative Study of the Process of Development*. New York: David McKay, 1970.

Rosa-Clot, Michele. "The Apportionment Act of 1842: 'An Odious Use of Authority.'" *Parliaments, Estates & Representation* 31, no. 1 (April 2011): 33–52.

Rosenthal, Howard L., and Keith T. Poole. "United States Congressional Roll Call Voting Records, 1789–1990: Reformatted Data." *ICPSR Find and Analyze Data*. 2000. http://www.icpsr.umich.edu/icpsrweb/ICPSR/studies/9822/version/2.

Rowell, Chester H. *A Historical and Legal Digest of All the Contested Election Cases in the House of Representatives from the First to the Fifty-Sixth Congress, 1789–1901*. H.R. Doc. No. 510-56 (1901).

Rusk, Gerald G. *A Statistical History of the American Electorate*. Washington, DC: CQ Press, 2001.

Scarrow, Howard A. "Vote Dilution, Party Dilution, and the Voting Rights Act: The Search for Fair and Effective Representation." In *The US Supreme Court and the Electoral Process*, 2nd ed., edited by David K. Ryden, 42–59. Washington, DC: Georgetown University Press, 2002.

Schattschneider, E. E. *Party Government*. New York: Farrar and Rinehart, 1942.

Schmeckebier, Laurence F. *Congressional Apportionment*. Washington, DC: Brookings Institution, 1941.

Schmidt, Gary J., and Robert H. Webking. "Revolutionaries, Anti-Federalists, and Federalists: Comments on Gordon Wood's Understanding of the American Founding." *Political Science Reviewer* 9, no. 1 (Fall 1979): 195–229.

Schwartz, Nancy L. *The Blue Guitar: Political Representation and Community*. Chicago: University of Chicago Press, 1988.

Shields, Johanna Nicol. "Whigs Reform the 'Bear Garden': Representation and the Apportionment Act of 1842." *Journal of the Early Republic* 5, no. 3 (Autumn 1985): 355–382.

Shotts, K. W. "Does Racial Redistricting Cause Conservative Policy Outcomes? Policy Preferences of Southern Representatives in the 1980s and 1990s." *Journal of Politics* 65, no. 1 (2003): 216–226.

Smith, Adam. *An Inquiry into the Nature and Causes of the Wealth of Nations* (1776). Edited with an introduction, notes, marginal summary and an enlarged index by Edwin Cannan. 2 vols. London: Methuen, 1904. http://oll.libertyfund.org/titles/171.

Smith, Melancton. "New York Ratifying Convention, June 20, 1788." In *The Founder's Constitution*, vol. 1, edited by Philip B. Kurland, and Ralph Lerner, ch. 13, document 37. Indianapolis: Liberty Fund, 1987.

Smith, Rogers M. "Beyond Tocqueville, Myrdal, and Hartz: The Multiple Traditions in America." *American Political Science Review* 87, no. 3 (September 1993): 549–566.

Squire, Peverill. *The Evolution of American Legislatures: Colonies, Territories and States, 1619–2009.* Ann Arbor: University of Michigan Press, 2014.

———. *The Rise of the Representative: Lawmakers and Constituents in Colonial America.* Ann Arbor: University of Michigan Press, forthcoming.

Squire, Peverill, and Keith E. Hamm. *101 Chambers: Congress, State Legislatures, and Future of Legislative Studies.* Columbus: Ohio State University Press, 2005.

The Statutes at Large of Pennsylvania, 1788. Internet Archive. https://archive.org/.

Sterne, Simon. *On Representative Government and Personal Representation: Based in Part upon Thomas Hare's Treatise, Entitled "The Election of Representatives, Parliamentary and Municipal."* Philadelphia: J. B. Lippincott, 1871.

Still, Jonathan W. "Political Equality and Election Systems." *Ethics* 91, no. 3 (1981): 375–394.

Storing, Herbert J., ed. *The Anti-Federalist: An Abridgement, by Murray Dry, of the Complete Anti-Federalist.* Chicago: University of Chicago Press, 1985.

———. *The Complete Anti-Federalist: Writings by the Opponents of the Constitution.* Chicago: University of Chicago Press, 1981.

———. *What the Anti-Federalists Were For: The Political Thought of the Opponents of the Constitution.* Chicago: University of Chicago Press, 1981.

Thomas, George. "Political Thought and Political Development." *American Political Thought* 3, no. 1 (Spring 2014): 114–125.

———. "What Is Political Development? A Constitutional Perspective." *Review of Politics* 73, no. 2 (Spring 2011): 275–294.

Tucker, Harvey J., and Arnold Vedlitz. "Does Heavy Turnout Help Democrats in Presidential Elections?" *American Political Science Review* 87, no. 4 (1986): 1291–1298.

Tufte, Edward R. "The Relationship between Seats and Votes in Two-Party Systems." *American Political Science Review* 67, no. 2 (1973): 540–554.

United States Census Bureau. "Lifetime Mobility in the United States: 2010." In *American Community Survey Briefs.* Washington, DC: United States Census Bureau, 2011.

———. *Projections of the Size and Composition of the US Population: 2014–2060.* http://census.gov/content/dam/Census/library/publications/2015/demo/p25-1143.pdf.

"United States Congressional Roll Call Voting Records, 1789–1998." ICPSR Find *and Analyze Data.* 2010. http://www.icpsr.umich.edu/icpsrweb/ICPSR/studies/4. doi:10.3886/ICPSR00004.v3.

"United States House of Representatives Elections, 2012." *Ballotpedia.* http://ballot pedia.org/United_States_House_of_Representatives_elections,_2012. Accessed April 18, 2015.

Wang, Sam. "The Great Gerrymander of 2012." *New York Times Sunday Review,* Opinion, February 2, 2013.

Wasserman, David. *The Cook Political Report Partisan Voter Index.* Cook Political Report, 2014. http://cookpolitical.com/story/5604.

Wesberry v. Sanders, 376 US 1 (1964). Opinions. https://www.law.cornell.edu/supreme court/text/376/1.

Wesberry v. Sanders, 376 US 1 (1964). *Oyez Project at IIT Chicago-Kent College of Law.* http://www.oyez.org/cases/1960-1969/1963/1963_22. Accessed February 1, 2016.

Wiebe, Robert H. *The Search for Order: 1877–1920.* New York: Hill and Wang, 1967.

Wittrock, Jill, Stephen C. Nemeth, Howard Sanborn, Brian DiSarro, and Peverill Squire. "The Impact of the Australian Ballot on Member Behavior in the US House of Representatives." *Political Research Quarterly* 61, no. 3 (September 2008): 434–444.

Wood, Gordon S. *The Creation of the American Republic, 1776–1787.* Chapel Hill: University of North Carolina Press, 1969.

———. *Empire of Liberty: A History of the Early Republic, 1789–1815.* New York: Oxford University Press, 2009.

———. *The Radicalism of the American Revolution.* New York: Knopf, 1991.

Woodburn, James Albert. *The American Republic and Its Government.* New York: G. P. Putnam's Sons, 1903.

Yarbrough, Jean. "Representation and Republicanism: Two Views." *Publius* 9, no. 2 (1979): 77–98.

Zagarri, Rosemarie. *The Politics of Size: Representation in the United States, 1776–1850.* Ithaca, NY: Cornell University Press, 1987.

INDEX